Microsoft Certified Azure Fundamental AZ-900

Technology Workbook

www.ipspecialist.net

Document Control

Proposal Name	:	Microsoft Certified: Azure Fundamentals
Document Version	:	Version 1
Document Release Date	:	
Reference	:	AZ-900

Copyright © 2018 IPSpecialist LTD.
Registered in England and Wales
Company Registration No: 10883539
Registration Office at: Office 32, 19-21 Crawford Street, London W1H 1PJ, United Kingdom
www.ipspecialist.net

All rights reserved. No part of this book may be reproduced or transmitted in any form or by any means, electronic or mechanical, including photocopying, recording, or by any information storage and retrieval system, without the written permission from IPSpecialist LTD, except for the inclusion of brief quotations in a review.

Feedback:
If you have any comments regarding the quality of this book, or otherwise alter it to better suit your needs, you can contact us through email at info@ipspecialist.net
Please make sure to include the book's title and ISBN in your message.

About IPSpecialist

IPSPECIALIST LTD. IS COMMITTED TO EXCELLENCE AND DEDICATED TO YOUR SUCCESS.

Our philosophy is to treat our customers like family. We want you to succeed, and we are willing to do everything possible to help you make it happen. We have the proof to back up our claims. We strive to accelerate billions of careers with great courses, accessibility, and affordability. We believe that continuous learning and knowledge evolution are the most important things to keep re-skilling and up-skilling the world.

Planning and creating a specific goal is where IPSpecialist helps. We can create a career track that suits your visions as well as develop the competencies you need to become a professional Network Engineer. We can also assist you with the execution and evaluation of your proficiency level, based on the career track you choose, as they are customized to fit your specific goals.

We help you STAND OUT from the crowd through our detailed IP training content packages.

Course Features:

- ❖ Self-Paced Learning
    - Learn at your own pace and in your own time
- ❖ Covers Complete Exam Blueprint
    - Prep-up for the exam with confidence
- ❖ Case Study Based Learning
    - Relate the content with real life scenarios
- ❖ Subscriptions that Suits You
    - Get more and pay less with IPS subscriptions
- ❖ Career Advisory Services
    - Let the industry experts plan your career journey
- ❖ Virtual Labs to test your skills
    - With IPS vRacks, you can evaluate your exam preparations
- ❖ Practice Questions
    - Practice questions to measure your preparation standards
- ❖ On Request Digital Certification
    - On request digital certification from IPSpecialist LTD.

About the Authors:

This book has been compiled with the help of multiple professional engineers who specialize in different fields e.g. Networking, Security, Cloud, Big Data, IoT etc. Each engineer develops content in his/her own specialized field that is compiled to form a comprehensive certification guide.

About the Technical Reviewers:

Nouman Ahmed Khan

AWS-Architect, CCDE, CCIEX5 (R&S, SP, Security, DC, Wireless), CISSP, CISA, CISM, Nouman Ahmed Khan is a Solution Architect working with a major telecommunication provider in Qatar. He works with enterprises, mega-projects, and service providers to help them select the best-fit technology solutions. He also works as a consultant to understand customer business processes and helps select an appropriate technology strategy to support business goals. He has more than fourteen years of experience working in Pakistan/Middle-East & UK. He holds a Bachelor of Engineering Degree from NED University, Pakistan, and M.Sc. in Computer Networks from the UK.

Abubakar Saeed

Abubakar Saeed has more than twenty-five years of experience, managing, consulting, designing, and implementing large-scale technology projects, extensive experience heading ISP operations, solutions integration, heading Product Development, Pre-sales, and Solution Design. Emphasizing on adhering to Project timelines and delivering as per customer expectations, he always leads the project in the right direction with his innovative ideas and excellent management skills.

Areeba Tanveer

Areeba Tanveer is a AWS Certified Solution Architect – Associate working professionally as a Technical Content Developer. She holds a Bachelor's of Engineering Degree in Telecommunication Engineering from NED University of Engineering and Technology. She also worked as a project Engineer in Pakistan Telecommunication Company Limited (PTCL). She has both the technical knowledge and industry sounding information, which she utilizes effectively when needed.

Syed Hanif Wasti

Syed Hanif Wasti is a Computer Science graduate working professionally as a Technical Content Developer. He is a part of a team of professionals operating in the E-learning and digital education sector. He holds a Bachelor's Degree in Computer Sciences from PAF-KIET, Pakistan. He has completed training of MCP and CCNA. He has both the technical knowledge and industry sounding information, which he uses efficiently in his career. He previously worked as a Database and Network administrator and obtained a good experience in software development.

Free Resources:

With each workbook purchased, IPSpecialist offers free resources to our valuable customers.

Once you buy this book you will have to contact us at support@ipspecialist.net or tweet @ipspecialistnet to get this limited time offer without any extra charges.

Free Resources Include:

Exam Practice Questions in Quiz Simulation: With 300+ Q/A, IPSpecialist's Practice Questions is a concise collection of important topics to keep in mind. The questions are especially prepared following the exam blueprint to give you a clear understanding of what to expect from the certification exam. It goes further on to give answers with thorough explanations. In short, it is a perfect resource that helps you evaluate your preparation for the exam.

Career Report: This report is a step-by-step guide for a novice who wants to develop his/her career in the field of computer networks. It answers the following queries:

- What are the current scenarios and future prospects?
- Is this industry moving towards saturation or are new opportunities knocking at the door?
- What will the monetary benefits be?
- Why to get certified?
- How to plan and when will I complete the certifications if I start today?
- Is there any career track that I can follow to accomplish specialization level?

Furthermore, this guide provides a comprehensive career path towards being a specialist in the field of networking and also highlights the tracks needed to obtain certification.

IPS Personalized Technical Support for Customers: Good customer service means helping customers efficiently, in a friendly manner. It is essential to be able to handle issues for customers and do your best to ensure they are satisfied. Providing good service is one of the most important things that can set our business apart from the others of its kind.

Great customer service will result in attracting more customers and attain maximum customer retention.

IPS offers personalized TECH support to its customers to provide better value for money. If you have any queries related to technology and labs, you can simply ask our technical team for assistance via Live Chat or Email.

Our Products

Technology Workbooks

IPSpecialist Technology workbooks are the ideal guides to developing the hands-on skills necessary to pass the exam. Our workbooks cover the official exam blueprint and explain the technology with real life case study based labs. The content covered in each workbook consists of individually focused technology topics presented in an easy-to-follow, goal-oriented, step-by-step approach. Every scenario features detailed breakdowns and thorough verifications to help you completely understand the task and associated technology.

We extensively used mind maps in our workbooks to visually explain the technology. Our workbooks have become a widely used tool to learn and remember the information effectively.

vRacks

Our highly scalable and innovative virtualized lab platforms let you practice the IP Specialist Technology Workbook at your own time and your own place as per your convenience.

Quick Reference Sheets

Our quick reference sheets are a concise bundling of condensed notes of the complete exam blueprint. It is an ideal and handy document to help you remember the most important technology concepts related to the certification exam.

Practice Questions

IP Specialists' Practice Questions are dedicatedly designed from a certification exam perspective. The collection of these questions from our technology workbooks are prepared keeping the exam blueprint in mind covering not only important but necessary topics as well. It's an ideal document to practice and revise your certification.

Content at a glance

Table of Contents

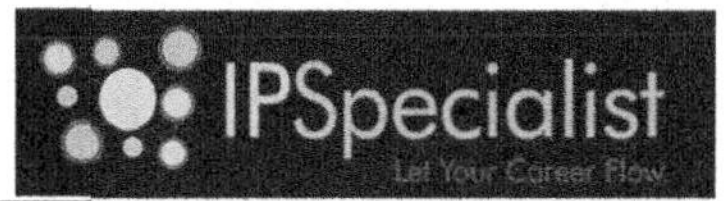

Microsoft Certifications

Microsoft Azure Certifications are industry-recognized credentials that validate your technical Cloud skills and expertise while assisting you in your career growth. These are one of the most valuable IT certifications right now since Azure has established an overwhelming growth rate in the public cloud market. Even with the presence of several tough competitors such as Amazon Web Services, Google Cloud Engine, and Rackspace, Azure is going to be the dominant public cloud platform today, with an astounding collection of proprietary services that continues to grow.

In this certification, we will discuss cloud concepts where we will learn the core benefits of using Azure like high availability, scalability, etc. We will talk about the Azure Architecture in which cloud resources are put together to work at best; Azure Compute where you will learn how to run applications in Azure; Networking in which the discussion is on how Azure resources communicate with each other; Storage, where you put all of your data and have different ways of storing it. We will also be covering Databases that are used for storage of data, its efficient retrieval as per demand, and to make sure that the users have the right access to the resources. Also, we will counter some complex scenarios with their solutions. We will have discussions on important topics like; Security, which makes Azure the best secure choice for your applications and functions; Privacy, Compliance and Trust that make sure how services ensure privacy and how you stay compliant with standards; As well as, Pricing in Azure to stay ahead on cost.

AZ-900 is the first certification of Microsoft Azure, which is the foundational certificate in Azure. After this certification, you can prove to the world that you are proficient and have the credibility to reach the highest point of your professional life.

Value of Azure Certifications

Microsoft places equal emphasis on sound conceptual knowledge of its entire platform, as well as on hands-on experience with the Azure infrastructure and its many unique and complex components and services.

For Individuals

- Demonstrate your expertise in designing, deploying, and operating highly available, cost-effective, and secured applications on Microsoft Azure.
- Gain recognition and visibility of your proven skills and proficiency with Azure.
- Earn tangible benefits such as access to the Microsoft Certified Community, get invited to Microsoft Certification Appreciation Receptions and Lounges, obtain Microsoft

Certification Practice Exam Voucher and Digital Badge for certification validation, Microsoft Certified Logo usage.

- Foster credibility with your employer and peers.

For Employers

- Identify skilled professionals to lead IT initiatives with Cloud technologies.
- Reduce risks and costs to implement your workloads and projects on the Azure platform.
- Increase customer satisfaction.

Types of Certification

Role-based Certification

- *Fundamental* - Validates overall understanding of the Azure Cloud.
- *Associate*- Technical role-based certifications. No pre-requisite required.
- *Expert*- Highest level technical role-based certification.

About Microsoft Certified: Azure Fundamentals Exam

Exam Questions	Case study, short answer, repeated answer, MCQs
Number of Questions	40-60
Time to Complete	85 minutes
Exam Fee	99 USD

The Microsoft Certified: Azure Fundamentals exam validates cloud concepts, core Azure Services, Azure pricing and support, and the fundamentals of cloud security, privacy, compliance, and trust. Example concepts you should understand for this exam include:

- Cloud Concepts
- Core Azure Services
- Security, Privacy, Compliance, and Trust
- Azure Pricing and Support

Recommended Knowledge

- The benefits and considerations of using cloud services
- The differences between Infrastructure-as-a-Service (IaaS), Platform-as-a-Service (PaaS) and Software-as-a-Service (SaaS)
- The differences between public, private and hybrid cloud models
- The core Azure architectural components
- Core products and solutions available in Azure
- Azure management tools
- Securing network connectivity in Azure
- Azure identity services, security tools, and governance methodologies
- Monitoring and reporting in Azure
- Privacy, compliance, and data protection standards in Azure
- Azure subscriptions, planning and management tools
- Azure support options, SLAs, and service lifecycle

	Domain
Domain 1	Cloud Concepts
Domain 2	Core Azure Services
Domain 3	Security, Privacy, Compliance and Trust
Domain 4	Azure Pricing and Support

Chapter 01: Introduction to Azure

Introduction:

Azure, like Google and Amazon Cloud Platforms, is Microsoft's Cloud Platform. It is typically a platform that allows us to use Microsoft tools. We need tremendous amount of money, energy, physical space, etc. to set up the huge IT infrastructure. In such circumstances, Microsoft Azure comes to our rescue. It offers us virtual machines, fast data processing, analytical tools, and monitoring instruments to simplify our work. Azure pricing is also simpler and cheaper. It is commonly referred to as "Pay as You Go", meaning you only pay for the services when you are using them. Microsoft launched Azure's Windows at the beginning of October 2008 but it became live in 2010. Microsoft later changed the name to Microsoft Azure in 2014, from Windows Azure. It has become one of the leading cloud services used today and is only growing bigger by the day.

What is Cloud Computing?

Cloud Computing is basically storing data and accessing the computers over the internet. It is the delivery of different computing services like servers, software, analytics, databases, and storage via the internet. Computing resources are delivered on-demand through a cloud service platform with pay-as-you-go pricing. The companies that are providing services termed as "Cloud Providers". There are numbers of cloud providers like Amazon, Google and Azure.

Benefits of Cloud Computing

We all know that Cloud Computing has brought a major change in the traditional business thinking for IT resources. There are many benefits of using Cloud Computing. Some of which are:

1. **Cost**

   Cloud computing eliminates the capital cost of buying hardware and software and of building and running in-house datacenters – server racks, 24 hours' electricity for power and cooling, etc.

2. **Scale Globally**

   Cloud computing services have the capacity to scale with elasticity. In cloud, it means that IT resources are provided more or less computing power, storage, bandwidth – as per requirement and from the right place.

3. **Increase Speed and Agility**

   New IT resources are readily available so that resources can be scaled up infinitely according to demand. This leads to a dramatic increase in agility for organizations.

4. **Reliability**

   Cloud computing allows data backup, disaster recovery and business continuity as data can be replicated in the network of the cloud supplier on multiple redundant sites.

5. **Security**

   The protection of their data is one of the main problems for any organization regardless of its size and industry. Infringements of data and other cyber-crimes can devastate the revenue, customer loyalty, and positioning of a company. Cloud provides many advanced security features to strengthen the security of the overall company. It also helps in protecting your data, application, and infrastructure.

The Economy of Cloud Computing

In the traditional environment of organizations, as there is a need for large investments on CapEx, Cloud is the best way to switch to the pay-as-you-go model. Cloud reduces the Capital Expenditure (CapEx) cost and also gives some other benefits. With Cloud Computing, you should move toward Operational Expenditure (OpEx).

Mostly in Azure, the pricing is based on an hourly basis like VMs, App Services, etc. There is also consumption based pricing which is on the basis of per execution of function, per second use of resource, or both. An example of consumption based pricing is Azure Function.

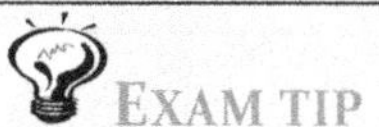

Capital Expenditure (CapEx) is the expenditure to maintain or acquiring fixed assets by spending money. This includes land, equipment, etc.

Operational Expenditure (OpEx) is the cost of a product or a system that is running on a day-to-day basis like electricity, printer papers, etc.

Technical Terms

In order to understand Cloud Computing, you need to understand some technical terms.

- **High Availability (HA)** - It is the core of cloud computing. As we know that in traditional server environments, companies own a number of hardware and the workload is limited to this hardware capacity. In case of extra load, capacity cannot

be increased whereas, sometimes this hardware seems extra for the workload. In cloud, you do not own any of the hardware and addition in servers is just a click away. This way, you get high availability for your servers by replacing instantly the failed server with the new one. HA depends on the number of VMs that you set up to eventually cover in case one goes down

- **Fault Tolerance** - For resilience in the cloud, fault tolerance is also an important factor. Fault tolerance gives you zero down time. Fault tolerance means that if there is any fault from the Azure side, then it is immediately mitigated by Azure itself
- **Disaster Recovery (DR)** - In case of any catastrophic disaster like cyber-attack. There is a plan in DR to recover your business from these critical systems or in normal operation if such an event occurs. DR has designated time to recover and a recovery point
- **Scalability** - In cloud computing, scalability means addition or removal of the resources in an easy and quick way as per demand. It is important in such a situation where you do not know the actual number of resources that are needed. Auto-scaling is an approach for scalability depending on your requirement by defining the threshold
- **Elasticity** - Elasticity is the capacity to dynamically extend or minimize network resources to respond to autonomous working load adjustments and optimize the use of resources. This can contribute to overall cost savings for services
- **Agility** - Agility is the capability to adapt quickly and efficiently to changes in the business environment. Agility also refers to the ability to quickly develop, test and deploy business-led software applications. Instead of providing and managing services, Cloud Agility lets them concentrate on other issues such as security, monitoring, and analysis

From the Exam perspective, one must be familiar with all the terms like HA, Fault Tolerance, DR, Elasticity, Scalability, and Agility.

Types of Cloud Computing

The cloud computing services are divided into four broad categories: IaaS, PaaS, Serverless, and SaaS. These are also known as a stack in cloud computing because each of them is built on top of another. Let's discuss each of them.

1. **Infrastructure as a Service (IaaS)**

   It gives you a basic IT infrastructure for Cloud IT like VMs, Data Storage, Networks, OS on a pay-as-you-go model.

2. **Platform as a Service (PaaS)**

   Cloud computing platforms that provide an on-demand environment to build, test, deliver and manage software applications are referred to as Platform as a Service. PaaS is designed to facilitate the fast development of web or mobile apps for developers without the concern of setting or maintaining the underlying server, storage, network, and database infrastructure that are needed for development.

3. **Serverless**

   Overlapping PaaS, serverless computing concentrates on creating application functionality, without continually spending time maintaining the required server and infrastructure. The cloud provider is responsible for the configuration, capacity planning, and server governance. The highly scalable and event-based serverless architectures only use resources when a particular task or trigger takes place.

4. **Software as a Service (SaaS)**

   Both servers and code are taken over by cloud providers. Cloud providers are hosting and maintaining the applications and underlying infrastructure for SaaS and handling updates such as software upgrades, and security patches. Users link the app over the Internet, usually through their phone, tablet or PC through their web browser.

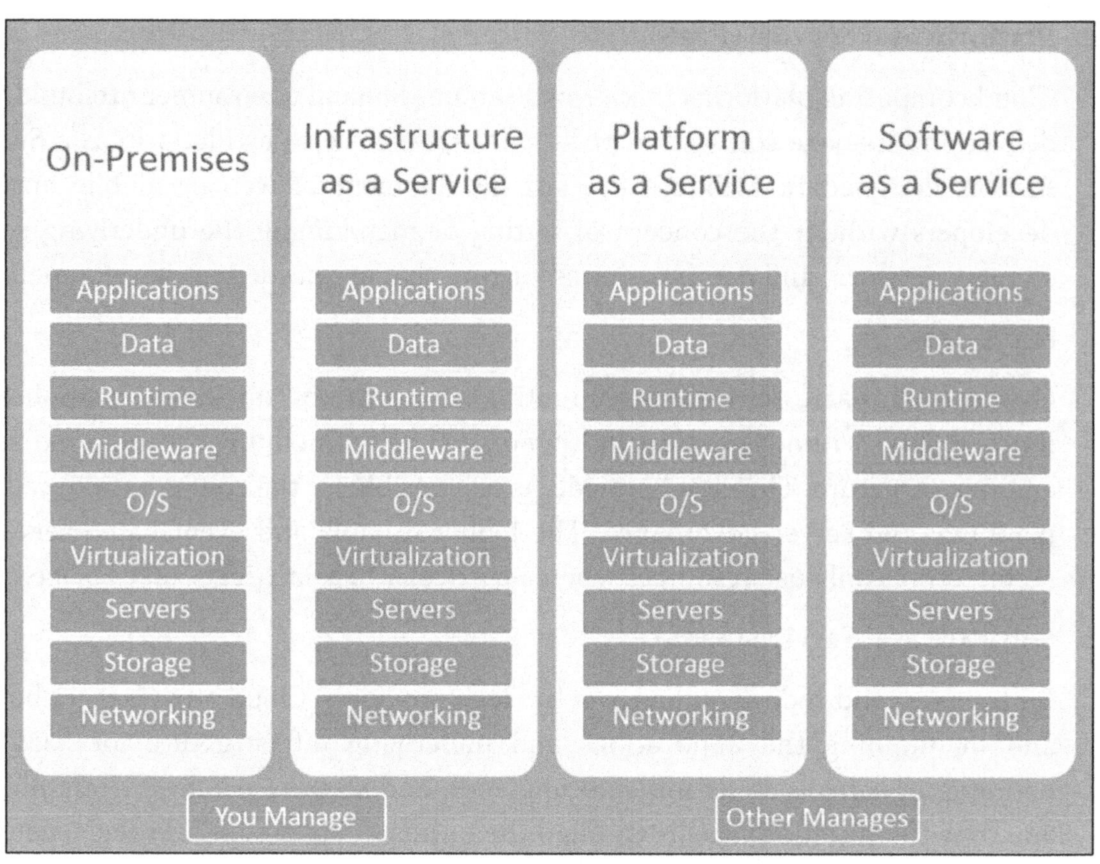

Figure 1-01: Iaas, PaaS and SaaS Overview

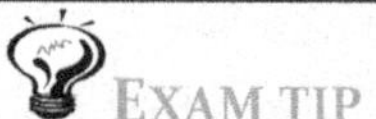

EXAM TIP

IaaS- servers, storage, and networking

PaaS-servers, storage, networking, management tools

SaaS- a complete application like Office 365

Serverless- no need of server; there is a single function that is hosted, deployed and managed on its own

Cloud Computing Deployments Models

We know that all clouds are not the same and not every business requirement for cloud computing is the same. So, in order to meet the requirements; different models, types and services have been used. Firstly, you have to decide how the cloud service is being applied by finding out the cloud deployment type or Architecture. There are three different types of Cloud Computing: Public, Private and Hybrid.

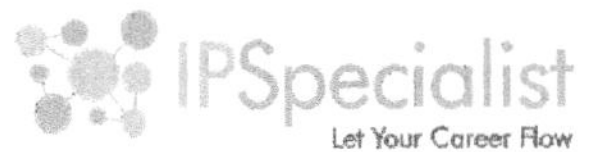

Public Cloud

- As the name says, Public Cloud is a deployment model that supports all type of users. Public cloud is owned and operated by third parties that are providing computing services like storage, software etc. With a public cloud, the cloud provider owns and manages all hardware, software and other supporting infrastructure. Users can use a web browser to access and manage these services. Microsoft Azure is an example of Public Cloud.

Private Cloud

- As the name says, Private Cloud only refers to one organization. On the company's on-site data center, a server is physically located. Many businesses also manage their private cloud with third-party service providers. A private cloud is a private network that manages services and infrastructure. The capital expenditure involved in the creation and management of private clouds is costlier than public clouds. Private clouds are more likely to respond to organizations' security and privacy concerns.

Hybrid Cloud

- Hybrid Clouds integrate public and private clouds together with the technology to share data and applications. The hybrid cloud provides greater versatility and allows further deployment. It improves the existing infrastructure, protection, and enforcement by allowing data and applications to migrate between private and public clouds.

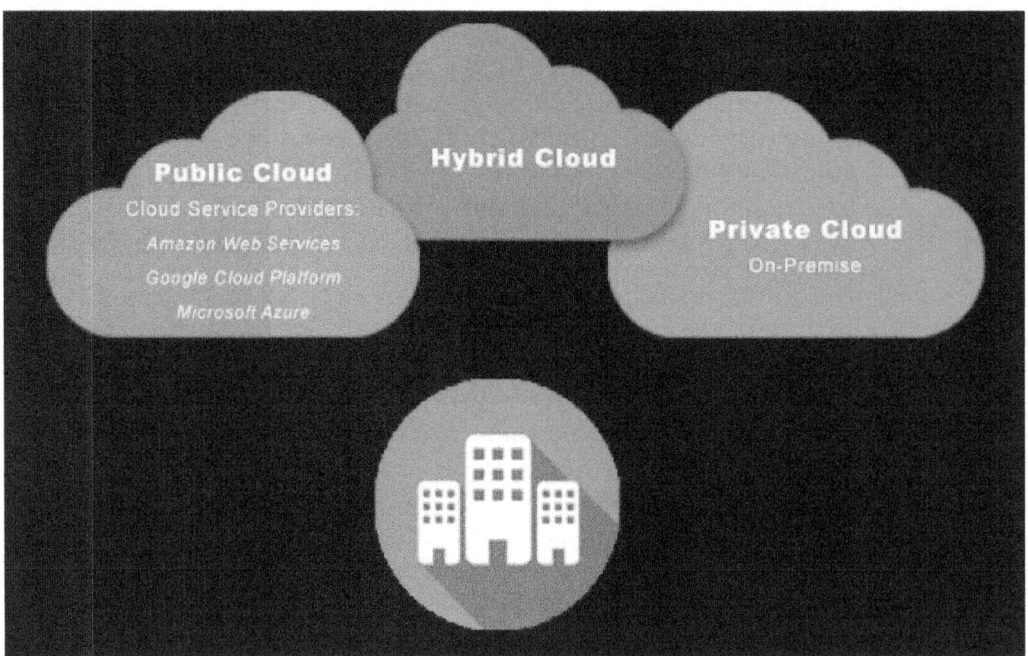

Figure 1-02: Public, Private and Hybrid Cloud

What is Azure?

Microsoft Azure is known as Windows Azure and it is a Public Cloud. We have already learned in the above discussion about Public Cloud. As for Azure, it is an expanding cloud service that helps the companies to meet their challenges. It is free to build, manage and deploy applications with your favorite tools and frames in a huge, global network. Azure is considered for offering both IaaS and PaaS. Azure offers over 100 services, from the execution of existing applications on virtual machines to exploration of new tech paradigms like smart bots and mixed reality.

In order to use Azure, you first need to setup an Azure account directly by going to "Azure.com" or with the help of a representative. You can sign-up to Azure as a Free account with free USD 200 credit and 25+ free services.

Azure, for example, offers AI and machine learning tools that can communicate with your customers through vision, hearing, and speech. It also offers solutions for the storage of massive amounts of data, which are increasing rapidly. Azure services give solutions that without Cloud resources, are much expensive.

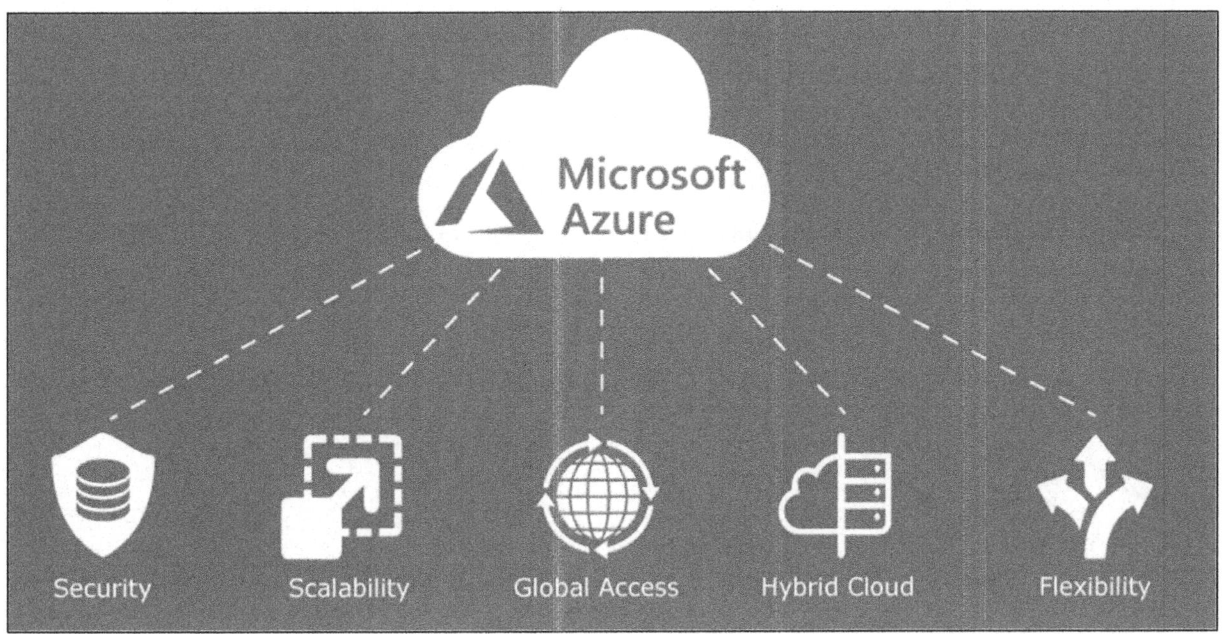

Figure 1-03: Azure Benefits

Azure Market Place

The Azure market place offers technical solutions and services from Microsoft and partners to build and extend Azure products and services. It has all kinds of services and applications like VMs, Templates, apps, and Azure managed services etc. There is an Azure App Store in your mobile for buying cloud services, where you have a variety of solutions including base OS, database, security, networking and developer tools. For accessing all of these you can either go directly to the website of market place or use Azure CLI or integrate with Powershell. From the catalog, you can add anything to subscription. Some services are free and some are charged. In order to publish your own product in the Market Place, you need to become partner with Microsoft so that it becomes a distribution channel for your business.

Global Footprint

Azure has more global regions than any other cloud provider — which offers the scale required to bring users around the world closer to applications, preserve residency and provide customers with comprehensive compliance and resilience options. There are 58 regions of Azure that are available around the world with 140 available in 140 countries.

Regions

Regions are geographical areas where Azure is present to deploy the Azure resources. It is a set of data centers with latency-defined perimeter connected via a dedicated regional low-

latency network. There are region specific services but some core services like storage and VMs are by default live in all regions.

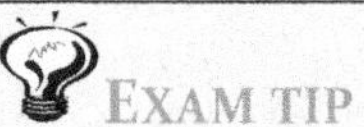

EXAM TIP

Dedicated Regional Low Latency network means there is a fiber connection between data centers in the region.

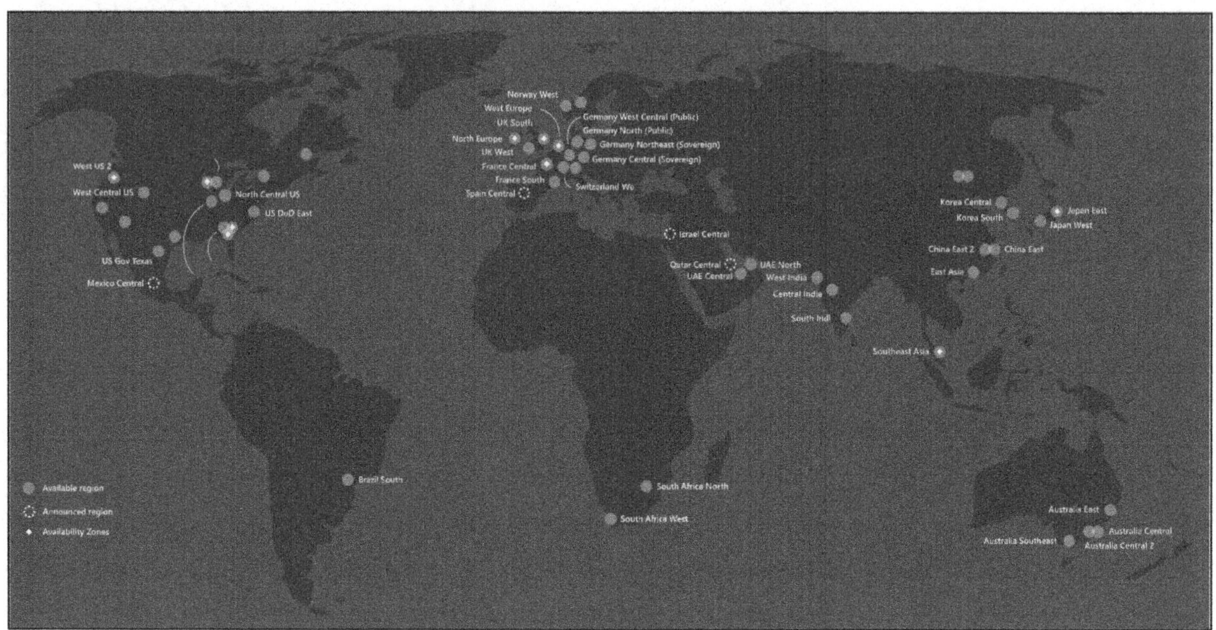

Figure 1-04: Azure Geographical Region

How to Choose a Region?

When you are choosing a region, you need to think about three things mainly:

- **Location**- in order to reduce the latency, choose a region closest to the user
- **Features**- all features are not available in all regions, so select a region where your specific feature is available
- **Price**- service prices in Azure vary from region to region

Geographies/Paired Regions

Geography is a distinct market that usually conserves data residence and compliance boundaries with two or more regions within the same geographic area.

Geographies enable customers with particular data residency needs to maintain their data and apps in close proximity. Geographical areas are fault tolerant to whole failures in the field by linking them to Azure's dedicated networking infrastructure. So if the primary

region goes down, it failovers to the secondary region. In the paired region, only one region is updated at a time. For some services, paired regions are used as replications.

Availability Set

An Availability Set is a logical grouping function that can be used to separate VM resources from each other. Azure must ensure that your VMs are operating across several physical servers, device tables, storage units and network switches within an availability set. If a hardware or software failure occurs, only the VMs will be impacted, and the overall solution will remain operational.

Availability Zone

Availability Zones (AZ) are locations within an Azure region that are physically separate. An availability zone is composed of one or more independently operating power, and network data centers. Each region has a minimum of three zones.

Availability zones allow clients to run high-availability and low-latency mission-critical applications.

Availability Set

Region

Availability Zone

Availability Zone

Region

Region

Region

Peered
Region

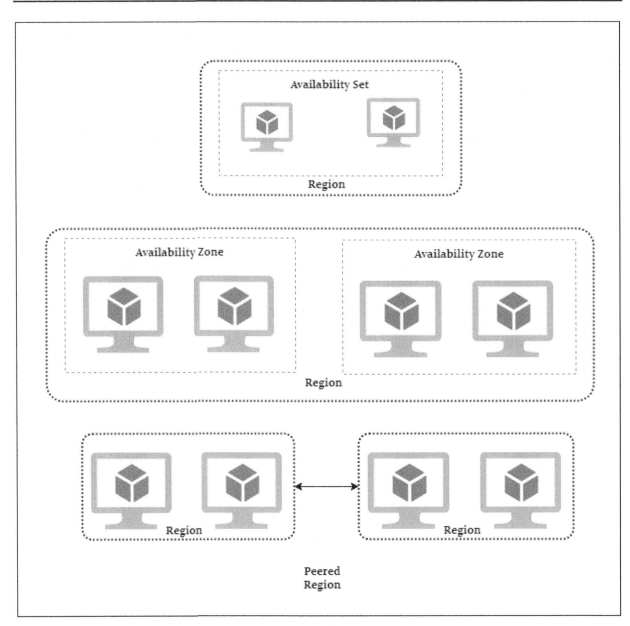

Figure 1-05: Region, AZ, and Paired Region

Azure Resource Manager (ARM)

It is an underlying service where the Azure resource deployment and management is done. It provides a management layer, which lets you create, upgrade, and uninstall your Azure subscription tools. You use management features such as access control, locks, or tags to ensure that your resources are protected and organized after deployment.

- **A Resource** is a manageable item that is available in Azure like VM, storage, databases, etc. Each resource can reside only in one resource group
- **Resource Groups** are the place where you deploy your resources. Here, you need to identify which resource group you want to deploy a resource. It is like a container where all resources of a solution or the resources that you want to manage in a group reside. The resource from the resource group can be added or removed at any time. You can move your resources from one group to another and the resource from multiple regions can be in one resource group as well. With the resource group, you have access control to the resource. The resources in different resource groups can interact with each other
- **Resource Provider** is a service that supplies the resources that you can deploy for a manageable resource for the resource manager
- **Resource Manager Template** is a JavaScript Object Notation (JSON) file that defines the resources deployed in the resource group. It also defines the dependencies between the deployed resources. With this template, resources can be deployed in a consistent and repeatable way

ARM Benefits

- You have group resource handlings like deploying, management, and monitoring
- You get consistency; For example, when you deploy resources, it will be happening in the same way as every time
- Define the dependencies between resources in the right order.
- Access Control, which is built-in to assign access to the users
- Tagging, which makes it easier to identify the resource in the future
- For billing, you can use tagging to stay on top

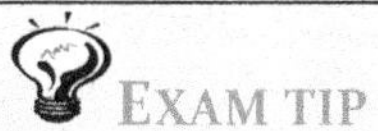

The resource group itself is not a resource, it helps in the structure of Azure Architecture.

Azure Services

There is a number of available services and features in Azure. The most commonly used categories are:

- Compute
- Networking
- Storage
- Mobile
- Databases

- Web
- Internet of Things
- Big Data
- Artificial Intelligence
- Security and Identity
- Monitoring and Management

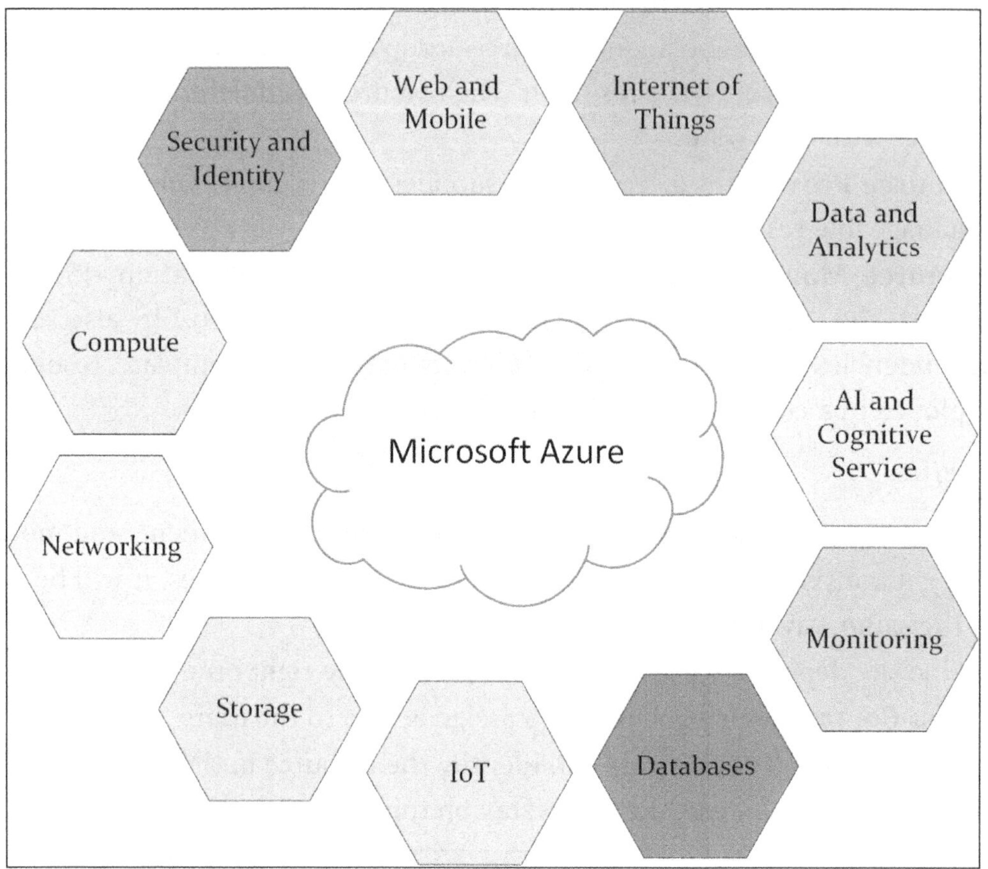

Figure 1-06: Azure Services

Compute

In Azure, there is a number of options that are available for application and service hosting. Azure Compute provides you an infrastructure where you can run your applications.

- **Azure Virtual Machine**- These are Linux and Windows VMs on demand with your desired configuration hosted in Azure. The supported Linux distributions are CentOS, Oracle Linux, RHEL, Debian, openSUSE, SUSE LES, and Ubuntu. There are 6 types of VMs with 28 families. There is a set amount of Memory, vCPUs and Temporary Storage. You can also attach additional data disks to these VMs. Pricing

is based on per minute billing. Reserved VMs are also available for significant discounts, like you can get discounts up to 72% on a pay-as-you-go model

- **App Service** - It is a PaaS that provides a fully managed platform for creating cloud applications for web and mobile. It is used to host web applications, mobile app back ends, RESTful APIs and automated business processes. The programming languages that are supported by App Service are .NET, .NET Core, Ruby, Java, PHP, Node.js and Python
- **Azure Function** – A serverless compute that enables you to automatically run code on demand. Azure Function is an event driven service for accelerating app development. It is FaaS that executes the code in response to an event or trigger. Its billing is done when code is executed; in the idle state, it is not charged. Its supported languages are C#, F# and JavaScript, and currently Java is in preview state. Azure Function is a part of App Services that can run in App Service Plans (from free to isolated plan). In free account, the first 1 million executions/month are free
- **Azure Batch** - A managed service for batch processing jobs like for running large-scale parallel and High-Performance Computing (HPC) applications. It has the ability to scale to tens, hundreds, or thousands of virtual machines as per requirement. It supports both windows and Linux compute nodes. This service is free and you only need to pay for the resource that are used in your task
- **Azure Kubernetes Service** - A managed Kubernetes Container Orchestration for simplifying the deployment, management, and operations of Kubernetes. It gives you automatic upgrades and patching. Azure Kubernetes Service enables you to manage the cluster of VMs on which containerized app is running. It also supports other orchestration like DC/OS, Docker, and Un-managed Kubernetes, but these are not managed. Here, you only need to pay for agent nodes not for the master node
- **Azure Container Instance** - A containerized service that is used to run an application on Azure without provisioning the VMs and servers. You can easily run the container with a single command. It gives you an individual container as a service. Azure Container Instance is the fastest and easiest way to run a container in Azure. It is good for applications that run in an isolated container. The applications are publically addressable and the container spec can be designed by you. The billing is per-second based
- **Service Fabric** - A distributed network framework that is capable of operating in various environments, Azure and on-site. It creates Windows and Linux micro services and orchestrates containers. Service Fabric is used by multiple Azure and Microsoft services like Skype, CosmosDB, Cortana, etc. It supports both stateful and

stateless micro services. Its supported community is .NET but it also supports other languages and containers

- **Cloud Services** - A managed service for cloud applications. It is actually a PaaS offered by Azure. It is similar to App Services but with the difference that you can remote it into VMs. It creates highly available, flexible cloud applications and APIs to concentrate on software rather than hardware. It has two types of services: Web Roles that are websites and web apps, and Worker Roles that are for asynchronous processing

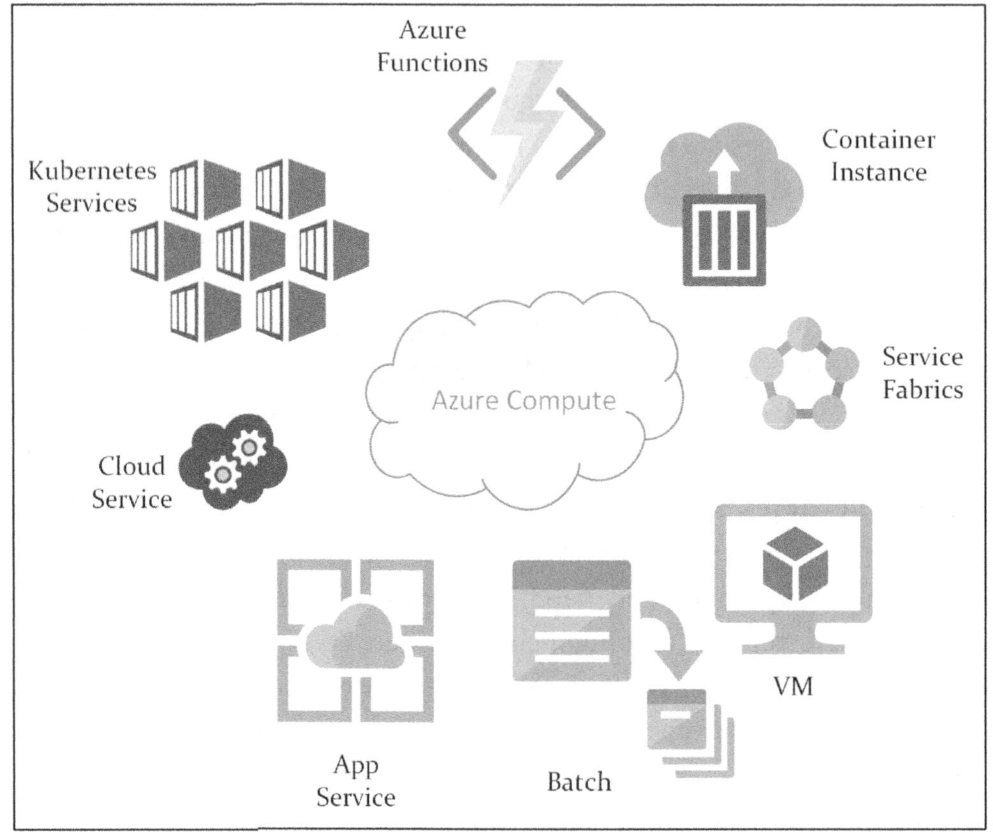

Figure 1-07: Azure Compute

Networking

The key function of Azure networking is the relation of compute resources and access to applications. In Azure, a network interface includes a number of options in global Microsoft Azure data centers that link the outside world to services and apps. There are various networking services in Azure that can be used individually or together. Azure networking provides you the most secure environment for your data as compared to any other Cloud Platform.

- **Virtual Networks** – This allows your Azure resources to communicate with each other over the internet or on-premises network, in a secure way. It is also known as VNET and is an isolated network where you host your VMs, VM Scale Sets and App Service environments. Virtual Networks are composed of subnets with user defined routes where you define the route to send the traffic and the destination from where it comes in. With Virtual Network, you can add Security Groups and outbound internet access to the resources. In Virtual Network, you have the capability of VNET Peering, where you connect two VNETs together. VNET peering can be done within the same region or across the region for global coverage. However, across-region VNET peering is supported in only a few regions currently. There is also a Service Endpoint feature that enables you to access the services within your VNET by creating a private connection to that resource rather than using the internet. This endpoint feature is only available in Storage account and SQL databases
- **Azure Load Balancer** – This balances the incoming and outgoing traffic to and from the application resources and service endpoints. It gives basic load balancing features to your VMs and operates at layer 4 (Transport layer of the OSI model). It has a public or internal load balancer. A public load balancer is internet facing while internal load balancer is used within the VNET. Azure Load Balancer provides regional load balancing by routing traffic over availability zones and into your VNets. It provides internal load balancing by routing traffic across and from your local resources within VNET. It has HTTP or TCP based probes for health checks and availability. It uses hash based load balancing to balance the load inside the VMs that are behind your load balancer
- **Application Gateway** – This is a cloud load balancing device to handle web app traffic. It is Layer 7 load balancing that uses HTTP based Round robin. It optimizes application server delivery while increasing security for applications with a web application firewall. It also offers some other features like SSL Offloading, stickiness for some cookies based session affinity at the backend to maintain the state for the user between the connection of user with a single VM. It also provides support for client connected applications by Web Socket. It has internal and external load balancing, similar to the public and internal load balancer but they are at higher level
- **VPN Gateway** – This sends encrypted traffic across the public internet between an Azure virtual network and an on-site location. Azure Virtual Networks are accessed through high performance VPN Gateways in a secure way over the internet. VPN Gateway supports both Site-to-Site VPN and Point-to-Site VPN. You have one VPN gateway per VNET then you have the ability to have multiple connections per VPN Gateway. In that, you can perform Static or Dynamic Routing

- **Azure DNS** – This hosts DNS domains with the same credentials of Microsoft Azure infrastructure to provide name resolution with fast DNS response and high domain availability. In Azure DNS, you cannot purchase the Domain name. For DNS, you pay per zone, per month, and then per million queries. The pricing of per zone changes depending upon the zone. Private domain support currently is in preview state
- **Traffic Manager** – This is a global traffic router that distributes DNS-based traffic to services across the Azure region in order to get the best available endpoint, providing high availability and responsiveness. It supports 4 routing methods: priority, weighted, geographic and performance. Depending on the routing method and health checks, the traffic will be sent. It can be used to build multi-region architecture like web applications
- **Content Delivery Network (CDN)** – This provides users with high bandwidth content. To reduce latency, CDNs save cached content on edge servers at POP locations near to end users. Edge servers are the smaller data centers. It is mainly used for static assets like media, images, etc. It also supports Dynamic Site Acceleration by optimizing the route between the requester and the origin for dynamic content because it does not cache the dynamic content on the edge servers. In Azure, CDN is actually provided by Akamai and Verizon. The billing is based per Gb outbound per month and the rates can change on zone basis
- **Express Route** - ExpressRoute allows you to extend your on-premises networks to Microsoft Cloud by a connectivity provider's private connection. This is a private connection. There is no traffic going on the internet. Connections to cloud services such as Microsoft Azure, Office 365, and Dynamics 365 can be built with ExpressRoute through stable high bandwidth connections. The dedicated link is up to 10Gbps. With that, you have two options: either you have connectivity to MPLS or to the on-premises network. This is good for DR or hybrid cases

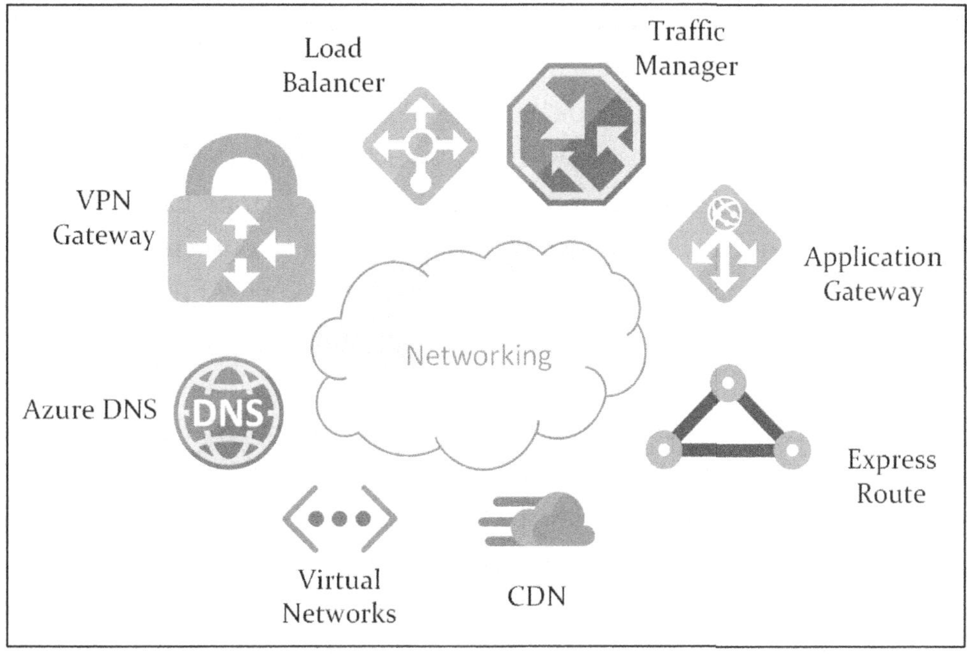

Figure 1-08: Azure Networking

Storage

Azure Storage is a cloud storage system from Microsoft that helps to store up-to-date files. Azure Storage offers an extremely scalable data object store, a cloud file system service, a reliable message store, and a NoSQL store. Azure Storage is secure, highly available and durable, scalable, managed and accessible. You must first create an account in Azure to use any kind of storage there, the storage account is the parent object. You can move your data to and from your storage account after your account has been established. You can also build a storage account for up to 500TB of cloud data because it has a limit of 500TB per storage account. To manage your expenses, use a Blob storage account and hot or cold access tiers depending on how often the object data is accessed. A storage account can be of two types: Standard and Premium accounts.

In Azure Storage, there are multiple types of replication: Locally Redundant Storage (LRS), Zone Redundant Storage (ZRS), Geo-Redundant Storage (GRS) and Read Access Geo-Redundant Storage (RA-GRS). In Azure Storage, there are also various tiers of Storage: Archive (for Blob only), Cool Storage (for infrequently accessed data) and Hot Storage (for frequently accessed data).

- **Blob Storage** - Azure Blob Storage is Microsoft's cloud object storage solution. Blob storage is for storage of large volumes of unstructured data, like text or binary data. It is an internet accessible Objet Store via HTTP or HTTPS. In that, you have an option to make your data either public or private. The hierarchy is like: Storage

Account -> Containers -> Blobs. A blob is an object which is in the container. It also has an archiving tier available

- **Queue Storage** – Azure Queue Storage is a data store for queuing and for the reliable provisioning of messages. It is a managed queuing service through which you get secure storage for communication between apps based on the message. Messages in the queue can be up to 64 KB and millions of messages can be stored in a single queue. A queue is generally used to store asynchronous lists of messages. It is useful for de-coupling applications. The life time of a message in the queue is 7 days
- **File Storage**- Azure File Storage makes the use of a regular SMB (Server Message Block), to set up a highly available network of file shares. You also can read files via the REST interface or libraries for the storage client. The cloud or on-site implementations of Windows, Linux, Mac OS installs Azure file shares concurrently. Azure file shares can also be cached with Azure file sync on Windows Servers for easy access close to the data point. You can also use it as a shared file system for the apps that lift and shift into the cloud. The maximum file share size is 5TB
- **Table Storage**- Azure Table Storage is a service that stores NoSQL unstructured data in the cloud and offers a schema less design for providing a key/attribute database. Since table storage is schema less, the development of your application will make it easy for you to adapt your data. In table storage, there can be as many entity and tables as you like. The maximum entity size can be up to 1MB. Access to table storage data for many types of applications is fast and cost effective and is typically lower than conventional SQL for similar data volumes. It has now become a part of Cosmos DB. A new Azure Cosmos DB Table API is introduced in addition to the Azure Table storage service, which offers optimized throughput tables, global distribution and automated secondary indexes
- **Disk Storage** – Azure Disk Storage provides a managed or unmanaged disk for your VMs. Managed disk takes care of the storage account and disks for you, and you pay for what you provisioned while in un-managed disk, as you have to manage the disk itself but you only have to pay for what you use. It has 99.999% availability with three replicas. The available types of disk storage are Ultra-Disks, Premium Solid-State Drives (SSDs), Standard SSDs, and Standard Hard Disk Drives (HDDs). In premium, you have an option of disk IOPS that are provisioned and these are mapped on disks not on VMs. However, not all VM families support the premium disk type. In Standard disk, the IOPS are not provisioned via disk so it varies with VMs. The size for the disk storage is from 32 GB to 4 TB, but you can attach multiple disks to a VM

Queue Storage
Table Storage
Azure Storage
File Storage
Blob Storage
Disk Storage

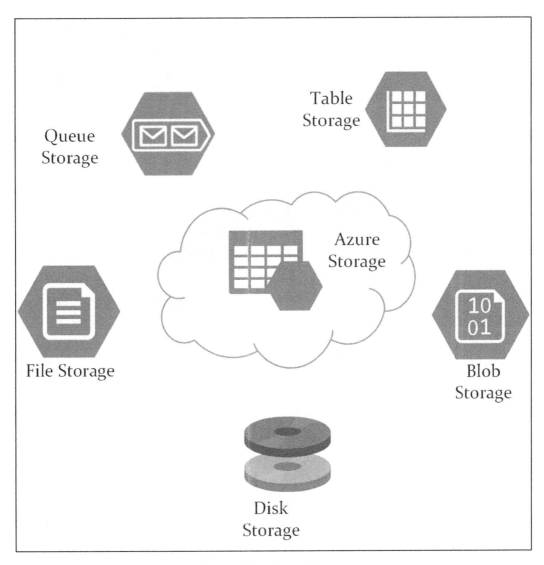

Figure 1-09: Azure Storage

Data and Analytics

Data is available in all sizes and formats. When they speak about Big Data, it means they refer to large volumes of information. Like, producing hundreds of gigabytes of data from weather systems, communications systems, genome analysis, imagery platforms, and many other scenarios. The volume of data makes it difficult to interpret and determine. It often is so large that it is no longer appropriate for traditional methods of processing and analysis.

To cope with these large data sets, Open Source cluster technologies have been developed. Microsoft Azure offers a wide range of Big Data and analytics tools and services.

- **HDInsight** – It is an open source fully managed analytic service. It processes huge amounts of data in the cloud with managed Hadoop clusters. The 99.9 percent SLA for your business is given by this. It is basically a Hadoop component from HDP

(Hortonworks Data Platform). It is used for running streaming and historical data analytics. The open framework for HDInsight includes hive, spark, Kafka, storm, etc. The use cases for this service are batch processing, data science, and many more

- **Event Hub** – It is a large scale telemetry ingestion that allows you to run millions of events per second. You can use it to load a large amount of data in to the cloud in real time. It captures data into the Azure Blob or Data Lake and then publishers send this data into the event hub. Then from these hubs, the consumer reads data. The retention period of an item in hub is 7 days
- **Data Lake Store and Analytics** - Azure Data Lake provides all the capabilities to make the storage of data of any scale, shape and speed, and all types of processing and analytics across platforms and languages simple for developers, data scientists, and analysts. This eliminates the complexity of ingesting and processing all your data and makes the process of batching, uploading and immersive analysis easier. Data Lake Store is a repository for the analytics workload and it is HDFS compatible and can integrate with HDInsight. It has no limit for data storage. Data Lake Analytics is a completely managed pay-per-job analysis service with corporate security, auditing and support. It uses U-SQL language that is specifically designed for Data Lake Analytics that combine SQL and uses C# code to perform analytics. Data Lake Analytics can work with Data Lake Store and others
- **Data Factory** – It is a fully managed cloud based data integration service. Big data demands for the service to organize and operationalize processes and refine these huge raw data stores into operational business insights. This is an integrated cloud service for complex hybrid Extract-Transform-Load (ETL), Extract-Load-Transform (ELT), and data integration projects. It is a service that automates the data movement along its process through various systems. SQL Server Integration Service built-in V2 of Data Factory is in preview, which is the transformation process of ETL
- **Azure Analysis Service** – It is an analytic engine as a service for enterprise grade. It uses advanced computing and mashup to combine data from several data sources, set metrics, and secure data in an advanced single table of the semantic data model for query purpose. The data model makes searching vast volumes of data for ad hoc data analysis easier and quicker for users. It supports hybrid network and it has built-in SQL Server Analysis Service

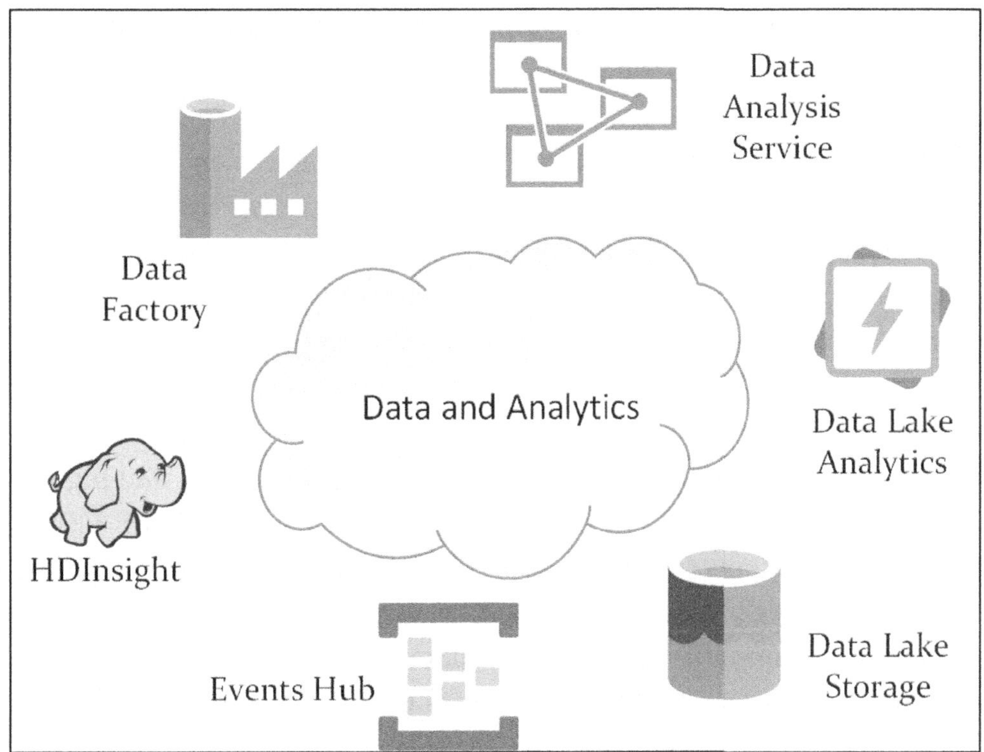

Figure 1-10: Data and Analytics

Databases

Azure Database is a fully managed service. It has business-grade efficiency with integrated high availability that ensures you can easily scale and hit global distribution without needing to pay attention to costly downtime.

- **SQL DB** – It is a fully managed relation database with high availability and performance data storage for applications. In that, you have two deployment options: Single DB and Elastic Pools. In Single DB, you pick a single service and scale it up or down in a single database while in Elastic Pools, a pool of resources is shared across number of databases. With Elastic Pool, you get better optimization. It has Database Transaction Unit (DTU) purchasing model. The purchasing model DTU provides a mixture of computing, storage and I/O services in three levels, supporting light to large databases. SQL DB shares its code base with MS SQL server, which means that SQL DB gets updated first before rolling out to the MS SQL server, this way, it will be up to date with the feature of an SQL server. It has built-in intelligence via auto tuning
- **Azure DB for MySQL and Postgre SQL** - Both of the databases are fully managed and relational databases. They both are scalable databases with security and high availability. They both have a pay-as-you-go pricing model

- **SQL Data Warehouse** – It is a managed petabyte data warehouse with complete security at all levels without additional costs. It uses massively parallel processing technique to run complex queries along with these data. The data is imported into the Data Warehouse by Polybase. The data storage is in Columnar storage in relational database that reduces the query time as well as storage. The billing is on compute Data Warehouse Unit (cDWU). In this, there are two performance tiers; one is Elasticity, which is for short burst and peak activity. The other is Compute Optimized performance, which is used SDD for frequently accessed data and recommended for fat performance requirements. With SQL Data Warehouse, you can map any type of data on it
- **Cosmos DB** – It is a non-relational database with low latency and high availability. It is a globally distributed and multi-model service which includes SQL, MongoDB, Cassandra, Table and Germlin (raph). It gives you a guaranteed throughput and within a single region, it gives you 99.99% availability. It offers you turnkey global replication. Cosmos DB replicates your data transparently wherever your users are so that they can interact with a replica of the data closest to them. It offers you five consistency models, from Strong SQL to relax NoSQL (the models include strong, bounded staleness, session, consistent prefix, and eventual consistency). It also automatically indexes all of your data
- **Redis Cache** - It is managed in-memory cache service with quick, scalable, open-source compatible data store for applications. It frequently uses caches and static data to minimize storage and latency of the application. It comes in three tiers: basic tier that is with a single node and used for test and dev, and non-critical workloads with volume of up to 350GB. Standard tier is two replicated nodes in primary and secondary configurations with a high-availability SLA (99.9%) and is managed by Microsoft. Premium tier offers caches with more functionality and with lower latencies and higher throughput. Premium tier caches are used on more powerful hardware that performs better than the basic or standard tier. It is useful for snapshots and VNET integration. Its size can be up to 530GB

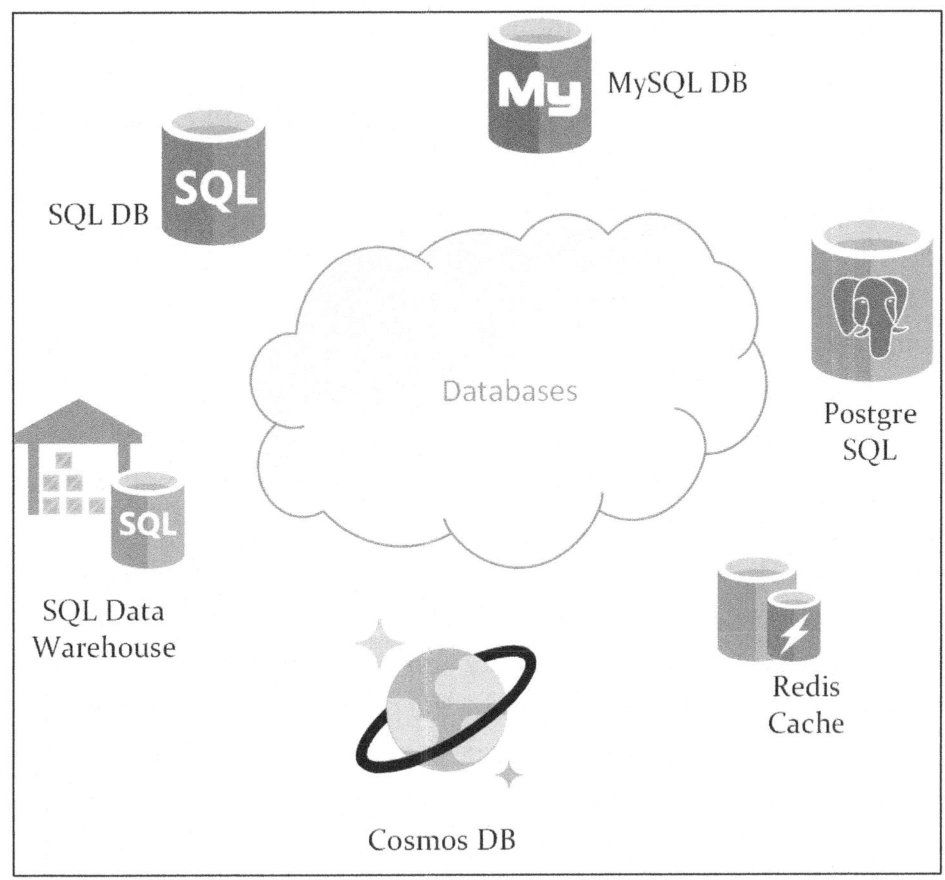

Figure 1-11: Azure Databases

Web and Mobile

Great web experience in today's business is important. Azure provides premium support for the creation and management of web applications and HTTP-based web services. Azure build engaging cross platforms for Android, iOS and Windows applications without any compromises that suit your business needs and reach to your customers everywhere. You can power your apps with smart back-end services and simplify your development cycle faster and more confidently.

- **App Service** - It is PaaS in Azure. It allows you to create and host web apps, mobile back ends and RESTful APIs without network maintenance in the programming language of your choice. It supports both Windows and Linux, automatic deployment from GitHub, Azure DevOps and any Git repo. It offers high availability and auto scaling. The supported languages are .NET, .NET Core, Ruby, Java, PHP, Node.js and python. App Service runs in various "App Service Plans" from free to isolated
- **API Management** - API Management (APIM) is a way of creating reliable and functional back-end API gateways. API Management enables companies to publish

APIs to external, partner, and internal developers to unlock their data and service potential. API Management consist of the following components:

1. API Gateway has a tunnel feature that accepts the API calls and routes it to the backend. API gateway offers authorization and caching.
2. Developer Portal is for developers that are used for developing the API. It is provided with documentation and different level or access requirements.
3. Azure Portal is for the user to develop the API. Users can import existing APIs and create API products.

- **Media Services** - Cloud-based media workflow platforms allow you to build solutions requiring encoding, packaging, content protection and live broadcasting of events. The protection of the content is done via encryption. It also has streaming URLs that you provide to the user to download the streaming asset
- **Notifications Hub** – This gives you an ability to send mobile push notifications from any back-end (cloud or on-site) to any platform (iOS, Android, Windows, Kindle, Baidu, etc). For both corporate and customer applications, the Notification Hubs work well. You can also segment the user notification on the basis of tags so that certain notifications are sent to a certain group of users. You can also tailor your notification using user's language and their location. Scheduling of notification is also available. With this, you can also send silent push notifications to your application
- **Azure Search** - Azure Cognitive Search is the only cloud search service that has built-in AI capabilities, enriching all kinds of information for easy content recognition and discovery. It also performs a full text search using simple or lucent query syntax. The data uploaded is in JSON format. It also has the ability to auto crawl various Azure services to get the data automatically. The supported services are Azure SQL DB, Cosmos DB and Azure Blob Storage. It supports filter, paging, and sort for the searches. It also has the ability for geo-based search.

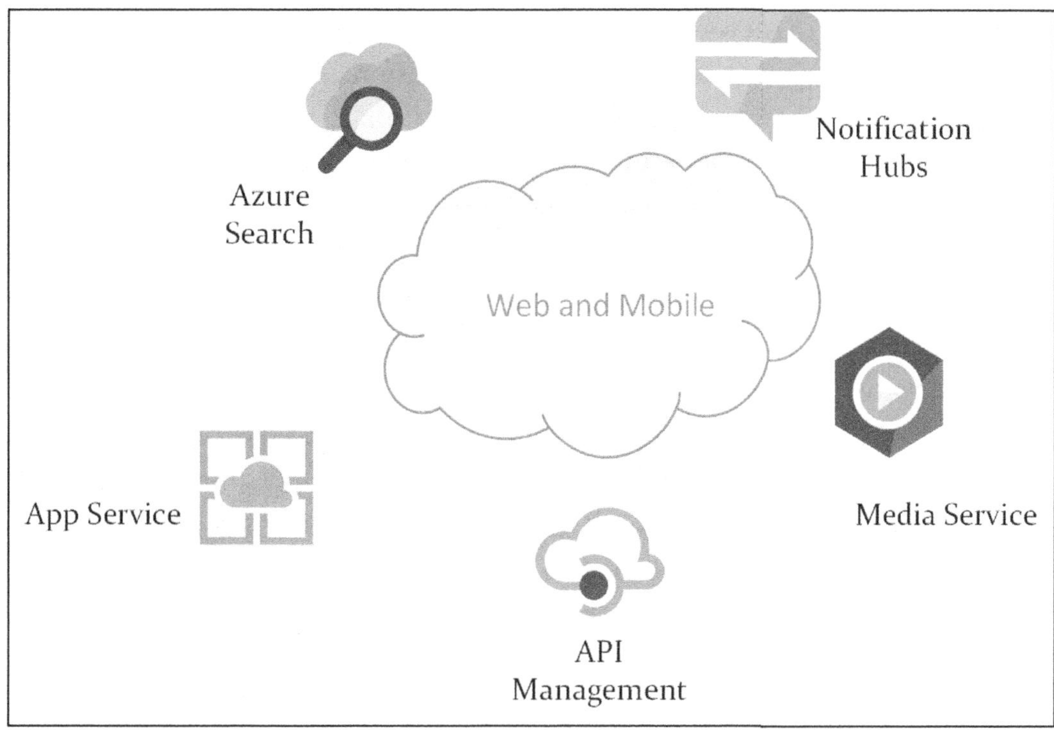

Figure 1-12: Web and Mobile

Security and Identity

We know that safety is one thing in the cloud and it is very important to have accurate and timely Azure Security information. Azure has a wide range of security tools and features that make it the best reason to use for your applications and services. Integrated Azure security services protect data, applications, and infrastructure quickly, this includes unparalleled security intelligence to help in identifying rapidly changing threats earlier, so you can react faster.

You can protect Azure identity and access management solutions for your applications and data on the front door. Defend malicious login attempts and secure passwords through risk-based access controls, identification security tools, and efficient authentication options, without interrupting productivity.

- **Azure Active Directory** – This is a cloud-based identity and access management service in Azure. It is one of the core services of Azure. With this service, the user can sign in and access the internal or external resources. The access can be role based and controlled access on various resources. With this, you can SSO for multiple clouds based SaaS applications with your company credentials. You can also authenticate your own applications by integrating it with this. You can also integrate your on-premises Windows AD

- **Azure Active Directory B2C** – This gives consumer identity and access management for your consumer based application. Your consumers can use their favorite social, company or local identity accounts to access your apps and APIs in an SSO interface. It is different from normal AD as it uses consumers to login and authenticate. It supports multiple languages
- **Azure Active Directory Domain Service** - Azure Active Directory Domain Services (Azure AD DS) offer fully Windows Server Active Directory-compatible, managed domain services such as Domain Join, Group policy, Lightweight Directory Access Protocol (LDAP) and Kerberos. There is no need of installing, maintaining and patching domain controllers in the cloud. You can use these domain services without a domain controller. It can be used in Cloud Only and Hybrid as well
- **Key Vault**- is a security service that can be used for key management in an encrypted form. When you deploy an application in the cloud, there are secrets and keys that are needed to access the DB or third party systems. So you need some service to store these and key vault is the most secure place for that. Keys in the key vault are protected by HSMs. For your own keys, it uses FIPS 140-2 Level 2 validated HSMs. With this, you can get real time usage logs of keys
- **Security Center** – This is a centralized network security management system that improves the security position of your data centers and provides advanced threat safety through your hybrid cloud workloads–whether in Azure or on site. It continuously checks your resources against the policy in order to inform you about any incident at its earliest. If it finds any incident, it gives you a recommended action in order to resolve the issue. It also gives you a prioritized alert functionality as well. It comes in two tiers: free or standard. The standard is $15 per server/month

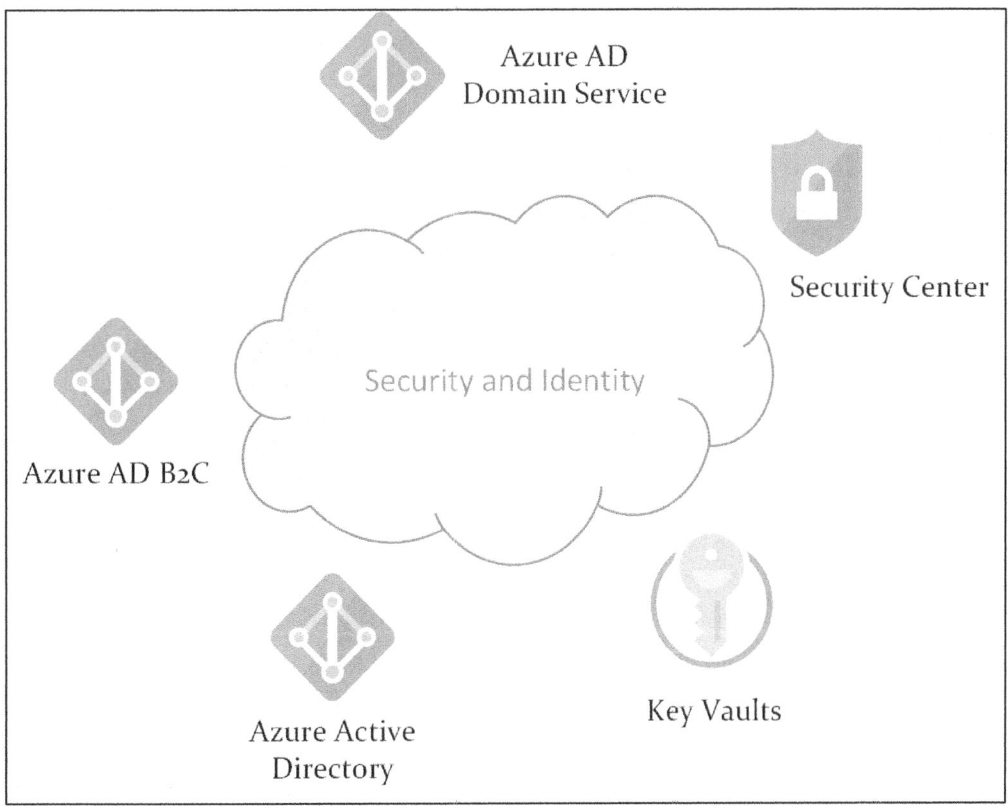

Figure 1-13: Security and Identity

Monitoring and Management

Azure management and governance tools help system managers and developers to secure and compliant the resources, both in-house and on the cloud. It monitors the infrastructure, software, system provision and set-up, app-updating, vulnerability detection, backup resources, disaster recovery, policy implementation, process automation, and even the management of costs— during the IT cycle.

- **Azure Policy** - Through this you can set and manage policies across the resources and monitor compliance
- **Azure Monitor** – This provides basic monitoring of Azure resources. It helps you understand how your applications work and recognize challenges and tools that impact them proactively. With this, you can monitor metrics, activity log and diagnostic log
- **Application Insights** – This is a feature of Azure Monitor, is a robust APM (Application Performance Management) tool for Developer and Technical DevOps. You can use it for live application monitoring. This operates with applications on a wide range of different platforms, including. NET, Node.js and Java EE, hosting on site, hybrid, and other public clouds

- **Log Analytics** – This collects data from various sources and visualizes the data from sources like on premise and cloud. Log Analytics is the primary tool for collecting interactive analysis of log queries within the Azure portal
- **Azure-Site Recovery** – This is a service used for business continuity and DR. It gives highly available and built-in DR solutions. It has failover and failback capability as well
- **Azure Backup** – This is a service in Azure that provides backup against data loss in cloud and on-premises. For backup, you have multiple options available

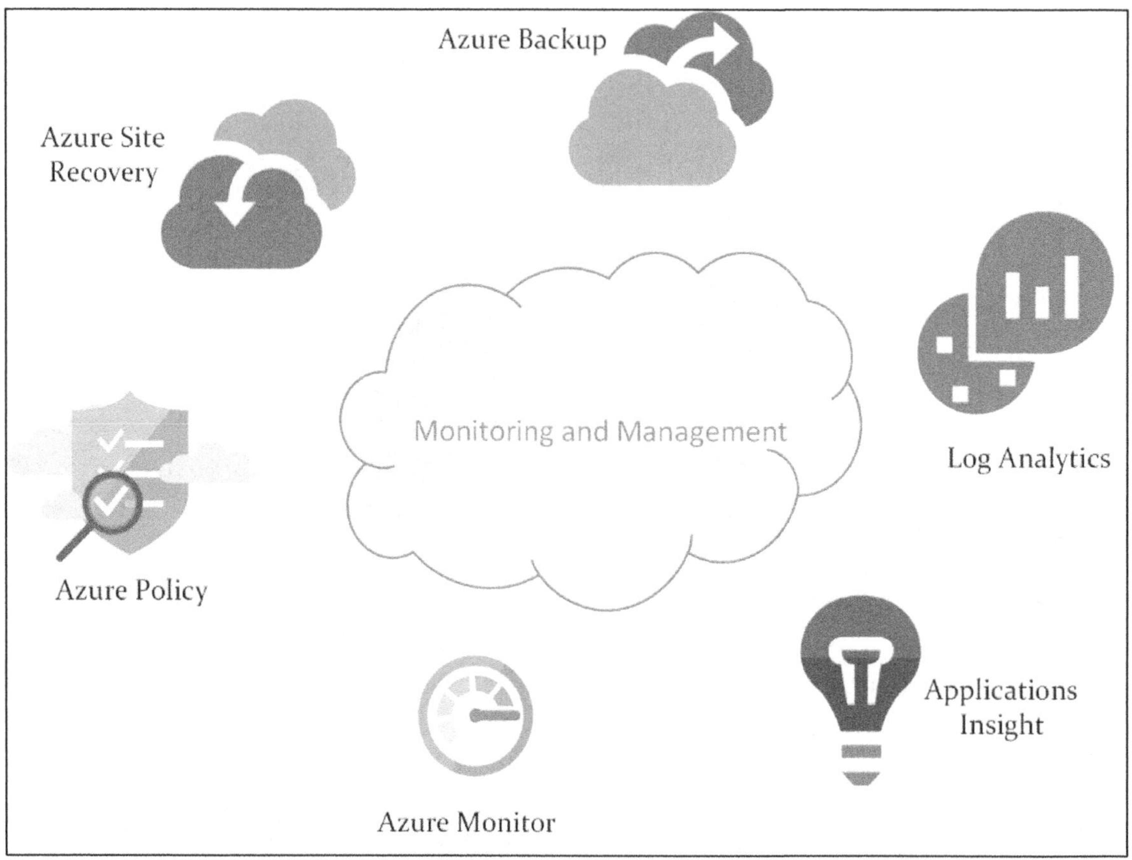

Figure 1-14: Monitoring and Management

MindMap

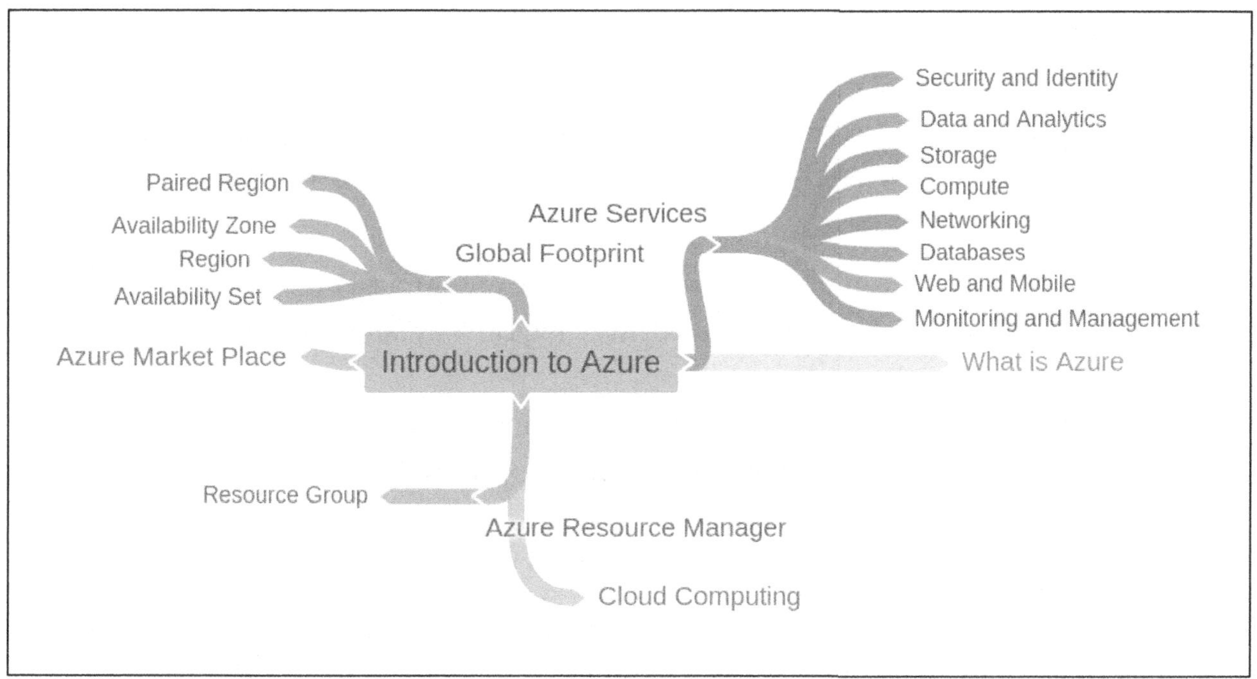

Figure 1-15: Mindmap

How to Interact with Azure

Azure Portal

In order to interact with Azure, Azure Portal is the most common way. Portal is just a website, where you fill your Microsoft account ID and password and login to Azure. With the portal, you get access to all the resources in Azure as well as on all its features. With the Azure portal, you can build, manage, and monitor everything like from simple apps to complex apps in a single console.

There are many benefits of using the Azure portal. Some of which are:

- You can personalize your Azure dashboard, layout, and workflow with colors
- With great accuracy, you can choose an access control on all resources that make your management and governance easier
- Cost management keeps an eye on the current and projected cost of resources
- It is like a One Stop shop where you have a single portal, single login for all of your Azure assets
- It has quick feature updates on products
- It has multi-platforms; it is available on the web and many other mobile devices

Azure CLI

Azure CLI is another tool that helps to interact with Azure services and features. It is only a text entry tool. In CLI, you need to enter a command to perform any action. Most Azure professionals use it frequently. Azure CLI can be downloaded from the website. The benefits of using Azure CLI are:

- It is stable, meaning commands do not change and can be used reliably
- The commands are structured in a logical way and all will follow the same pattern
- It is cross-platform, so it can work on Windows, Mac, and Linux
- As the command changes rarely in CLI, you can automate the commands for future purposes
- With CLI, you can keep track of who did what with the CLI command

You can always test the CLI that you installed to see if it has the proper version by running az --version. The CLI is designed to simplify scripting, query details, long term operations and more. The current version in use is 2.0.79. To login to azure, the first thing you need to do is write the "az login" command. A browser window will open asking you for login credentials. After logging in, you will see a list of all subscriptions associated with your account.

In order to install Azure CLI, write "Invoke-WebRequest -Uri https://aka.ms/installazurecliwindows -OutFile .\AzureCLI.msi; Start-Process msiexec.exe -Wait -ArgumentList '/I AzureCLI.msi /quiet'" in Windows PowerShell.

You can also use the following link to download the CLI: https://docs.microsoft.com/en-us/cli/azure/install-azure-cli-windows?view=azure-cli-latest

Azure PowerShell

It is just like Azure Command Line Interface (CLI). PowerShell is pre-installed in your windows machine and if it is not, then simply install it from the internet. PowerShell lets you use cmdlet that are small light weight groups of command through which you can perform simple tasks by calling a script, like to create a VM, you use command "New-AzVm". With PowerShell, you can also use Azure Resource Manager just like the Azure portal. It can be used for any other tasks as well. PowerShell version 5.1 or higher can work on Windows while PowerShell core6.x and later versions can work on any other platforms. In order to check PowerShell version, type: `$PSVersionTable.PSVersion:`

Windows PowerShell

```
Windows PowerShell
Copyright (C) Microsoft Corporation. All rights reserved.

Try the new cross-platform PowerShell https://aka.ms/pscore6

PS C:\Users\a> _
```

```
PS C:\Users\a> $PSVersionTable.PSVersion

Major  Minor  Build  Revision
-----  -----  -----  --------
5      1      18362  145


PS C:\Users\a>
```

Azure Cloud Shell

An interactive browser-accessible shell for managing Azure resources. The shell experience is the best option, whether you work Bash or PowerShell as it offers flexibility. With Cloud Shell, you can either use a fully stand-alone browser or use the portal component to experience bash, which is similar to Azure CLI or PowerShell. With Cloud Shell, you get authenticated and secure access to the resources using any web or mobile app from anywhere. Choose between Bash (CLI) or PowerShell. Tools included are interpreter, Azure tools, modules and different language support like Node.js, Python or .NET. In order to persist the data between sessions, it has its own dedicated storage. It also has integrated file editor.

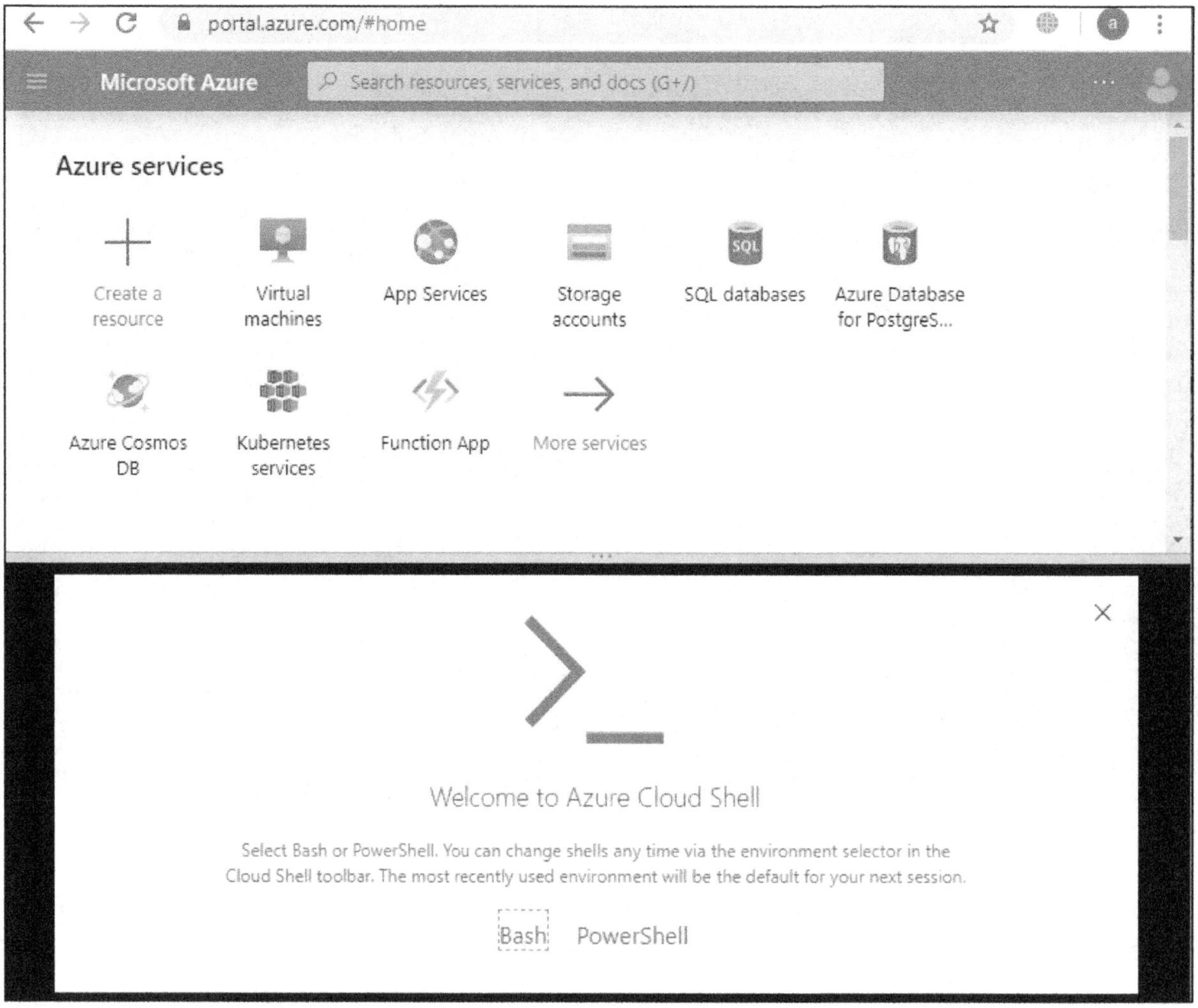

Creating an Account on Azure

1. Create an account on Microsoft using your email address then go to "Azure.com".
2. Click on "Start free". Now Sign-in with the email address.
3. Go to the window of the sign-up process for creating a new account. In "About You" page, enter all the required details for sign-up then click "Next".
4. Now in "Identity verification by phone", enter the number with country code. Then you will get a message or call option to get the verification code.
5. After verifying the code, enter the card information in "Identity verification by card".
6. Click "Next".
7. Then you have an agreement. Select the agreement then select "Sign-up".
8. After signing up, click on "Go to Portal". You will now get a pop-up window of Welcome to Azure with "start tour" or "maybe later" options.

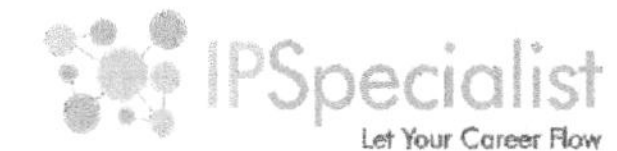

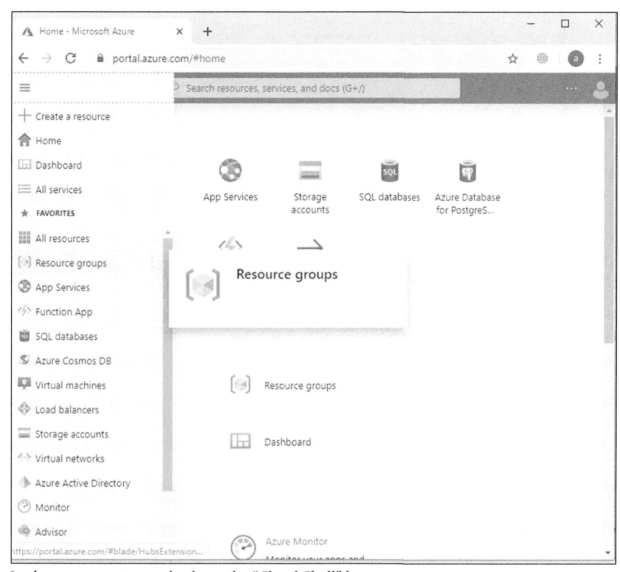

9. In the top corner, you also have the "Cloud Shell" button.

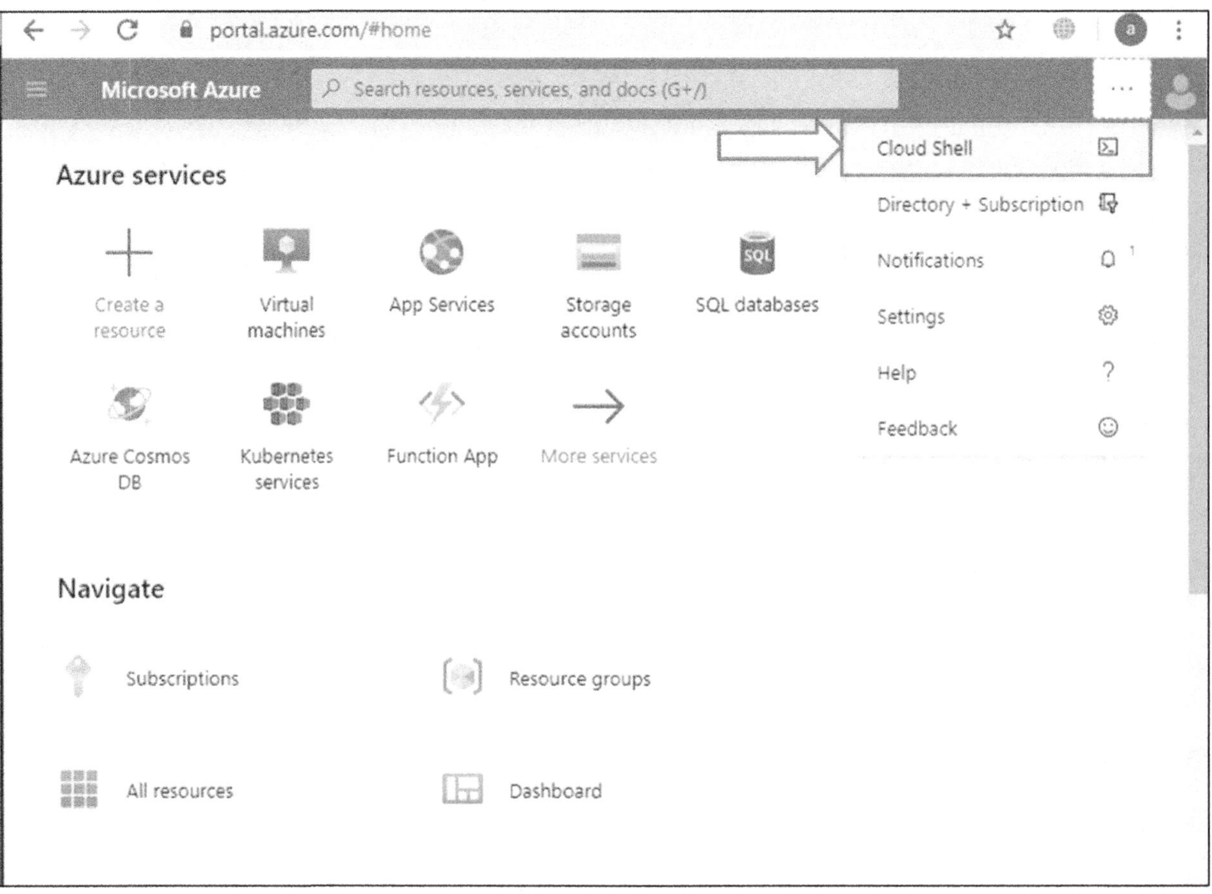

10. You also have the "Directory and Subscription" filter on the top corner.

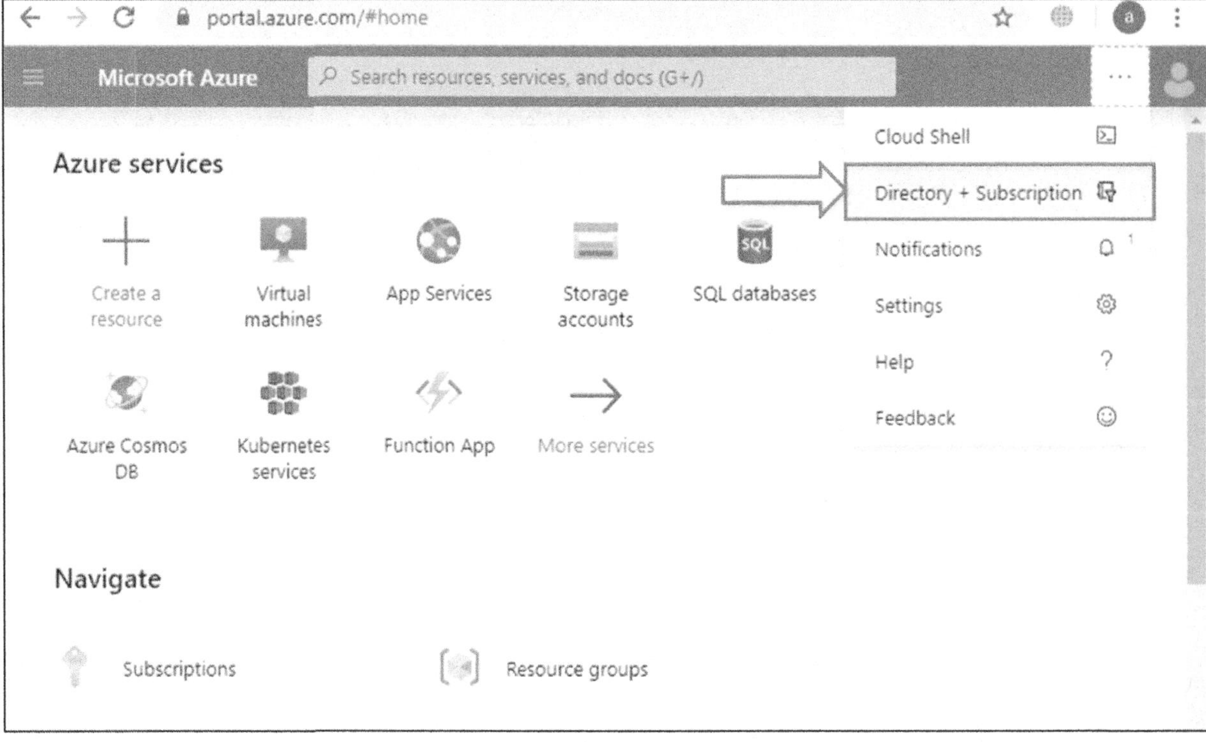

Note: The limitation of the free Azure Account is that you get free services for 12 months with credit expiration after 30 days.

Practice Questions:

1. Any service you use on Azure has a consumption component as part of the pricing is known as consumption-based pricing. True or false?
A. True
B. False

2. What does Infrastructure-as-a-Service mean?
A. Services on Azure that are updated automatically to provide a stable infrastructure for your applications
B. The layer of services that enable a complete cloud infrastructure for your business
C. Any hardware service provided by Azure such as Virtual Machines and Virtual Networks
D. Any service on Azure that you can rent and do not have to buy upfront

3. Which Azure service should you use to correlate events from multiple resources into a centralized repository?
A. Azure Log Analytics
B. Azure Monitor
C. Azure Events Hub
D. Azure Analysis Service

4. What is Cloud Agility?
A. To automatically improve the fidelity of resource usage and utilize the platform better
B. Quickly scale resource as per demand
C. Focus on business rather than provisioning and maintaining the resources
D. Using cloud elasticity to increase the return on investment

5. As resource demand increases, Azure can split the demand over more resources and scale the application. True or false?
A. True
B. False

6. In case any resource goes down, then instantly replacing it with a new one is known as________.
A. Scalability
B. Elasticity
C. Fault Tolerance
D. High Availability

7. What is the difference between OPEX and CAPEX?
A. OPEX is the cost for acquiring or maintaining assets. CAPEX is an ongoing cost for running a business

B. OPEX has a better return on investment in the short term. CAPEX has a better return on investment in the long term
C. OPEX is an ongoing cost for running a business. CAPEX is the cost of acquiring or maintaining assets
D. OPEX is a cost on services you do not own, such as cloud computing. CAPEX is a cost of ownership

8. What is an Availability Zone?
A. One or more datacenters equipped with independent power, cooling, and networking
B. A collection of software that can enable high scalability at short notice
C. A set of data centers close together
D. One of the more datacenters that are close together to provide backup

9. How many zones must each region have?
A. 2
B. 3
C. 5
D. 6

10. What is Azure Region?
A. One or more datacenters equipped with independent power, cooling, and networking
B. A collection of software that can enable high scalability at short notice
C. A set of datacenters close together
D. One of the more datacenters that are close together to provide backup

11. A cloud server is being migrated to Azure. External users can access the web application. To reduce the administrative effort needed to manage the web application, which would you suggest from the following?
A. IaaS
B. SaaS
C. FaaS
D. PaaS

12. Azure VM resource is a PaaS. True or false?
A. True
B. False

13. For daily operations, Azure resources are needed for every business unit. The same form of Azure services is expected for all businesses. To automate the development of Azure resources, which solution would you suggest?
A. Azure API Management Service
B. Resource Manager Template
C. Management Groups
D. None of the above

14. What is the limit of the amount of storage in Azure Storage?
A. 30TB
B. 500GB
C. 500TB
D. 10TB

15. Which Azure Service is relevant to the AWS IAM service?
A. Azure VM
B. Azure Blob
C. Azure MySQL DB
D. Azure Active Directory

16. From the following option, which is the best reason to use the Azure CLI?
A. It makes it cheaper to use Azure, as you do not have to pay for the Azure Portal
B. You can use products and services that are not available in the Azure Portal
C. It rarely changes, and the commands stay the same for the most part
D. You can use Azure CLI with more than one cloud provider

17. Why would you prefer to use Cloud Shell rather than CLI or PowerShell?
A. The Cloud Shell can be used entirely in a web browser and can be used across multiple devices
B. The Cloud Shell gets new features first
C. The Cloud Shell is free for 12 months
D. You can update the Cloud Shell independently of Azure CLI and Azure PowerShell

18. What is the limitation of Azure free account?
A. Azure free accounts are valid only for certain times of promotion such as the launch of new services
B. Credit will expire after 30 days and free resources expire after 12 months
C. Free account resources can only be created when using the USA address
D. You are only allowed to create resources for 30 days

19. What is a PowerShell cmdlet?
A. A PowerShell scripting language specifically for Azure
B. A piece of advice from Microsoft about PowerShell updates
C. A lightweight version of PowerShell that can run on mobile devices
D. A small lightweight group of commands to perform an action

20. Only products that are available globally can be accessed through Azure Portal. True or false?
A. True

a) False

Chapter 02: Compute

Introduction

In advance computing, compute means activities, applications or workloads that involves processing more resources than its memory requirements. In general, compute is used to describe concepts and objects focused on computation and processing. For example, CPUs, APUs and GPUs are considered compute resources while graphics processing applications like 3-D rendering and video games are defined as compute-intensive applications.

Compute is commonly encountered in advance computing concepts such as cloud computing and big data technologies where resources are used or served in the server and datacenters. With respect to Azure, compute is a term that covers all services, which enable computation in the cloud. This lesson will cover the topics including Virtual Machines (VMs), Scale Sets, App Services, Container Instances, Kubernetes Service and Azure Functions.

Virtual Machines (VMs)

Virtual machine is a server or computer created within a computer that actually behaves like a computer. It works on windows machine much like any other programs, providing the same end user experience as they would be hosting the operating system itself. VM does not have its own exclusive hardware. Multiple virtual machines can run simultaneously on the same physical hardware. Each virtual machine has its own virtual hardware, including CPUs, memory, hard drives, network interfaces, and other devices. On the physical computer, the virtual hardware is then mapped to the actual hardware, which saves costs by reducing the need for physical hardware systems along with the related maintenance costs, also the power and cooling demand.

Features

Following are the features provided by Azure to deploy the virtual machines on their own:

Infrastructure as a Service: Virtual machines are a part of the IaaS offering on Azure where you can manage everything except the hardware. You have complete control on the operating system, application installation and maintenance. It provides networking for VM as well.

Tools: If you want to buy your own hardware and run your own services with Azure, you can add additional tuning to manage up to thousands of VMs. Use the Azure Portal to control your hybrid cloud that includes VMs on Azure and on premises.

Compliance: You can ensure virtual machines compliance with your company guidelines by using Azure blueprints, these blueprints give instructions on how to create VMs.

Recommendations: Azure recommendations of improvements to ensure better security, higher availability, lower cost and greater performance.

Choice: Azure offers you to run VMs on both Linux or Windows, you can choose the amount of RAM and number of CPUs of your choice.

EXAM TIP

Virtual machines are the core of Azure compute and are widely used. VM is the machine that you can access exclusively.

Pricing

Azure charges for Virtual Machines on hourly basis and the resources you used. In simpler word, the more CPUs and RAMs on your VMs you use, the larger the amount you have to pay per hour.

Use Cases

Before you create a VM, you have all the necessary information regarding the VM that includes both its pros and cons.

Pros

Control: You need to control all aspects of an environment or machine before using virtual machines.

Application: you must install specific applications on your Windows or Linux machines.

Existing Infrastructure: You can move existing resources and virtual machines to Azure from on-premises or another cloud provider.

Cons

Not for Everything: If you want to use different service on Azure like hosting a website with an App service, then you do not need a VM.

Maintenance: If you have your own VM, a lot of maintenance requirements is involved such as operating system updates, patches, security concerns and others.

Scale Sets

Azure virtual machine scale sets allow you to create and manage a group of load balanced VMs that are identical. In this, a single VM is provided as baseline with which you can create VMs instantly. In response to demand or a given schedule, the number of VM instances will automatically increase or decrease. Scale sets make your applications highly accessible and allow you to centrally manage, configure and upgrade a large number of VMs. You can create significant services with virtual machine scale sets for the areas including compute, big data, and container workloads.

Benefits

Azure virtual machine scale sets provide management capabilities for applications running through multiple VMs, automated resource scaling, and traffic load balancing. The following key benefits are offered by the scale sets:

Scale sets are identical VMs, they can be activated or deactivated upon the demand.

Easy to create and manage multiple VMs

- It is important to maintain a consistent configuration across your environment when you have multiple VMs that operates your application. The VM size, disk configuration, and device configurations should be the same across all VMs for reliable performance of your application
- All VM instances are created from the same base OS image and configuration in the scale set. This approach allows you to easily control hundreds of VMs without additional network management or configuration tasks
- Scale sets allow the use of the Azure load balancer for basic layer-4 traffic distribution, and Azure Application Gateway for further advanced layer-7 traffic distribution and SSL termination

Allows your application to automatically scale as resource demand changes

- Customer demand for your application may change frequently. Scale sets will increase the number of VM instances automatically as application demand increases to fulfil customer demand, and also decrease the number of VM instances as demand decreases
- This ability of auto-scaling helps to reduce costs and create Azure resources efficiently as needed

Works at large-scale

- Scale sets support up to 1,000 VM instances. If your own custom VM images are created and uploaded, the limit is 600 VM instances
- Use Azure Managed Disks to achieve the highest performance for development workloads

Use Case

Imagine you are running an online store, everyday customers come, browse your shop and buy your items. As it is with online habits, your traffic usually increases in the evening or in the weekends. Obviously, your sells and traffic increase further. Your part of online store runs on VM that process the data. As demand increases, so does the data you need to process. If you are scaling manually as well as creating new VMs when needed, you would be constantly doing it and you probably would be very accurate. Scale set would be monitoring usage constantly to make sure you have both enough resources and VMs as well as removing them when they are not needed. In effect, you would save more money.

App Services

Azure App Service is a fully managed Platform as a Service (PaaS), which means servers, networks, storage and other fundamental infrastructures are all managed and control by Azure; you just have to focus on business values and logics.

Azure App Service is an HTTP-based service for hosting web applications, REST APIs, and mobile backends. You can develop it in your favorite programming languages, like .NET, .NET Core, Java, Ruby, Node.js, PHP, or Python. Applications run and scale easily on both Windows and Linux-based environments.

App Service not only adds the features of Microsoft Azure to your application, such as security, auto-scaling, load balancing, and automated management but also take benefits of its DevOps capabilities, such as continuous deployment from Azure DevOps, GitHub, Docker Hub, and other sources, package management, staging environments, custom domain, and SSL certificates.

App services is an easy way to host and manage your web application.

Features

Some key features of App Service are outlined here:

Multiple Languages and Frameworks: App Service has exceptional support for Java, Ruby ASP.NET, ASP.NET Core, Node.js, PHP, or Python. You can also run background services like PowerShell and other scripts or executables.

DevOps Optimization: Set up ongoing Azure DevOps, GitHub, BitBucket, Docker Hub, or Azure Container Registry integration and deployment. Encourage updates via environments for testing and staging. Using Azure PowerShell or the cross-platform Command-Line Interface (CLI) to control the applications in App Service.

Global Scale with High Availability: Scale up or down manually or automatically. Host your apps anywhere in the global data center infrastructure of Microsoft, and the App Service SLA assures high availability.

Connections to SaaS Platforms and On-premises Data: Choose from over 50 interfaces for enterprise (such as SAP), SaaS (such as Salesforce) and Web (such as Facebook) applications. Use Hybrid Connections and Azure Virtual Networks to access on-premises data.

Security and Compliance: App Service is compatible with ISO, SOC, and PCI. Authenticate users with Azure Active Directory or social login (Google, Facebook, Twitter, and Microsoft). Build limitations on IP addresses and control identities of the service.

Application Templates: Choose from a wide-ranging list of application templates in the Azure Marketplace, such as WordPress, Drupal and Joomla.

Visual Studio Integration: Dedicated tools in Visual Studio streamline the development, deployment and debugging work.

API and Mobile Features: App Service provides RESTful API scenarios with turn-key CORS support and simplifies mobile app scenarios by allowing authentication, offline data sync, push notifications, and more.

Serverless Code: Run a code snippet or on-demand script without having to provide or manage resources directly, and pay only for the compute time your code actually uses.

App Services Categories

Azure App services divided into three main categories:

Web Apps

Web Apps, as supported by Azure App Service, is a fully managed platform that allows you to create, deploy and scale Web Apps in seconds to enterprise-grade.

These are the main features:

- Runs on both Windows and Linux environment

- Supports a lot of languages such as.NET, Java, PHP, Node.js, Python and Ruby
- Has built-in auto-scale and load balancing
- High availability with auto-patching
- Continuous deployment with Git, TFS, GitHub
- Web Apps Gallery: WordPress, Umbraco, Joomla, Drupal

EXAM TIP

Web Apps are used to host web sites and web applications.

Web Apps for Containers

Web Apps for containers allow deploying and running containerized applications in Azure. A container is a self-contained unit of software. All the code programs and applications are shipped inside the container. This means, you can deploy your applications anywhere with consistent experience. Web Apps for Containers allow developers to bring their own Docker formatted container images and easily deploy and run them at scale with Azure. Containers makes software run reliably between environments.

Following are the features of Web Apps for containers:

- Easily deploy and run containerized applications that scale with the business
- Take benefit of built-in auto scaling and load balancing
- Use a fully-managed platform to achieve infrastructure maintenance
- Update CI/CD with Docker Hub, Azure Container Registry and GitHub

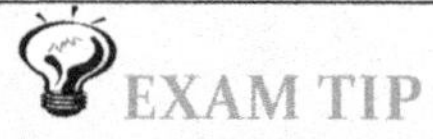

EXAM TIP

Web Apps for Containers can host your existing container images on Azure.

API Apps

API App is an efficient way to connect and expose any data backend you have. API is an Application Programming Interface that does not have graphical user interface, i.e., no user interface, no frontend. API provides the interface to connect other applications programmatically. API Apps offered by Azure App Service provide a rich framework and ecosystem for developing, using and distributing APIs in the cloud and on-premises.

The main features provided are as follows:

- Incorporate with SaaS and business applications
- Generate client proxies or APIs in your chosen language
- Automate API provisioning and deployment
- Safe APIs through OAuth Active Directory and Single Sign-On
- Exchange APIs internally through corporate galleries

API Apps can host your data backend services and does not have a graphical front end.

Azure Container Instances

Containers become the preferred way for cloud applications to be packaged, deployed and managed. Azure Container Instances is the simplest and fastest way to run a container in Azure without having to manage any virtual machines and without having to follow a higher-level service.

Azure Container Instances is a great solution for any situation that can be used in isolated containers, including simple apps, task management and job building.

ACI Features

Manage Application Dependencies

All the dependencies for an application are included in the container image. You can manage the application and its dependencies with confidence.

Less Overhead

Virtual machines require a lot more maintenance and updates. Containers do not have any operating system components that require maintenance.

Increased Portability

Applications running on containers can be deployed easily to multiple different operating systems and hardware platforms.

Efficiency

Containers are much more efficient when it comes to the development life cycle of deploying and maintaining them. Scaling and patching is much simpler as well.

Consistency

The operations team can rely on containers being the same every time, regardless where they are being deployed to.

Container in Azure Workflow

The workflow to using a Container in Azure is following:

Software Development Cycle: Develop a desired software application through various processes of software development cycle. When it is ready, it will go through the container placement phase.

Application Placed in Container: When the software application is ready for deployment or publishing, it is placed in a container image.

Azure Container Instances: When the software application is placed in a container, it can be deployed or published to Azure Container Instances (ACI).

Benefits of ACI

Azure Container Instances (ACI) have following benefits:

Run containers without managing servers

By running your workloads in Azure Container Instances (ACI), you can concentrate on designing and building your applications instead of managing the infrastructure.

Increase agility with containers on demand

Deploy unparalleled flexibility and speed containers to the cloud — with a single command. Use ACI to provide additional computation whenever you need challenging workloads.

Secure applications with hypervisor isolation

Gain the security of virtual machines for your container workloads, while keeping the efficiency of lightweight containers. In order to ensure that containers operate in isolation without sharing a kernel, ACI provides hypervisor isolation for each container group.

Works with your favorite tools

Azure Container Instances can be accessed by using Azure Portal, Azure CLI or PowerShell, whichever you like the most.

Azure Kubernetes Service

Kubernetes

Kubernetes is an open-source container orchestration system for automating application deployment, management, and scaling.

Let's briefly understand the above terms;

Open Source: It is an open source platform, which means the code based is public and anyone can submit the fixes and provisioned and get involved and invested to the product.

Orchestration: It orchestrates a cluster of Azure VMs; Scheduled containers automatically manages service discovery, incorporates load balancing and tracks resource allocation. It makes sure that all the configuration of containers is correctly configured to work properly.

Automatic Application Deployment: Kubernetes will deploy more images of containers as demanded. This will be needed as per demand of your application.

Automatic Scaling: Automatic monitoring of application load to determine when to increase or decrease the number of containers.

Azure Kubernetes Service

Azure Kubernetes Service (AKS) enables the simplest deployment of a managed Kubernetes cluster in Azure. AKS eliminates the complexity and operating overheads of Kubernetes management by offloading many responsibilities to Azure. Azure performs essential tasks such as health monitoring and maintenance for you as a hosted Kubernetes provider. The masters of the Kubernetes are managed by Azure. Only the agent nodes are managed and maintained by you. As a managed Kubernetes service, AKS is free; you only pay for the agent nodes within your clusters, not for the masters.

In the Azure portal, you can build an AKS cluster with the Azure CLI, or template-driven deployment solutions such as templates for Resource Manager and Terraform. The Kubernetes master and all nodes will be deployed and configured for you when you deploy an AKS cluster. Additional features such as advanced networking, integration with Azure Active Directory, and monitoring during the deployment process can also be configured.

Azure Container Registry

ACR is a service that keeps track of current valid container images. It manages files and artifacts for containers. When your Azure container instances and Kubernetes service need to create a new container, the images come from ACR. You can use Azure identity and security features as well to make sure the container images are safe.

AKS Cluster Architecture

Azure Kubernetes Service cluster architecture is based on the following main components:

Node

You need a Kubernetes node to run your applications and support services. An AKS cluster has one or more nodes, an Azure Virtual Machine (VM) running the components of the Kubernetes nodes and container runtime.

Node Pools

Nodes of the same configuration are grouped together into node pools. A cluster of Kubernetes contains one or more node pools. Once you create an AKS cluster, which generates a default node pool, you specify the initial number of nodes and size. This default node pool in AKS contains the underlying VMs that run your agent nodes.

Pods

Kubernetes uses pods to run an application instance. A pod represents a single application instance. Pods usually have a 1:1 container mapping, although there are advanced cases where several containers may be found in a pod. Such multi-container pods are arranged on the same node together, and allow containers to share similar resources.

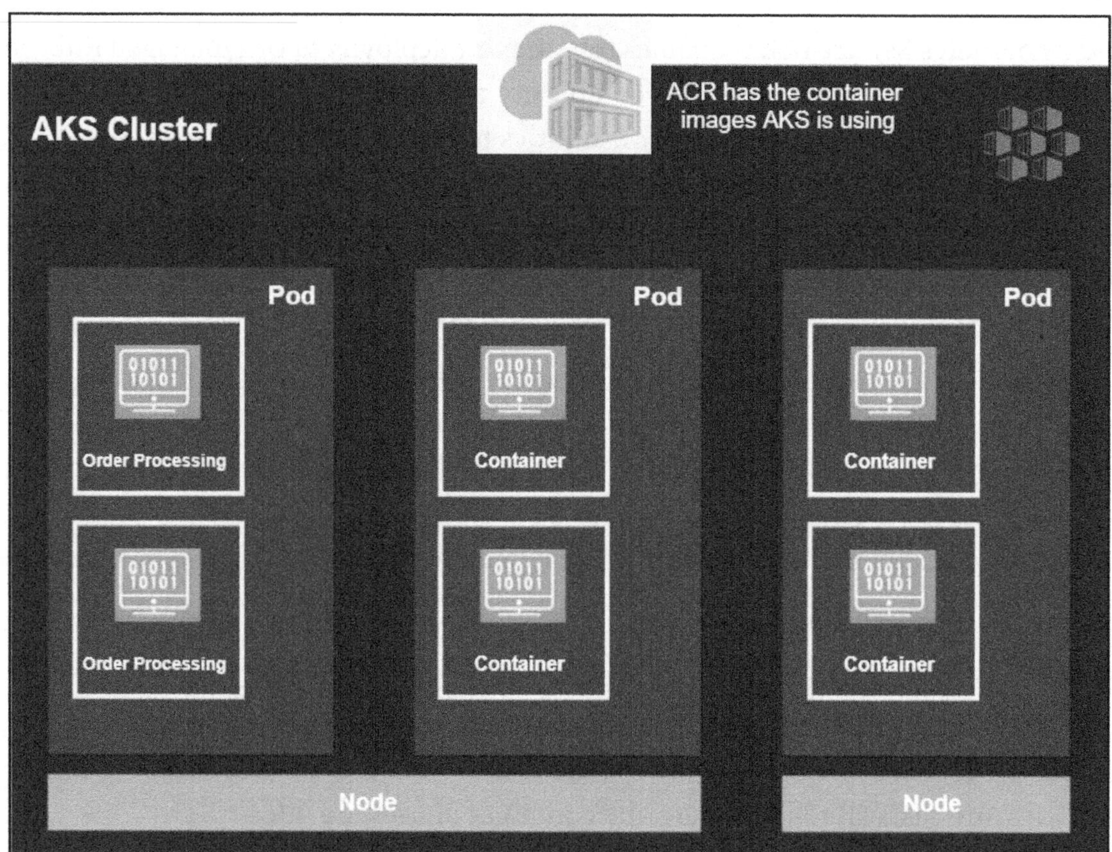

Figure 2-02: AKS Cluster Architecture

AKS supports Kubernetes clusters running multiple node pools to support varied operating systems and containers on the Windows Server (currently previewed). Linux nodes run a customized Ubuntu OS image and a modified Windows Server 2019 OS image runs on Windows Server nodes.

As demand for resources change, the number of cluster nodes or pods that run your services can automatically scale up or down. You can use both the horizontal pod auto-scaler or the cluster auto-scaler. This approach to scaling lets the AKS cluster automatically adjust to demands and only run the resources needed.

As the demand for resources increases, you can automatically scale up or down the number of cluster nodes or pods running your services. You can use either the pod auto-scaler or the cluster auto-scaler. This scaling approach allows the AKS cluster to adapt to demands automatically and only run the necessary resources.

Azure Functions

Azure Function is smallest compute on Azure. It is a single function and an easy way to run small pieces of code or "functions" in the cloud. For the problem at hand, you can write only the code you need without worrying about a whole application or the infrastructure to run it. Functions can make development even more productive, and you can use your development language of choice, such as C#, Java, JavaScript, PowerShell, and Python. It is invoked by a standard web address URL. It triggers the events to run at once and then stops.

Azure Functions is the serverless computing service that is hosted on the public cloud of Microsoft Azure. In general, Azure Functions and serverless computing are designed to accelerate and simplify the development of applications. The idea behind serverless computing, also known as function as a service, is to remove the infrastructure for user considerations. A user can create and upload code with serverless, and then define the triggers or events to execute the code. Triggers may come from a wide variety of sources, including the application of another user or other cloud services, such as databases, events and hubs for notification.

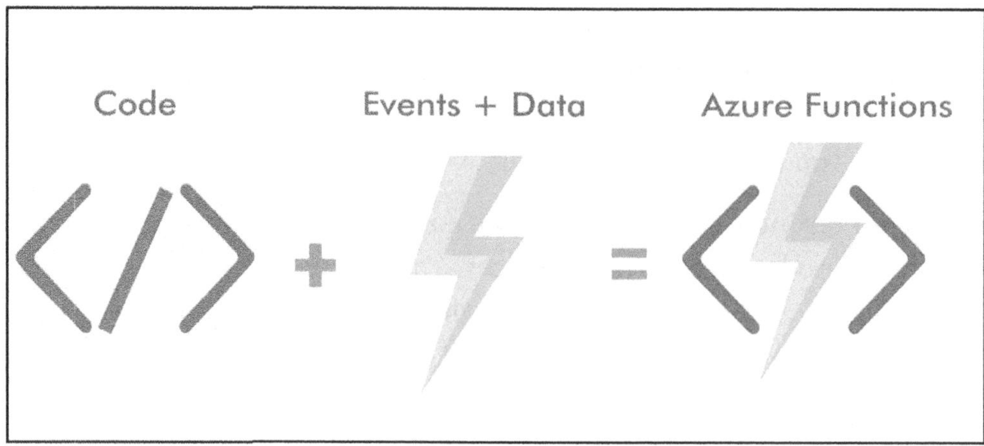

Figure 2-03: Azure Functions

It is the responsibility of the cloud provider to load the code into a suitable execution environment once a trigger or event occurs, then run the code and release the computing resources. Servers are still involved, but the user no longer has to provide or manage instances. In addition, users pay for serverless computing based on the amount of time a function runs in a given billing cycle instead of paying for those compute instances and other associated resources each month.

Microsoft Azure Functions are an event-driven, on-demand computation experience that builds on the Azure's best offering (PaaS platform).

Use Case

A website named funnyferret lets users upload pictures. These images need both processing and optimization for web display and storage. When a user uploads a picture on the funnyferret website, Azure function receives that image. The job of function here is to process the image to compress it and change into the correct file format. The function then places the image in the database of the online application for future use.

Features

Here are some key features of Functions:

Choose Language: Write functions using C#, Java, JavaScript, Python, and other languages of your choice.

Pricing Model for Pay-per-use: Only pay for the time spent running the code.

Integrated Security: Protects functions enabled by HTTP with OAuth providers such as Azure Active Directory, Facebook, Google, Twitter, and Microsoft Account.

Simplified Integration: Azure infrastructure and Software-as-a-Service (SaaS) systems can be easily leveraged.

Open-source: The functions runtime is open-source and available on GitHub.

Lab 2-01: Azure App Services

Scenario

An organization wants to deploy a web app by using an Azure service that provides a fully managed infrastructure environment for customers and developers to develop and manage applications without having to worry about managing the infrastructure. How will this be done?

Solution

Azure App Service is a fully managed Platform as a Service (PaaS), which means servers, networks, storage, and other fundamental infrastructures are all managed and controlled by Azure. Web Apps allow to create, deploy and scale Web Apps in seconds to enterprise-grade.

Step-by-Step Guide

Below are some steps to create a Web App by using Azure App services.

1. Login to "Azure portal". Select the "App Services" from the dashboard.

Search resources, services, and docs (G+/)

Create a resource
Home
Dashboard
All services
FAVORITES
All resources
Resource groups
App Services
Function App
SQL databases
Azure Cosmos DB
Virtual machines
Load balancers
Storage accounts
Virtual networks
Azure Active Directory
Monitor
Advisor

App Services

Create
View

Description

Create, build, deploy, and manage powerful web, mobile, and API apps for employees or customers using a single back-end. Build standards-based web apps and APIs using .NET, Java, Node.js, PHP, and Python.

Free training from Microsoft

Host a web application with Azure App servi...
7 units · 1 hr 5 min

Deploy and run a containerized web app wit...
8 units · 46 min

Scale an App Service web app to efficiently ...
6 units · 46 min

Useful links

Overview

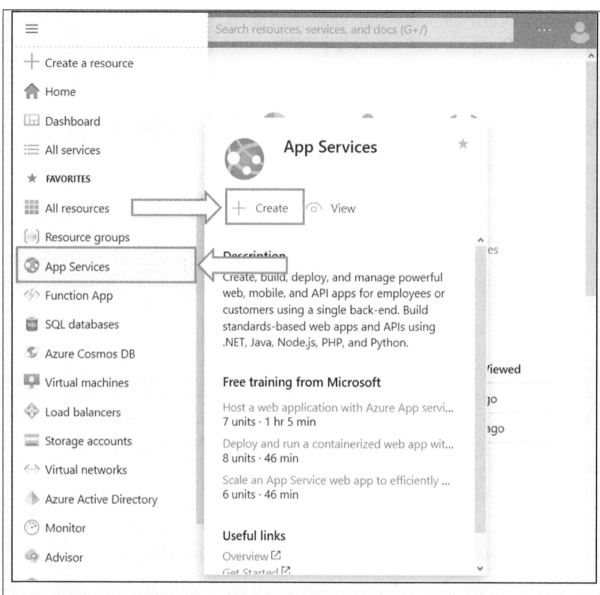

2. Click the "+ Add" icon to create Web App by providing required details such as name of the App, resource group name, etc.

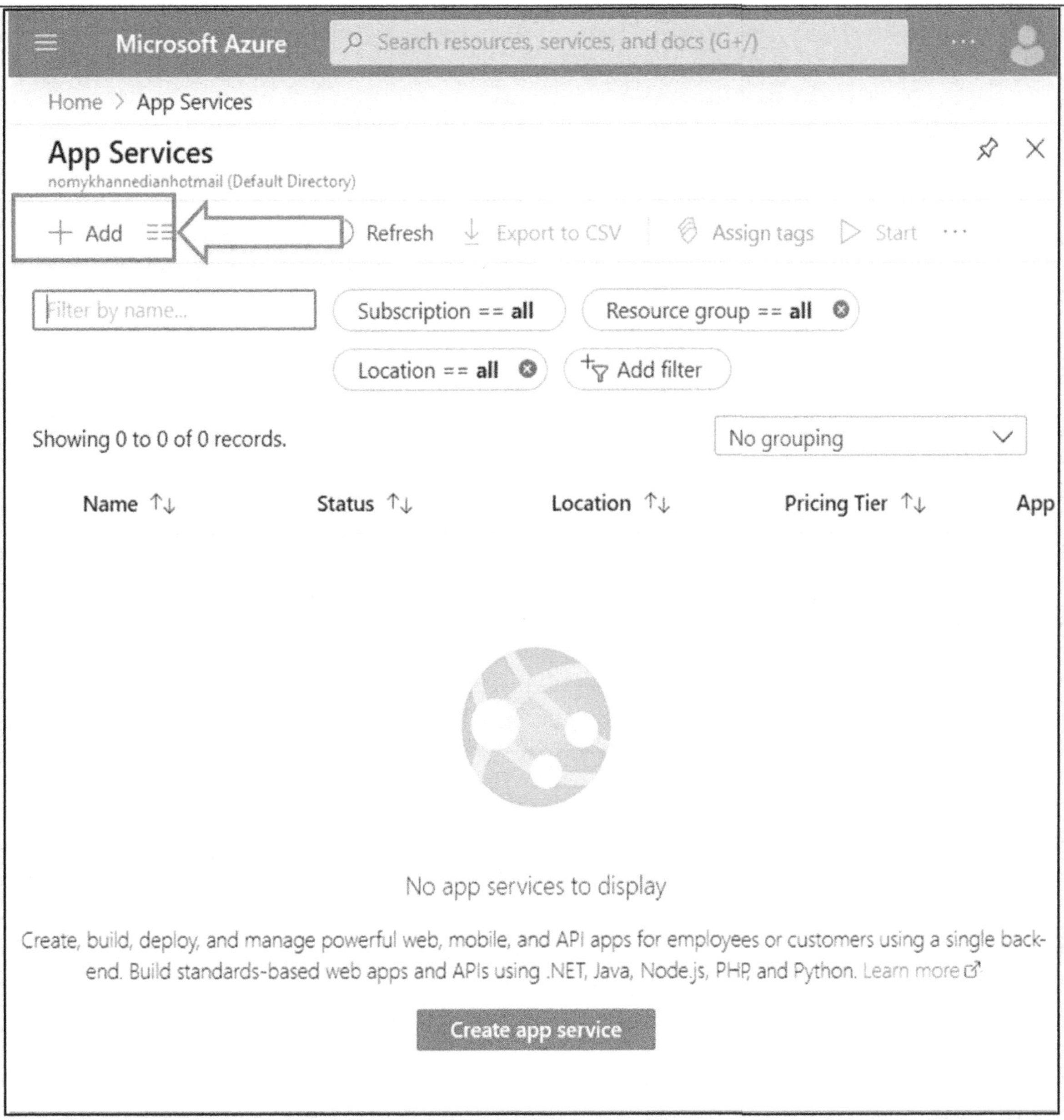

3. When you click on the "+ Add button", you will see a screen where you can enter all the information needed to create a web app. All required fields are marked using an asterisk (*) symbol.
4. Select the "Subscription" and create a resource group.

Microsoft Azure
Search resources, services, and docs (G+/)

Home > App Services > Web App

Web App

Basics | Monitoring | Tags | Review + create

App Service Web Apps lets you quickly build, deploy, and scale enterprise-grade web, mobile, and API apps running on any platform. Meet rigorous performance, scalability, security and compliance requirements while using a fully managed platform to perform infrastructure maintenance. Learn more

Project Details

Select a subscription to manage deployed resources and costs. Use resource groups like folders to organize and manage all your resources.

Subscription * : Pay-As-You-Go

Resource Group * : Select existing... / Create new

Instance Details

Name * : Web App name.
.azurewebsites.net

Publish * : Code | Docker Container

Review + create | < Previous | Next : Monitoring >

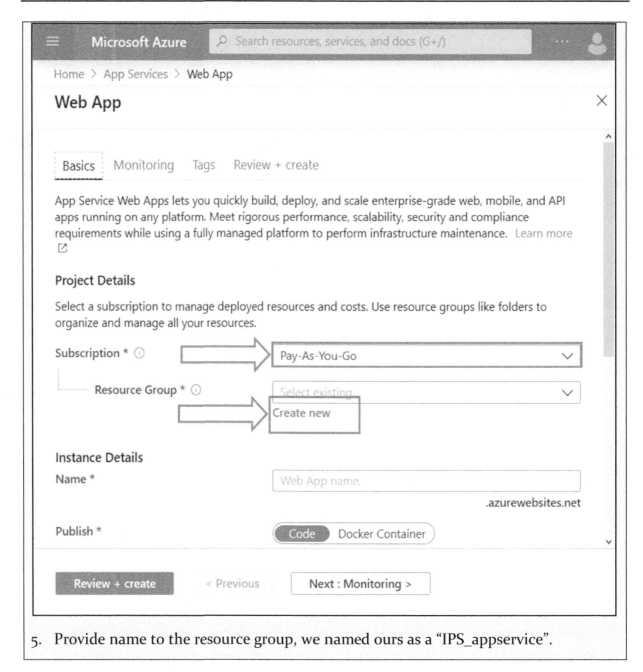

5. Provide name to the resource group, we named ours as a "IPS_appservice".

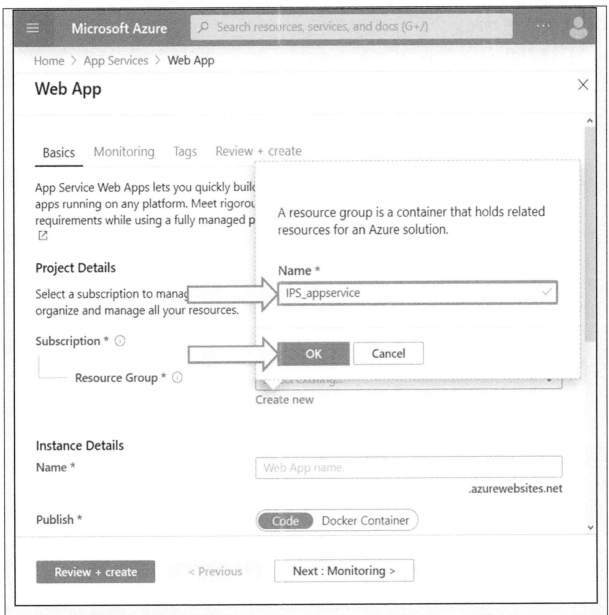

6. Provide instance details such as name, publish, runtime stack, operating system, and region.

Home > Web App

Web App

Project Details

Select a subscription to manage deployed resources and costs. Use resource groups like folders to organize and manage all your resources.

Subscription * — Pay-As-You-Go

Resource Group * — (New) IPS_appservice

Create new

Instance Details

Name * — testlabipsapp .azurewebsites.net

Publish * — Code | Docker Container

Runtime stack * — .NET Core 2.2

Operating System * — Linux | Windows

Region * — Australia Southeast

Not finding your App Service Plan? Try a different region.

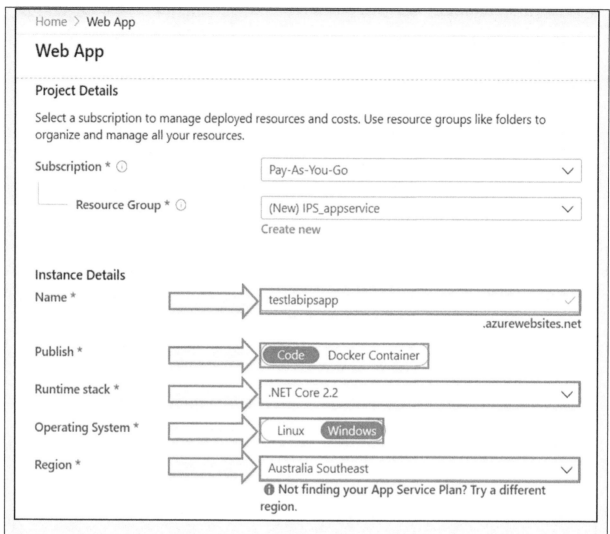

7. Create an App Service Plan.
8. When you click on "App Service Plan", you will see a screen with the "+ Create new" button, allowing for the creation of a new App Service Plan.

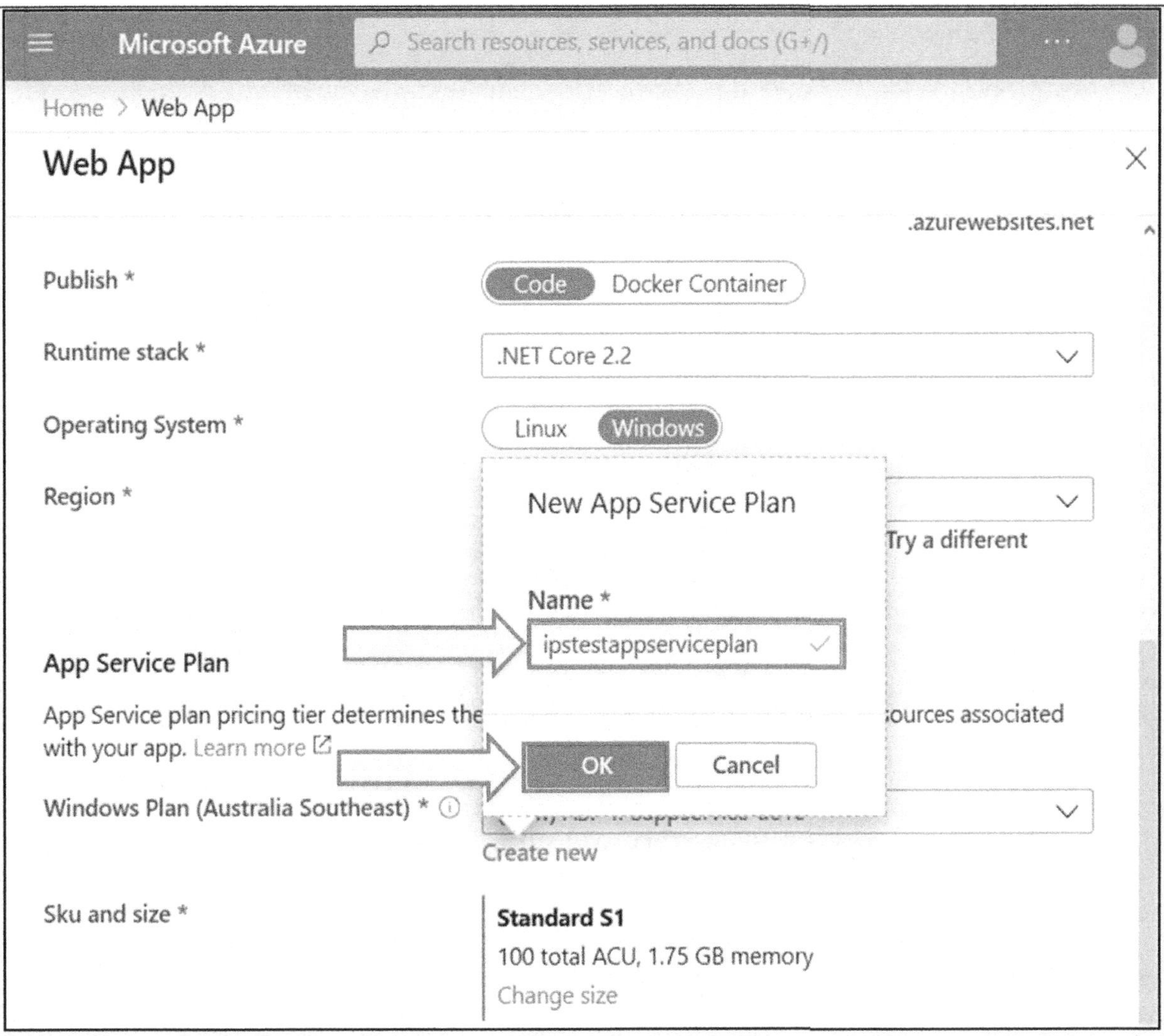

Microsoft Azure
Search resources, services, and docs (G+/)
Home > Web App
Web App
.azurewebsites.net
Publish * Code Docker Container
Runtime stack * .NET Core 2.2
Operating System * Linux Windows
Region *
New App Service Plan
Name *
ipstestappserviceplan
Try a different
App Service Plan
App Service plan pricing tier determines the ... sources associated with your app. Learn more
OK Cancel
Windows Plan (Australia Southeast) *
Create new
Sku and size *
Standard S1
100 total ACU, 1.75 GB memory
Change size

9. Change the pricing tier.
10. When you click on this option, you will see another screen presenting available features for different available tiers. This choice is really important feature-wise, and will depend, in most cases, on the environmental characteristics you are planning such as Dev/Test environments, Production applications.

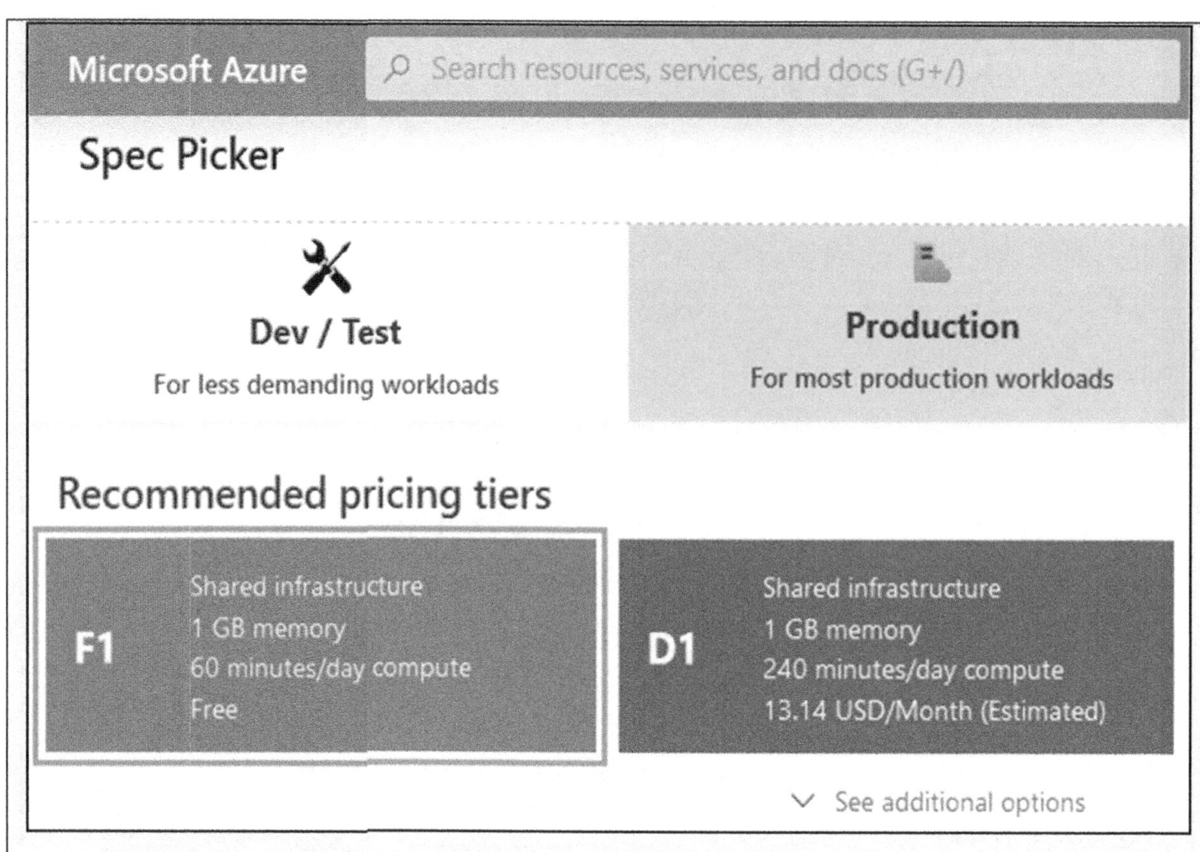

11. The "Dev/Test" category shows F, D, and B tiers (which stand for free, shared, and basic). They are designed for simple dev/test scenarios and lightweight web applications that do not need features such as auto-scaling or backups.
12. Select the recommended pricing tiers that is F1.

Microsoft Azure

Search resources, services, and docs (G+/)

Spec Picker

Dev / Test

For less demanding workloads

Production

For most production workloads

Recommended pricing tiers

F1
Shared infrastructure
1 GB memory
60 minutes/day compute
Free

Shared infrastructure
1 GB memory
minutes/day compute
13.14 USD/Month (Estimated)

See additional options

Included harc

Every instance of you
configuration:

Memory
Memory av
App Service

Storage
1 GB disk st
plan.

Apply

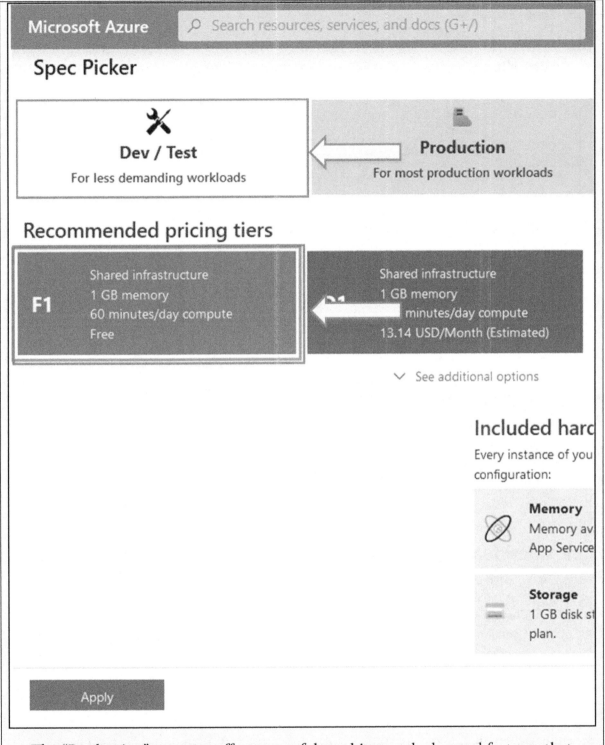

13. The "Production" category offers powerful machines and advanced features that are useful in many realistic scenarios, such as APIs, ecommerce, and popular portals.
14. Select the recommended pricing tiers.
15. After selecting, click the "Apply" button.

Microsoft Azure

Search resources, services, and docs (G+/)

Spec Picker

Dev / Test
For less demanding workloads

Production
For most production workloads

Recommended pricing tiers

S1
100 total ACU
1.75 GB memory
A-Series compute equivalent
91.98 USD/Month (Estimated)

210 total ACU
3.5 GB memory
-2-Series compute equivalent
183.96 USD/Month (Estimated)

P3V2
840 total ACU
14 GB memory
Dv2-Series compute equivalent
735.84 USD/Month (Estimated)

See additional options

Included features
Every app hosted on this App Service plan will have access to these features:

Custom domains / SSL
Configure and purchase custom domains with SNI and IP SSL bindings

Included har
Every instance of you
configuration:

Azure Co
Dedicated

Apply

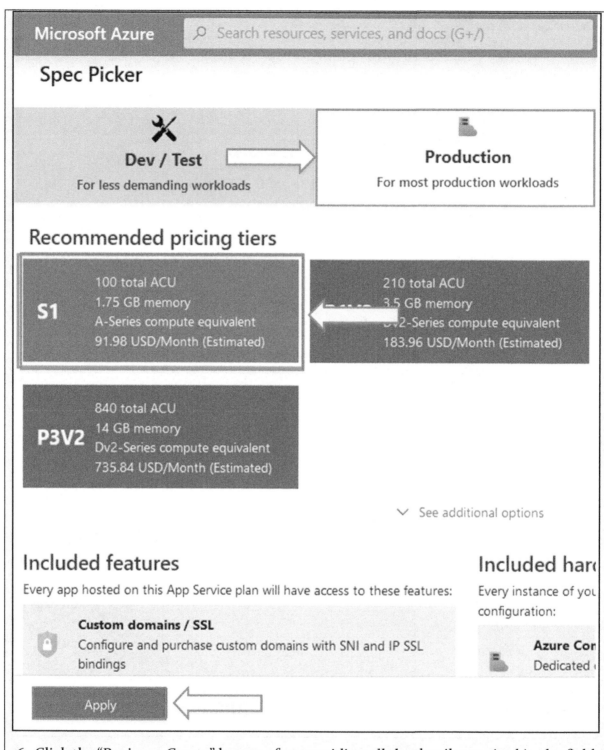

16. Click the "Review + Create" button after providing all the details required in the field.

Microsoft Azure
Search resources, services, and docs (G+/)

Home > Web App

Web App

.azurewebsites.net

Publish * Code Docker Container

Runtime stack * .NET Core 2.2

Operating System * Linux Windows

Region * Australia Southeast

Not finding your App Service Plan? Try a different region.

App Service Plan

App Service plan pricing tier determines the location, features, cost and compute resources associated with your app. Learn more

Windows Plan (Australia Southeast) * (New) ipstestappserviceplan

Create new

Sku and size * **Standard S1**

100 total ACU, 1.75 GB memory

Change size

Review + create Next : Monitoring >

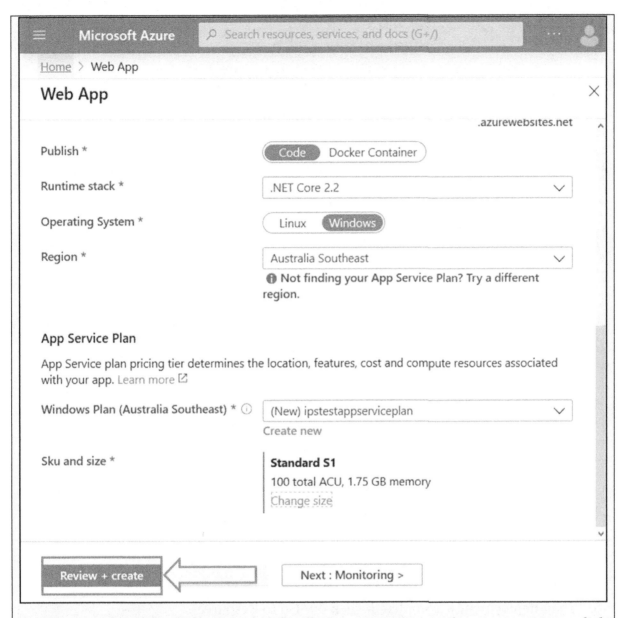

17. After viewing that all the provided details are appropriate in the summary page, click the 'Create button' and you will see the notification about deployment initializing.

Microsoft Azure
Search resources, services, and docs (G+/)

Home > Web App

Web App

Initializing deployment... 4:39 PM
Initializing template deployment to resource group 'IPS_appservice'.

Basics Monitoring Tags Review + create

Summary

Web App
by Microsoft

Details

Subscription	797152d3-23c4-499f-bfef-bb103da7d054
Resource Group	IPS_appservice
Name	testlabipsapp
Publish	Code
Runtime stack	.NET Core 2.2

App Service Plan (New)

Name	ipstestappserviceplan
Operating System	Windows
Region	Australia Southeast
SKU	Standard

Create Next > Download a template for automation

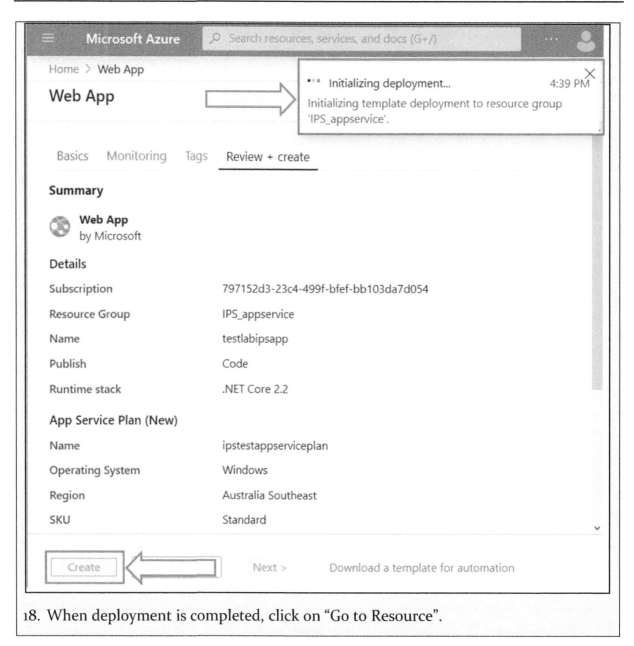

18. When deployment is completed, click on “Go to Resource”.

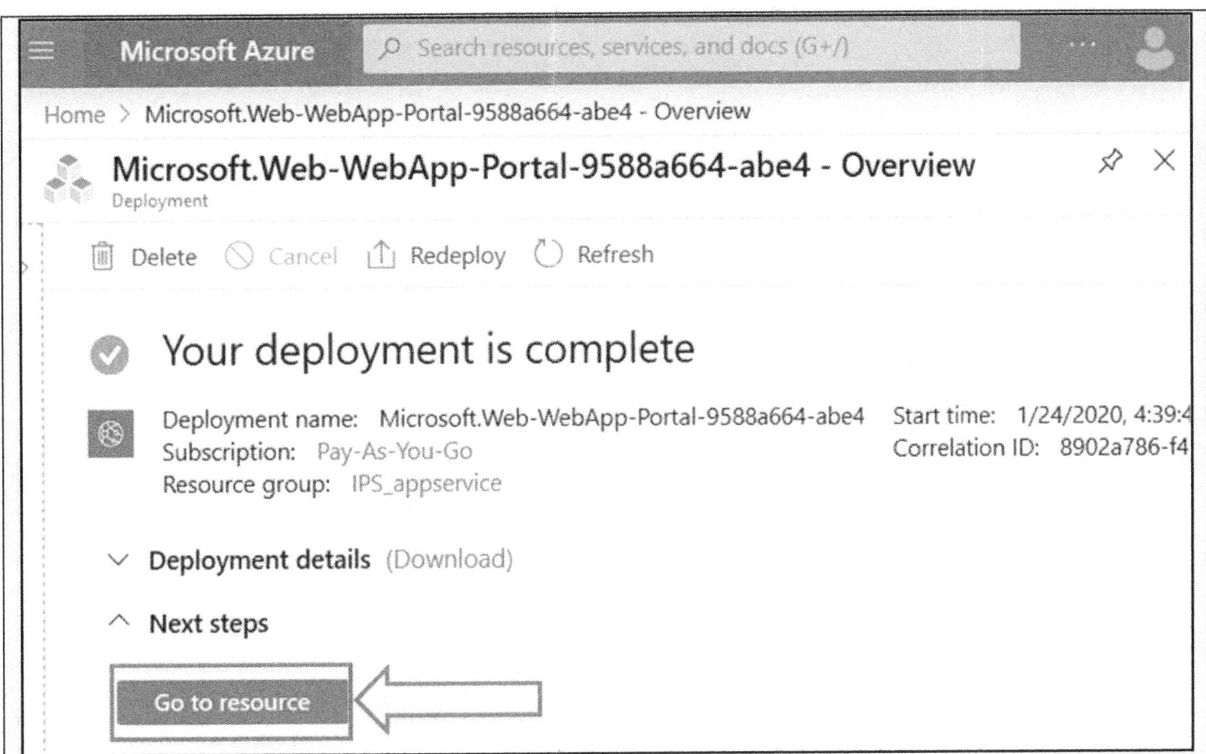

19. Go to the overview tab of the resource group, it will show the details of the app details.
20. Click on the URL, it is the link of the web app that we created.

Microsoft Azure
Search resources, services, and docs (G+/)

Home > Microsoft.Web-WebApp-Portal-9588a664-abe4 - Overview > testlabipsapp

testlabipsapp
App Service

Browse | Stop | Swap | Restart | Delete | Get publish profile | ···

Click here to access our Quickstart guide for deploying code to your app →

Resource group (change)
IPS_appservice

Status
Running

Location
Australia Southeast

Subscription (change)
Pay-As-You-Go

Subscription ID
797152d3-23c4-499f-bfef-bb103da7d054

Tags (change)
Click here to add tags

URL
https://testlabipsapp.azurewebsites

App Service Plan
ipstestappserviceplan (S1: 1)

FTP/deployment username
No FTP/deployment user set

FTP hostname
ftp://waws-prod-ml1-017.ftp.azurew

FTPS hostname
ftps://waws-prod-ml1-017.ftp.azure

Diagnose and solve problems
Our self-service diagnostic and troubleshooting experience helps you identify and resolve issues with your web app.

Application Insights
Application Insights helps you detect and diagnose quality issues in your apps, and helps you understand what your users actually do with it.

App Service
App Service Adv
insights for impr
experience on th
platform. Recom
sorted by freshn
impact to your a

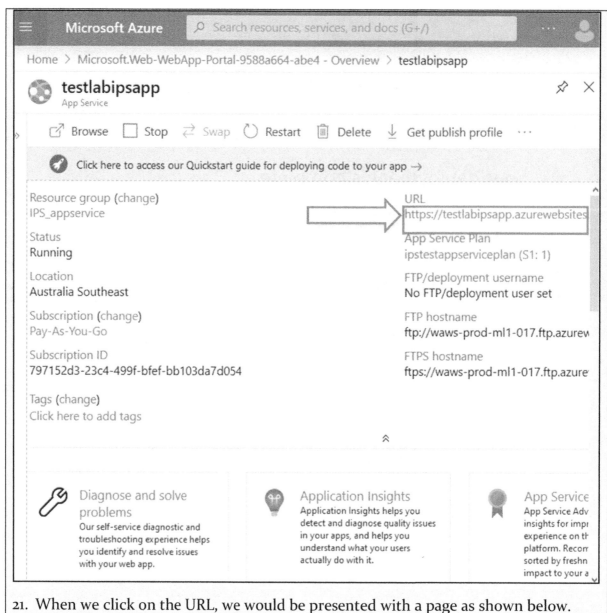

21. When we click on the URL, we would be presented with a page as shown below.

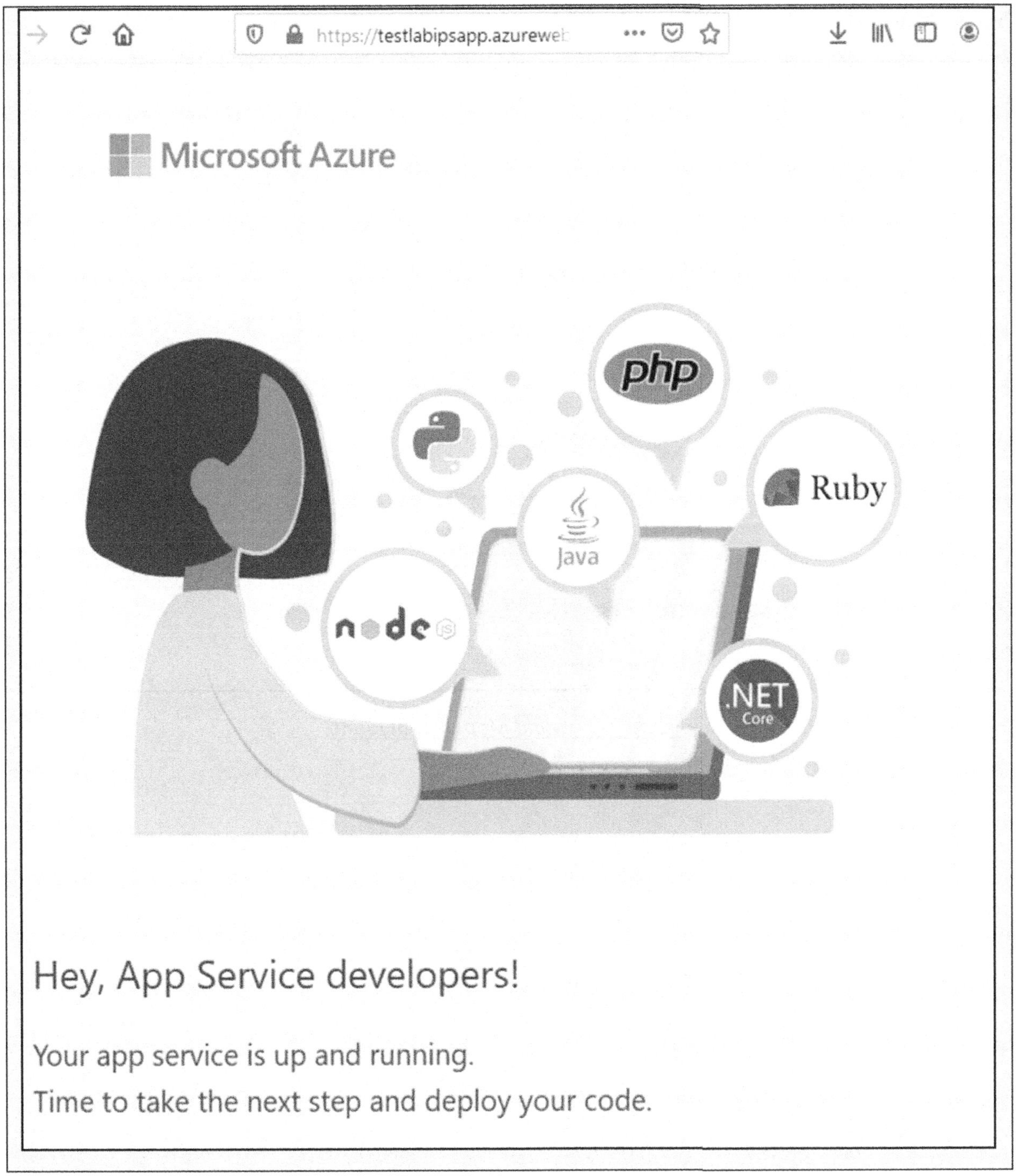

https://testlabipsapp.azureweb

Microsoft Azure

php

Ruby

Java

node

.NET Core

Hey, App Service developers!

Your app service is up and running.

Time to take the next step and deploy your code.

Mind Map

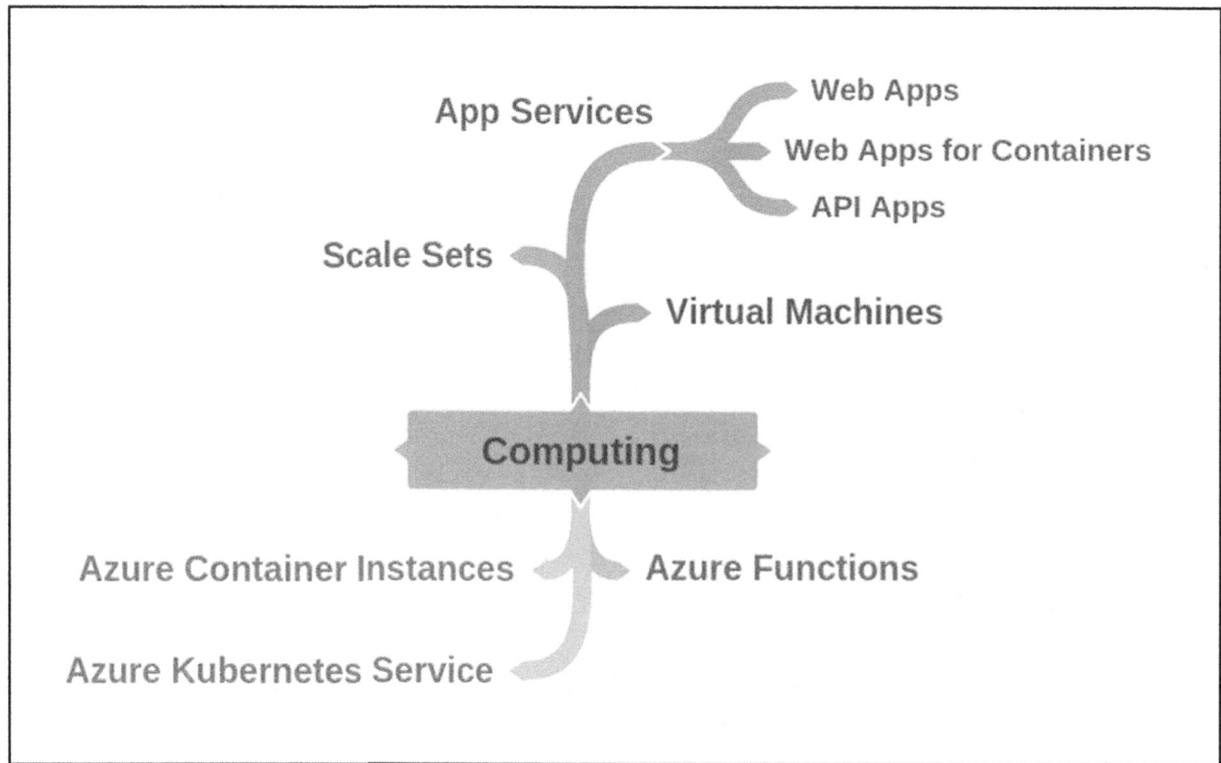

Figure 2-04: Mind Map of Computing

Practice Questions:

1. Which of the following is the right category to which the Azure Virtual machine belongs?
   A. PaaS
   B. SaaS
   C. IaaS
   D. FaaS

2. On which basis will Azure Virtual Machines be charged?
   A. Hardware utilization
   B. Resources utilization
   C. Nodes utilization on VMs
   D. All of the above

3. Which is the simplest and fastest way to run an Azure container without having to manage any virtual machines and without having to follow a higher-level service?
   A. App Service
   B. Web App for Containers
   C. Function Service
   D. Azure Container Instances

4. With respect to Azure, compute is a term that covers any services in azure that enables ________ in the cloud.
   A. Migration
   B. Calculation
   C. Computation
   D. Virtualization

5. Which of the following is the right category to which the Azure App services belongs to?
   A. PaaS
   B. SaaS
   C. IaaS
   D. FaaS

6. Scale sets support up to _______ VM instances.
   A. 6000
   B. 600
   C. 50
   D. 1000

7. Which of the following programming service is supported by API app?
   A. Backend Service
   B. Frontend Service
   C. Graphical User Interface

D. All of the above

8. ________ is the preferred way for cloud applications to be packaged, deployed and managed.
   A. Azure Scale Set
   B. Azure VM
   C. Azure Container
   D. Azure Load Balancer

9. Which Azure service is an open-source container orchestration system for automating application deployment, management, and scaling?
   A. Azure Functions
   B. Kubernetes
   C. Azure VM
   D. Azure Container Instances

10. On which of the following components is Azure Kubernetes Service cluster architecture based on?
   A. Node
   B. Trigger
   C. Node Pools
   D. Pods

11. ________ is the serverless computing service that is hosted on the public cloud of Microsoft Azure.
   A. Azure Functions
   B. Kubernetes
   C. Azure VM
   D. Azure Container Instances

12. Which of the following would help reduce the administrative effort required to deploy the machines?
   A. Azure Functions
   B. Kubernetes
   C. Azure Scale Sets
   D. Azure Container Instances

13. Which one of the following is a great solution for data processing, systems integration, internet-of-things (IoT) work, and simple APIs and microservices development?
   A. Kubernetes
   B. Azure Scale Sets
   C. Azure Functions
   D. Azure Container Instances

14. Which definition best describes compute on Microsoft Azure?
   A. A Virtual Machine
   B. An optional component to improve the efficiency of Azure

C. Any service that performs or enables a computation
D. Any serverless service, such as Azure Functions

15. Which cloud service model does Function Service belong to?
    A. Platform-as-a-Service
    B. Serverless
    C. Software-as-a-Service
    D. Infrastructure-as-a-Service

16. What is a scale set?
    A. A range of sizes of Virtual Machines ready to take over a workload
    B. A set of similar services that all work together for a service or application
    C. A pool of identical VMs that can be activated or deactivated as needed
    D. A set of Virtual Machines running in the same datacenter

17. What is an Azure Function?
    A. An add-on to any paid Azure subscription that allows using Azure services as functions in your applications
    B. A function to update any resources on Azure
    C. A single unit of compute that is triggered by a separate process
    D. A foundational component of any Azure infrastructure

18. What is the function of a fully managed platform on Azure?
    A. You can pay a monthly fee to have Microsoft look after the maintenance of your applications and services on Azure
    B. Servers, network, storage and more is all managed by Azure. You focus on your business value and logic
    C. Every part of your Azure services are looked after by Microsoft. This means you only have to worry about your application development
    D. The fully managed platform on Azure is a specific subscription that provides extra support for your Azure services

19. What are the three kinds of App Service? (Choose 3)
    A. Web Apps for Containers
    B. Event Grid for App Services
    C. Web Apps for Linux
    D. Web Apps
    E. API Apps

20. What are some benefits of using a Virtual Machine on Azure?
    A. Much higher performance of your applications
    B. Owning the hardware but Azure maintains it
    C. No maintenance of hardware and only paying for what you use
    D. Much cheaper than running your own servers

Chapter 03: Networking

Introduction

Networking creates long-lasting connections with others. It is the connecting point between the entities for resource sharing or other purposes as well. In cloud computing, networking is the base. Multiple networks are present in the cloud to provide high speed connection opportunities for users to use its services and play online game, use online Photoshop and other applications. Cloud networking enables cloud computing in order to develop network with low latency, better security and storage capabilities, and optimized performance.

Keep in mind that Microsoft Azure is a PaaS (Platform as a Service) cloud provider, that provides the number of services for their customers as discussed in chapter 01. This chapter is concentrated to give an overview of networking services that Microsoft Azure has to offer for its users when running and building their on-demand applications in the cloud. All of the networking services provide a high level based service for the customer to fulfil their demands. Azure networking is considered as the key component in building a successful public cloud into Microsoft Azure and its fundamental part. The networking service of Microsoft Azure not only provides the connectivity toward users and serves as connectivity between the service elements. Most of the money bank companies use Microsoft Azure networking services for fulfilling the monitoring and management responsibility of the networks.

So with Networking, you can give your users and customers the best possible experience by connecting the cloud and on-premises infrastructures.

All networking services provided by Microsoft Azure offer a variety of featured services that are discussed in the following sections systematically. Figure 3-01 gives a summarized overview of the networking services offered by Microsoft Azure.

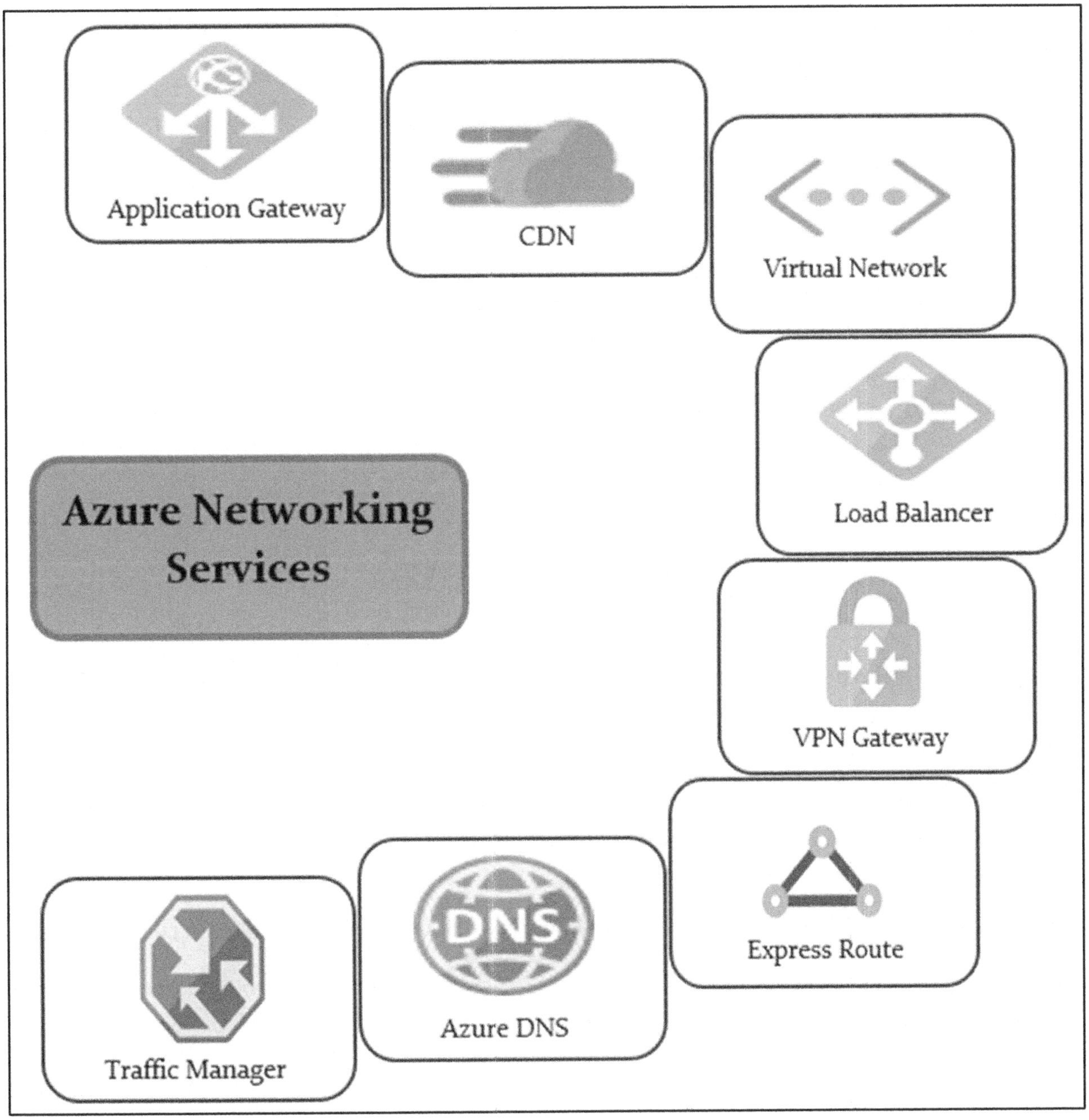

Azure Networking Services

Application Gateway

CDN

Virtual Network

Load Balancer

VPN Gateway

Express Route

Azure DNS

Traffic Manager

Figure 3-01: Azure Networking Services

Virtual Network

A Virtual Network (or VNet) is used as a networking service to host the infrastructure resources within Microsoft Azure. It is the most essential part of the Azure network. It is a logical isolation of the Azure cloud dedicated to your subscription. You can use VNets to provision and manage virtual private networks (VPNs) in Azure.

Azure Virtual Network or VNet enables many Microsoft Azure resources like Azure Virtual Machines (VM), to safely communicate with each other over the internet and on-premises

network without any access to the physical hardware. Figure 3-02 shown a simple Virtual Network containing two VMs along with the internet.

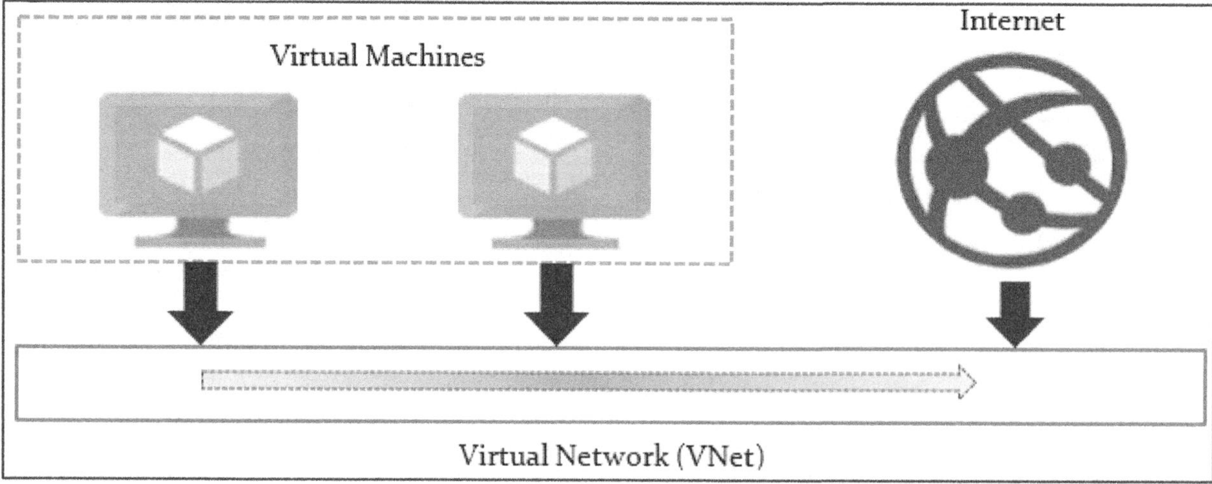

Figure 3-02: Virtual Network

IP Address

Without the internet, while sending a letter, there is a letter that is sent to the letterbox and after it is processed, the letter is delivered to the right destination using the address that is already written in the letter. With the internet, the same procedure is followed, with the addition of an IP address. Each traffic has its own IP address, which ensures that traffic delivers to the right destination (server). An IP address serves two main functions: network interface and address.

A virtual network is similar to the traditional network when operating from the datacenter. VNet consists of four main aspects.

Address Space

An address space is the range of IP addresses. Every resource, service or connected device that is present on a particular VNet has its own IP address on that VNet within the address space. This way, services in the subnet can communicate with each other. Address space assigned to VNet will automatically get an IP address by each entity present on that VNet.

Subnets

A subnet is a feature that enabling segmentation. A virtual network is divided into two or more virtual subnetworks and assigned a range of IP addresses (address space) for each subnet. Therefore, multiple networks can operate simultaneously within the same virtual network.

The major advantage of the subnetting is to make the virtual network more route efficient, reliable. Management control groups and security groups can play important in securing the individual subnet as well.

Subnet Regions

Each virtual network within Azure belongs to a single region. Therefore, the resources and service on VM must be physically present in that particular region. VNet can be connected to provide communication across regions.

Subscription

Each virtual network has only one subscription and every subscription has multiple virtual networks.

The virtual network including the above defined features is shown in figure 3-03.

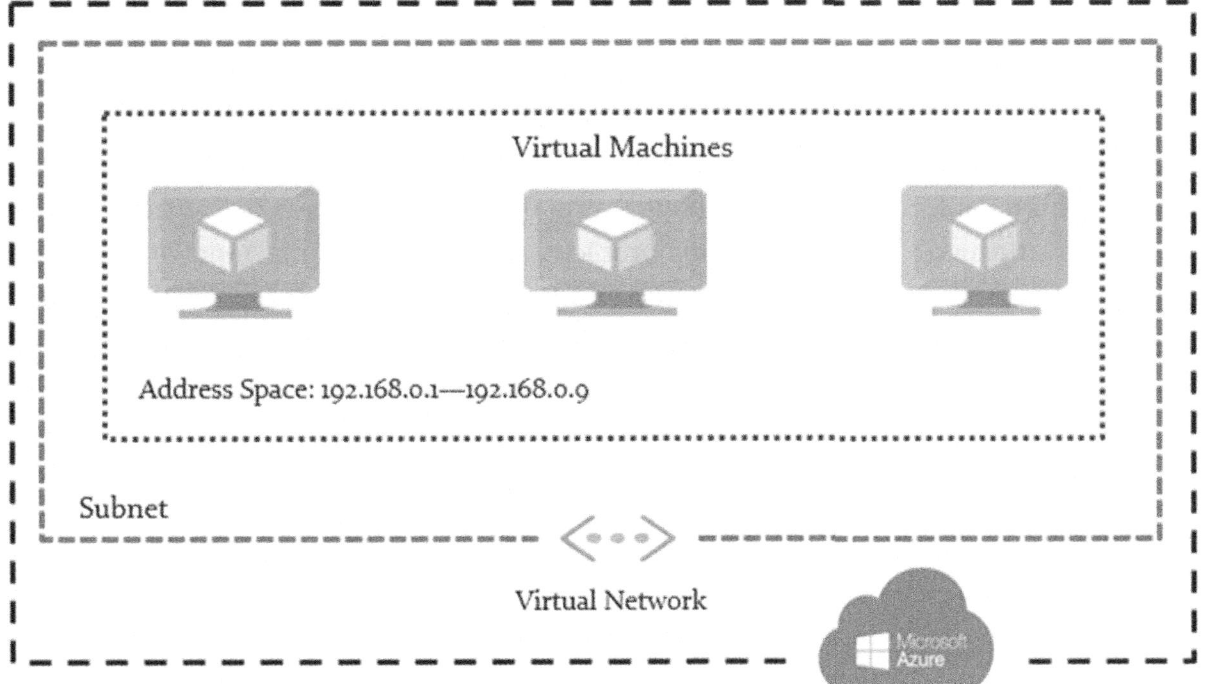

Figure 3-03: Azure Virtual Network

Cloud Advantages

- **Scaling:** Virtual network is the fundamental part of Microsoft Azure. It is also beneficial for scaling due to a wide range of address space that helps in generating more subnets or you can add more VNets
- **Isolation:** Resources and Services can be managed, organized and isolated more efficiently in VNets using subnets and network security groups

- **Security:** The inbound and outbound traffic can be control by VNets, virtual subnets, and VMs to ensure high security
- **High Availability:** In VNet, the peering feature of the network ensures high availability of services and resources. Peering means connecting of two networks together. VNets can communicate via a load balancer or a Virtual Private Network (VPN) gateway

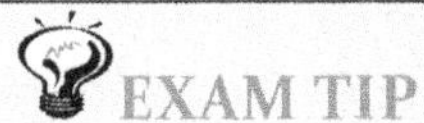

VNet is an essential part of Azure infrastructure, responsible for communicating the resources and services that are present in your VNet.

VNet is in a single region and belongs to a single subscription.

Load Balancer

Consider an example as shown in Figure 3-04. There is an online booking app introduced by a client. The app is working well. At a time, the app is simultaneously accessing by a large number of customers. Initially, there is only a single virtual machine responsible for processing the data. As the simultaneous traffic demands increases, the virtual machine becomes overloaded. To overcome this problem, another virtual machine is added. The addition of a second virtual machine creates another problem that how traffic is shared between the two VM. A load balancer is used in front of two VM to access the data before reaching the destination. Therefore, multiple users can access the service at the same time more efficiently.

Load balancer, in general is used to distribute the traffic arrived on the front end to the backend pool as per rules and health status.

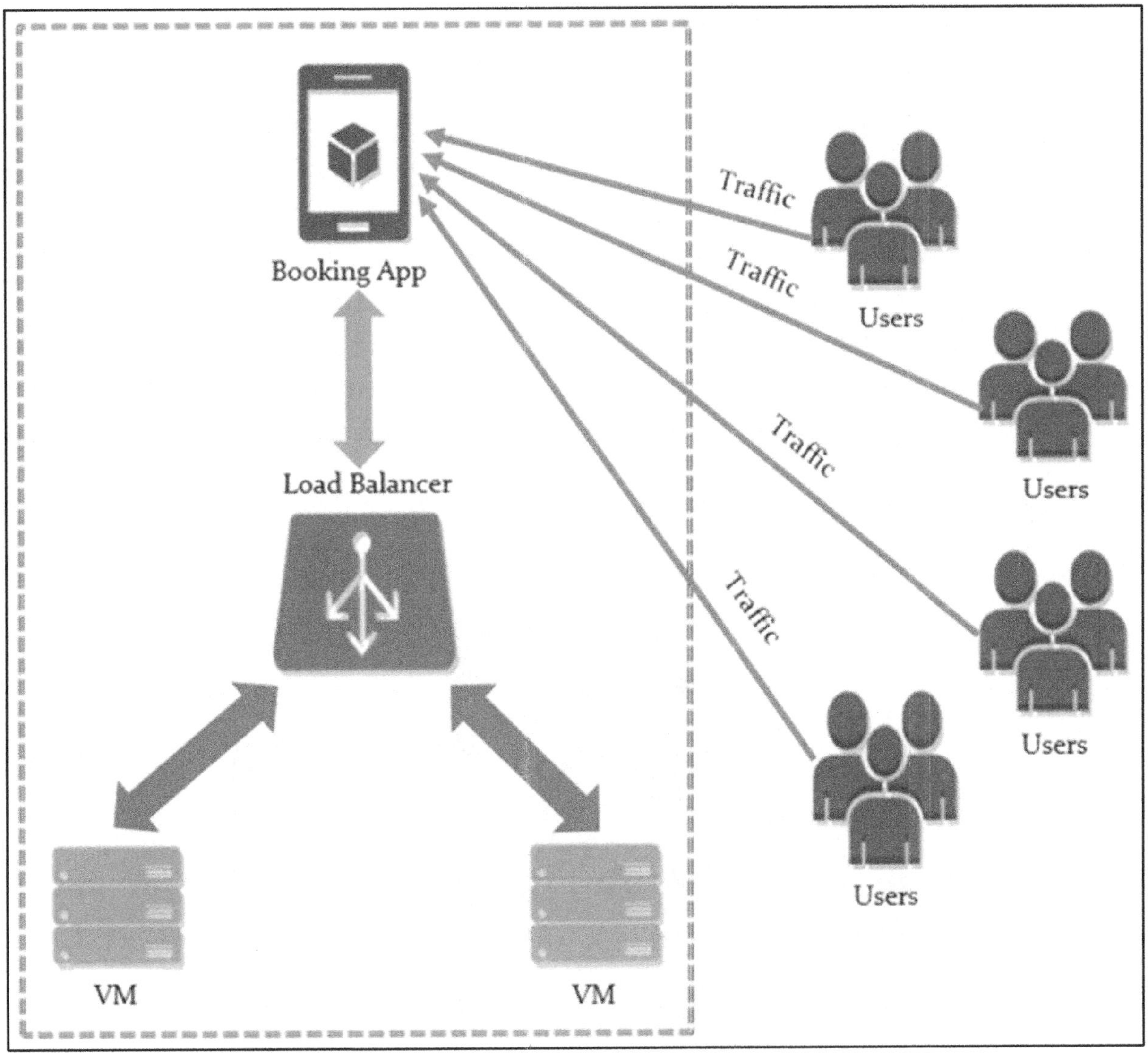

Figure 3-04: Scenario-Load Balancer

Azure load balancer serves the load-balancing feature to the connected virtual machines within Microsoft Azure. It operates at the transport layer (Layer 4) of the OSI model. When there are multiple VMs serving an application within VNet, a load balancer decides which VM belongs to the particular user.

The two types of load balancers are public and internal. Public load balancer converts the private IP address of VM to public IP address for outbound access and internet-facing. Whereas, internal load balancer is capable of managing the traffic inside the VNet. For example, load balancer is only used when there is a private IP address required only. For checking the availability, HTTP and TCP based probes are used by the load balancer.

Technical Terms of Load Balancer

- **Inbound Flow:** Inbound flow is traffic that comes from either the internet or local network. This traffic is then received by the load balancer
- **Outbound Flow:** Outbound flow is used for establishing the connection between public frontend and virtual machine backend
- **Frontend Pool:** Frontend pool connects clients to the load balancer via IP addresses. It manages traffic to the VM. All the traffic arrives here first
- **Backend Pool:** Backend pool allows VM to receive the traffic from a load balancer
- **Rules and Health Probes:** Rules refer to the load balancer rule for directing the traffic and health probes ensure that VM is ready to receive traffic before the load sends any, as load balancer always sends traffic to healthy VM. Health probe can be HTTP, HTTPS or TCP

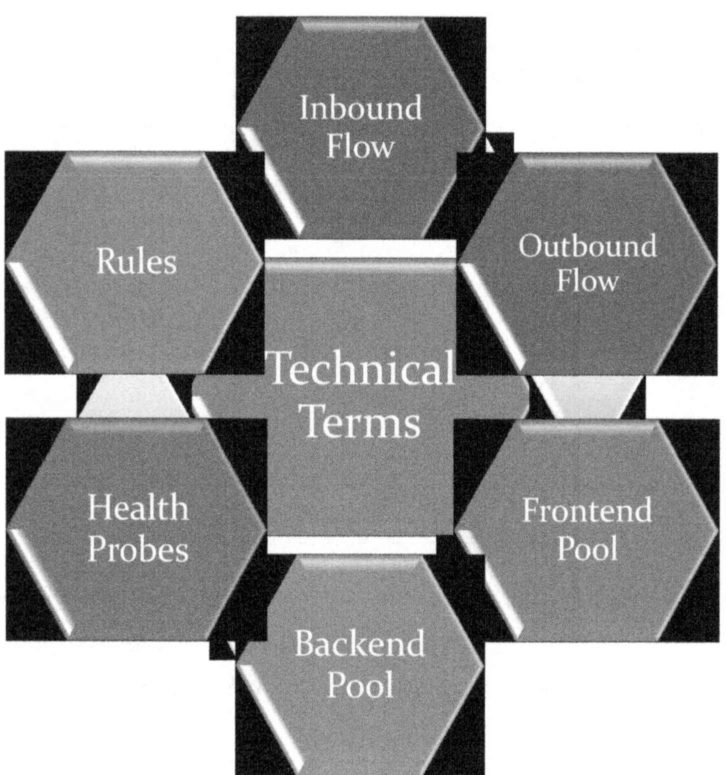

Figure 3-05: Technical Terms of Load Balancer

Benefits of Load Balancer

- **Internet Traffic:** It helps to balance internet traffic when there is a large number of users

- **Internal Network:** Balances the traffic that is generated from internal running applications within Azure
- **Port Forwarding:** Serves as a forwarding point of traffic. We can easily forward traffic to a specific port or specific machine in a backend pool
- **Outbound Traffic:** Load balancer also ensures the outbound connectivity for the VM in the backend pool

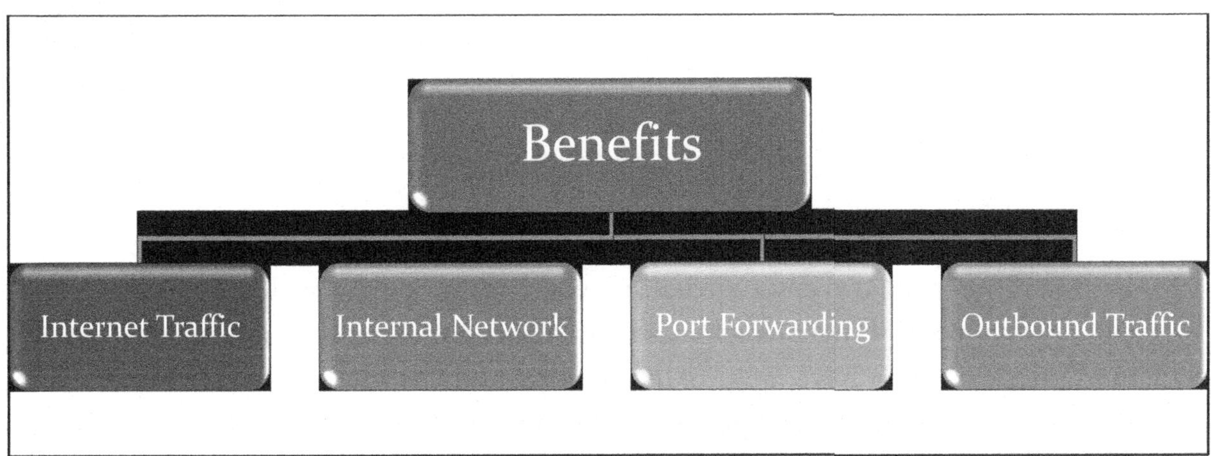

Figure 3-06: Benefits of Load Balancer

VPN Gateway

VPN Stands for Virtual Private Network, a VPN gateway is useful for establishing the private connection between Azure resource and an on-premises environment, offices, the cloud or other premises within the cloud in order to establish a private secure connection. In Microsoft Azure, VPN gateway provides the managed services within the cloud. VPN gateway is used for site-to-site connection, point-to-site or multi-site connection. It is also used for generating the encrypted connection between services. The encrypted connection can be used between Azure to on-premises or Azure-to-Azure connections. There is only a single VPN gateway per Virtual Network (VNet). VPN gateway is responsible for two types of routing, one is static and the other is dynamic routing.

Considering that there are two services with data for the company, some of the data is available on-premises and some data is available at the Azure cloud to run the applications more reliably and increase scalability. For the connection between two entities, there is a need for adding a gateway, which is the VPN gateway. Figure 3-07 shows a simple VPN gateway within the network, which provides encrypted communication between on-premises and Azure. For secure, available and hybrid cloud architecture, VPN gateway is a key part.

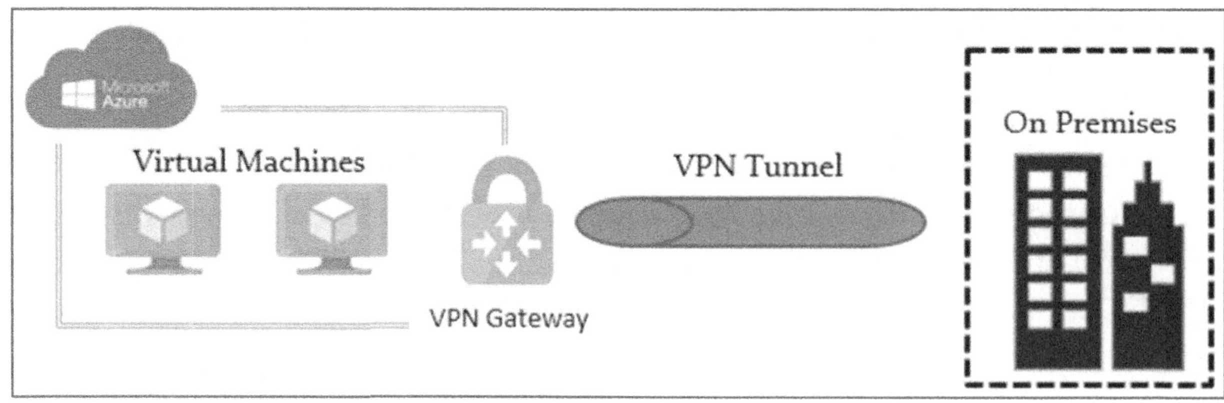

Figure 3-07: Network with VPN Gateway

Virtual Network Gateway

VPN gateway is a specific type of virtual network gateway. A virtual network gateway is composed of a number of virtual machines (VMs) within the specific subnet called Gateway Subnet. A gateway subnet has a range of IP addresses and VM within that subnet containing the address under the designed specific range. A typical example of VNet with gateway subnet is shown in figure 3-08.

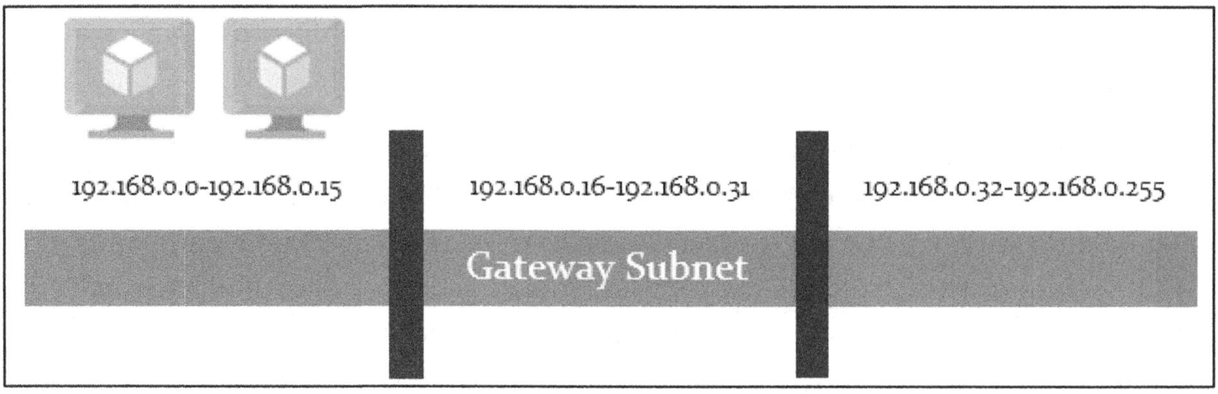

Figure 3-08: VNet Gateway

Components of VPN Gateway

The main components of the VPN gateway consist of Azure VNet, VPN gateway, VPN tunnel, and on-premises services. Within Azure VNet, there is a VPN gateway present. VPN gateway has its own public IP address. A secure connection called a tunnel is responsible for enabling multiple encrypted connections for security purposes. VPN Tunnel provides encrypted communication between the on-premises network and Azure VNet. On on-premises network, there is a complementary gateway that accepts encrypted data. Figure 3-09 shows a network employing all the components of the VPN gateway. The network in figure 3-09 is called site-to-site connection between two entities.

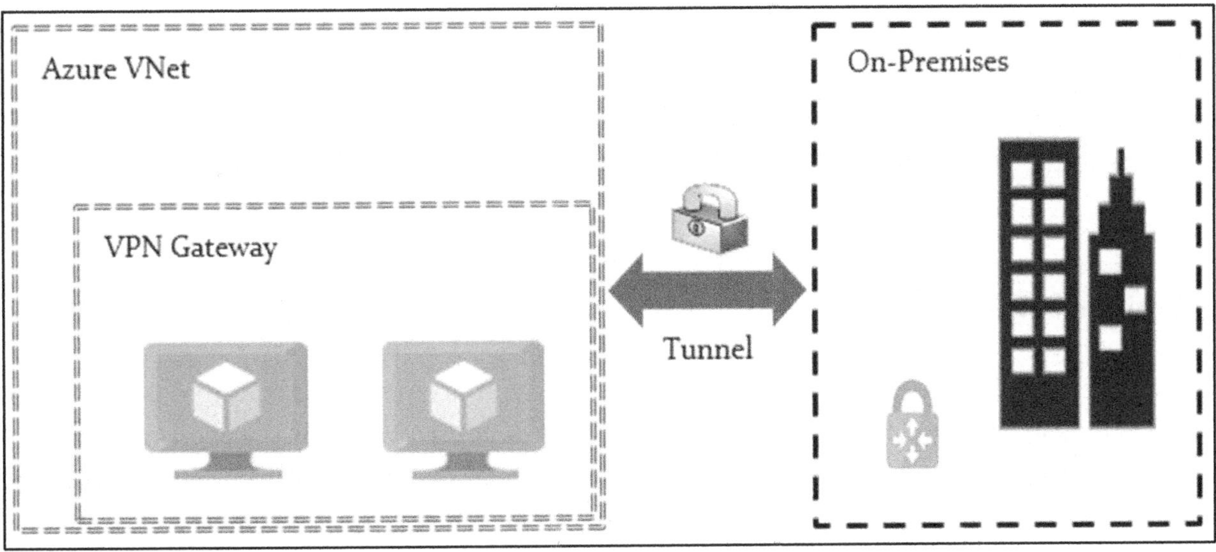

Figure 3-09: Site-to-Site Connection

One possible network configuration is also shown in figure 3-10, which is called a multi-site connection between two entities. In such a network, there is a single VPN gateway with multiple on-premises networks connected.

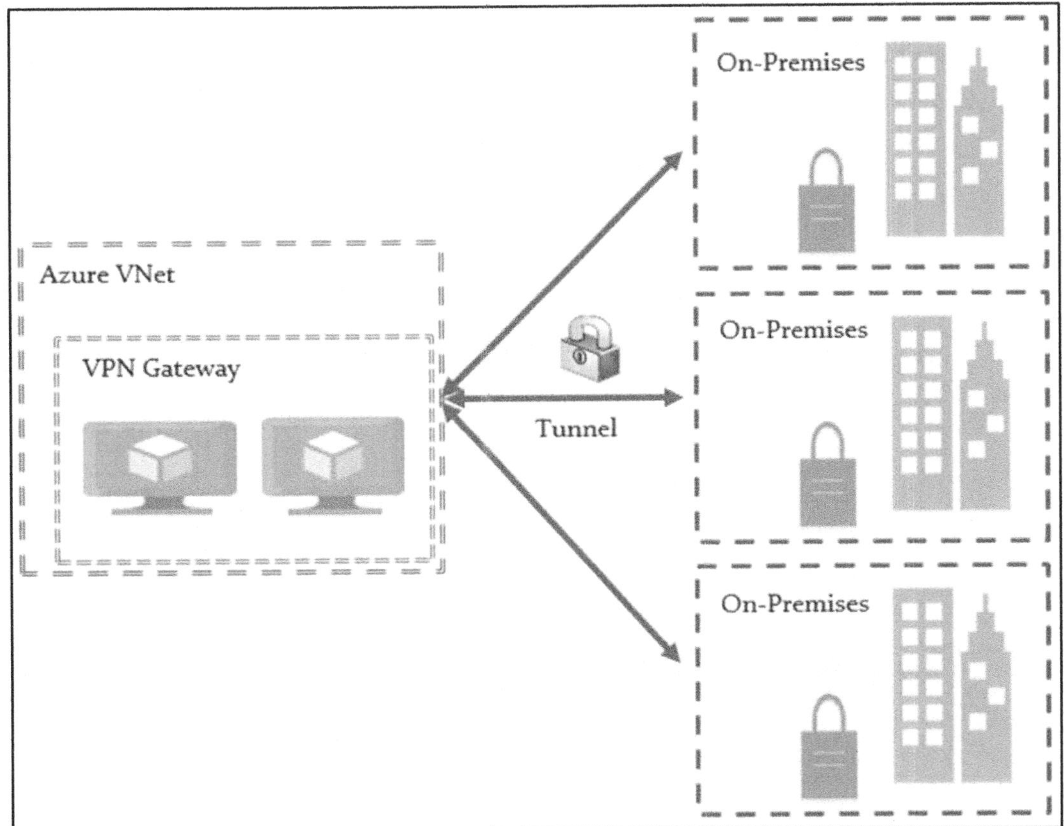

Figure 3-10: Multi-Site Connection

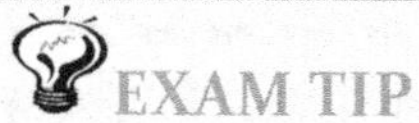

VPN gateway can provide efficient cloud computing services within the hybrid cloud infrastructure. VPN gateway is composed of VNet gateway and virtual private network.

Application Gateway

One type of VPN gateway is the application gateway. It is considered as the most advanced load balancer that enables the balancing of web traffic to manage the web applications using an HTTP request. Because of its services, the gateway is called layer 7 load balancer within Microsoft Azure. It also supports ADC (Application Delivery Controller) functionality. Figure 3-11 shows a network specifying the contribution of the application gateway. In figure 3-11, with application gateway, routing decisions are based upon additional characteristics of the HTTP request. This request is in the form of data format so that any type of internet traffic would be able to receive the request. Uniform Resource Identifier (URI) is the web address while host request is the piece of information that is sent with the request. The configured network is able to send a request to a specific web address to a specific machine present at the backend pool.

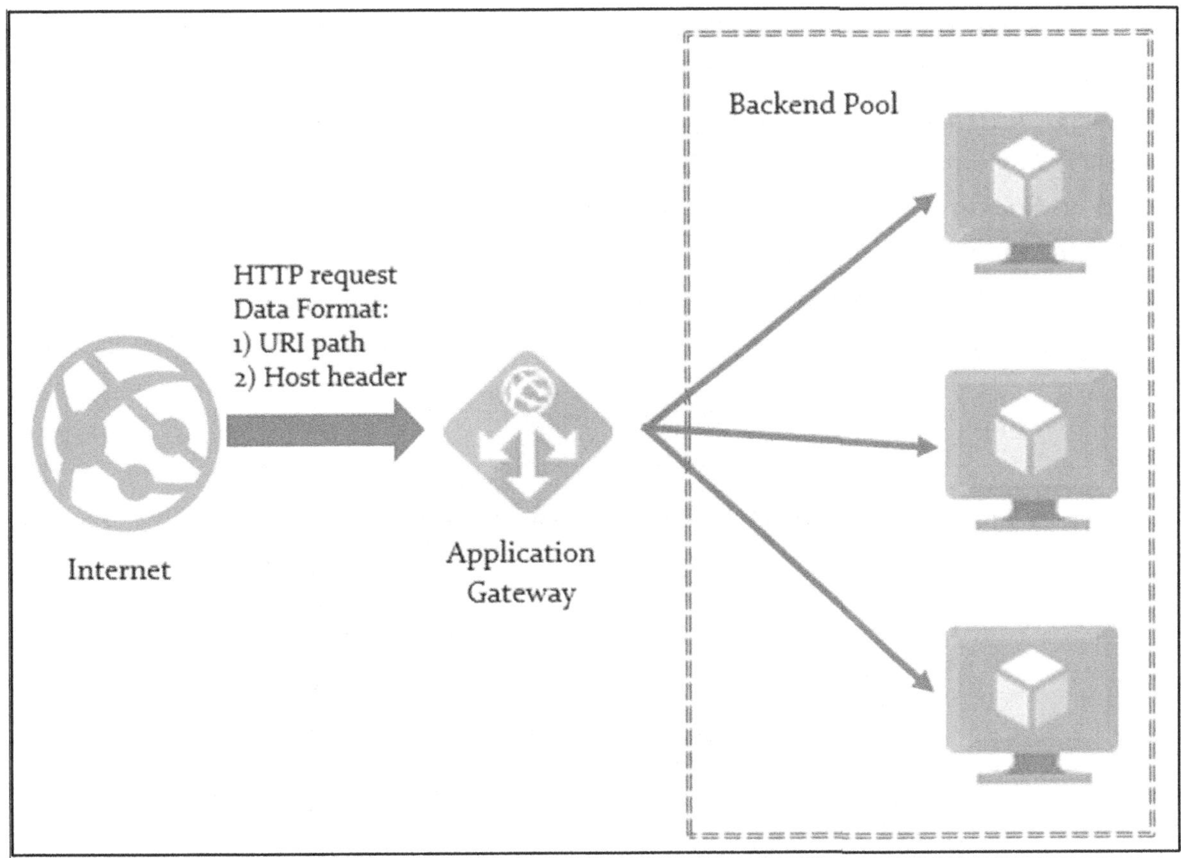

Figure 3-11: Network with Application Gateway

Benefits of Application Gateway

The benefits of the application gateway are as follows;

- **Scaling:** Application gateway can be scaled due to the abrupt change of traffic load
- **High Availability:** The use of a layer 7 based load balancer increases the availability of resources for the web application in Microsoft Azure
- **Encryption:** Application gateway is responsible for providing the end-to-end encrypted communication between the services. You can enable or disable the traffic encryption to backend pool to improve the processing time
- **Zone Redundancy:** Application gateway supports multiple zones to improve flexibility and fault resiliency
- **Multi-Site Hosting:** By using multi-site hosting, a single application gateway is used for a number of web applications and providing a secure connection between the entities
- **SSL Offload:** After routing traffic to the right destination, SSL offloads are supported by the application gateway to provide relief towards the webserver

- **Cost-Effective:** As an application gateway, hosting multiple web applications results in saving cost and minimizing complexity
- **Session Affinity:** Application Gateway allows keeping the user on the same web server by directing the user traffic on the same web server
- **Web Socket Support:** Application gateway allows web socket for client connected applications. Web socket pushes specific client applications within a browser
- **Web Application Firewall:** Application gateway also provides protection features like web application firewall that protect internet requests and applications

Figure 3-12: Benefits of Application Gateway

EXAM TIP

Application gateway is more efficient in delivering web application services as compared to other gateways.

It works on HTTPS rather than IP address/port.

Content Delivery Network

When the users are present far from datacenters (online resource) in which they want to get data from, one way of getting the data is that user accesses the data but that takes much time and provides a low performance of the application due to the distance. Another way

of getting the data is by using the Microsoft Azure service called Content Delivery Network (CDN). It is a distributed network of servers that can deliver web content close to users. Within Azure, CDN places the duplicates of data at the datacenter present closer to the user side and users can easily log into the application into which they want. The datacenters present closer to the users is called edge nodes/edge servers containing a cache of files that provide the edge of the internet closest to the users. The information present in these edge nodes is limited for a few days because each node has an expiry date. Using edge nodes, users can easily access data from datacenters. One problem behind the edge node is how users get informed by the update. The solution for this is that when information is about to expire, the user will get the updated data from far datacenter at once such that the user can create a new datacenter in which all the update is available.

The main reason behind the use of Content Delivery Network (CDN) is to deliver data to the user with the lowest latency by providing data that is present at edge nodes. The data usually consist of image, file, media, etc. The delivery of data content can be improved by using a feature called Dynamic Site Acceleration (DSA). DSA finds the best route for the request of the traffic from the user to the server. DSA in Content Delivery Network stores the dynamic contents for improving the performance of the network.

Figure 3-13 shows the concept of Content Delivery Network (CDN). The given network is spread over the geographical area and users from any area can access the data such as logs of an online application using edge node. The edge node is the service of Azure CDN.

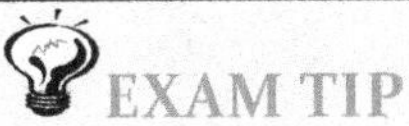

Origin server is the original location of files such as web application that hold the master copy of all data.

Edge Datacentre

Russia

Datacentre

Edge Datacentre

Australia

Europe

Edge Datacentre

America

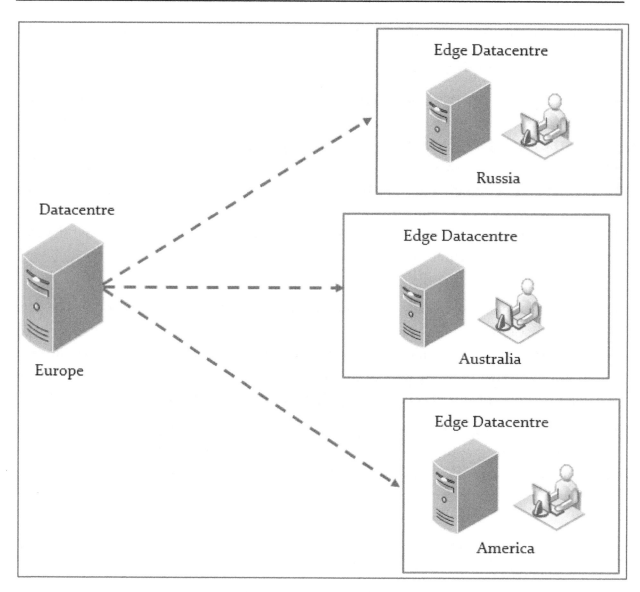

Figure 3-13: Concept of CDN

Benefits of CDN

- **Global Coverage:** Content Delivery Network (CDN) provides global coverage using the multiple edge node across the region
- **Better Performance:** Providing optimized performance due to the fast delivery of data and increased user experience
- **Scaling:** CDN can be scaled up or down due to the instantaneous high traffic load and protect by hidden other data from the backend
- **Distribution:** Edge nodes help deliver less content from the main server to the user, all of the request data can be easily achieved by the user from edge nodes

Cache is a collection of duplicate copies of a file. The main purpose of the cache is to provide fast online application services to end-users.

Lab 3-01: Creating a Virtual Network Connection

Scenario

An organization wants to deploy a secure network in Azure Cloud for its application. How can this be done?

Solution

Using the VNet and VM, you can deploy your application in a secure network.

1. Log in to the Microsoft Azure portal and go to the portal menu.
2. Now click on "Virtual networks" from the portal menu. 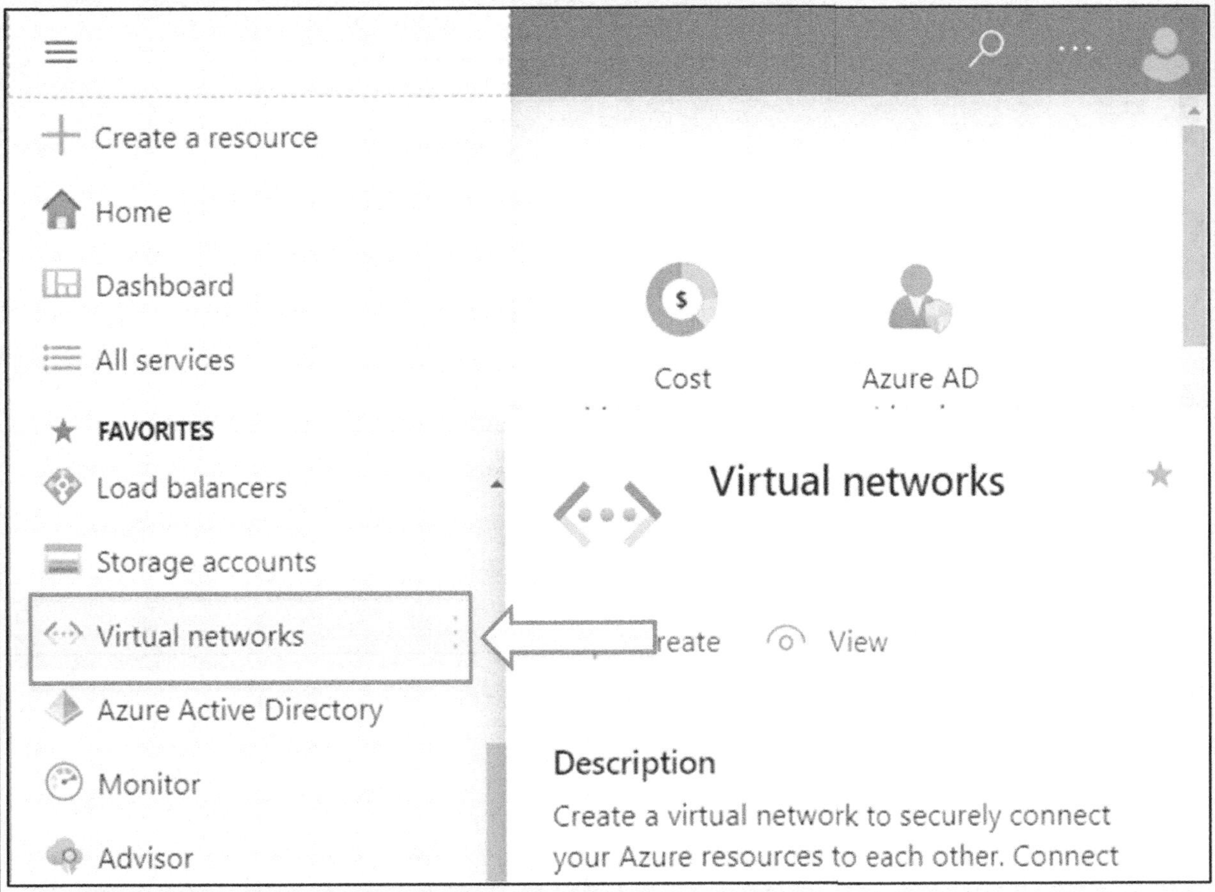
3. Click on "Add" for the creation of a virtual network.

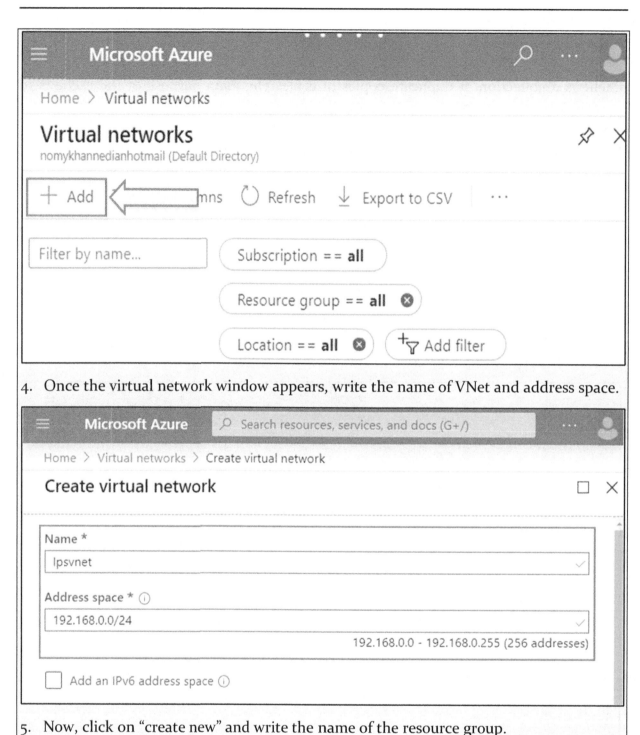

4. Once the virtual network window appears, write the name of VNet and address space.

5. Now, click on "create new" and write the name of the resource group.

Microsoft Azure

Home > Virtual networks > Create virtual network

Create virtual network

Subscription *

Pay-As-You-Go

Resource group *

Select existing...

Create new

A resource group is a container that holds related resources for an Azure solution.

Name *

vnetRG

OK Cancel

(0 addresses)

Basic Standard

Create Automation options

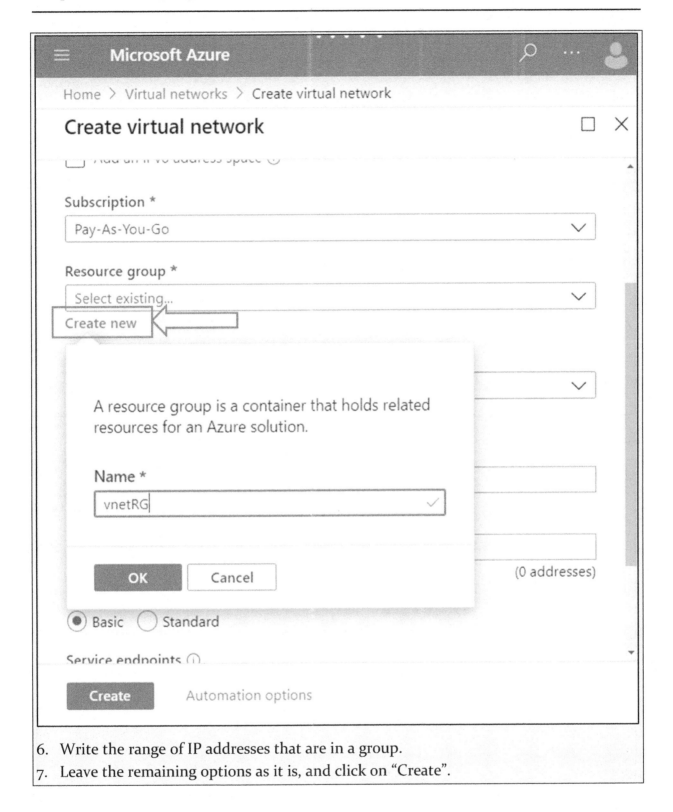

6. Write the range of IP addresses that are in a group.
7. Leave the remaining options as it is, and click on “Create”.

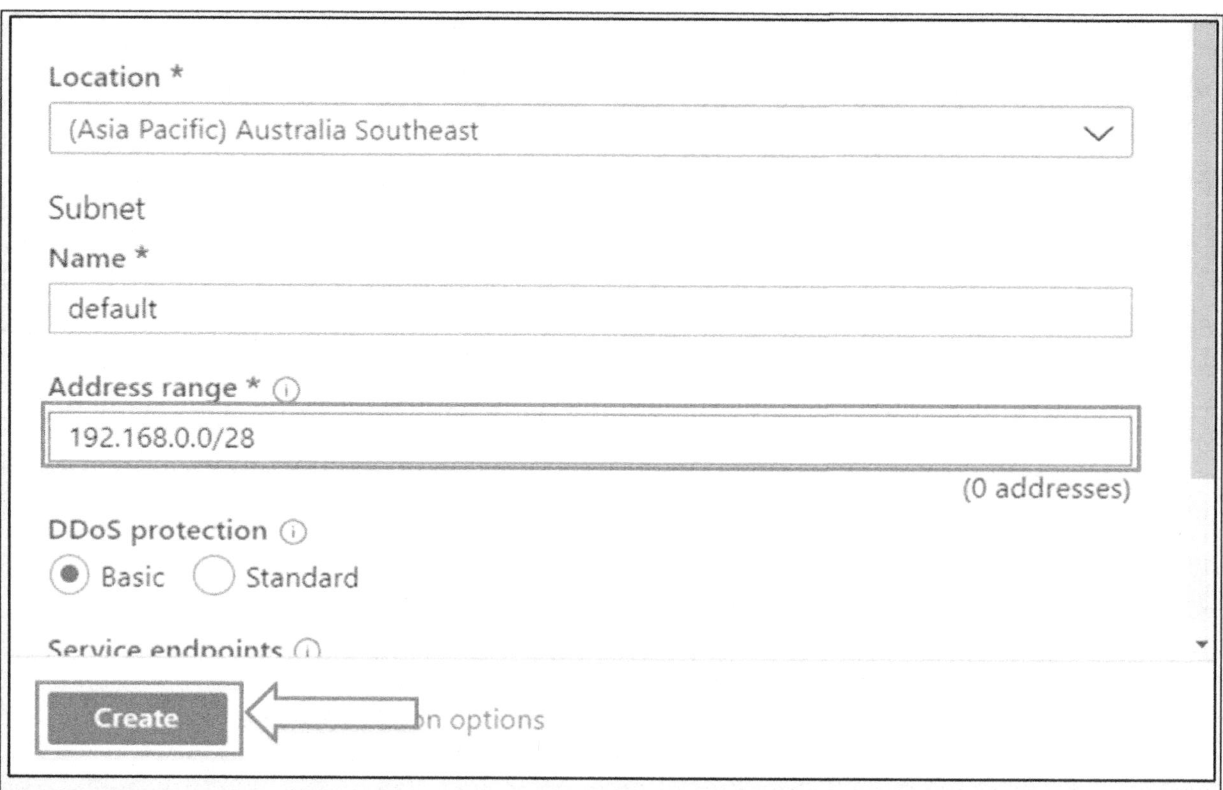

8. Your VNet will now be created, click on "Refresh" to see the created VNet.

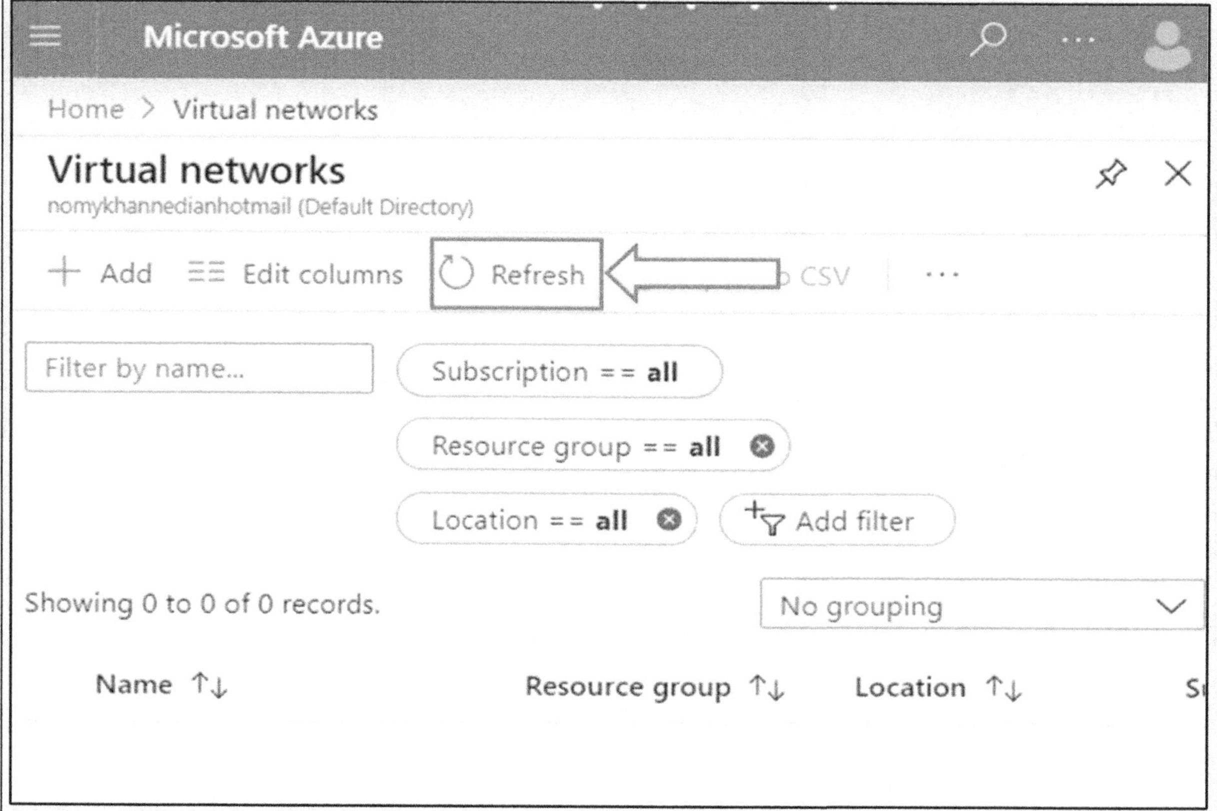

Microsoft Azure | Search resources, services, and docs (G+/)

Home > Virtual networks

Virtual networks

nomykhannedianhotmail (Default Directory)

+ Add | Edit columns | Refresh | Export to CSV | Assign tags | Feedback

Filter by name... | Subscription == **all** | Resource group == **all** | Location == **all** | Add filter

Showing 1 to 2 of 2 records. | No grouping

Name	Resource group	Location	Subscription
Ipsvnet	vnetRG	Australia Southeast	Pay-As-You-Go
NAK-vnet	NAK	Central US	Pay-As-You-Go

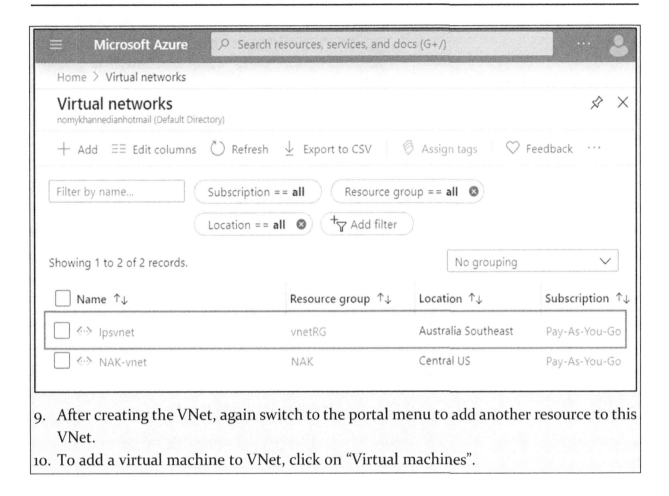

9. After creating the VNet, again switch to the portal menu to add another resource to this VNet.
10. To add a virtual machine to VNet, click on "Virtual machines".

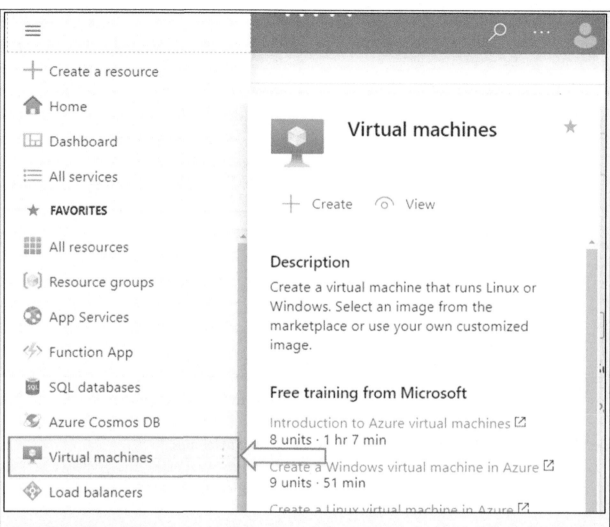

11. A virtual machine window will appear, click on "Add" for the creation of a virtual machine to VNet.

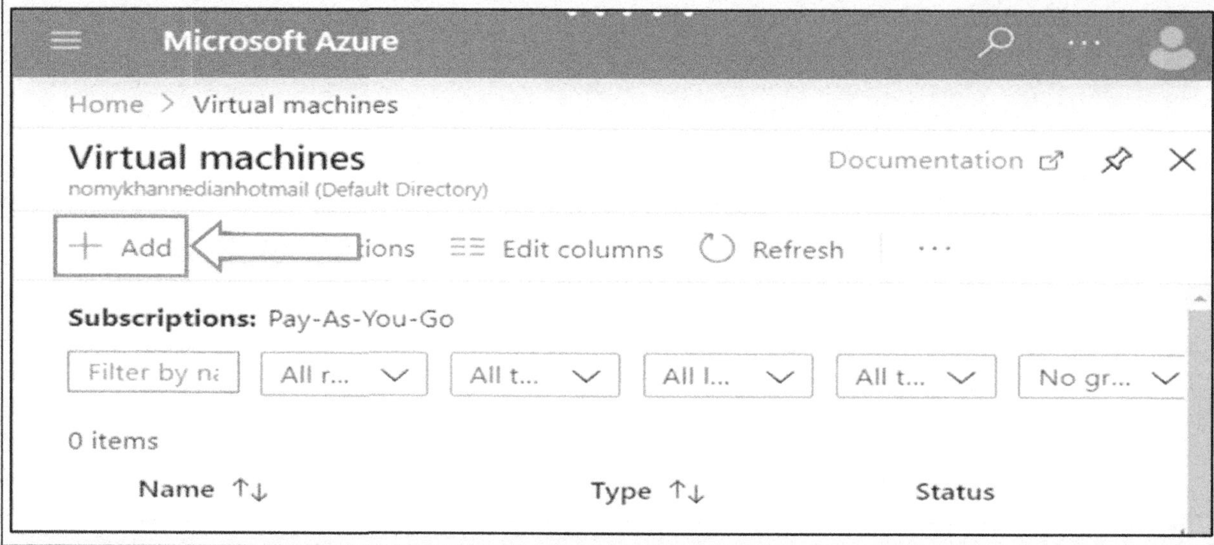

12. Write the name of the resource group for which the virtual machine is going to be created.

Microsoft Azure
Search resources, services, and docs (G+/)
Home > Virtual machines > Create a virtual machine
Create a virtual machine
Subscription *
Pay-As-You-Go
Resource group *
Select existing...
Create new
Instanc
Virtual
A resource group is a container that holds related resources for an Azure solution.
Region
(Asia P
Name *
vnetRG
Availabi
No inf
OK
Image *
Ubuntu Server 18.04 LTS
Review + create
< Previous
Next : Disks >

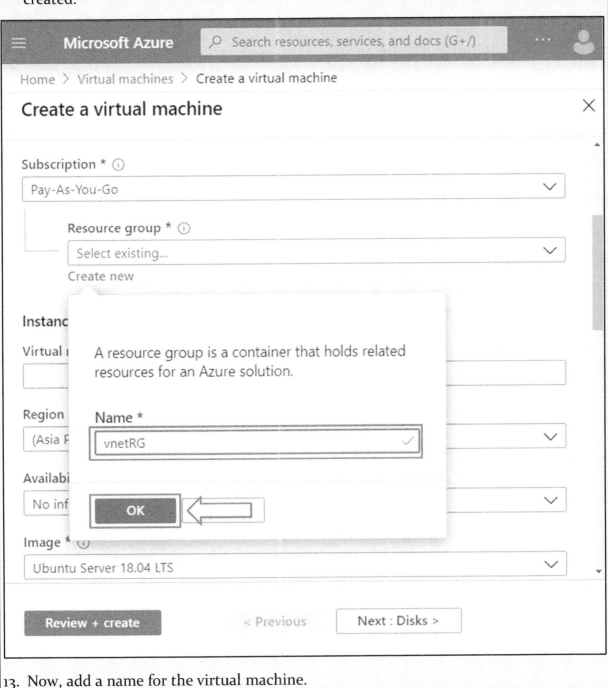

13. Now, add a name for the virtual machine.

Microsoft Azure   Search resources, services, and docs (G+/)

Home > Virtual machines > Create a virtual machine

Create a virtual machine

Subscription * ⓘ

Pay-As-You-Go

Resource group * ⓘ

(New) vnetRG

Create new

Instance details

Virtual machine name * ⓘ

ipsvm

Azure resource names cannot contain special characters \/""[]:|<>+=;,?*@& or begin with '_' or end with '.' or '-'

Virtual machine name must be unique in the current resource group.

The value is in between 1 and 64 characters long.

All characters are valid for Linux OS computername.

Image * ⓘ

Ubuntu Server 18.04 LTS

Review + create   < Previous   Next : Disks >

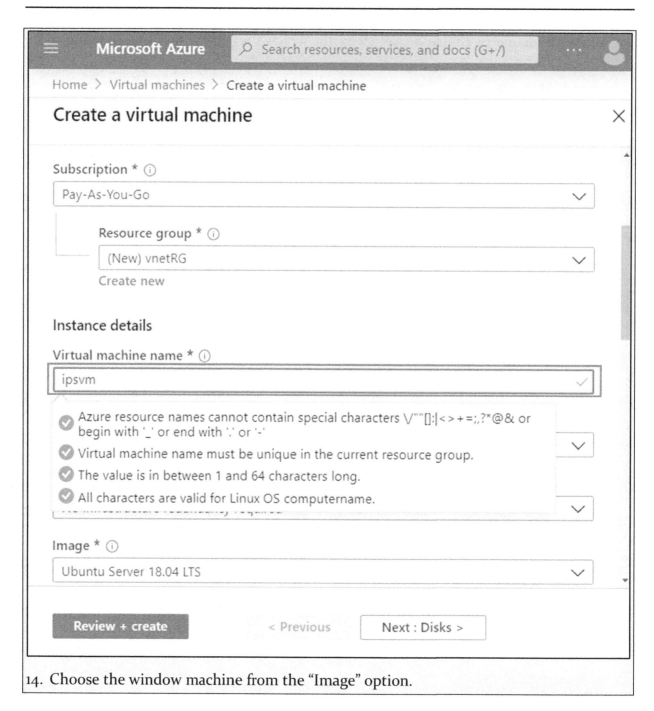

14. Choose the window machine from the “Image” option.

Microsoft Azure

Home > Virtual machines > Create a virtual machine

Create a virtual machine

(Asia Pacific) Australia Southeast

Availability options

No infrastructure redundancy required

Image *

Windows Server 2019 Datacenter

Ubuntu Server 18.04 LTS

Red Hat Enterprise Linux 7.7

SUSE Linux Enterprise Server (SLES) 15

CentOS-based 7.7

Debian 9 "Stretch" with backports kernel

Oracle Linux 7.7

Ubuntu Server 16.04 LTS

Windows Server 2019 Datacenter

Windows Server 2016 Datacenter

Review + create | < Previous | Next : Disks >

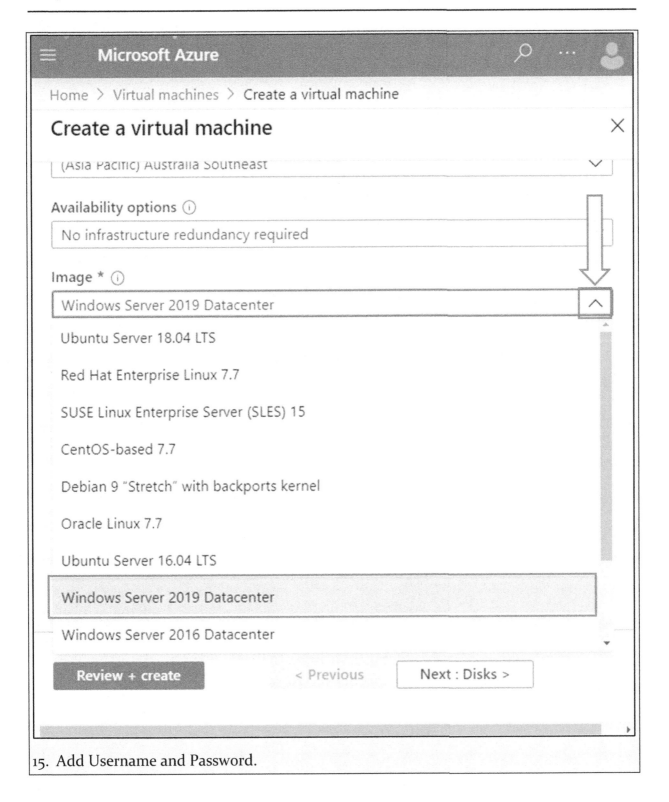

15. Add Username and Password.

Microsoft Azure | Search resources, services, and docs (G+/)

Home > Virtual machines > Create a virtual machine

Create a virtual machine

Username *

ipsadmin

Password *

•••••••••••••

Confirm password *

•••••••••••••

Inbound port rules

Select which virtual machine network ports are accessible from the public internet. You can specify more limited or granular network access on the Networking tab.

Public inbound ports *

None | Allow selected ports

Select inbound ports *

SSH (22)

Review + create | < Previous | Next : Disks >

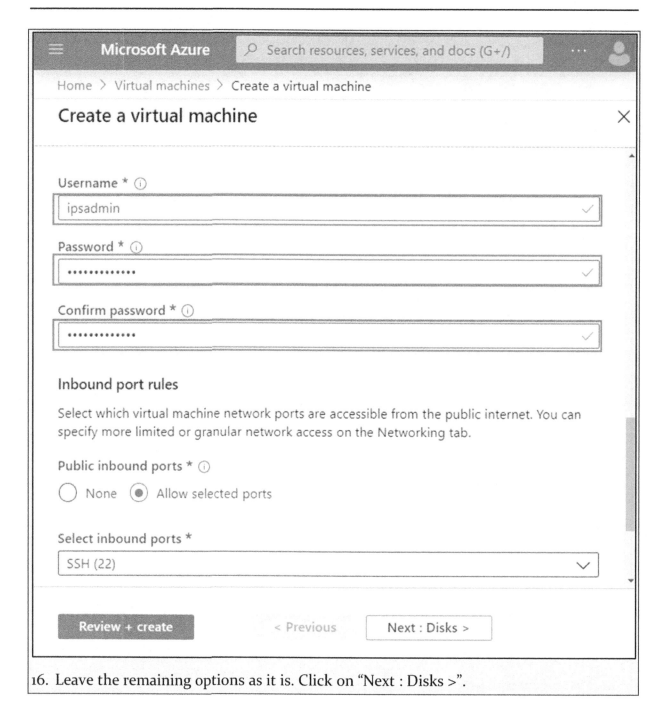

16. Leave the remaining options as it is. Click on "Next : Disks >".

Microsoft Azure
Search resources, services, and docs (G+/)

Home > Virtual machines > Create a virtual machine

Create a virtual machine

Username *
ipsadmin

Password *
•••••••••••••

Confirm password *
•••••••••••••

Inbound port rules

Select which virtual machine network ports are accessible from the public internet. You can specify more limited or granular network access on the Networking tab.

Public inbound ports *
None
Allow selected ports

Select inbound ports *
SSH (22)

Review + create
Next : Disks >

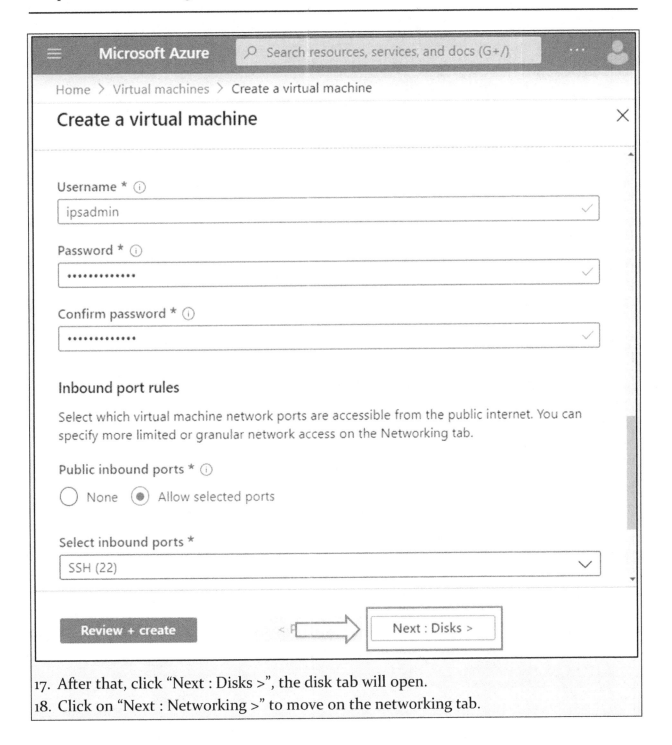

17. After that, click “Next : Disks >”, the disk tab will open.
18. Click on “Next : Networking >” to move on the networking tab.

Microsoft Azure

Home > Virtual machines > Create a virtual machine

Create a virtual machine

Basics Disks Networking Management Advanced Tags ...

Azure VMs have one operating system disk and a temporary disk for short-term storage. You can attach additional data disks. The size of the VM determines the type of storage you can use and the number of data disks allowed. Learn more

Disk options

OS disk type * ⓘ

Premium SSD

Enable Ultra Disk compatibility ⓘ

Yes No

Ultra Disk compatibility is not available for this VM size and location.

Data disks

You can add and configure additional data disks for your virtual machine or attach existing disks. This VM also comes with a temporary disk.

Review + create < Pre Next : Networking >

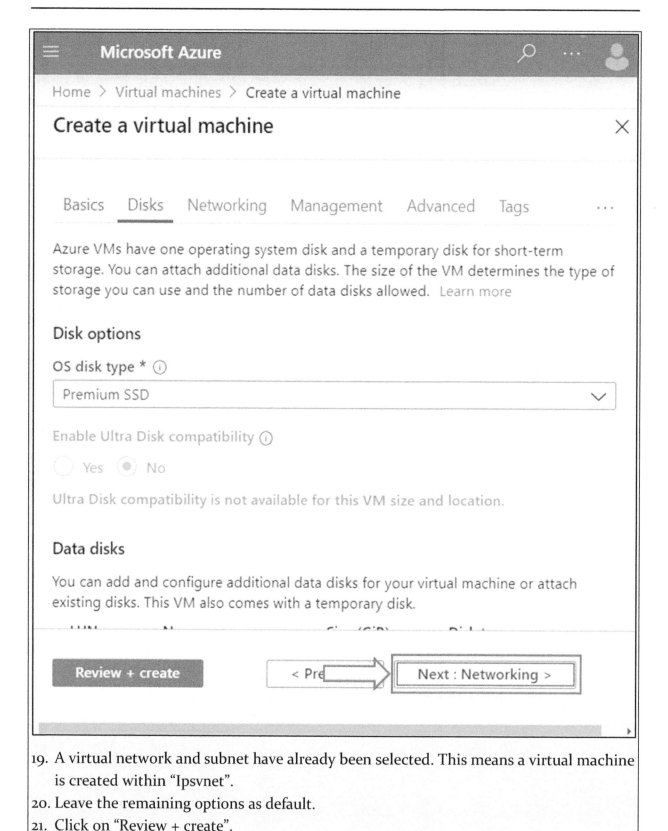

19. A virtual network and subnet have already been selected. This means a virtual machine is created within “Ipsvnet”.
20. Leave the remaining options as default.
21. Click on “Review + create”.

Microsoft Azure
Search resources, services, and docs (G+/)
Home > Virtual machines > Create a virtual machine
Create a virtual machine
Basics Disks Networking Management Advanced Tags
Define network connectivity for your virtual machine by configuring network interface card (NIC) settings. You can control ports, inbound and outbound connectivity with security group rules, or place behind an existing load balancing solution. Learn more
Network interface
When creating a virtual machine, a network interface will be created for you.
Virtual network * ⓘ
Ipsvnet
Create new
Subnet * ⓘ
default (192.168.0.0/28)
Manage subnet configuration
Public IP ⓘ
(new) ipsvm-ip
Create new
Review + create
< Previous
Next : Management >

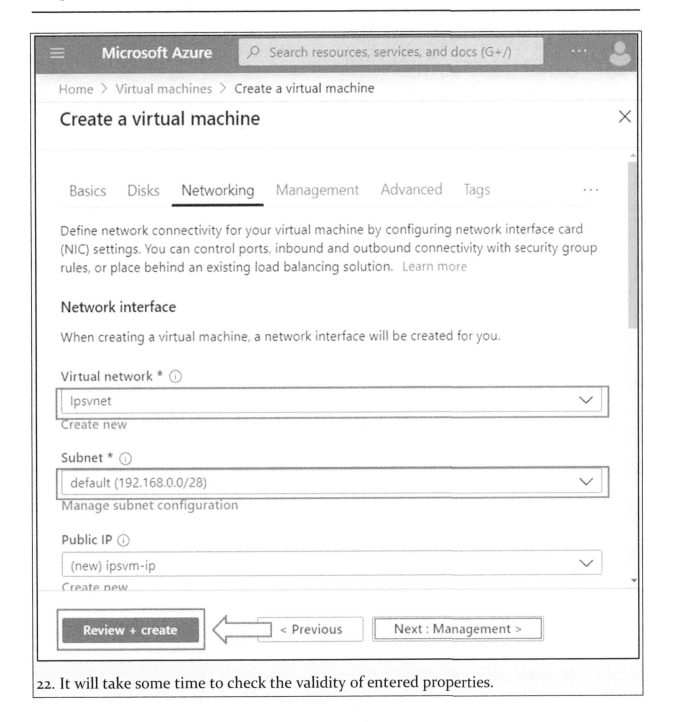

22. It will take some time to check the validity of entered properties.

Microsoft Azure

Home > Create a virtual machine

Create a virtual machine

Validation passed

Basics Disks Networking Management Advanced Tags ...

PRODUCT DETAILS

Standard DS1 v2
by Microsoft
Terms of use | Privacy policy

Subscription credits apply
0.1400 USD/hr
Pricing for other VM sizes

TERMS

By clicking "Create", I (a) agree to the legal terms and privacy statement(s) associated with the Marketplace offering(s) listed above; (b) authorize Microsoft to bill my current payment method for the fees associated with the offering(s), with the same billing frequency as my Azure subscription; and (c) agree that Microsoft may share my contact, usage and transactional information with the provider(s) of the offering(s) for support, billing and other transactional activities. Microsoft does not provide rights for third-party offerings. See the Azure Marketplace Terms for additional details.

Create < Previous Next >

Download a template for automation

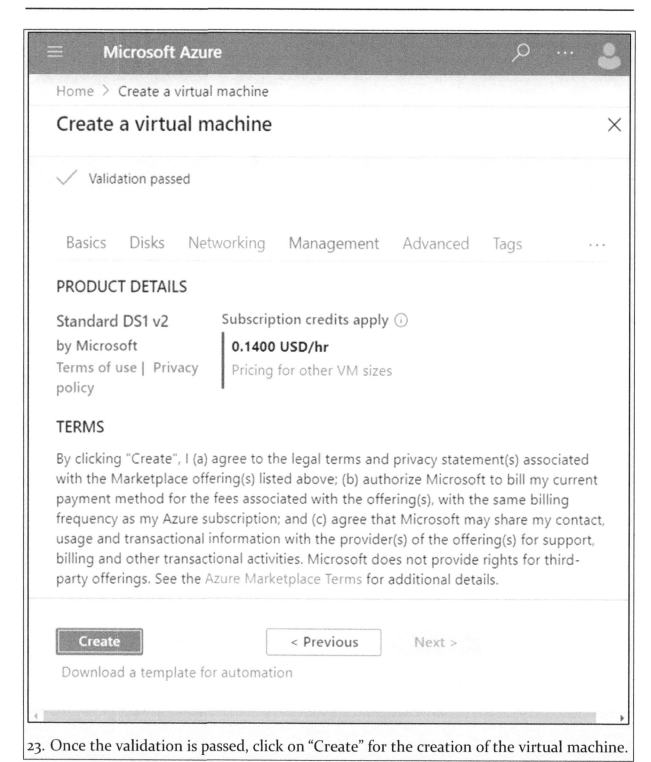

23. Once the validation is passed, click on "Create" for the creation of the virtual machine.

Microsoft Azure

Home > Create a virtual machine

Create a virtual machine

Validation passed

Basics Disks Networking Management Advanced Tags ...

PRODUCT DETAILS

Standard DS1 v2
by Microsoft
Terms of use | Privacy policy

Subscription credits apply
0.1400 USD/hr
Pricing for other VM sizes

TERMS

By clicking "Create", I (a) agree to the legal terms and privacy statement(s) associated with the Marketplace offering(s) listed above; (b) authorize Microsoft to bill my current payment method for the fees associated with the offering(s), with the same billing frequency as my Azure subscription; and (c) agree that Microsoft may share my contact, usage and transactional information with the provider(s) of the offering(s) for support, billing and other transactional activities. Microsoft does not provide rights for third-party offerings. See the Azure Marketplace Terms for additional details.

Create   < Previous   Next >

Download a template for automation

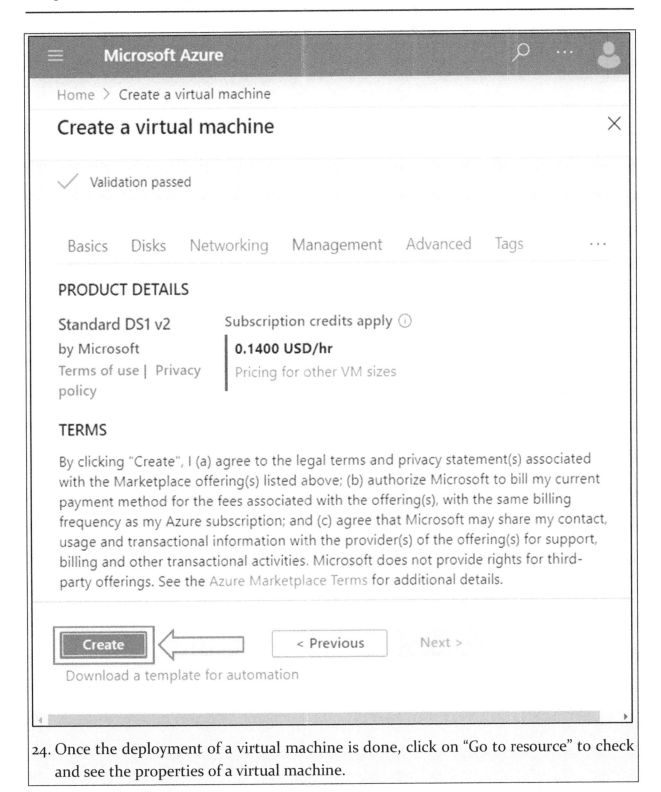

24. Once the deployment of a virtual machine is done, click on "Go to resource" to check and see the properties of a virtual machine.

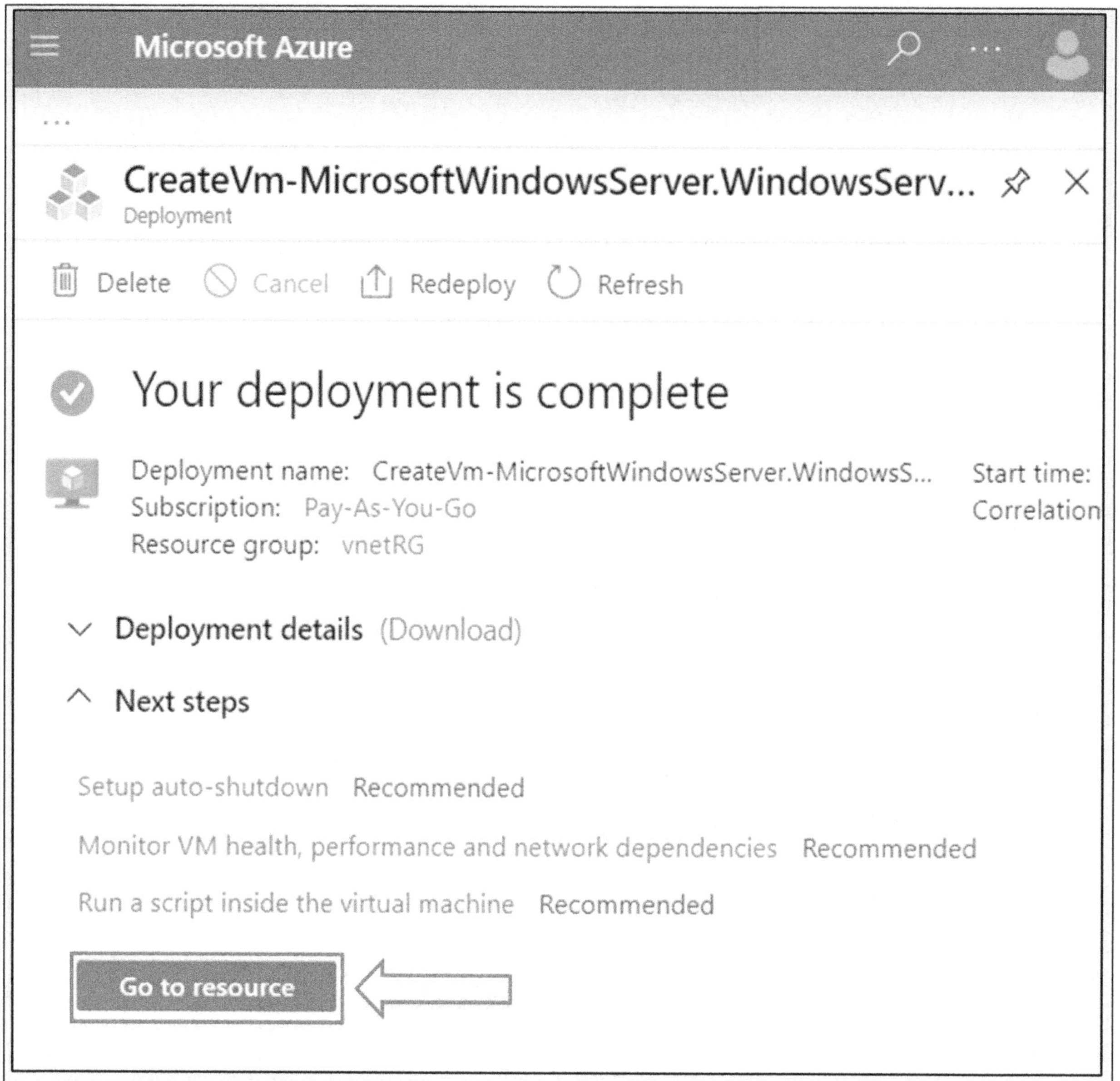

Microsoft Azure

CreateVm-MicrosoftWindowsServer.WindowsServ...
Deployment

Delete Cancel Redeploy Refresh

Your deployment is complete

Deployment name: CreateVm-MicrosoftWindowsServer.WindowsS... Start time:
Subscription: Pay-As-You-Go Correlation
Resource group: vnetRG

Deployment details (Download)

Next steps

Setup auto-shutdown Recommended

Monitor VM health, performance and network dependencies Recommended

Run a script inside the virtual machine Recommended

Go to resource

25. The virtual network and subnet are the same as those that were configured before.

Microsoft Azure | Search resources, services, and docs (G+/)

... > CreateVm-MicrosoftWindowsServer.WindowsServer-201-20200122121640 - Overview > ipsvm

ipsvm
Virtual machine

Connect | Start | Restart | Stop | Capture | Delete | Refresh

Resource group (change) vnetRG	Azure Spot N/A
Status Running	Public IP address 13.77.42.20
Location Australia Southeast	Private IP address 192.168.0.4
Subscription (change) Pay-As-You-Go	Public IP address (IPv6) -
Subscription ID 797152d3-23c4-499f-bfef-bb103da7d054	Private IP address (IPv6) -
Computer name (not available)	Virtual network/subnet Ipsvnet/default
Operating system Windows	DNS name Configure
Size Standard DS1 v2 (1 vcpus, 3.5 GiB memory)	Scale Set N/A
Tags (change) Click here to add tags	

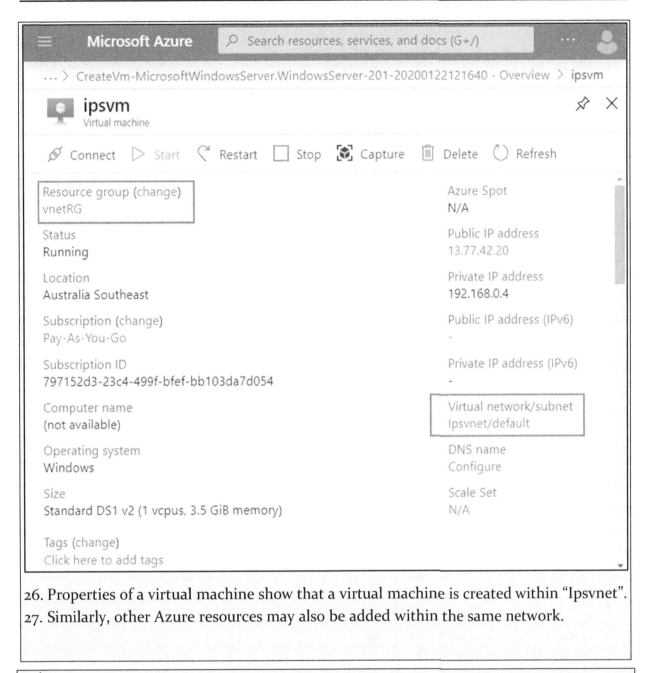

26. Properties of a virtual machine show that a virtual machine is created within "Ipsvnet".
27. Similarly, other Azure resources may also be added within the same network.

Resources should be deleted after being used by the customer from the Azure portal otherwise, the customer will be highly charged according to the subscription criteria.

MindMap

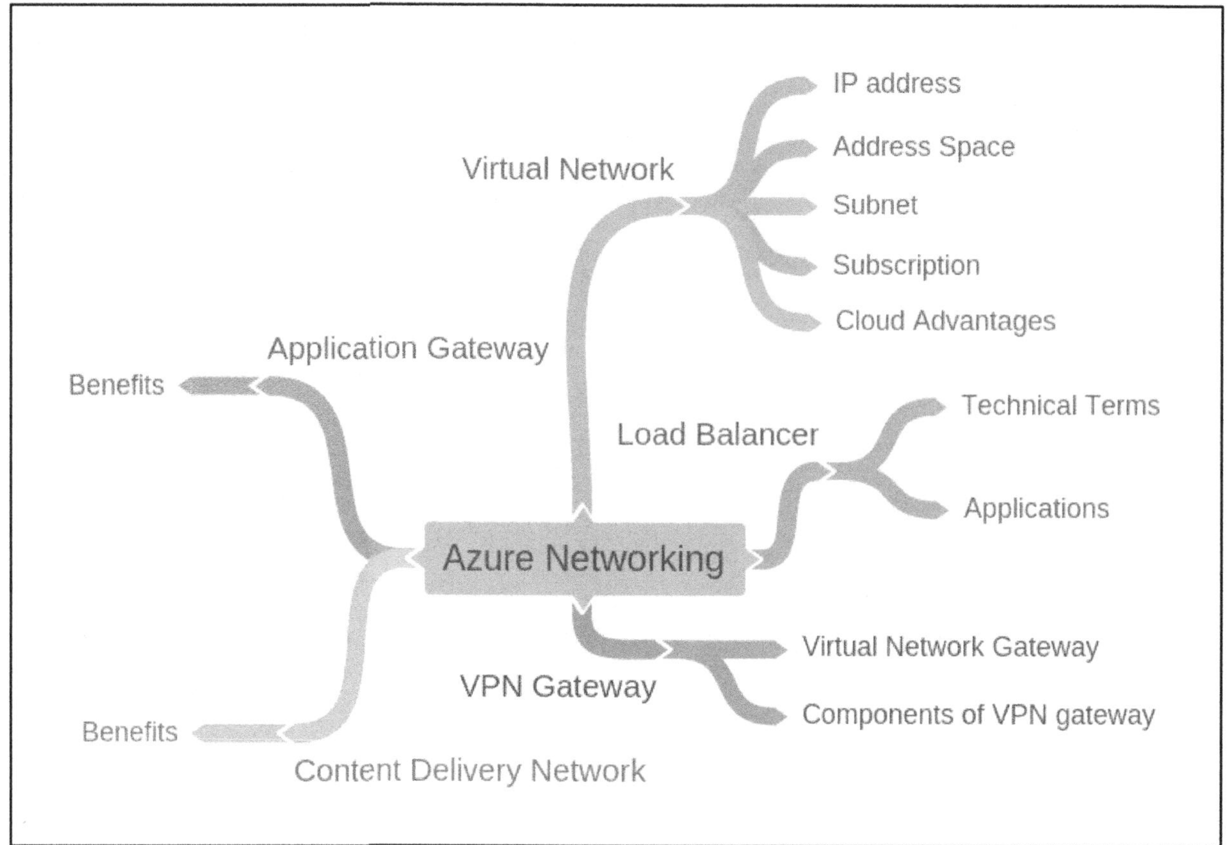

Figure 3-14: MindMap

Practice Questions:

1. What is Azure Networking?
A. Representation of a network in the cloud
B. The network made up optical fiber
C. It provides 4G connectivity
D. None of these

2. Which of the following Azure networking service is similar to the load balancer service?
A. VPN Gateway
B. Virtual Network (VNet)
C. Application Gateway
D. Traffic Manager

3. Which feature of CDN helps to improve performance?
A. Dynamic Site Acceleration (DSA)
B. Provides data such as image, files, media, etc.
C. Is able to work with internet
D. Has resource management capabilities

4. Which networking service launches edge nodes?
A. Azure Load Balancer
B. Azure DNS
C. MPLS Network
D. Content Delivery Network (CDN)

5. If a person wants to use their data that is present on both Azure and on-premises, how can a secure connection between the entities be possible?
A. By using VPN Gateway
B. By adding extra resources to VNet
C. By adding traffic router
D. By utilizing the cipher key

6. Which problem will be solved by adding the application gateway?
A. Web traffic management
B. Equally balances the traffic
C. Creating a private connection
D. Performance degradation

7. What type of information is provided by the Content Delivery Network (CDN)?
A. Encrypted data in binary format
B. Images, file, and media
C. Sequence of alphabets
D. Characteristics of VM

8. What is the purpose of the VPN gateway in Azure?
A. Distributes the traffic load
B. Manages the power of all entities in the network
C. Provides encrypted connection
D. None of these

9. If a virtual network is configured in such a way that it has a number of subnets, then which additional feature does it possess?

A. Delivers multiple networks features
B. Saves power
C. Cost-effective
D. All of the above

10. Which service is responsible for managing the traffic flow in the network?
A. Traffic Manager
B. Express Route
C. Load Balancer
D. Azure DNS

11. Why do we need the Azure portal?
A. To manage the resources
B. To create VNet with Azure services
C. To configure a network with Azure services
D. All of the above

12. Which of the following provides better security and storage capabilities?
A. Cloud Networking
B. Local Area Network
C. Logical Network
D. None of the above

13. For how many connections, a VPN gateway can be used?
A. 2
B. 3
C. 4
D. 10

14. Which of the following services is provided by a VPN gateway?
A. Offers open-source availability
B. Creates multiple layers of service for security purpose
C. Is used in private cloud architecture only
D. Provides a secure connection between Azure resources and the on-premises network

15. Which of the following main resources and services should be present in a VNet?
A. VM, internet, on-premises network
B. 10 internet users only
C. Traffic manager, route finder and online services

D. All possible gateways

16. Which of the following is not suited for networking service?
A. Network failure
B. Abrupt behavior of VM
C. Scalability
D. Global coverage

17. Which of the following services is offered by a load balancer?
A. Encrypts the incoming traffic among services
B. Provides internet connection for the communication
C. Works as a port forwarding point
D. None of these

18. While creating a VNet using the Azure portal, what specific things should be assigned in the network?
A. User name and password
B. Address space, resource group, subnets and location
C. App services only
D. Compute resources

19. We can add a maximum of two resources in Azure to VNet. True or false?
A. True
B. False

20. How is a load balancer different from an application gateway?
A. Layer 1, layer 5
B. Layer 7, layer 2
C. Layer 4, layer 7
D. Layer 3, Layer 6

Chapter 04: Storage

Introduction

As we know that no matter what compute we perform, we need some form of storage. We need storage for transient data, data that is used for a single session, storing user details, storing customer data, storing orders, and everything else. In this chapter, we will discuss four ways to create Storage on Azure. These ways include Blob, which is used in tons of different scenarios and is incredibly flexible; Disk Storage, which is just like a disk for you to stored data; File Storage, which is a fully managed file storage in cloud used in order to extent your on-premises storage. And, the last one is Archive Storage, which is a cheap way to store massive archived data. You need to make the right decision in storage as it makes your application sufficient. Choose the right storage option for your required job is one of the most critical steps. Nowadays, storage is scaling up constantly and we need modern storage solutions. So, Microsoft introduced Azure Storage, which provides us the best solution.

Storing data in the cloud omits the need for any hardware or physical space and also makes scaling of storage as per requirement very easy. By storing data in cloud, you can also increase the availability of data.

Storage Account

Before we go deep into Azure Storage, we need to understand what is Storage Account. A Storage Account is like an access point for Azure Storage. All of your Azure Storage Data Objects like blobs, files, queues, tables, and disks are on an Azure storage account. The storage account provides a unique namespace for your Azure Storage data, which is available via HTTP or HTTPS from anywhere in the world. Data on your Azure Storage Account are durable, highly accessible, safe, and scalable. The unique namespace means that every storage data has its webpage with its unique name. It is written in the format: "https://<Storage-Account-Name>.<Storage-type>.core.windows.net". The name of the storage account must be unique all over Azure. It is a base for all storage types as we know. The limit size of the Storage Account was already discussed in Chapter 1. All storage accounts are encrypted for data at rest using SSE (Storage Service Encryption). While naming your Storage Account, you must remember two things:

- The name length must be in between 3 to 24 characters and may only contain numbers and lowercase letters

- Your name for your storage account must be Azure-specific. There can be no two storage accounts with the same name

Two types of storage accounts are available. Users have access to Blob Storage, Table Storage, Queue Storage, and File Storage through the "Standard" storage account. The alternative is a "Premium" account, which is a new option that allows users to save data on SSD drives to boost IO capacity. There are 5 different types of storage account available that depends on different features and pricing.

- General-purpose v2 accounts
- General-purpose v1 accounts
- BlockBlobStorage accounts
- FileStorage accounts
- BlobStorage accounts

Azure Storage

Azure Storage is a Microsoft Cloud storage for storing data. It is a highly scalable object store and a message store for messaging. It also offers file system service. It is a NoSQL store that provides a number of benefits like:

- **Durability and Highly Availability** - In case of hardware failure, it provides you replicas by placing the data in a replicated form in different geographical locations. So your data is always highly secure and available
- **Security** - The data stored in Azure Storage is not able to access as it provides encryption of all data stored in Storage. It has restricted access to the data
- **Accessibility** - The data stored in Azure Storage can be accessible from anywhere in the world over HTTP or HTTPS
- **Scalability** - It can easily scale in order to meet the performance requirements

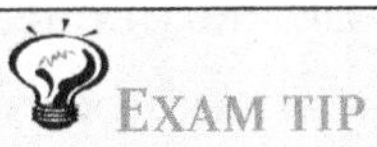

You must first create an account in Azure to use any kind of storage; the Storage account is the parent object.

Blob Storage

Blob means Binary Large Object, which is used for storage of Binary or text data. It is used for storage of huge amounts of data. Inside the storage account, these blobs are stored in a

container. A container is a place of organizing a set of blobs. Within the storage account, you have unlimited containers with unlimited capacity for storing blobs. As we have seen earlier that each object has its unique address, so here individual blob also has its unique address.

In different scenarios, you can use blob storage like for storing images, which belong to different sizes and formats, for storing all kind of file with distributed access to them via Azure Storage. It can be used for streaming audio and video directly from blob storage, for writing logs files regardless of size and frequency of writing, for storing backup data, for restoring, for DR or any other sort of archiving, and much more. For further basic information about Blob storage, you can refer to Chapter 1 "Storage" in Azure Services.

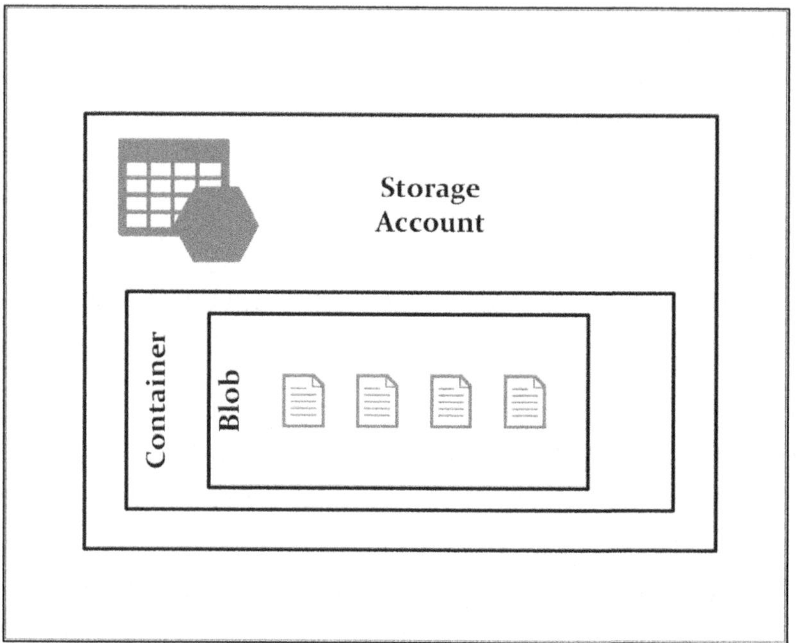

Figure 4-01: Blob Storage

In Azure, three types of Blobs are supported;

1. Block blobs store text and binary data up to 4.7TB. It is made up of blocks of data that can be managed individually. In one block blob, you can have 50,000 blocks.
2. Append blobs are used for log data and can be up to 195GB in size. It is usually used for optimizing the append operation.
3. Page blobs are used for frequent read and write operations on data. It sizes up to 8TB. The files stored in page blobs can be accessed with any part of the file at any time. It is used for storing virtual hard drive then serves as a disk for the virtual machine.

During the time of creation, you need to select the type of a storage account, which is based on different pricing options.

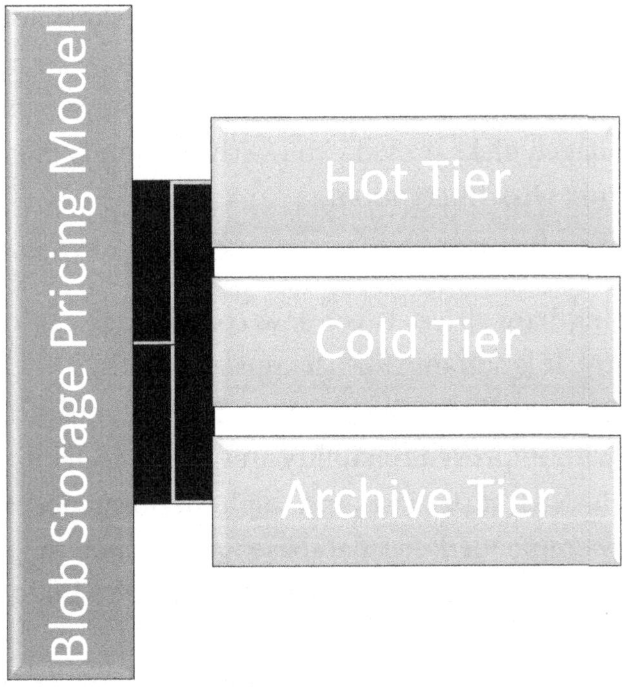

Figure 4-02: Pricing Model

1. **Hot Tier** - It is for frequently accessed data and is the most optimized. The access costs are low (read-write) but storage costs are the highest.
2. **Cold Tier** - It is for data that is not frequently accessed. Data is stored in cold tier for 30 days. Its storage cost is low but accessing cost is high. It is used for short term backup or for telemetry data.
3. **Archive Tier** - It is used to store rarely accessed data and it has the lowest cost for storage but the highest accessing cost.

The archive tier can be set to blob only while the Hot/Cool tier is enabled at the storage account level or blob level. All three levels of storage access can be found in the same storage account and a blob default level is inherited from the account level setting. However, blob-level tier can be used to set the level of the object.

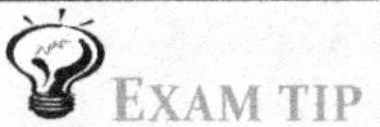

Blob Storage is a general kind of storage in which you can store any kind of data. Mainly, it has three pricing tiers: Hot, Cold and Archive.

Disk Storage

It is a disk to which you can store your data. A managed disk is the disk that is attached to your VM. Here, managed means that Azure will look after this disk for you and managed the uptime and backup. You also do not need to take care of the size and performance, as it is a part of the agreement with Microsoft Azure. With disk storage, you can easily upgrade the disk size and type. Managed disks provide you with two kinds of encryptions: Storage Service Encryption and Azure Disk Encryption.

There are four different types of disk.

- **HDD** - It's a spinning hard drive. It is a low cost storage option for data that are accessed infrequently. It is suitable for backups and testing
- **Standard SSD** - It is generally for the production environment. It gives you a lower latency than HDD with improved reliability and better scalability
- **Premium SSD** - It is a super-fast and high performance storage for critical workloads. It is recommended for database installation in particular with low latency. It is better than the standard SSD. Only VM series that are compatible with premium storage can use premium SSDs
- **Ultra Disk**- It is for the most demanding and data intensive workload. It provides extremely scalable performance with sub milliseconds latency. It can be up to 64TB in size. It is recommended for analytical models, gaming, etc.

Comparison between all disk types:

	Ultra disk	**Premium SSD**	**Standard SSD**	**Standard HDD**
Disk type	SSD	SSD	SSD	HDD
Scenario	IO-intensive workloads such as SAP HANA, top tier databases (for example, SQL, Oracle), and other transaction-heavy workloads	Production and performance sensitive workloads	Web servers lightly used enterprise applications and dev/test	Backup, non-critical, infrequent access
Max Disk Size	65,536 gibibyte (GiB)	32,767 GiB	32,767 GiB	32,767 GiB
Max Throughput	2,000 MiB/s	900 MiB/s	750 MiB/s	500 MiB/s

Max IOPS	160,000	20,000	6,000	2,000

Table 4-01: Comparison between Disk Storage Types

File Storage

We know that mostly companies have a file storage where they store the company's assets. In order to work with these files, they can upload, delete, synchronize and more. But on-premises storage can have issues like disk limitation for storage amount. You also need to configure and maintain backups. Security of data at on-premises storage is also difficult to maintain and you may need to hire security specialists for this. Also, file sharing across the team and organization becomes difficult. So by using file storage, all of these issues can be resolved. With File Storage, you get the following benefits:

- Share files across multiple Azure machines and be able to connect with the on-premises infrastructure
- It is fully managed and you do not need to worry about OS or hardware
- Highly available with super resistance against outages
- It has built-in redundancy

Some common scenarios in which you can use file storage are:

- In a hybrid network where your on-premises storage is out of space
- For lift and shift of existing file storage to Azure
- It can also be used as a centralized location for monitoring logs and config. files.

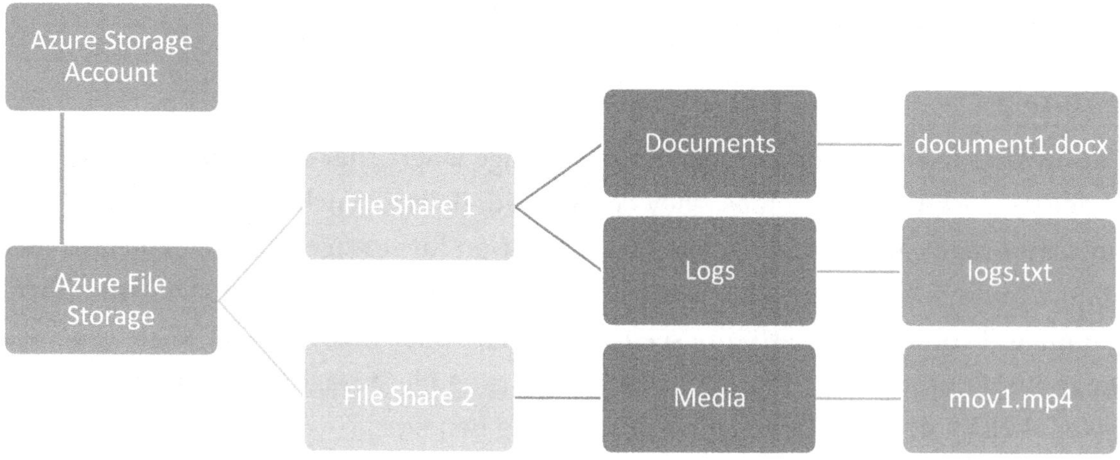

Figure 4-03: File Storage System

EXAM TIP

File Storage mitigates the on-premises file storage system.

Archive

Azure Archive Storage is used generally for archiving data and paying less for it. Most of the company's policies, legislations and recovery scenarios storing a large amount of archive data is required, so Azure Archive service can prove to be really handy for them. It is one of the lowest priced storage in Azure, which means you can store terabytes of data in just few dollars per month; with Azure Archive, growth in business data does not necessarily have to mean that there should be a growth in the cost of storage. It is a good storage option for the data that are not needed frequently, it is durable, encrypted and stable. With archive storage option, you can free up the most important storage in on-premises. It is secure for storing any personal data like banking data, medical data etc. It secures data at rest with 256-bit AES keys.

In the first chapter, we mentioned that archive storage is blob storage so the tools that even work for blob can work for archive data.

Use cases for Archive Storage are:

- Security and public safety data retention

- Magnetic tape replacement
- Healthcare Data Archiving
- Long term backup retention
- Digital media content retention

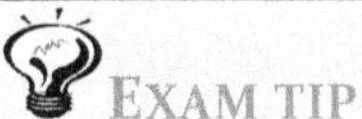

EXAM TIP

Archive Storage is a blob storage type.

Lab 4-01: Creating a Storage Account

Scenario

John has an organization for which he wants storage in Azure Cloud to store important documents. Which storage option can he use to store the documents?

Solution

By using Azure Storage, he can store his organization's important documents.

1. Login to the Azure portal and go to the "Storage Account" service.

portal.azure.com/#home
Search resources, services, and docs (G+/)
Create a resource
Home
Dashboard
All services
FAVORITES
All resources
Resource groups
App Services
Function App
SQL databases
Azure Cosmos DB
Virtual machines
Load balancers
Storage accounts
Virtual machines
Virtual networks
SQL databases
Azure Database for PostgreS...
Type
Last Viewed

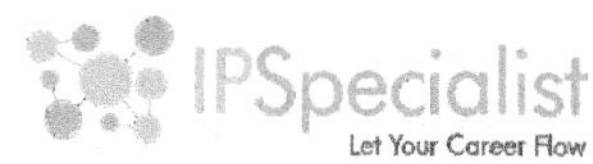

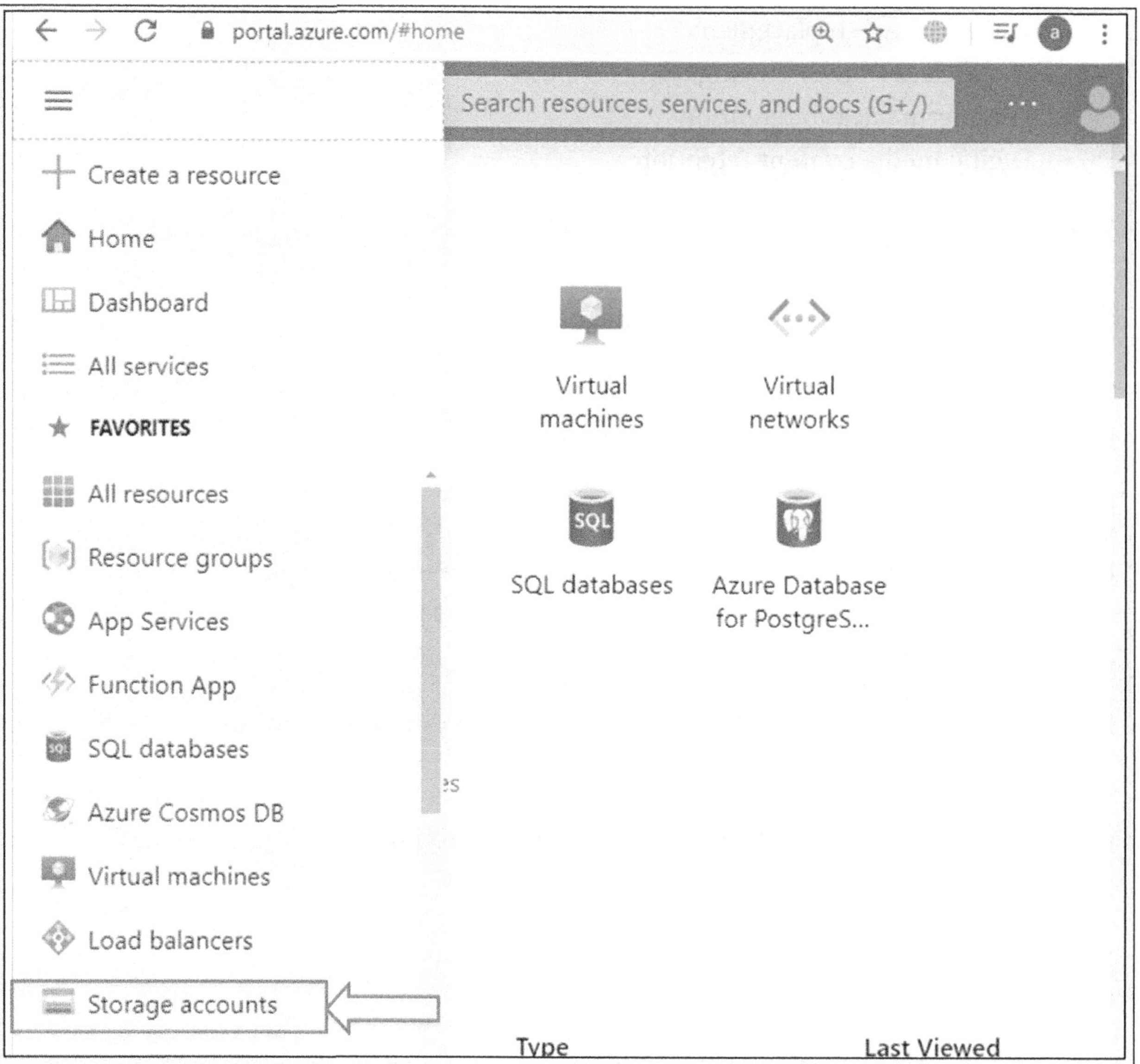

2. Click "Add"

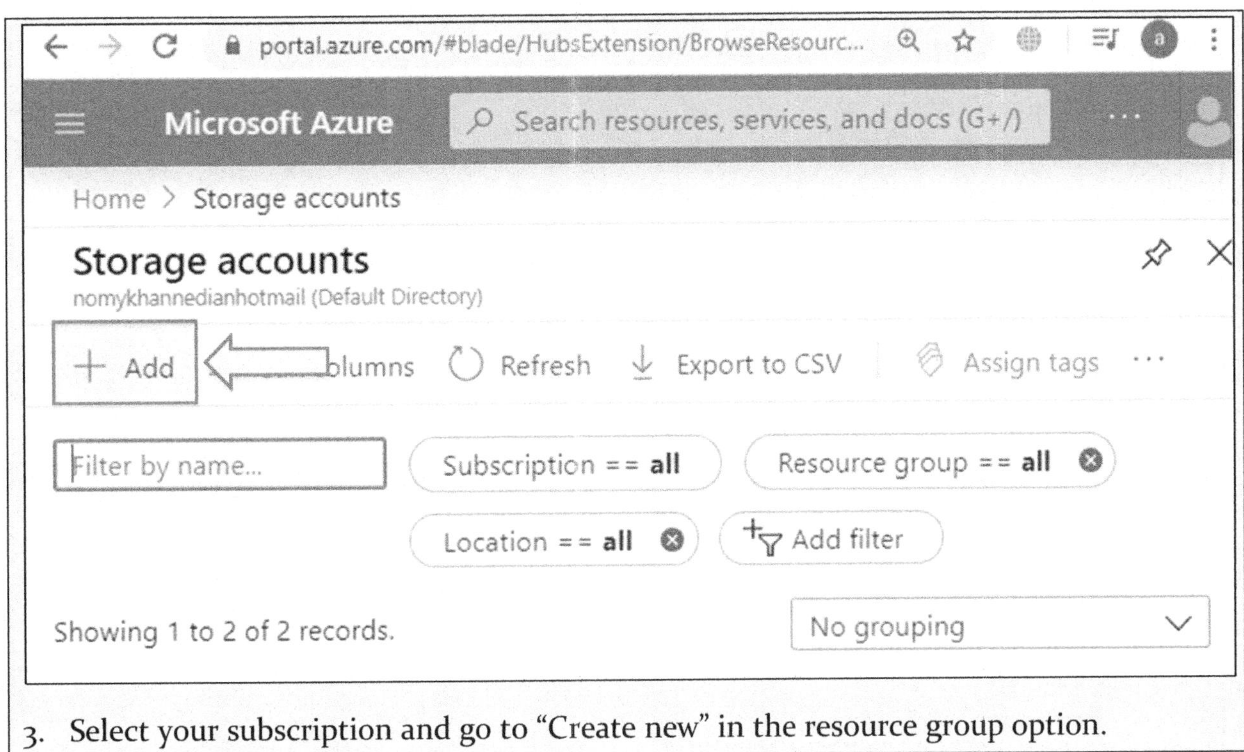

3. Select your subscription and go to "Create new" in the resource group option.

portal.azure.com/#create/Microsoft.StorageAccount

Microsoft Azure

Search resources, services, and docs (G+/)

Home > Storage accounts > Create storage account > Create storage account

Create storage account

Basics Networking Advanced Tags Review + create

Azure Storage is a Microsoft-managed service providing cloud storage that is highly available, secure, durable, scalable, and redundant. Azure Storage includes Azure Blobs (objects), Azure Data Lake Storage Gen2, Azure Files, Azure Queues, and Azure Tables. The cost of your storage account depends on the usage and the options you choose below.
Learn more about Azure storage accounts

Project details

Select the subscription to manage deployed resources and costs. Use resource groups like folders to organize and manage all your resources.

Subscription *
Pay-As-You-Go

Resource group *
Select existing...
Create new

Review + create   < Previous   Next : Networking >

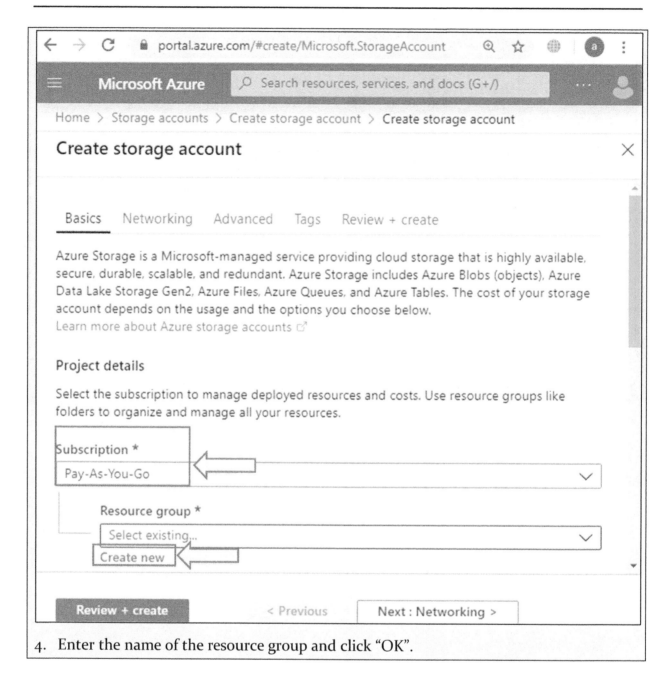

4. Enter the name of the resource group and click "OK".

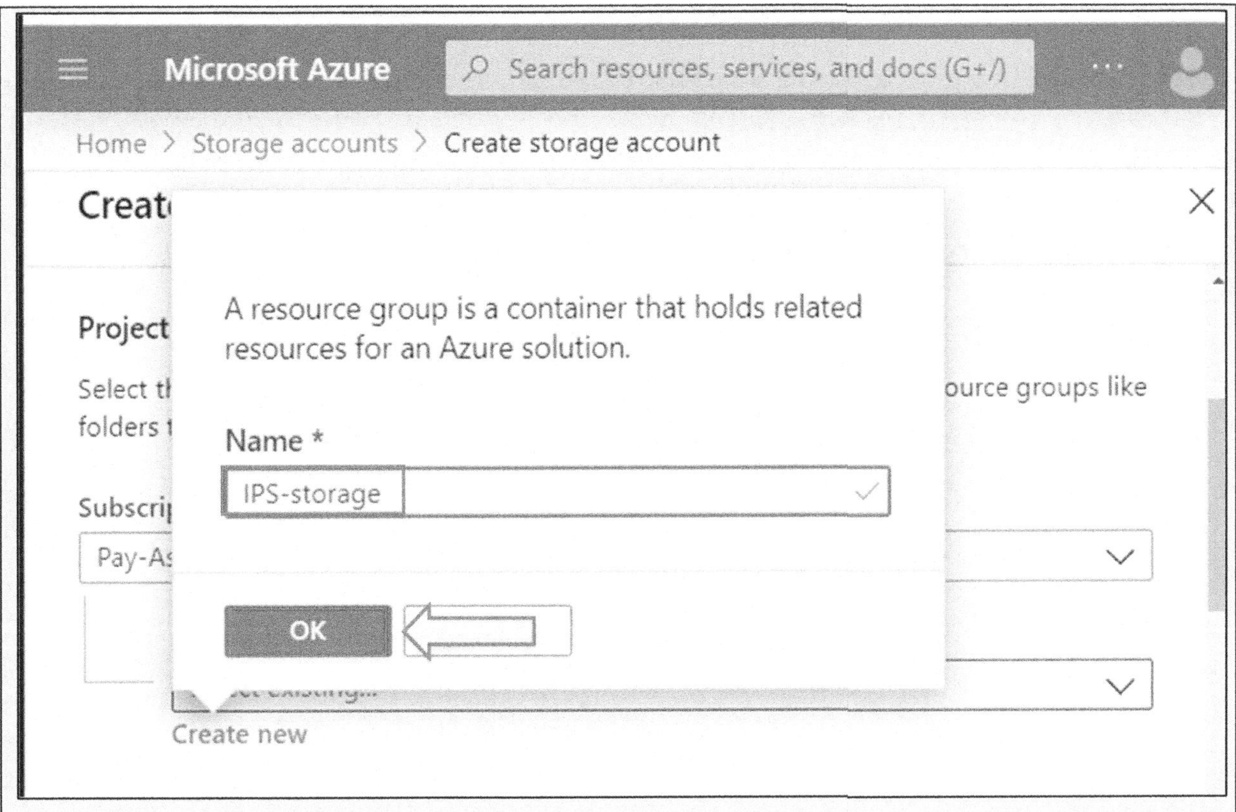

5. In the instance detail, enter "Storage account name" (the name should be in lowercase).

portal.azure.com/#create/Microsoft.StorageAccount

Microsoft Azure

Search resources, services, and docs (G+/)

Home > Storage accounts > Create storage account

Create storage account

Instance details

The default deployment model is Resource Manager, which supports the latest Azure features. You may choose to deploy using the classic deployment model instead.
Choose classic deployment model

Storage account name *

ipsteststorage1

Location *

(Asia Pacific) Australia Southeast

Performance

Standard Premium

Account kind

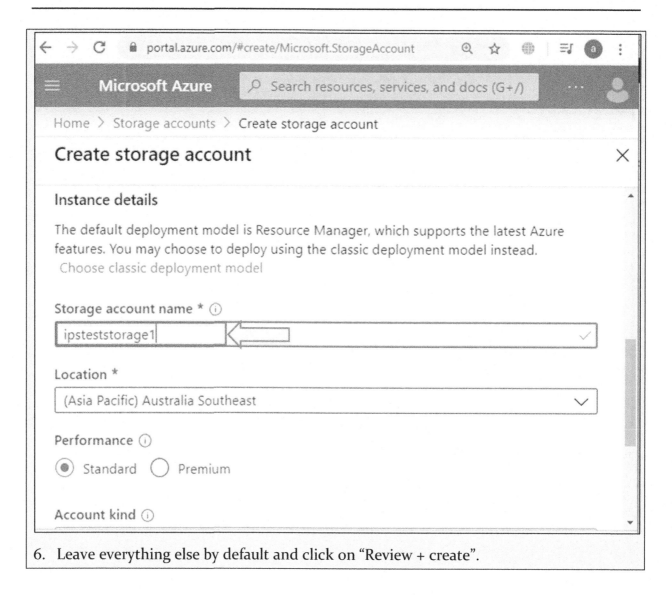

6. Leave everything else by default and click on "Review + create".

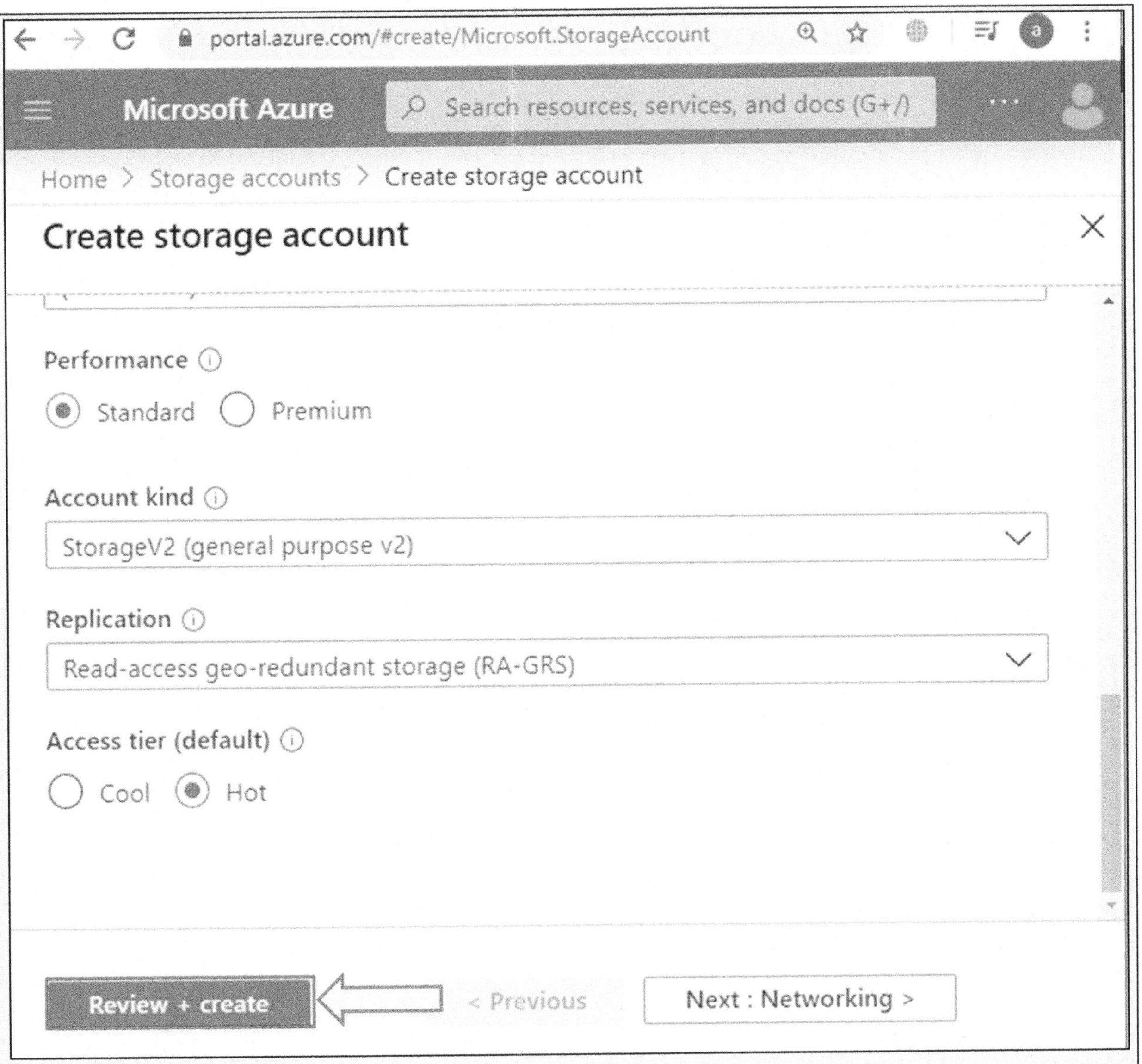

portal.azure.com/#create/Microsoft.StorageAccount

Microsoft Azure

Search resources, services, and docs (G+/)

Home > Storage accounts > Create storage account

Create storage account

Performance

Standard Premium

Account kind

StorageV2 (general purpose v2)

Replication

Read-access geo-redundant storage (RA-GRS)

Access tier (default)

Cool Hot

Review + create < Previous Next : Networking >

7. Click "Create".

portal.azure.com/#create/Microsoft.StorageAccount

Microsoft Azure

Search resources, services, and docs (G+/)

Home > Storage accounts > Create storage account

Create storage account

Validation passed

Basics Networking Advanced Tags Review + create

Basics

Subscription	Pay-As-You-Go
Resource group	(New) IPS-storage
Location	(Asia Pacific) Australia Southeast
Storage account name	ipsteststorage1
Deployment model	Resource manager
Account kind	StorageV2 (general purpose v2)

Create < Previous Next >

Download a template for automation

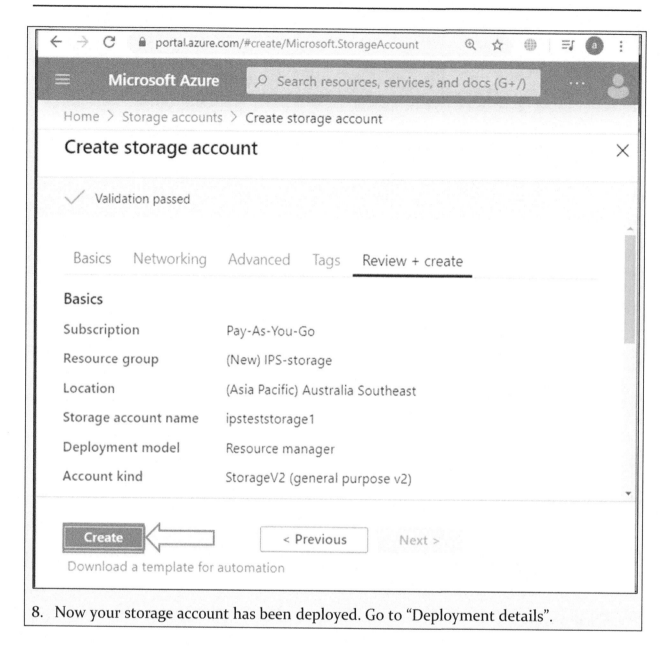

8. Now your storage account has been deployed. Go to "Deployment details".

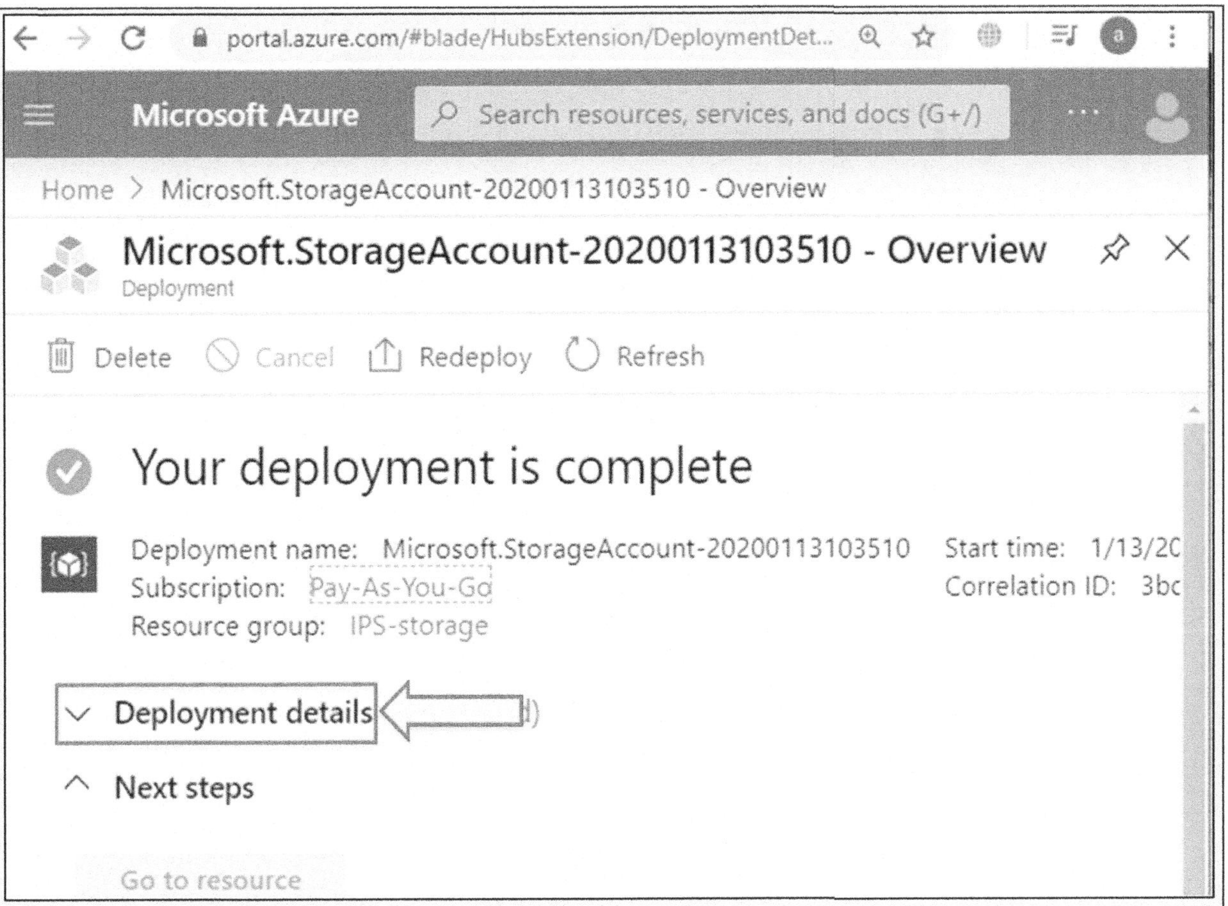

portal.azure.com/#blade/HubsExtension/DeploymentDet...

Microsoft Azure

Search resources, services, and docs (G+/)

Home > Microsoft.StorageAccount-20200113103510 - Overview

Microsoft.StorageAccount-20200113103510 - Overview

Deployment

Delete Cancel Redeploy Refresh

Your deployment is complete

Deployment name: Microsoft.StorageAccount-20200113103510 Start time: 1/13/2C

Subscription: Pay-As-You-Go Correlation ID: 3bc

Resource group: IPS-storage

Deployment details

Next steps

Go to resource

9. Click on the resource that you created. You will see the overview of the storage account.

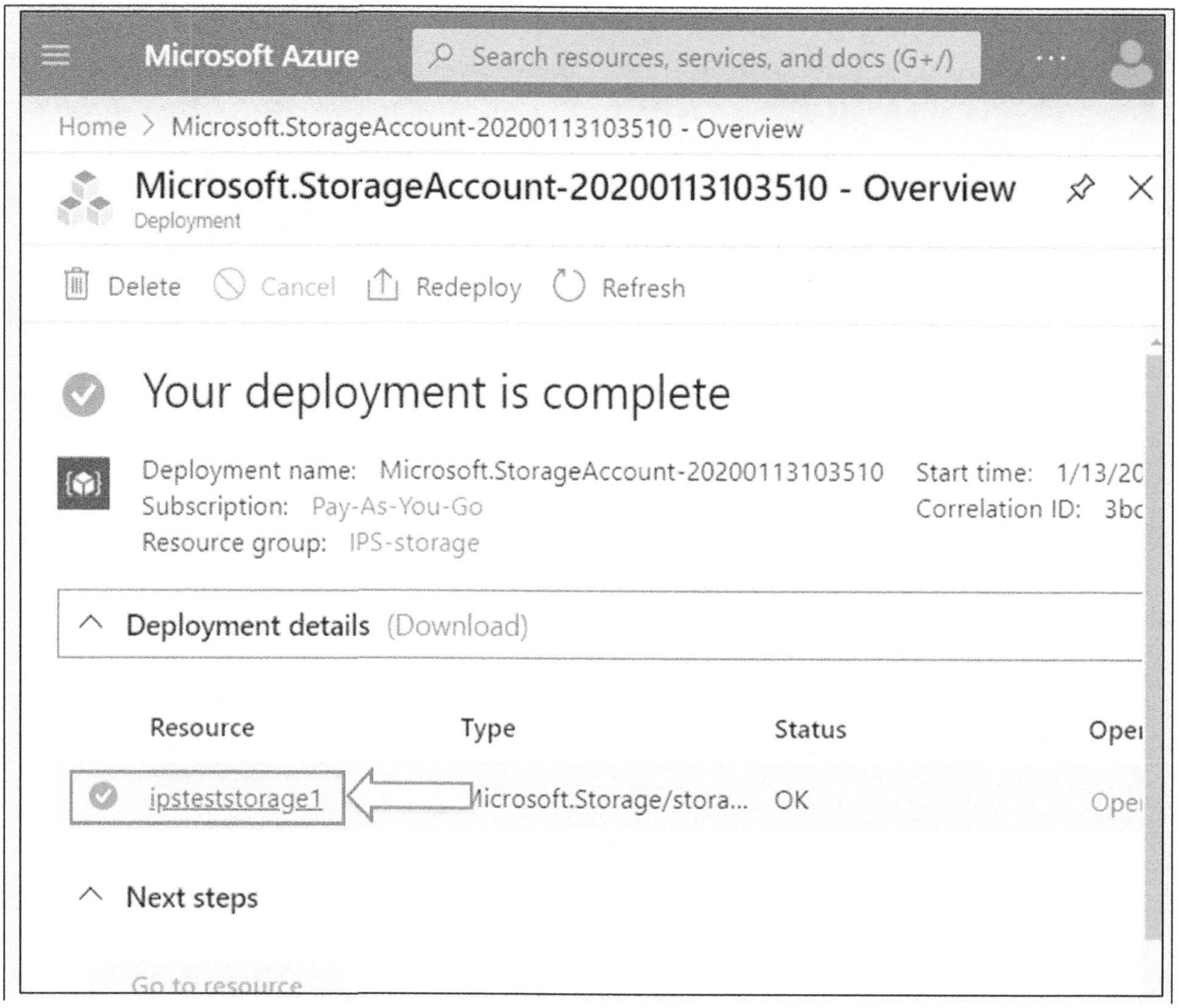

Microsoft Azure
Search resources, services, and docs (G+/)
Home > Microsoft.StorageAccount-20200113103510 - Overview
Microsoft.StorageAccount-20200113103510 - Overview
Deployment
Delete Cancel Redeploy Refresh
Your deployment is complete
Deployment name: Microsoft.StorageAccount-20200113103510 Start time: 1/13/20
Subscription: Pay-As-You-Go Correlation ID: 3bc
Resource group: IPS-storage
Deployment details (Download)

Resource	Type	Status	Ope
ipsteststorage1	Microsoft.Storage/stora...	OK	Ope

Next steps
Go to resource

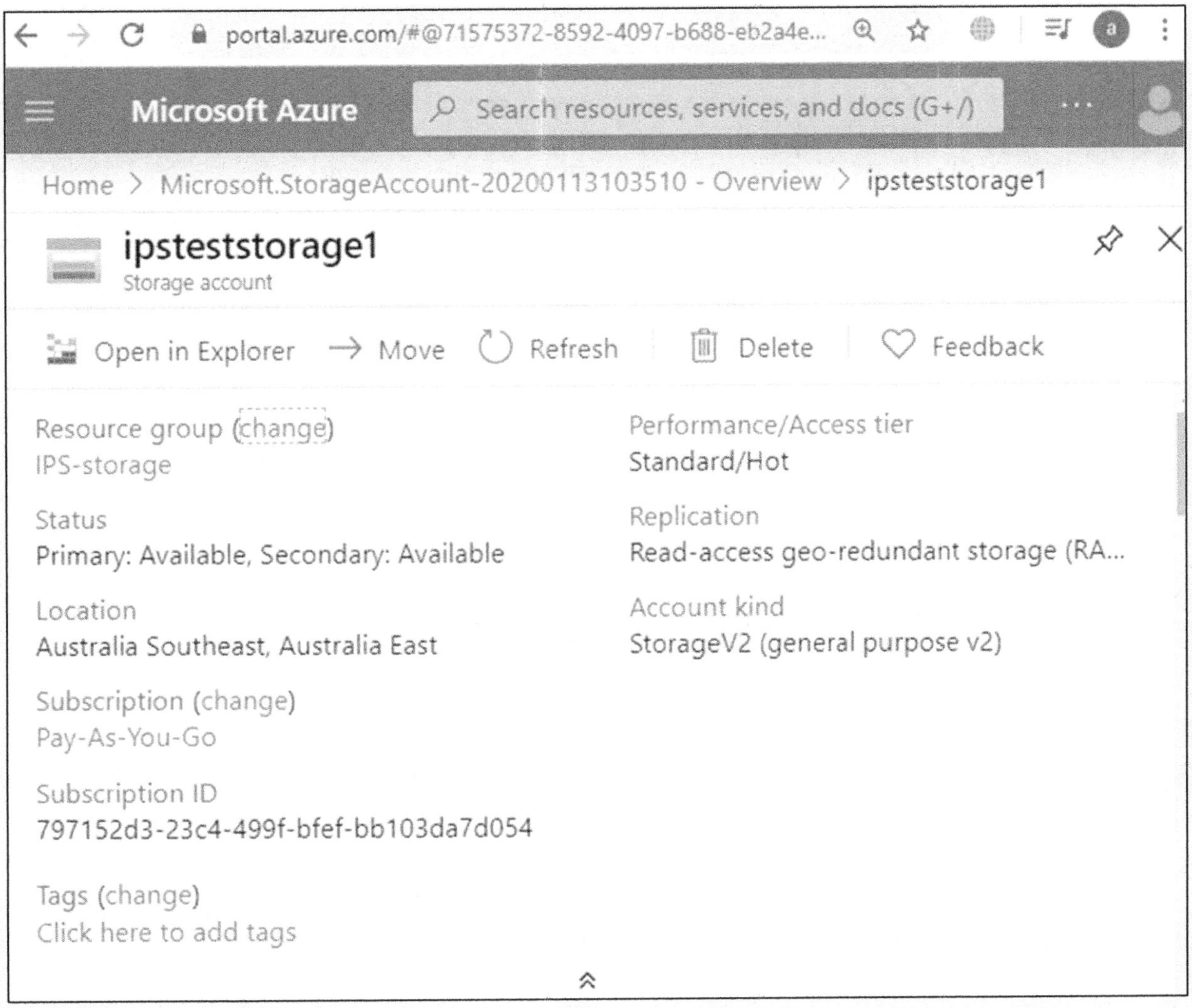

portal.azure.com/#@71575372-8592-4097-b688-eb2a4e...

Microsoft Azure

Search resources, services, and docs (G+/)

Home > Microsoft.StorageAccount-20200113103510 - Overview > ipsteststorage1

ipsteststorage1

Storage account

Open in Explorer → Move Refresh Delete Feedback

Resource group (change)
IPS-storage

Status
Primary: Available, Secondary: Available

Location
Australia Southeast, Australia East

Subscription (change)
Pay-As-You-Go

Subscription ID
797152d3-23c4-499f-bfef-bb103da7d054

Tags (change)
Click here to add tags

Performance/Access tier
Standard/Hot

Replication
Read-access geo-redundant storage (RA...

Account kind
StorageV2 (general purpose v2)

10. Now, you will see the service option where you get multiple storage options. Click on "Containers".

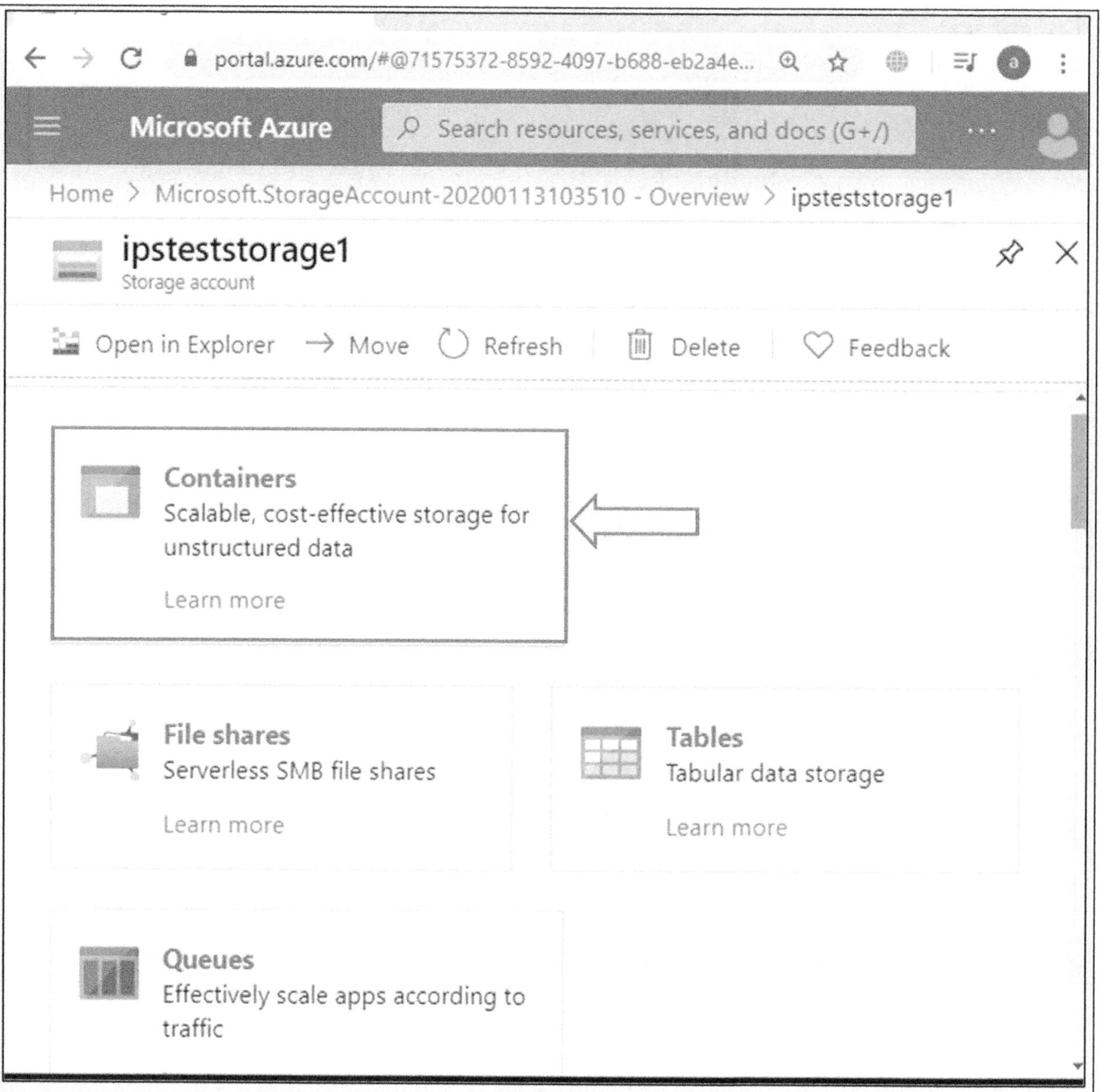

11. Click on "Container".

Microsoft Azure
Search resources, services, and docs (G+/)
... > Microsoft.StorageAccount-20200113103510 - Overview > ipsteststorage1 - Containers
ipsteststorage1 - Containers
Storage account
+ Container | access level | Refresh | Delete
Search containers by prefix

Name	Last modified	Public access...	Lease state

You don't have any containers yet. Click '+ Container' to get started.

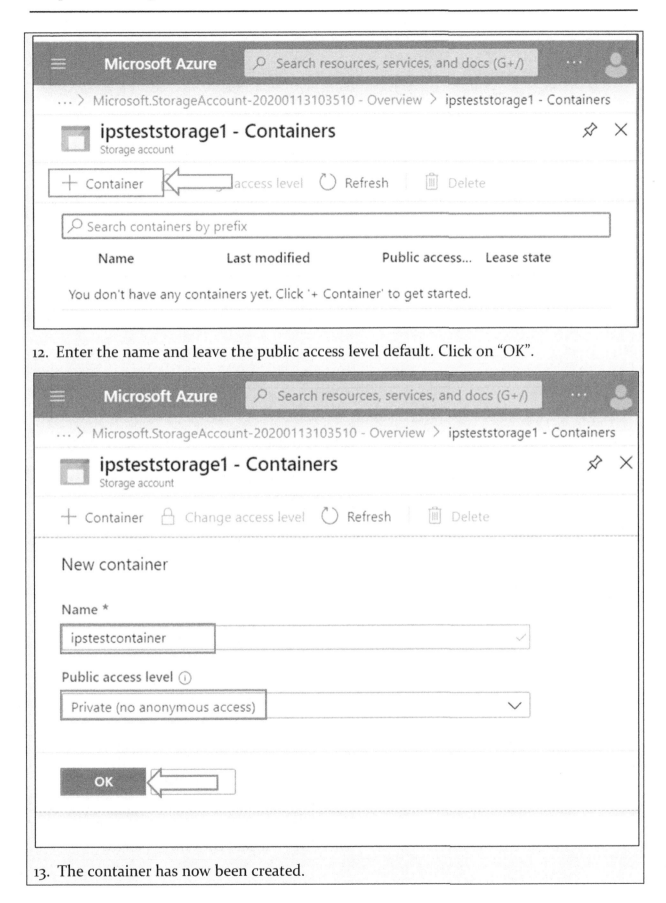

12. Enter the name and leave the public access level default. Click on "OK".

Microsoft Azure
Search resources, services, and docs (G+/)
... > Microsoft.StorageAccount-20200113103510 - Overview > ipsteststorage1 - Containers
ipsteststorage1 - Containers
Storage account
+ Container | Change access level | Refresh | Delete

New container

Name *
ipstestcontainer

Public access level
Private (no anonymous access)

OK

13. The container has now been created.

Microsoft Azure
Search resources, services, and docs (G+/)
Home > ipsteststorage1 - Containers
ipsteststorage1 - Containers
Storage account
+ Container | Change access level | Refresh | Delete
Search containers by prefix

Name	Last modified	Public access...	Lease state
ipstestcontainer	1/13/2020, 10:42:35 AM	Private	Available

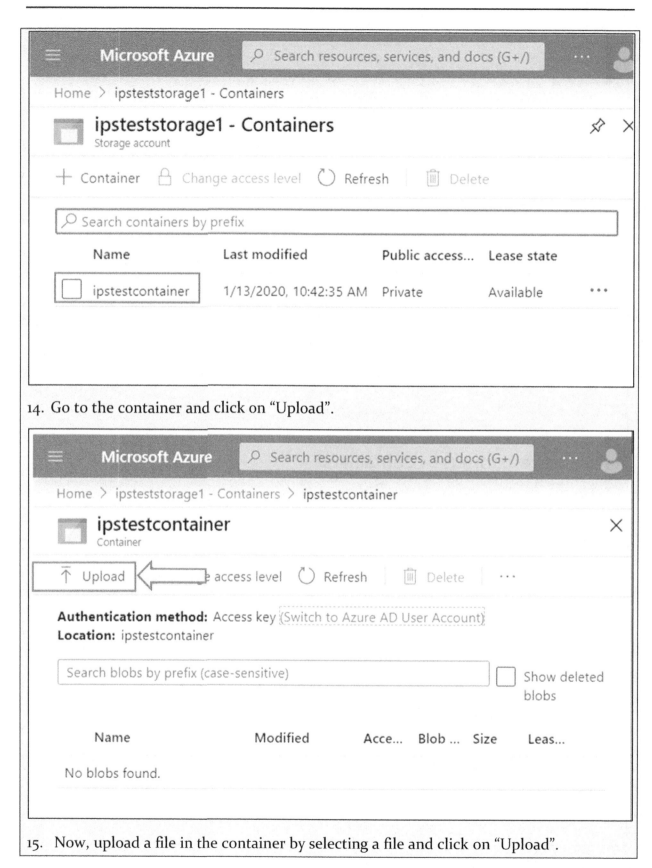

14. Go to the container and click on "Upload".

Microsoft Azure
Search resources, services, and docs (G+/)
Home > ipsteststorage1 - Containers > ipstestcontainer
ipstestcontainer
Container
Upload | access level | Refresh | Delete
Authentication method: Access key (Switch to Azure AD User Account)
Location: ipstestcontainer
Search blobs by prefix (case-sensitive)
Show deleted blobs

Name	Modified	Acce...	Blob ...	Size	Leas...
No blobs found.					

15. Now, upload a file in the container by selecting a file and click on "Upload".

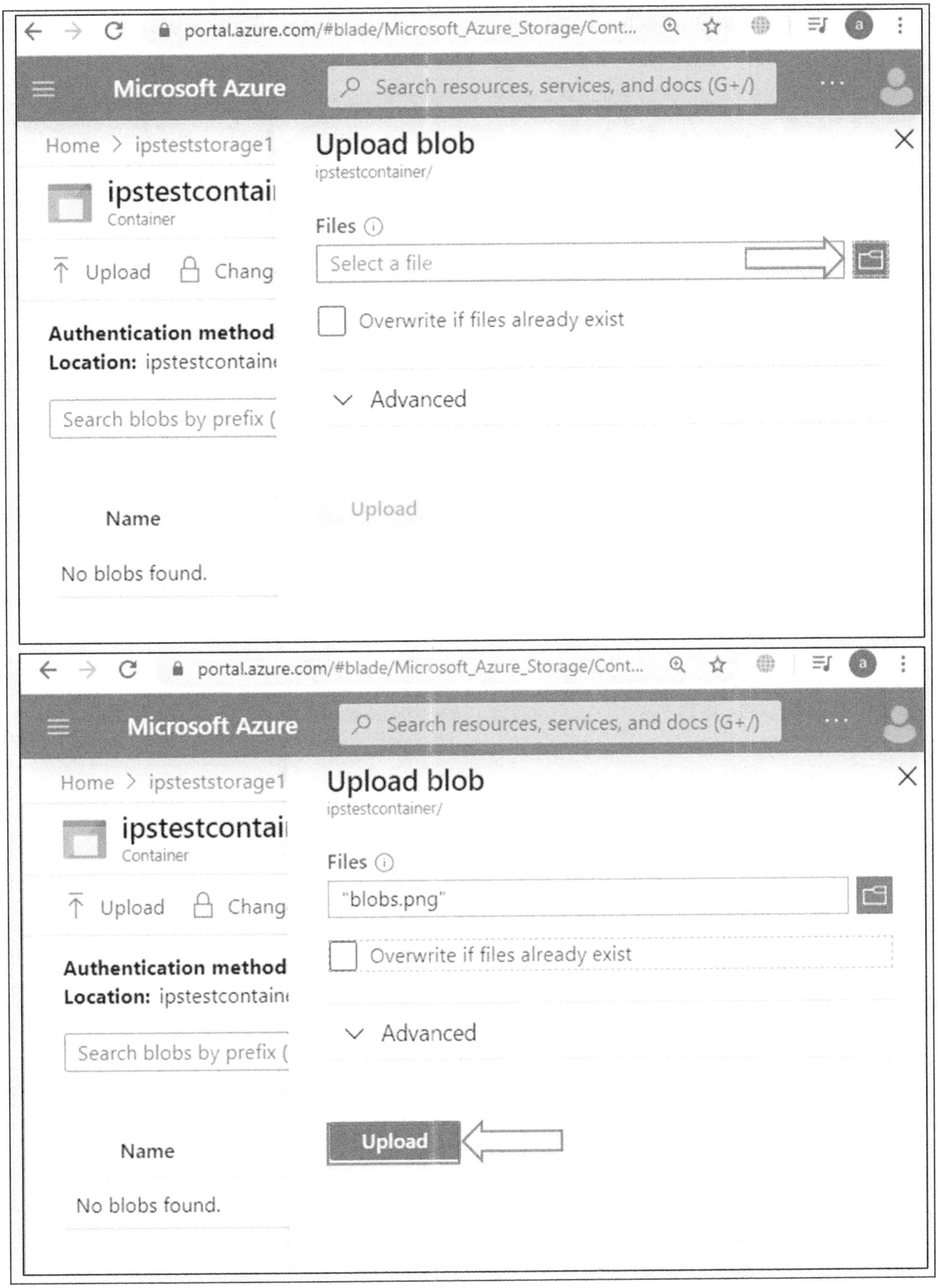

portal.azure.com/#blade/Microsoft_Azure_Storage/Cont...

Microsoft Azure

Search resources, services, and docs (G+/)

Home > ipsteststorage1

ipstestcontai

Container

Upload Chang

Authentication method

Location: ipstestcontain

Search blobs by prefix (

Name

No blobs found.

Upload blob

ipstestcontainer/

Files

Select a file

Overwrite if files already exist

Advanced

Upload

portal.azure.com/#blade/Microsoft_Azure_Storage/Cont...

Microsoft Azure

Search resources, services, and docs (G+/)

Home > ipsteststorage1

ipstestcontai

Container

Upload Chang

Authentication method

Location: ipstestcontain

Search blobs by prefix (

Name

No blobs found.

Upload blob

ipstestcontainer/

Files

"blobs.png"

Overwrite if files already exist

Advanced

Upload

16. You will see that the file has been uploaded inside the container. If you want to change the access level, then go to the "Change access level" option.

Microsoft Azure
Search resources, services, and docs (G+/)
Home > ipsteststorage1 - Containers > ipstestcontainer
ipstestcontainer
Container
Upload Change access level Refresh Delete ...
Authentication method: Access key (Switch to Azure AD User Account)
Location: ipstestcontainer
Search blobs by prefix (case-sensitive) Show deleted blobs

Name	Modified	Acce...	Blob ...	Size	Leas...
blobs.png	1/13/2020, 10:...	Hot (I...	Block...	37.08...	Availabl ...

Microsoft Azure
Search resources, services, and docs (G+/)
Home > ipsteststorage1 - Containers > ipstestcontainer
ipstestcontainer
Container
Upload Change access level Delete ...
Authentication method: Access key (Switch to Azure AD User Account)
Location: ipstestcontainer
Search blobs by prefix (case-sensitive) Show deleted blobs

Name	Modified	Acce...	Blob ...	Size	Leas...
blobs.png	1/13/2020, 10:...	Hot (I...	Block...	37.08...	Availabl ...

17. Change it to read only access for blobs. Click "OK".

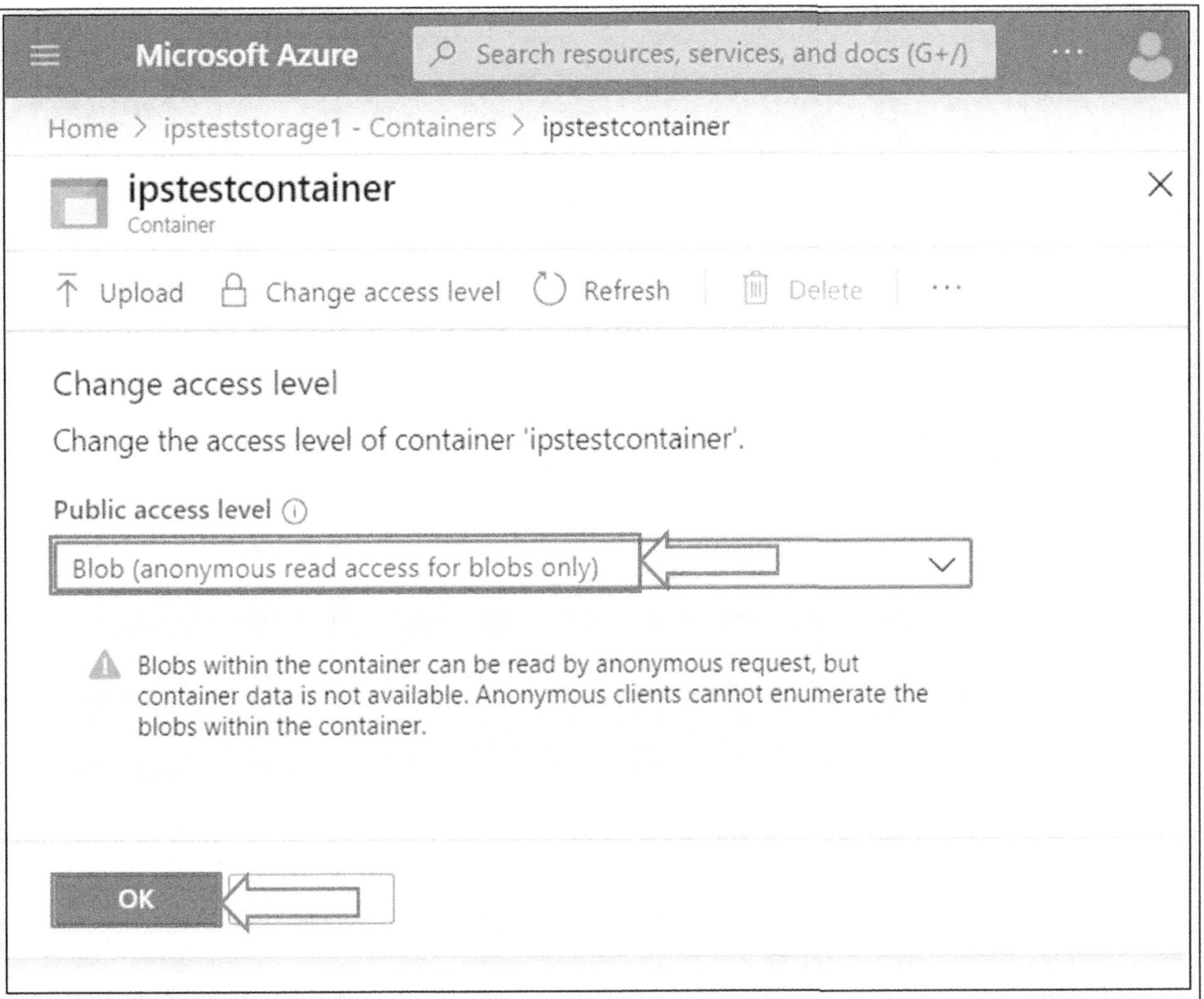

Microsoft Azure
Search resources, services, and docs (G+/)

Home > ipsteststorage1 - Containers > ipstestcontainer

ipstestcontainer
Container

Upload Change access level Refresh Delete ...

Change access level

Change the access level of container 'ipstestcontainer'.

Public access level

Blob (anonymous read access for blobs only)

Blobs within the container can be read by anonymous request, but container data is not available. Anonymous clients cannot enumerate the blobs within the container.

OK

18. You can now access this file over the internet by its URL. Click on the file and copy the URL.

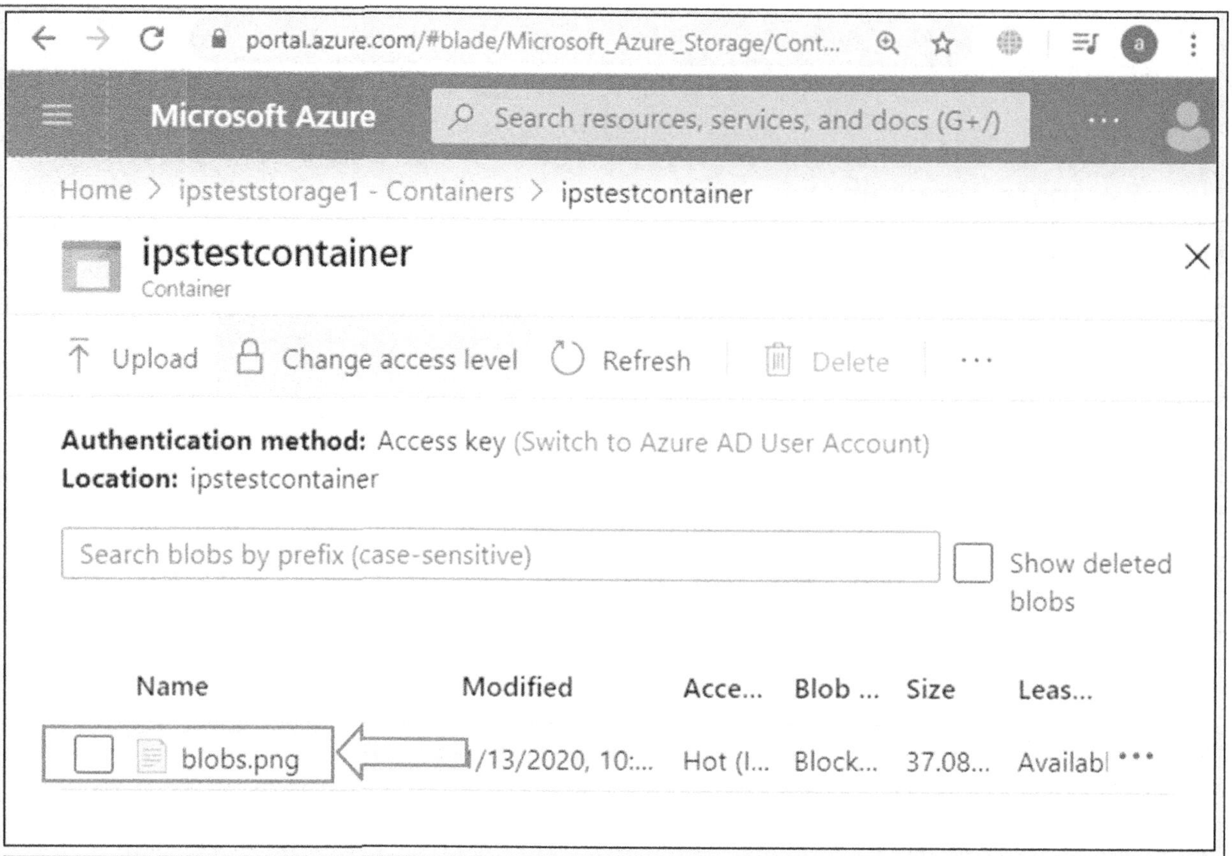

portal.azure.com/#blade/Microsoft_Azure_Storage/Cont...

Microsoft Azure

Search resources, services, and docs (G+/)

Home > ipsteststorage1 - Containers > ipstestcontainer

ipstestcontainer

Container

Upload | Change access level | Refresh | Delete | ...

Authentication method: Access key (Switch to Azure AD User Account)

Location: ipstestcontainer

Search blobs by prefix (case-sensitive)

Show deleted blobs

Name	Modified	Acce...	Blob ...	Size	Leas...
blobs.png	1/13/2020, 10:...	Hot (I...	Block...	37.08...	Availabl

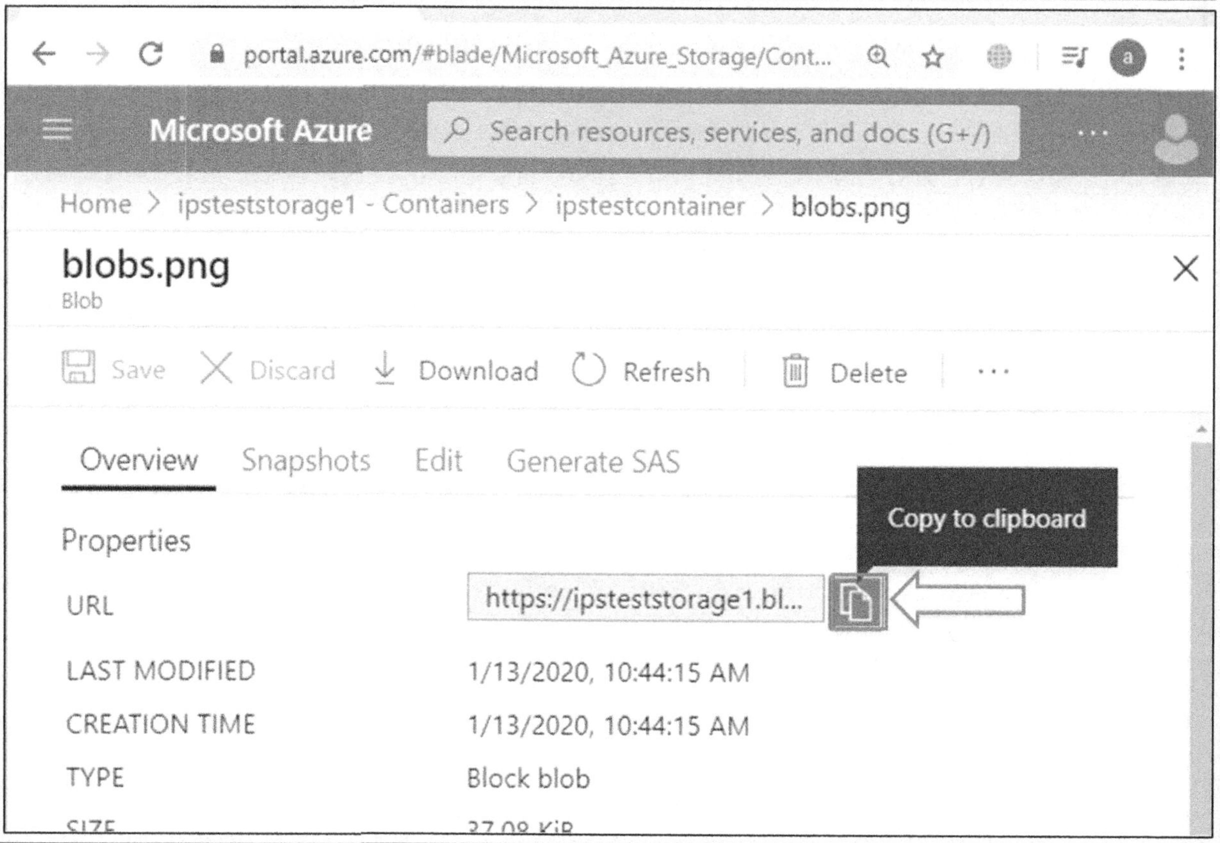

portal.azure.com/#blade/Microsoft_Azure_Storage/Cont...

Microsoft Azure

Search resources, services, and docs (G+/)

Home > ipsteststorage1 - Containers > ipstestcontainer > blobs.png

blobs.png

Blob

Save | Discard | Download | Refresh | Delete | ...

Overview | Snapshots | Edit | Generate SAS

Properties

Copy to clipboard

URL	https://ipsteststorage1.bl...
LAST MODIFIED	1/13/2020, 10:44:15 AM
CREATION TIME	1/13/2020, 10:44:15 AM
TYPE	Block blob
SIZE	37.08 KiB

19. Paste it in the browser and then you will see that the file is accessible over the internet.

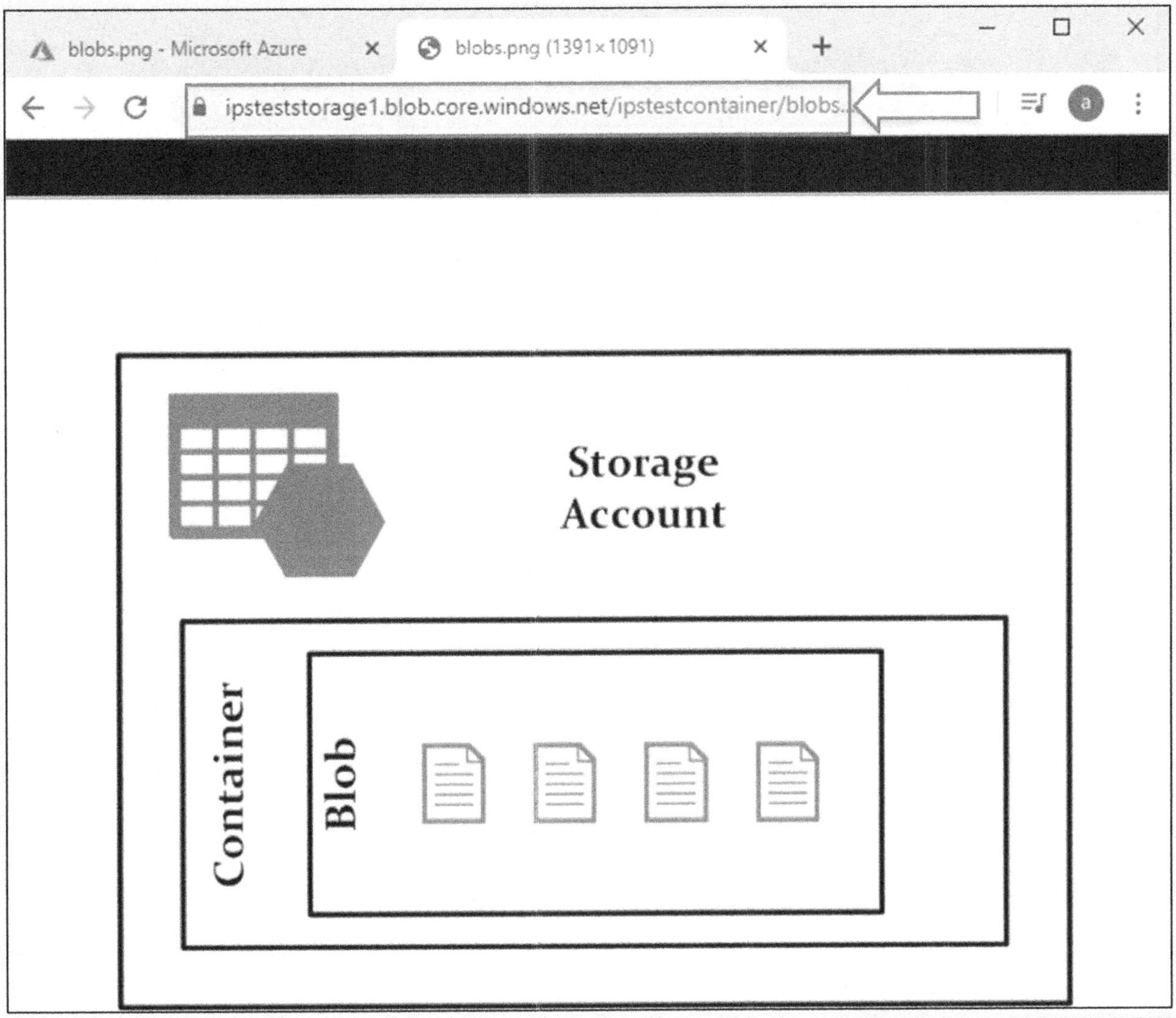

MindMap

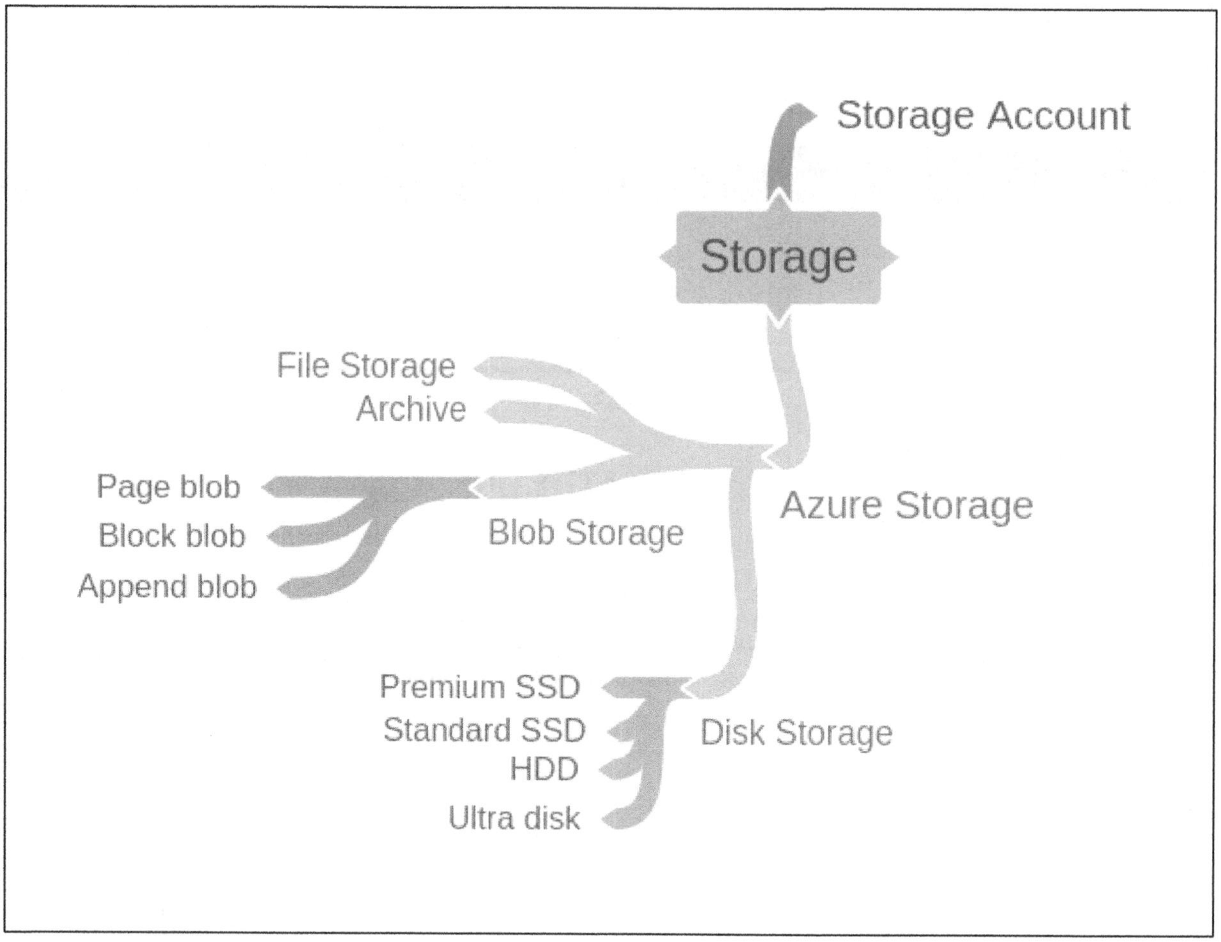

Storage Account
Storage
File Storage
Archive
Page blob
Block blob
Append blob
Blob Storage
Azure Storage
Premium SSD
Standard SSD
HDD
Ultra disk
Disk Storage

Figure 4-04: Mindmap

Practice Questions

1. In order to create a VM, you need a storage service that is used to store data of VM disk. Which storage option should you use?
A. Blob
B. File
C. Queue
D. Disk

2. In blob container, what type of data can you store?
A. Only binary known format
B. Binary files that comply with the Azure data types defined for the storage type
C. Any sort of binary files
D. The binary file that is less than 500KB

3. A network drive will be mapped from multiple computers running Windows 10 to Azure Storage. For the planned mapped drive, you need to create a storage solution in Azure. Which storage option is suitable for this?
A. Blob
B. File
C. Queue
D. Disk

4. From the following option which storage is also known as Archive storage?
A. File Storage
B. Blob Storage
C. Archive its own
D. Disk Storage

5. When creating a storage account, the name must contain a capital letter and special characters? True or false?
A. True
B. False

6. When creating an Azure storage account, what is the most significant?
A. The name you give the storage account becomes the main web address for accessing the files in it. It must be unique across all of Azure
B. The name you give the storage account becomes the main web address for accessing the files in it. It must be unique within your Azure subscription
C. Each storage account name is linked to a set of users that can access it

D. No significance. You can name a storage account as you want

7. From the following options, which storage solution can you use as an extension to your on-premises storage.
A. Blob
B. Queue
C. File
D. Disk

8. From the following, what are the types of disk storage? (Choose 2)
A. Slow HDD
B. Ultra disk
C. Premium HDD
D. Standard HDD

9. In storage account, encryption of data at rest is done via RSA. True or false?
A. True
B. False

10. Which type of blob you can use to store log data?
A. Page Blob
B. Fast Blob
C. Block Blob
D. Append Blob

11. Which pricing model of blob storage can you use to store the most frequently accessed data?
A. Cold
B. Hot
C. Archive
D. All of the above

12. Which disk storage type gives super-fast and high performance storage for critical workloads?
A. Standard HDD
B. Standard SSD
C. Premium SSD
D. Ultra Disk

13. What URL format can Blobs be accessed from?
A. http://<storage account>.blob.core.windowsazure.net/<container>/<blob>
B. http://<storage account>.core.windows.net/<container>/<blob>
C. http://<storage account>.blob.core.windows.net/<container>/<blob>

D. http://<storage account>.core.windowsazure.net/<container>/<blob>

14. You need to create a Storage account first before using any Azure Storage option. True or false?
A. True
B. False

15. The maximum size of data that you can store in block blob storage is ________.
A. 10TB
B. 15TB
C. 45TB
D. 4.7TB

Chapter 05: Databases

Introduction

In modern business, we know that managing data is much more important as a huge amount of data is collected from various sources and you want these data stored safely at a database. Azure has a service known as Azure Databases that fulfils your business requirement. In this chapter, we will discuss some keys that Azure databases offer, which are important from the exam perspective. We will discuss Cosmo DB, which scales globally and is a fully managed database service. It has fast read and write capability. Azure SQL is a managed database, which we will discuss in this chapter. We also learn about MySQL database, which is one of the most popular community databases. We will also learn about the PostgreSQL database, which is an open source database with some unique features.

In this chapter, we learn about the migration of databases to Azure by using Database Migration Services. With database, your data will be stored in an organized manner so that you get exactly the data you want at no time at all.

Databases

Microsoft Azure helps you unlock your potential, wherever you have your data. You can support quick growth and save innovation time by supporting open source database engines with a secure, corporate-grade, fully managed database service. Azure provides a variety of data types and volume storage facilities. And this data is available to users immediately via global connectivity. No matter what you create, Azure helps you get it to the market quickly, distribute it widely and handle it with ease and confidentiality. There are multiple Azure Database Services provided by Azure, which are:

- Cosmos DB
- Azure SQL
- Azure Database for MySQL
- Azure Database for Postgre SQL

Users can create multiple databases on a single MySQL server, and there is no limit to the number of databases that can be created.

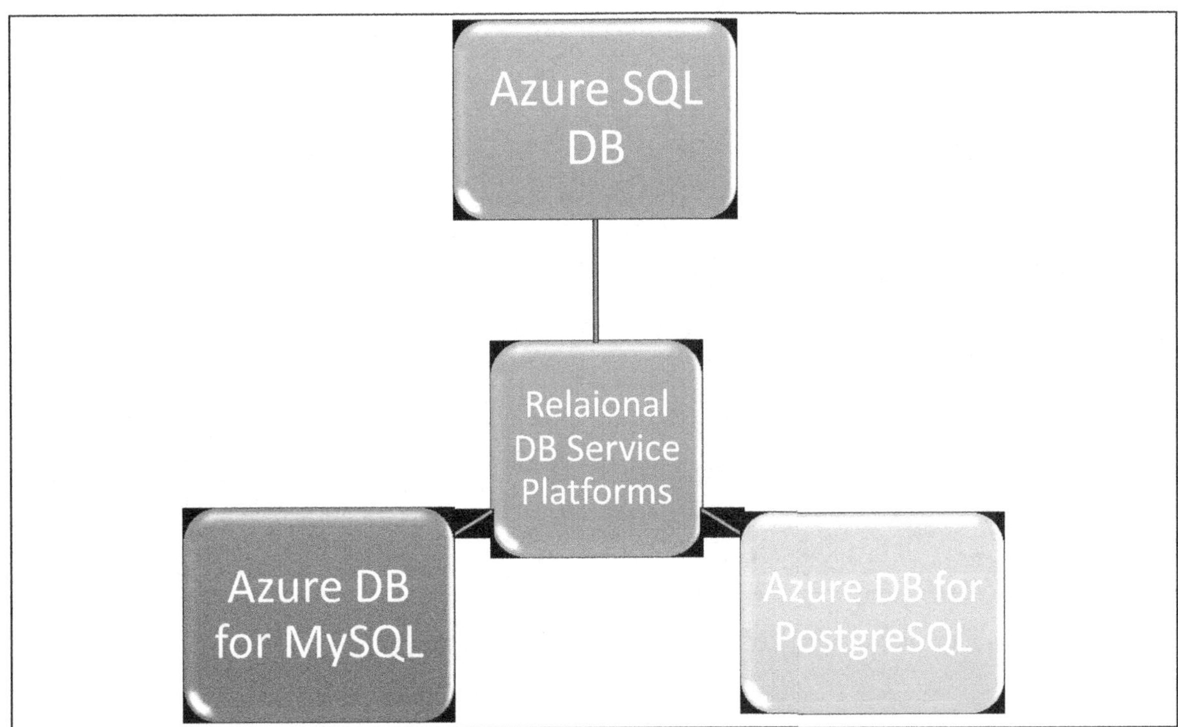

Figure 5-01: Relational Database

Cosmos DB

Cosmos DB is a global service provided from the beginning. With Cosmos DB, you can put the data closest to the user. This is one of the key features with great user experience as well. To put the databases at multiple locations can be such a difficult thing with synchronization but with Cosmos DB, Azure takes care of this synchronization for you. With a single click, you can add your Cosmos DB to more regions. Then Azure takes care of keeping that data and keeps it in Sync with the other region. The pricing of Cosmos DB is dependent on the throughput and consumed storage per hour.

All the data stored in Cosmos DB are encrypted at rest or in motion.

Multi-data templates can be provided with one backend. It is therefore ideal for documents, key values, relational, and graph models. It is a NoSQL database more or less because it does not rely on schemas. Nonetheless, as it has SQL-like query language and can easily support ACID transactions, some people have categorized it as a NewSQL database type.

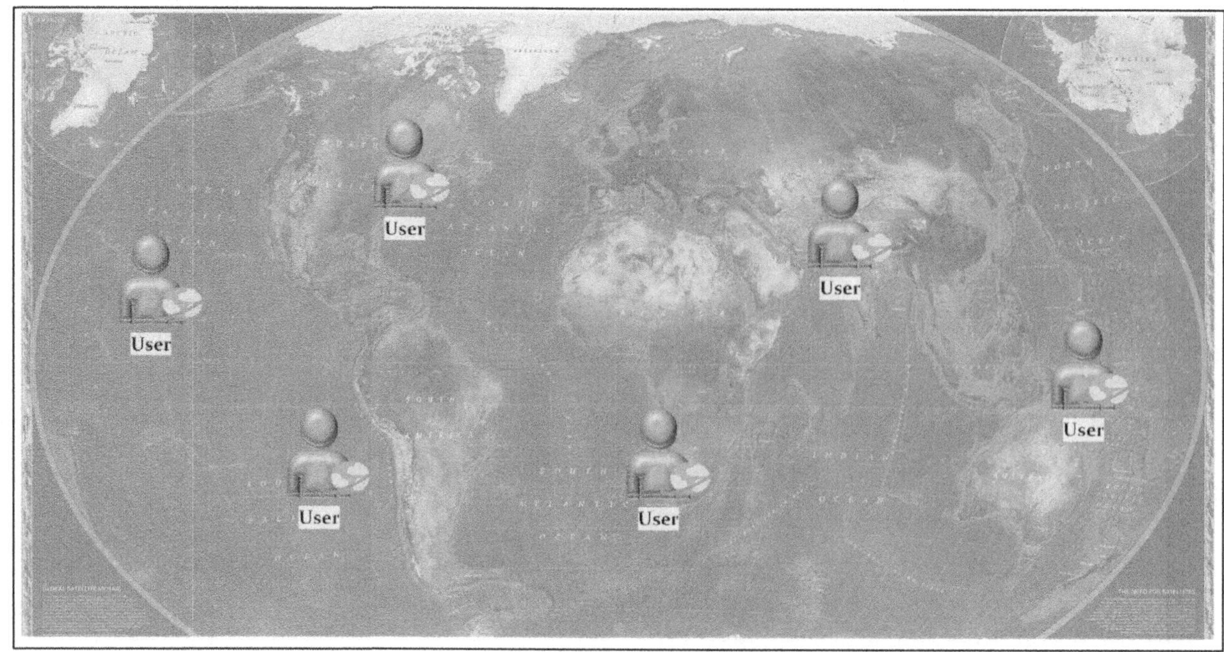

Figure 5-02: Globally Distributed

Latency

We all know that latency is the time taken by the data to travel. The higher the latency, the longer the data takes time to reach the user. With Cosmos DB, the latency is limited to a single digit millisecond (0-9) to anywhere in the world.

Scalability

With Cosmos DB, you can scale your database automatically to infinity when the requirement goes up in order to meet the resources. When you add more resources, then there is no limit on the number of users it can support. Scaling is automatic but you only need to pay for what you use, which means it is available at the lowest price.

Connectivity

With Cosmos DB, you can work in various ways for example, if you are a developer, then you can choose from multiple built-in ways in order to connect to Cosmos DB such as SDKs or APIs. You can also use different languages such as C#, Java or Node.js. It can also integrate with SQL, MongoDB or Cassandra.

With Cosmos DB, a disadvantage is that it gets really expensive even though you have to pay for what you use; As the Cosmos DB scales up, the cost automatically increases.

When you are embedding data in Azure Cosmos DB, then treat your data as a self-contained document in JSON.

Lab 5-01: Creating Cosmos DB

Scenario

John wants to create a database for the storage of data for his company and also needs that database to scale as per requirement. The scaling of that particular database must be global and easy. How he can do that?

Solution:

Using Cosmos DB as a database gives you benefit of scaling your database by replicating multiple geographical locations in single click.

1. Login to Azure Portal and go to the "Azure Cosmos DB" service.

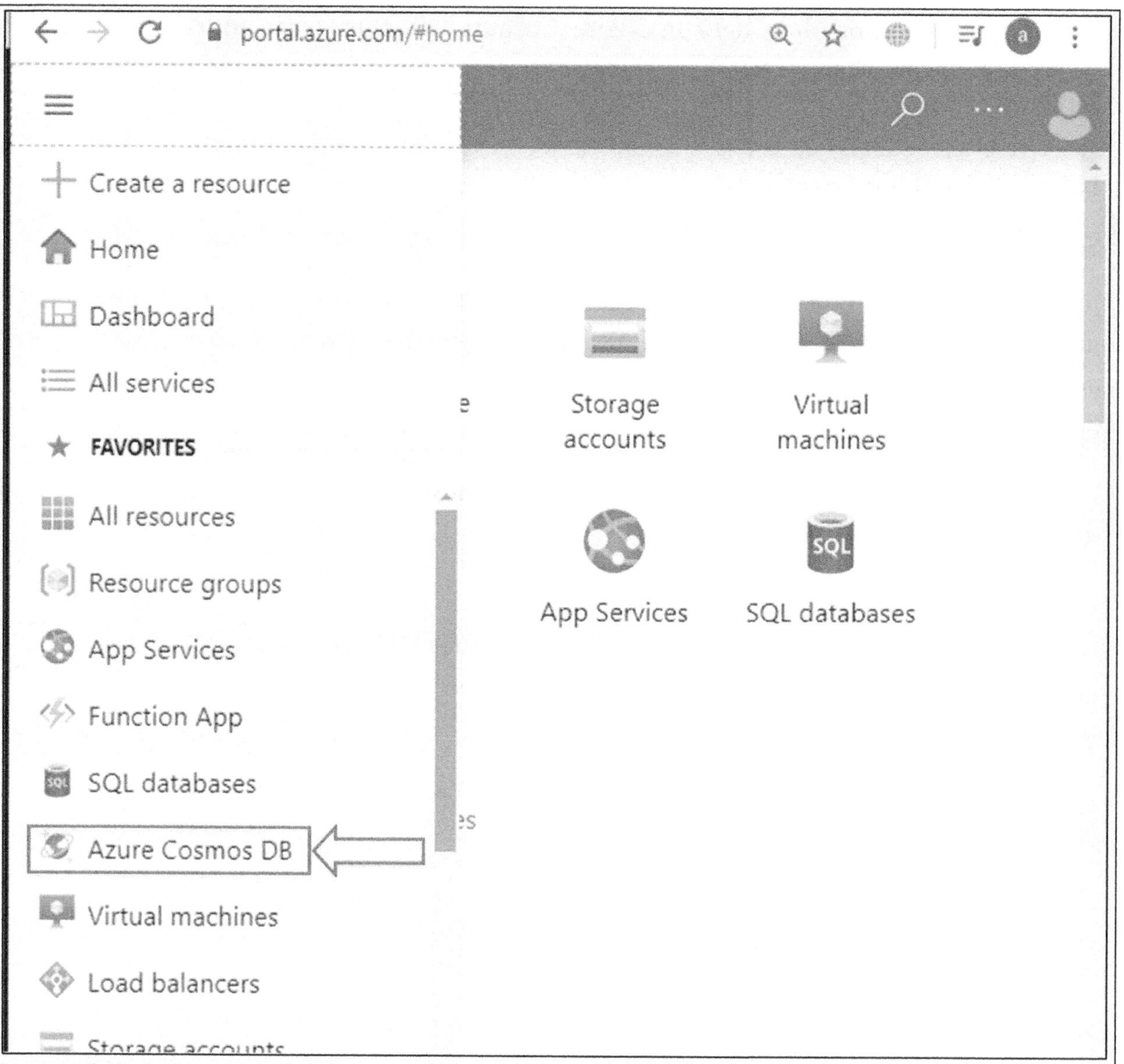

2. Click on "Add".

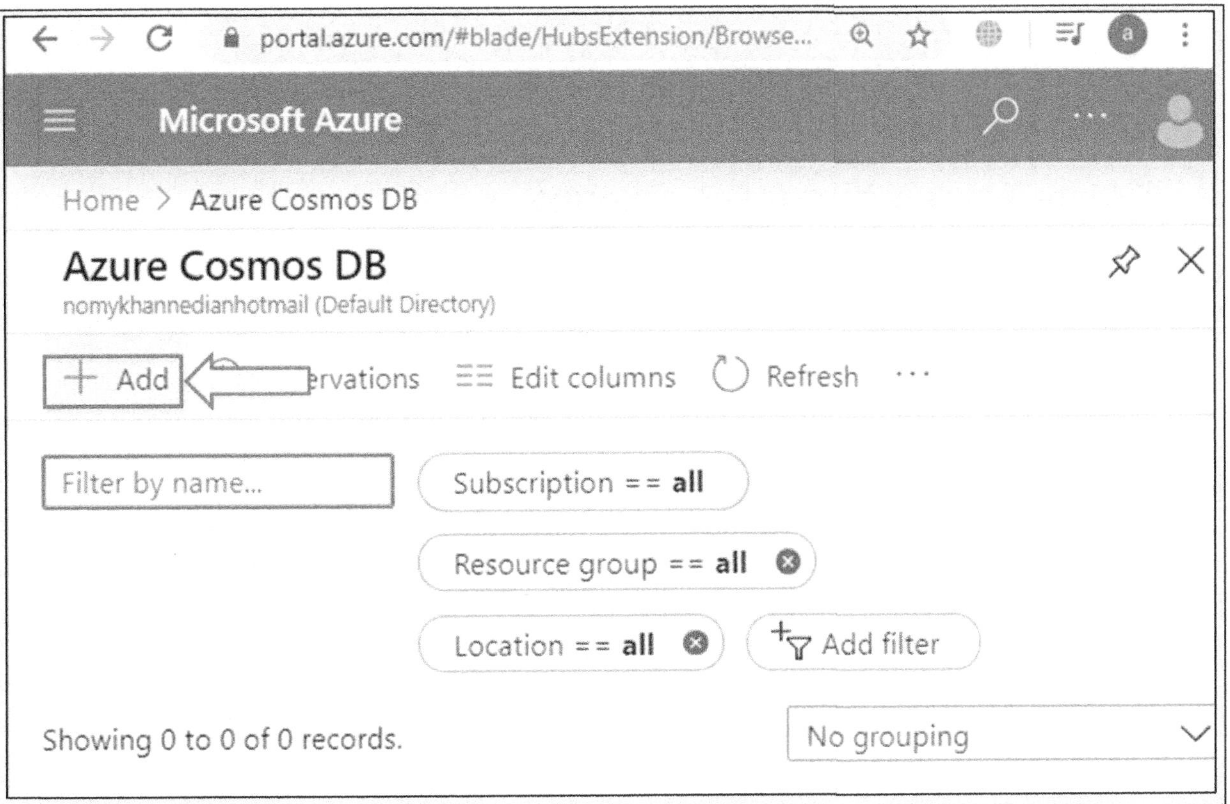

3. Click on "Create new" in the resource group. Enter the name of the resource group then click "OK".

Microsoft Azure

Home > Azure Cosmos DB > Create Azure Cosmos DB Account

Create Azure Cosmos DB Account

Create a new Azure Cosmos DB account with multi-region writes in any region by February 29, 2020 and receive up to 33% off for the life of your account. Restrictions apply.*

Basics Networking Tags Review + create

Azure Cosmos DB is a globally distributed, multi-model, fully managed database service. Try unlimited renewals. Go to production starting at $24/month per database, multiple containe

Project Details

Select the subscription to manage deployed resources and costs. Use resource groups like fc your resources.

Subscription *

Pay-As-You-Go

Resource Group *

Select existing...

Create new

Review + create Previous Next: Networking

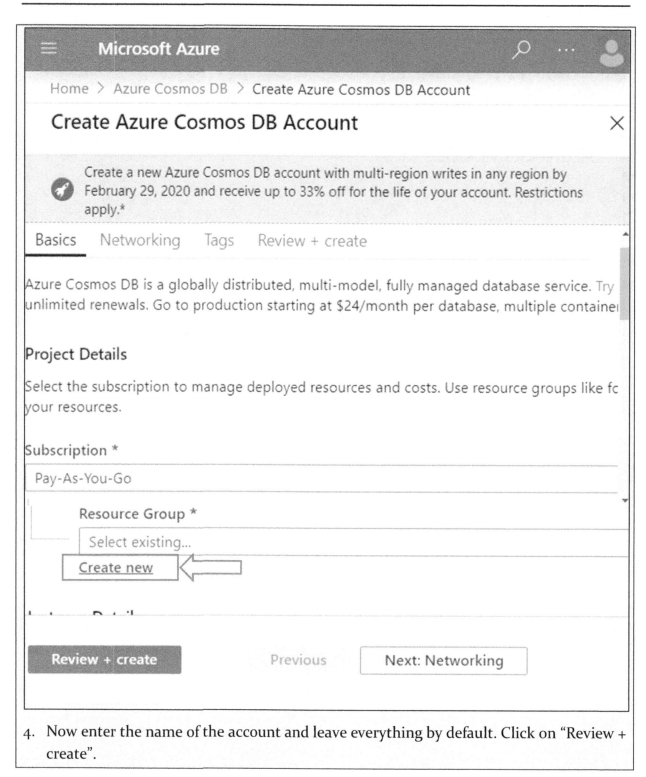

4. Now enter the name of the account and leave everything by default. Click on "Review + create".

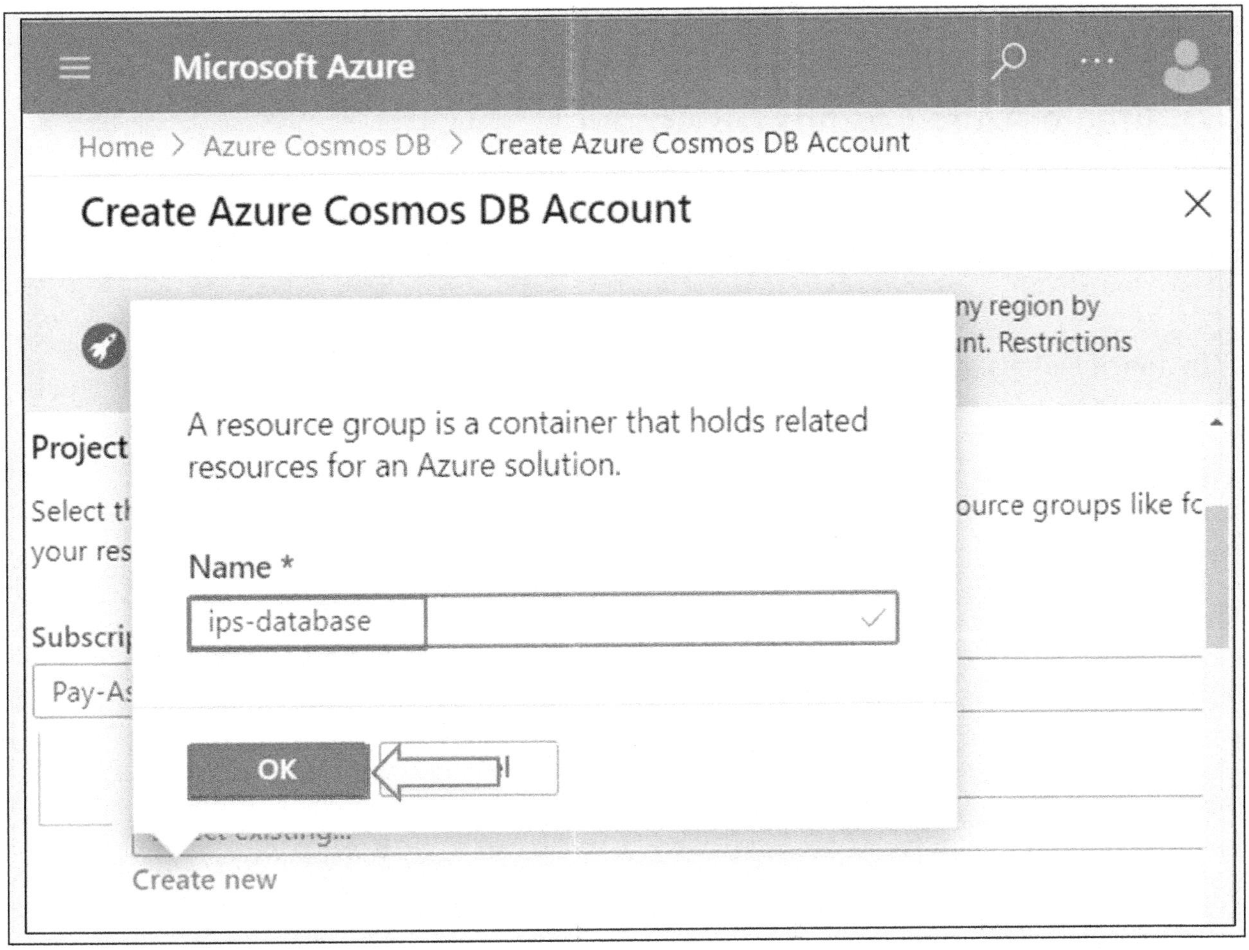

Microsoft Azure

Home > Azure Cosmos DB > Create Azure Cosmos DB Account

Create Azure Cosmos DB Account

A resource group is a container that holds related resources for an Azure solution.

Name *

ips-database

OK

Create new

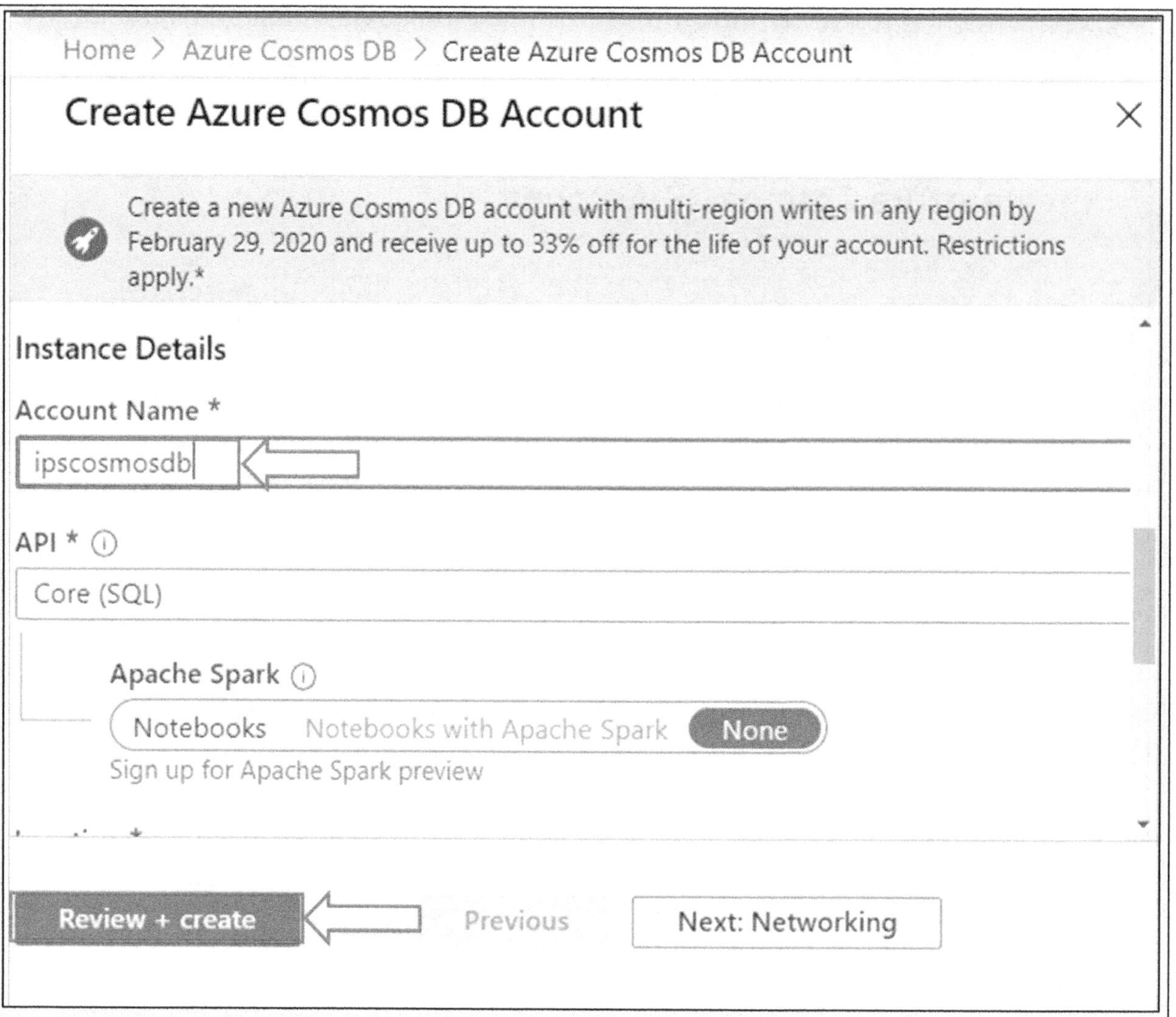

Home > Azure Cosmos DB > Create Azure Cosmos DB Account

Create Azure Cosmos DB Account

Create a new Azure Cosmos DB account with multi-region writes in any region by February 29, 2020 and receive up to 33% off for the life of your account. Restrictions apply.*

Instance Details

Account Name *

ipscosmosdb

API *

Core (SQL)

Apache Spark

Notebooks | Notebooks with Apache Spark | None

Sign up for Apache Spark preview

Review + create | Previous | Next: Networking

5. Click "Create".

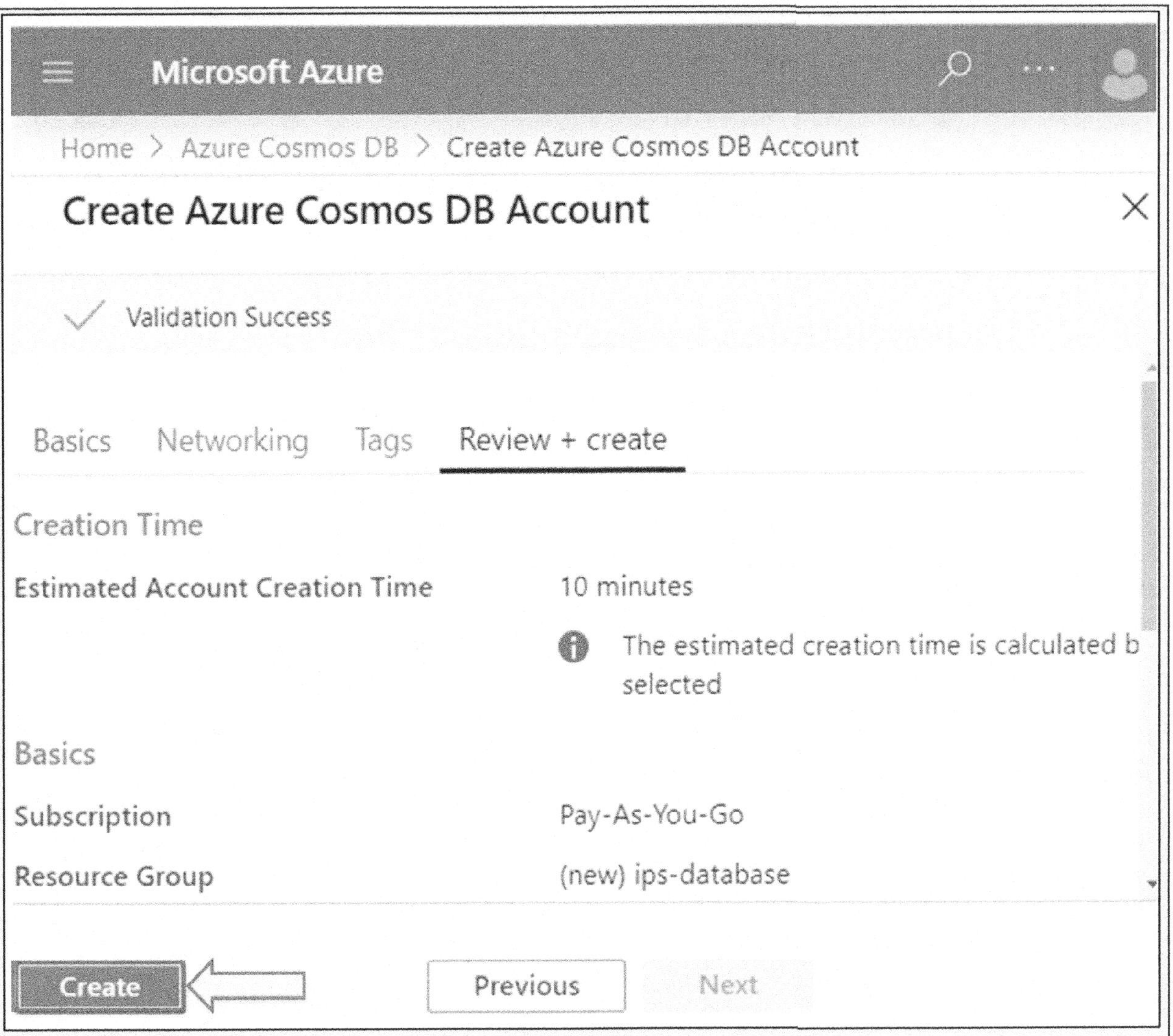

Microsoft Azure

Home > Azure Cosmos DB > Create Azure Cosmos DB Account

Create Azure Cosmos DB Account

Validation Success

Basics Networking Tags Review + create

Creation Time

Estimated Account Creation Time 10 minutes

The estimated creation time is calculated b selected

Basics

Subscription Pay-As-You-Go

Resource Group (new) ips-database

Create Previous Next

6. Once the deployment is complete, click on "Go to resource".

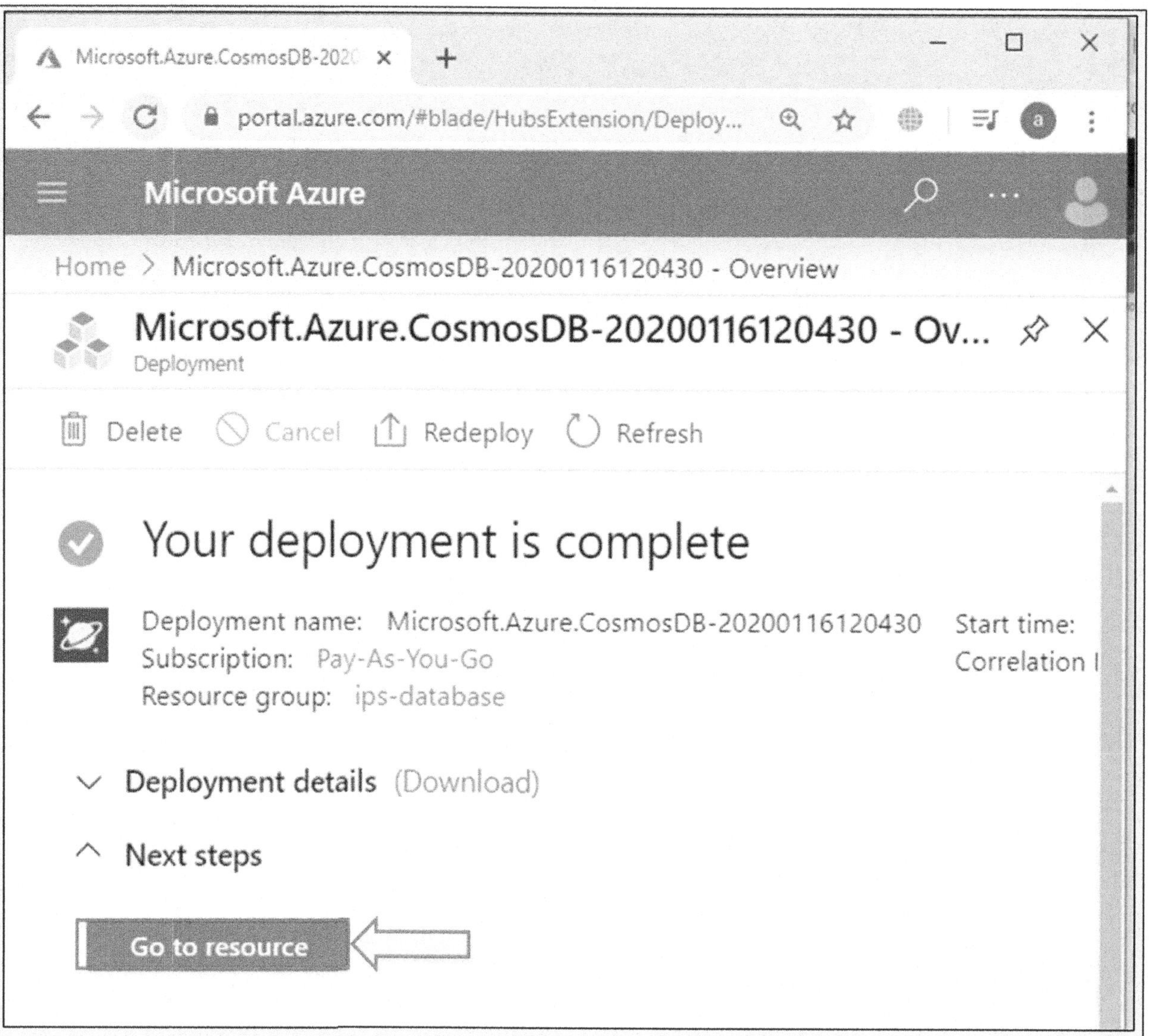

7. You can see the URL here, which you can use to access the data in Cosmos DB if accessing outside Azure.

Microsoft Azure

Home > Microsoft.Azure.CosmosDB-20200116120430 - Overview > ipscosmosdb

ipscosmosdb
Azure Cosmos DB account

+ Add Container | Refresh | → Move | Delete Account | ...

Status
Online

Resource group (change)
ips-database

Subscription (change)
Pay-As-You-Go

Subscription ID
797152d3-23c4-499f-bfef-bb103da7d054

Read Locations
West US

Write Locations
West US

URI
https://ipscosmosdb.documents.azure.c...

Containers

Looks like you don't have any containers yet. Data Explorer

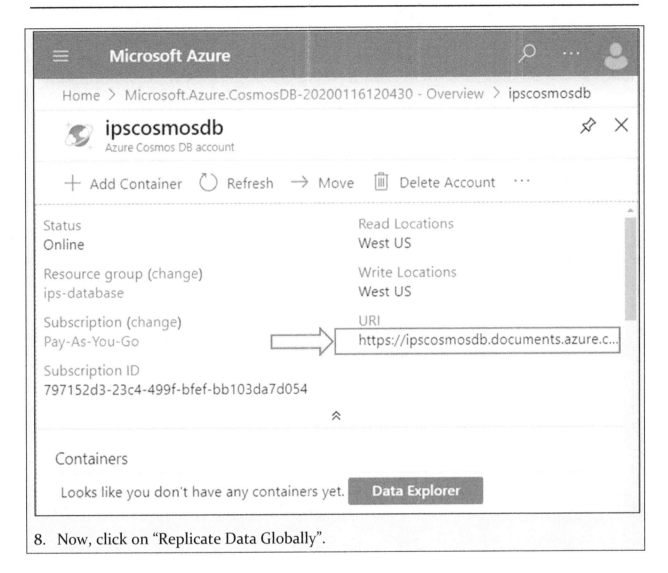

8. Now, click on "Replicate Data Globally".

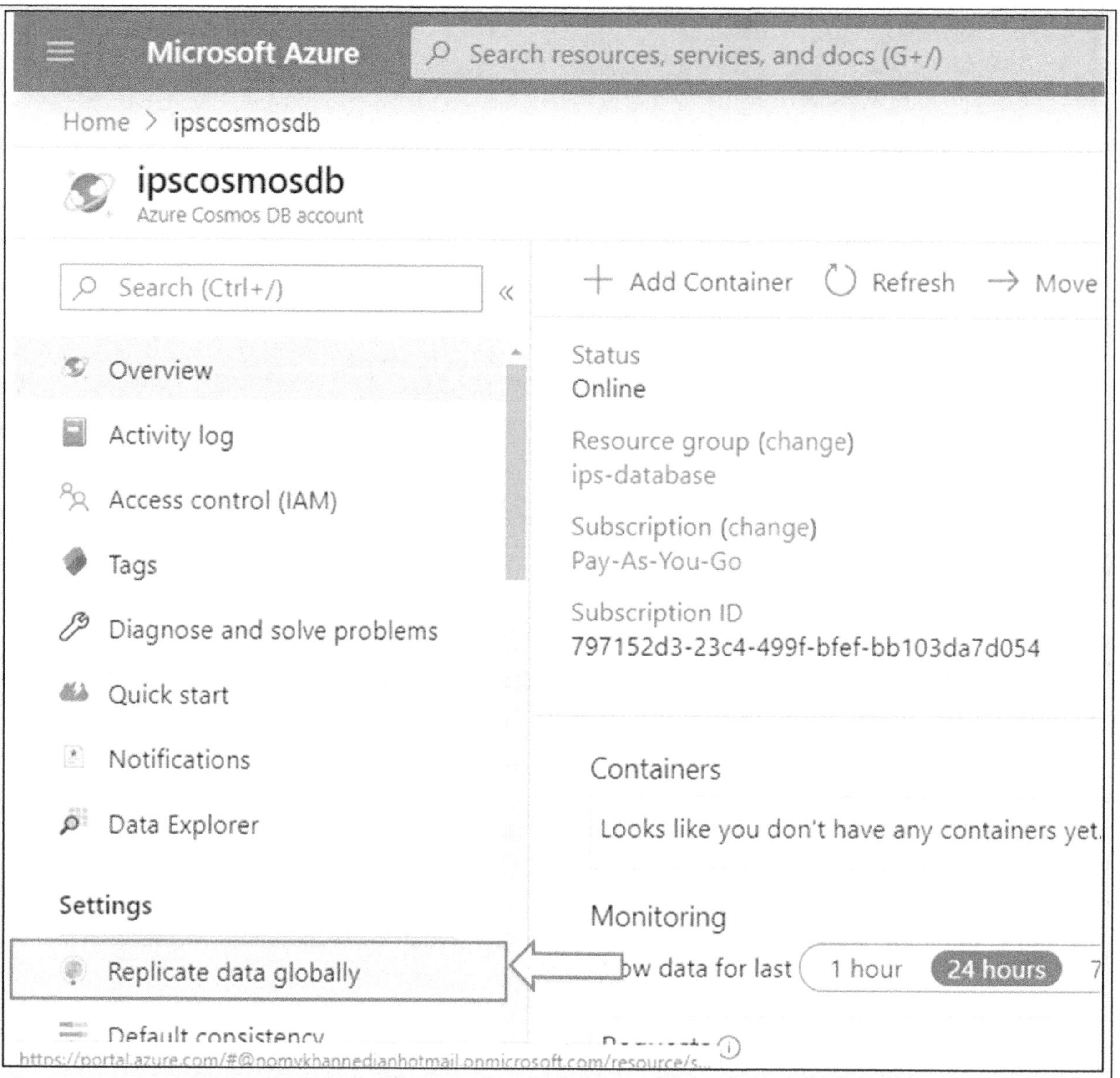

9. Here, you can enable more datacenters. The blue ticks in the map indicate where your actual data center is.

Microsoft Azure

Home > ipscosmosdb - Replicate data globally

ipscosmosdb - Replicate data globally

Azure Cosmos DB account

Save Discard Manual Failover Automatic Failover

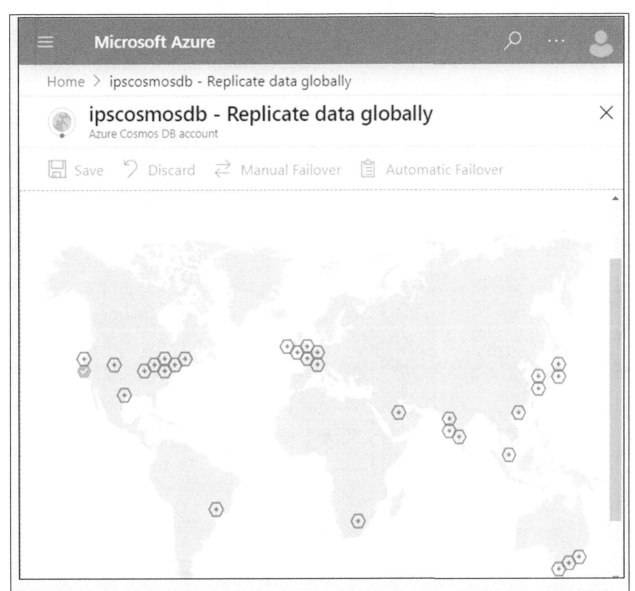

10. Now, click on the region where you want to replicate the data, then click "Save". After that, the data is replicated all across the two regions.

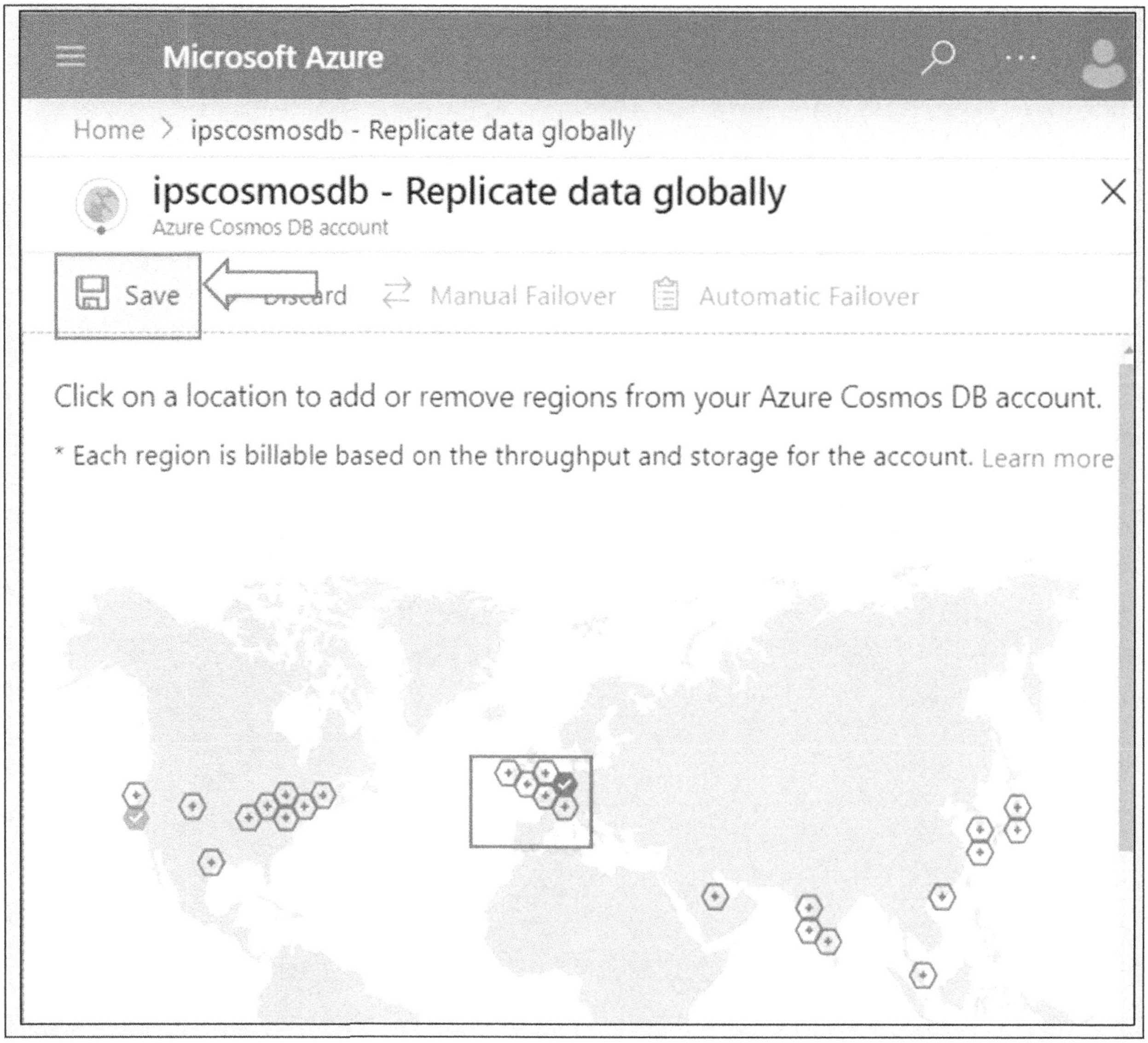

Azure SQL

Azure SQL database was launched in 1989 and is now one of the most stable products. It is a managed Azure SQL service. For a wide range of hybrid cloud applications, SQL Database can be a good choice, because it helps you to handle both relational and non-relational data structures like graphs, JSON, spatial, and XML. It is a managed Database as a Service, as another service in Azure takes care of hardware and IaaS levels. Azure SQL is on top of this and provides you basic business logic and functions as per requirement. A cloud-based Database Management System (DBMS) is provided in the Microsoft Azure SQL Database. With Azure SQL, you can easily migrate your on-premises SQL database to Azure SQL and get benefits of that. All of this is done without any change in code and with a frictionless process. This technology allows on-site and cloud apps to store data in Microsoft datacenters. Like other cloud-based services, a company pays for only what it requires,

increasing and reducing usage and cost as per requirements. The use of a cloud service, therefore, helps capital expenditure such as storage and DBMS investment to be translated into operating costs. With Azure SQL, you can store 100TB of data within a minute.

Integrated with ML

With Azure SQL, you can also take advantage of integrated Machine Learning tools. Depending on the usage pattern, database optimization and performance improvement suggestions are given. With ML, you get the benefit of getting notified about any degradation or anything bad happening in your database.

Scalability

As it is a cloud based service, it also offers excellent scalability through which you get high availability. And, it gives 99.995% availability. Azure SQL Database enables you to easily scale your database by adding more compute power (scale-up) or adding more database units (scale-out).

Security

With Azure Cloud Platform, security is a built-in feature that gives you benefit in terms of security of your data. Improved data security in a single glass window, includes discovery and authentication of files, vulnerability identification, and automated threat detection. You can get continuous security from the Azure Security Center with deeper insights.

Azure Database for MySQL

Azure Database for MySQL is the database built-in by the community while Azure SQL is Microsoft's product. MySQL is an open source project where anyone can contribute to the community. It is a relational database like SQL, which means that data is related to itself or other connections in it via defined connections. Currently, there are millions of MySQL database used as it has a developed and proven architecture for stability.

Azure MySQL platform provides a full-managed, business-ready MySQL cloud database. The MySQL Community Version quickly upgrades and migrates into the cloud with the choice of your language and framework, of which, some of the most popular are PHP or WordPress. Therefore, high flexibility and robust scaling are built in to help you adapt easily to changes in customer requirements. In fact, the protection and security, including the Azure IP advantage, as well as the leading market scope of Azure are incomparable. With a transparent price model, you can pick services without any hidden costs for your workload. Azure Server for MySQL was designed to provide high availability with 99.99% SLA and does not require additional setup, replica features or costs to guarantee that your apps run as necessary. It has automated batching and backup with monitoring. All of these are included without any cost.

Azure database for MySQL is PaaS, which is managed by Microsoft. By using this, you can focus on developing the business strength rather than focusing on managing servers or networks.

You can also use all security features of Azure with Azure database for MySQL like advance threat protection, monitoring, and identity management.

Use Cases

- Web Application
- E-Commerce
- Mobile Application
- Digital Marketing
- Finance Management
- Gaming

Azure Database for Postgre SQL

It is an open source relational database similar to MySQL. The first version of this database is based on ingress database and the new version can post the ingress database that is why it is called PostgreSQL. SQL is the language that is used to query the data in the database. PostgreSQL is in the market since 1996 and it is free. It is a default database from MacOS. It is good for mission-critical workloads with predictable performance, security, high availability, and dynamic scalability. It is deployed as a single server and as a Citus cluster. The Hyperscale (Citus) choice scales queries in a horizontal manner through multiple sharding tools and offers more scaled and productive applications.

Features

- You can integrate this database with lots of extensions like JSONB (Binary version of JSON), geospatial functions, rich indexing and integration with code like Ruby, Python, etc.
- With this, you can perform horizontal scaling, which gives you very high performance in order to access the distributed data sets across many PostgreSQL instances. You can scale also up to 100 nodes with no application reads and writes
- The performance recommendation in this is based on the usage of data on the database. It has a feature that detects the disruptive events that effect performance on which you can perform actions
- Similar to Azure Database for MySQL, it also offers fully managed database services like automatic patching, automatic backups, and built-in monitoring

Use Cases

- Financial Applications - it is good for online transactions and integrates with mathematical software such as MATLAB
- For geometric data (GIS) the government mostly uses Postgres. PostGIS is the GIS extension that gives hundreds of functions to process geometric data in multiple formats
- It provides automatic failover or full redundancy, which is good for manufacturing purposes

Database Migration Service

We already know that we can migrate our data server in particular Azure SQL servers but how? By using Database Migration Services, you can do that. In Azure, you have a dedicated tool for migrating databases from on-premises to Azure. With a single tool, you can move your existing SQL server; there is no need to use multiple tools. In order to do that, you have step-by-step documentation. There is also complete documentation for non-Microsoft database migration. The Azure Server Migration Service is a fully managed program that permits smooth migration to Azure Data systems with minimal downtime from various server providers. The service is currently available in general, with ongoing efforts for growth focused on:

- Reliability and performance
- Addition on source/target pairs
- For friction, free migration used for continuous investment

Pre-migration

Discover
Inventory database assets, & application stack discovery.

Assess
Assess workloads & fix recommendations.

Convert
Convert the source schema to work in the target environment.
(Only relevant for heterogeneous migrations)

Migration

Migrate
Migrate the source schema, source data & objects to the target.

Sync Data
Sync your target schema & data with the source.
(only relevant for minimal-downtime migrations)

Cutover
Cut over from the source to the target environment.
(Only relevant for minimal-downtime migrations)

Post-migration

Remediate Applications
Iteratively make any necessary changes to your applications.

Perform Tests
Iteratively run functional & performance tests.
(only relevant for minimal-downtime migrations)

Optimize
Based on tests, address performance issues & then retest to confirm the performance improvements.

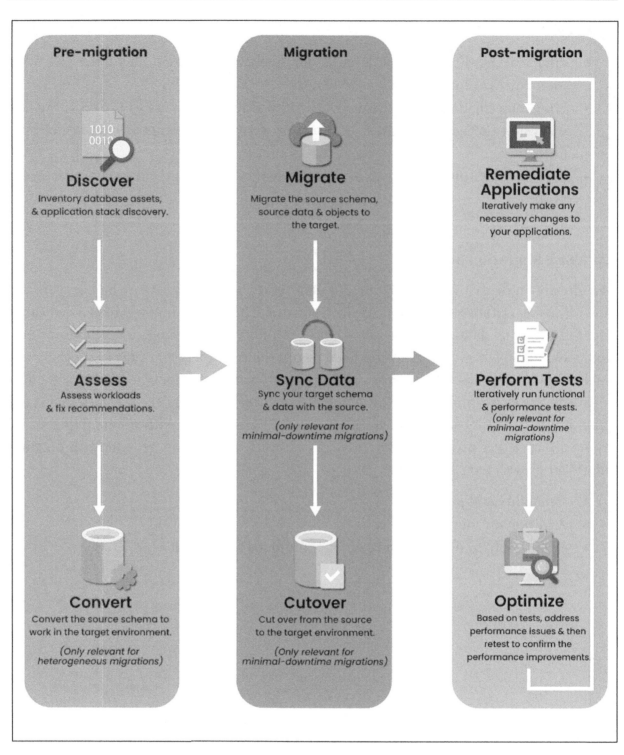

Figure 5-03: Migration Process Overview

Use Case

Consider a company that has everything on its on-premises location. The current database in use is Microsoft SQL. With the use of Database Migration Services, you can easily move

your SQL server to a managed Azure SQL instance in cloud. Similarly, if you have MySQL server, then you can also move that too.

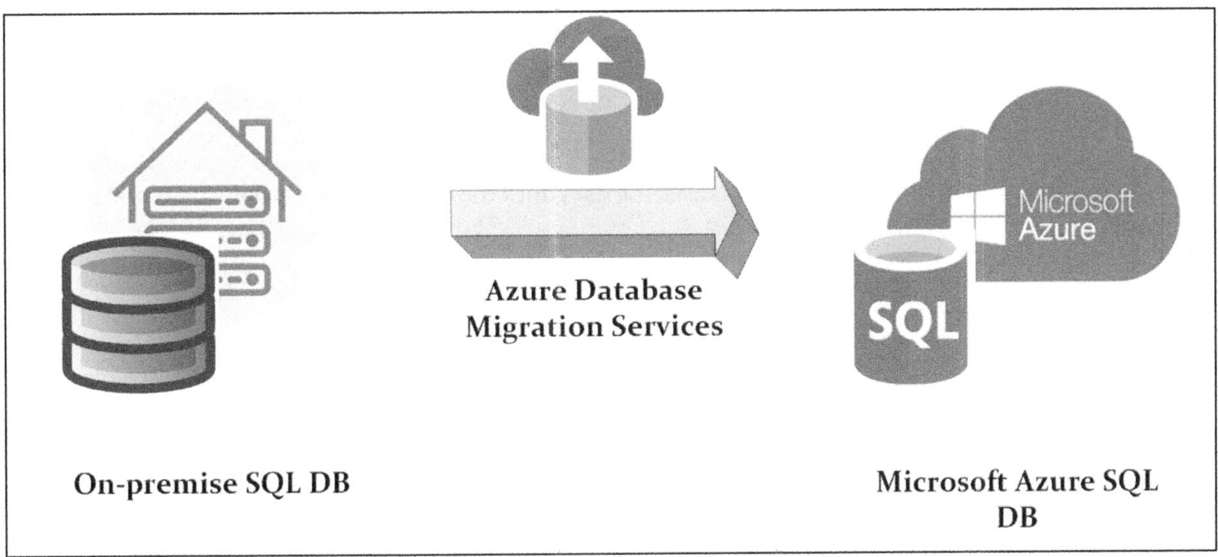

Figure 5-04: Azure DMS

MindMap

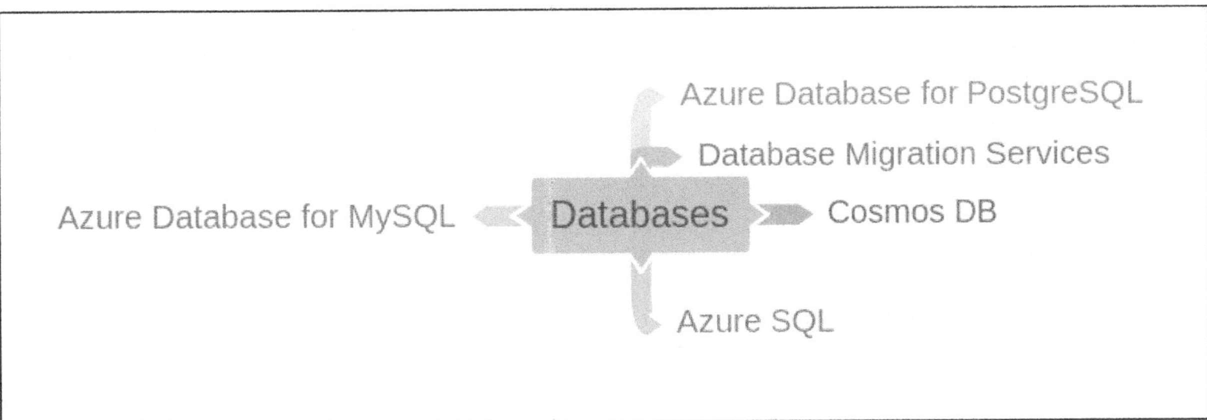

Figure 5-05: Mindmap

Practice Question

1. Cosmos DB is a Relational DB. True or false?
A. True
B. False

2. Latency is the time when you keep inserting data until the complete data is uploaded True or false?
A. True
B. False

3. How much latency is guaranteed by CosmosDB?
A. Single digit milliseconds
B. Two digit milliseconds
C. Single digit second
D. Single digit minutes

4. From the following DBs, which is best suited for migrating on-premises DB to Azure DB with all benefits?
A. Cosmos DB
B. Azure DB for MySQL
C. Azure DB for PostgreSQL
D. Azure SQL DB

5. How much data can you store with Azure SQL DB in a minute?
A. 100GB
B. 100MB
C. 100TB
D. 10TB

6. With Azure SQL DB, you can get the benefits of ML. True or false?
A. True
B. False

7. Azure DB for MySQL provides high availability with SLA __________.
A. 99.9%
B. 99.95%
C. 99.89%
D. 99.99%

8. From the following options, which one is an open source database in Azure?
A. Cosmos DB
B. Azure SQL
C. Azure DB for MySQL
D. None of the above

9. Azure database for MySQL is __________, which is managed by Microsoft.
A. IaaS
B. FaaS
C. PaaS
D. SaaS

10. From the following, which one is the default database for MacOS?
A. SQL
B. PostgreSQL
C. MySQL
D. None of the above

11. From the following options, which one is the best reason to choose database as storage of data?
A. You can store more data in less space due to the compression algorithms used by databases
B. Databases are more secure for storing data than regular Azure Storage
C. You can manage access to data in a database more granularly than for any other type of storage
D. It is a very powerful way of getting the data out in the exact format you want

12. Cosmos DB offers very low latency and is able to work with many tools like SDKs, APIs, etc. True or false?
A. True
B. False

13. From the following options, which are the targets for DMS?
A. HDInights
B. Azure Data Lake
C. Azure SQL
D. Microsoft SQL Server

14. How many methods of configuring Azure DB for MySQL are there?
A. 2
B. 3
C. 4
D. 5

15. From the following, which database is used for geometric data?

A. SQL

B. MySQL

C. PostgreSQL

D. All of these

16. If you want to store data that are frequently accessed, which data storage layer would you use?

A. Data Warehouse

B. Data Lake

C. Azure Cosmos DB

D. All of the above

Chapter 06: Authentication & Authorization

Introduction

Any technology service with IT applications that control the access of data from illegal users is very important in order to provide a secure environment. In addition, it is also very critical to find which user access which part of the infrastructure. In this chapter, we will discuss the fundamentals of authentication and authorization of users in Azure. Both of them are two major steps for ensuring network security. Authentication is a way of finding out whether the user exists in the database or not. Once the user is found from the database user ID and password, the next step is to ensure how many services that user has the right to access.

Authentication and Authorization in Azure includes:

- **Identity Services:** Identity services identify the platform for the user and ensures user validations for the application
- **Azure Active Directory:** This directory service is able to provide access and control of access to users with different directory services
- **Multi-Factor Authentication:** Provides security features by getting multiple information about the user for authentication

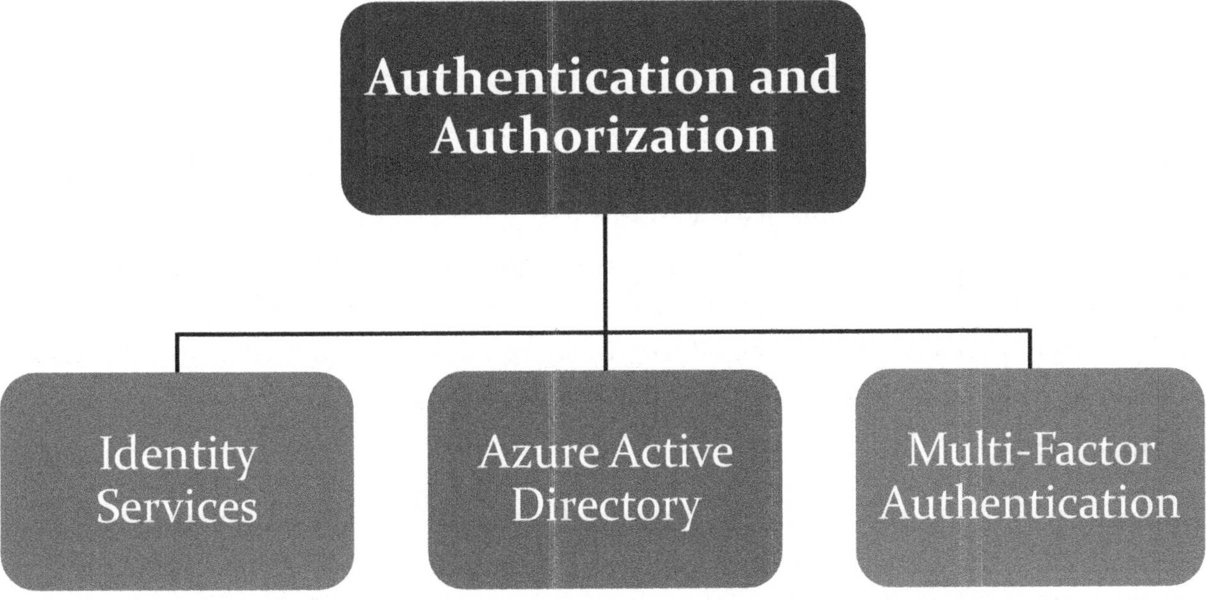

Figure 6-01: Azure Authentication and Authorization

Identity Services

When any user uses an online service that has any privacy criteria, then the user requires at least a username (that is the User ID) and password. Identity services include authentication, authorization and access management policies.

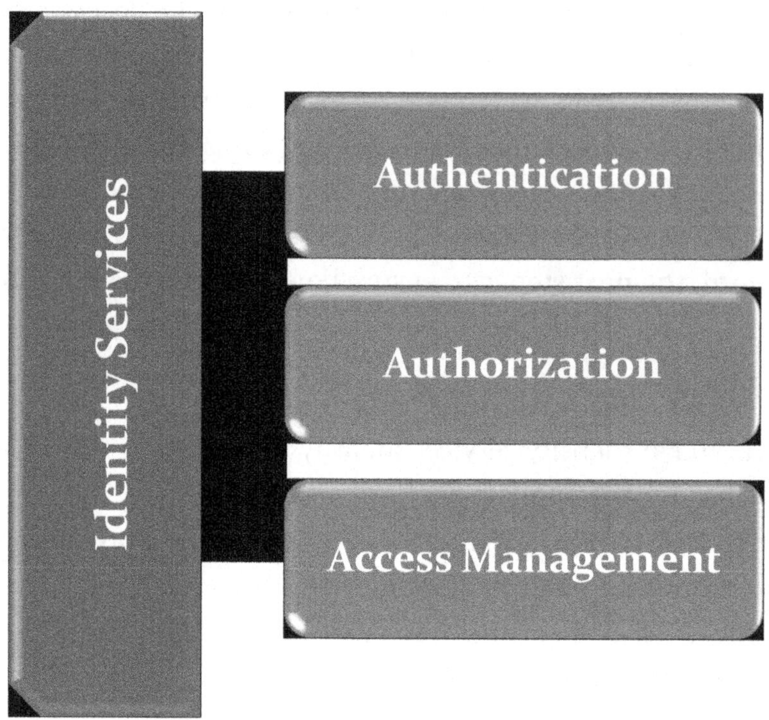

Figure 6-02: Identity Services

Authentication

Authentication is a way of identifying the user with the help of a user ID and password from the database. For example, if a user wants to use the Yahoo mail service, he/she cannot just access it easily by opening the Yahoo mail page. The user must have a valid ID and password to log in to the Yahoo mail page and then he/she will be able to use its services such as view Newsbeat, send an email, etc. In short, Authentication confirms the validity of the user by using its ID and password for the desired application.

Authorization

Authorization is the process that is conducted after authentication. When the user is authenticated, then the next step is to find which kind of data access is available for the authenticated user. For example, an Azure user is restricted to use limited Azure resources and services such as SQL Database, Virtual Network or Virtual Machine. If that Azure user tries to use those resources for which he/she is not authorized, Azure will not give access to that resources. Likewise, if a diabetes person visits an online shopping app, Azure service

has a profile of diabetes person. According to his profile, he is only allowed to purchase sugar-free items. That is, the person is authorized to buy only sugar-free items.

The process of identity service is clearly shown in the scenario defined in figure 6-03.

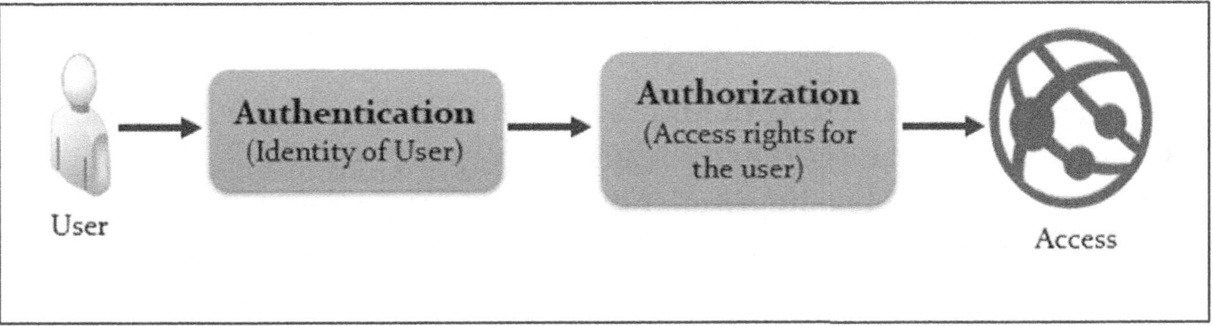

Figure 6-03: Process of Identity Management

Authentication vs Authorization

Authentication and authorization have very little differences. The summarized table shows the difference between these two entities.

Authentication	Authorization
The first step toward accessing resources	A person can be authorized only when its authentication has been done
A way to verify the customer or user's identity	Authorization allows authenticated users to access a file, database, mail, etc.
Normally, a user can be authenticate using user ID and password	Controls user access
Factor-based authentication is usually preferred for security purposes	Authorization is the granular part of identity services

Table 6-01: Authentication vs. Authorization

EXAM TIP

Authentication is the process of verification of users using user ID and password. Authorization is the method of providing the rights to authenticated users.

Access Management

Access management is a critical part of any cloud infrastructure as it ensures the restriction of access to service toward other users. It provides confidentiality, integrity, and availability. This means that access to any online application should be confidential for an unauthorized user and immediately available to authorized users. Access management policies should also be responsible for the following:

- **Authentication and Authorization:** User must be authenticated first, then authorized for the particular application
- **Faraway from Unauthorized Users:** Access management policies must be designed in such a way that no unauthorized person can access the information. Azure provides a number of ways to access management depending upon the application.

Azure Active Directory

Azure Active Directory (AAD) is the main tool to manage and monitor the dedicated users' information present in Microsoft Azure.

Active Directory

Active Directory (AD) is a directory service formed by Microsoft for the storage of information about the user, resources and other things present in the network. AD is commonly used in offices, educational institutes, and management departments.

- **Limitation of Active Directory:** Active Directory provides information for authentication and authorization, but it has some limitations;
  - **Traditional Use Only:** Active Directory provides directory services for physical access only. It is most commonly used in the on-premises network
  - **Not Permitted for Web Applications:** Active Directory is not applicable to serve its services for web applications
  - **Authentication:** Active Directory provides such directory services for authentication that is not available on Azure

Figure 6-04 shows the conceptual view of the Microsoft Active Directory (AD) services.

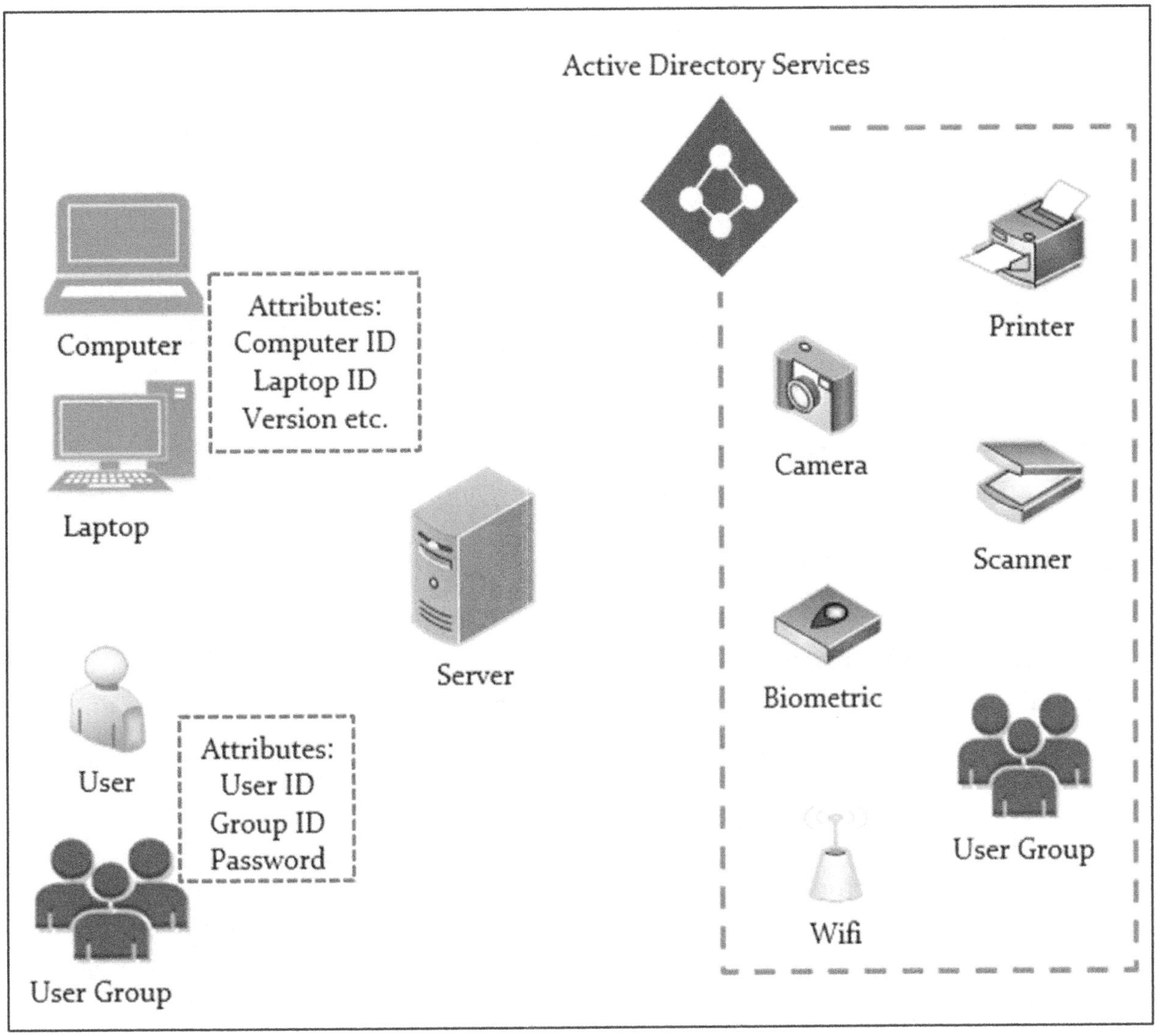

Figure 6-04: Active Directory Services

Azure Active Directory

Azure Active Directory (AAD) is different from the Active Directory (AD). AD provides its directory service to those companies who designed this service. Whereas, Azure Active Directory services are available for everything present on Azure. It is the first service given when a user creates an account in Azure.

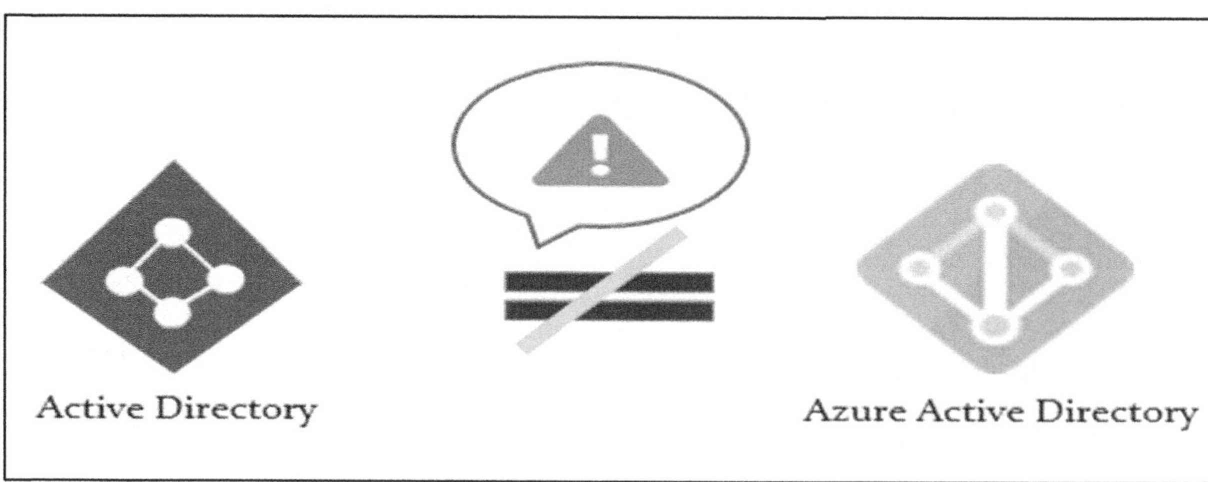

Figure 6-05: AD and AAD

AAD Services

- **Mandatory Service:** Users on Microsoft Azure are unable to create an account without AAD services
- **First User:** Every Azure account has the first user and owner. To become an Azure user, AAD service is needed

Microsoft Active Directory (AD) is the identity management solution for an on-premises network whereas, Azure Active Directory (AAD) is the Azure service for identity management.

Tenant

A tenant is the representation of an organization in Azure. A tenant is a dedicated instance of AAD service. It is the first ADD service when a user creates an account in Azure. Each AAD tenant is separate from other AAD tenants. A single user belongs to one tenant only. Each tenant contains a user or group of users. All users and tenants are a part of the AAD instance. Users may become a guest for other tenants for some duration.

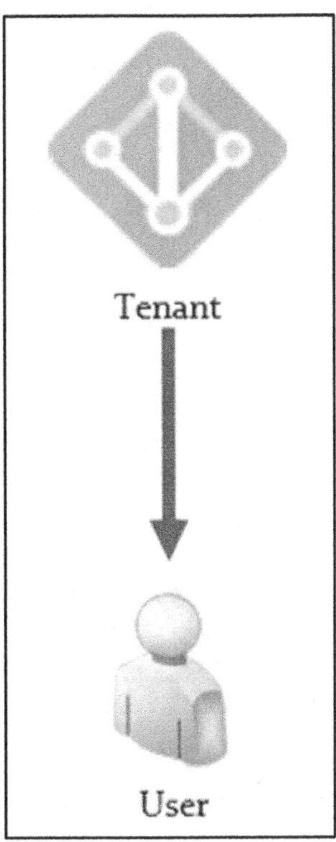

Figure 6-06: Concept of Tenant

EXAM TIP

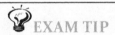

Tenant is a particular instance of AAD. It is the first AAD instance generated when a user creates an Azure account. Each user belongs to a single-tenant at a time.

Subscription

All Azure services require subscription in order to get access to using Azure resources and services.

- **Billing Entity:** All the resources used by the user in Azure is charged according to the subscription criteria
- **Cost:** A user can have multiple subscriptions within a single tenant to pay separately
- **Subscription Blockage:** Subscription of the Azure user may be blocked for a time until he/she pays the bills

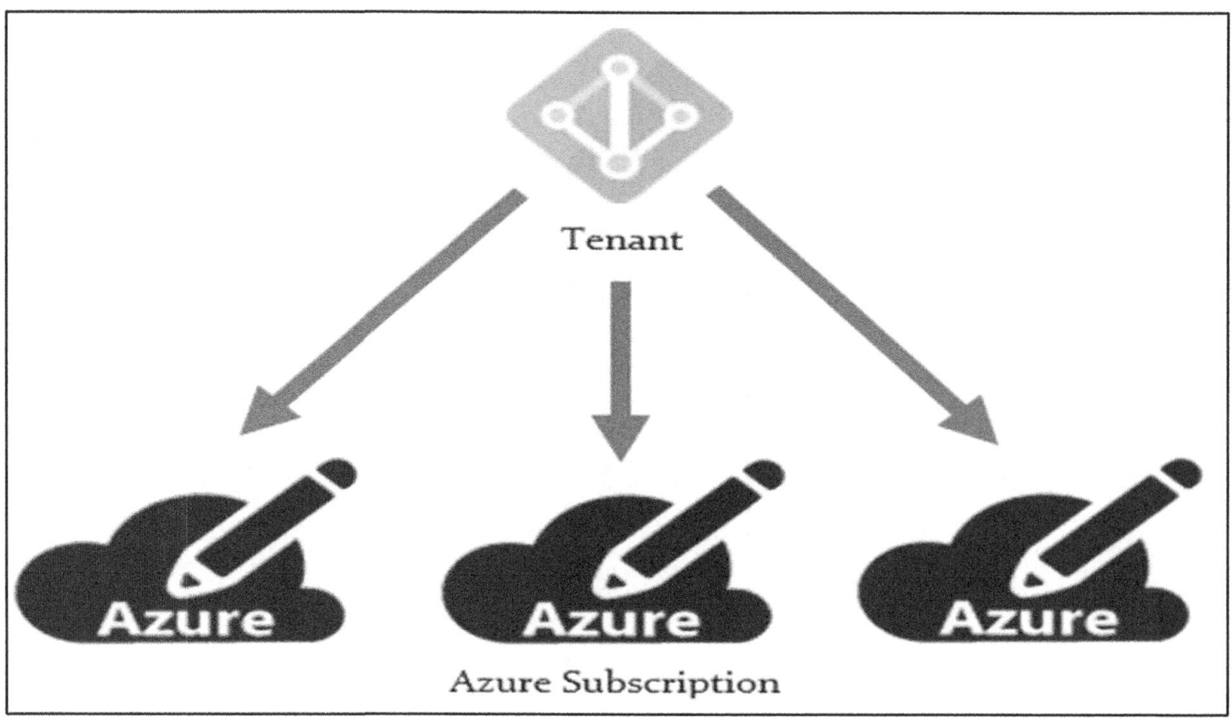

Figure 6-07: Azure Subscription

Hybrid Cloud Architecture

Within a hybrid cloud architecture, there are some services present on-premises and some services hosted on the cloud. When a user wants to set the hybrid cloud infrastructure, AAD instance can be used in hybrid cloud architecture. AAD can help users manage services on both the on-premises network and on cloud. It is considered a significant part of hybrid cloud infrastructure and is allowed for any organization. There are several services that AAD uses on Azure for management purposes.

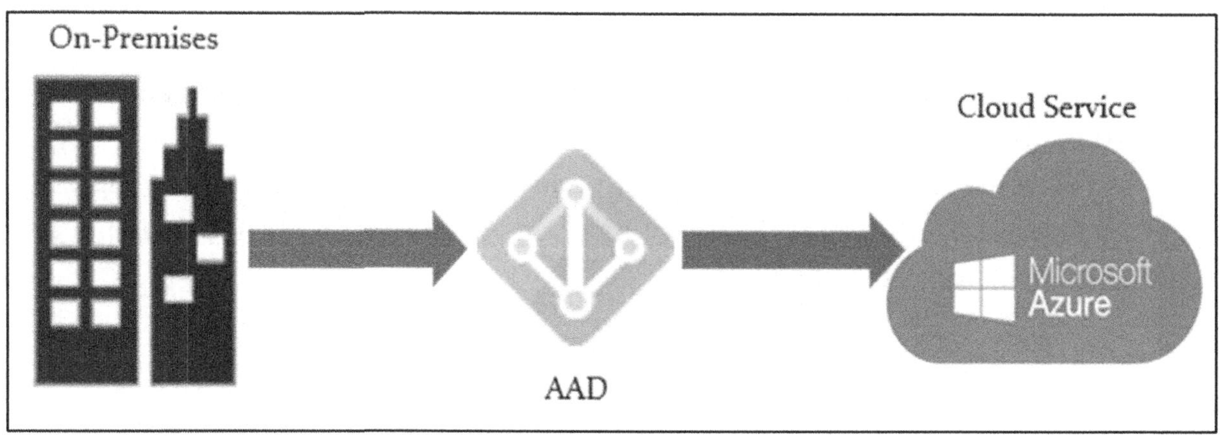

Figure 6-08: Hybrid Cloud Architecture

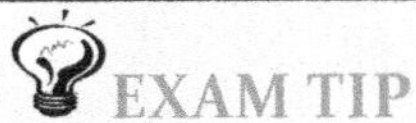

EXAM TIP

A hybrid cloud architecture can be achieved by using AAD instance, which provides the connection between Azure and on-premises networks.

Multi-Factor Authentication

Multi-Factor Authentication (MFA) provides a layer-based authentication using more than one form of authentication. This means, if one is compromised by attackers then they will still not able to get in. MFA is recommended as a default. It is a part of AAD that enables other ways to authenticate users. MFA is needed in organizations that have a large number of users, devices, and resources. To avoid any collapse, extra security is required for protection and efficient throughput.

How MFA Works

Multi-Factor Authentication (MFA) conducts the authentication of the user in multiple steps. The first step is to verify the user with a user ID and password. The second step is to send a code on the user's phone for further verification. The third step is the biometric verification. This step is optional.

For example, an Azure user wants to log in to the online booking web app. A large number of people are already accessing that web application due to its efficient throughput and fast response. Using MFA, the simplest way to use the application requires the user to put user ID and password for verification. Once the ID and password are correctly entered by a user, the second step of MFA verification is to confirm the user's credentials from the database by sending code on the user phone. A combination of numbers in the form of code is sent to the user's phone to confirm the user. When the user gets the code, he/she is required to put the code in the given area to confirm the validity. Once the code is entered, the authentication of the user is complete. Another way to authenticate the user is biometric verification but this step is only needed for highly advanced security purposes. Figure 6-09 shows the layer-based services offered by MFA.

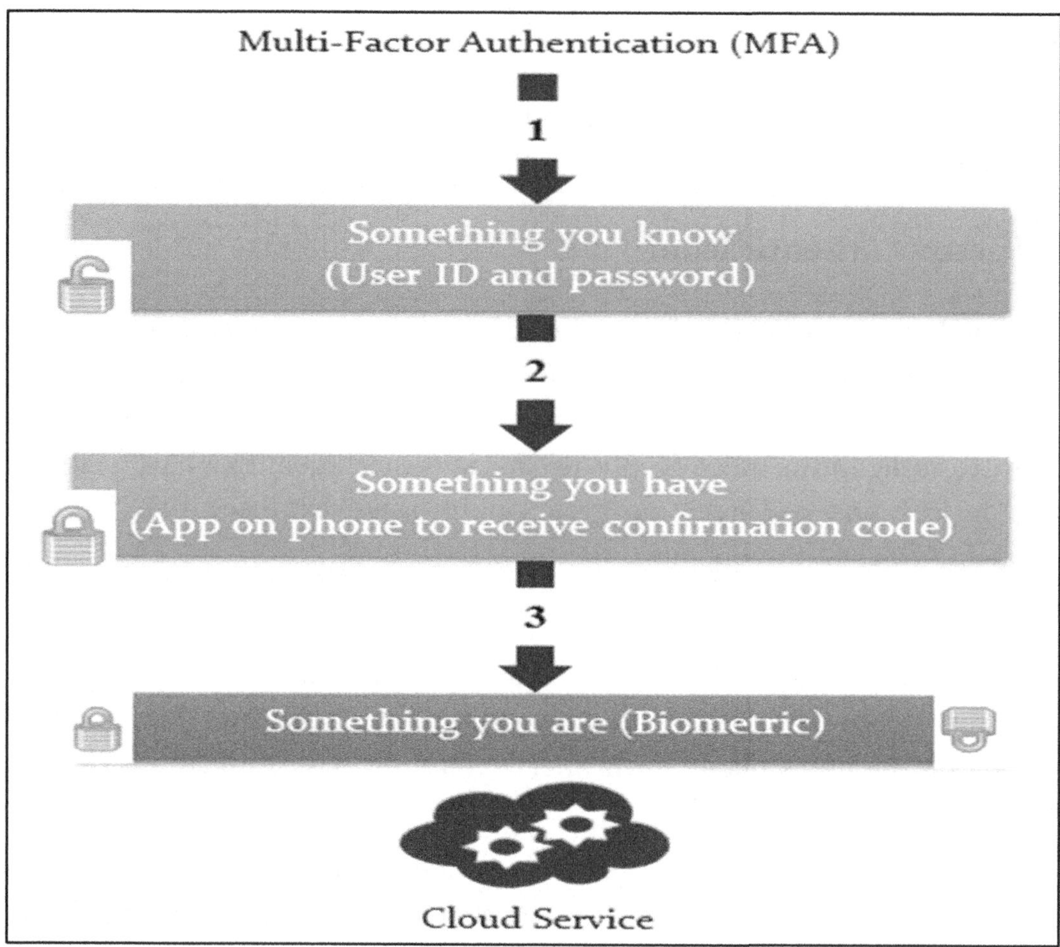

Figure 6-09: Multi-Factor Authentication

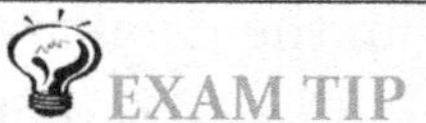

Multi-Factor Authentication (MFA) provides the combined version of authentication that results in an advanced level of security and protection.

Lab 6-01: Azure Active Directory

Scenario

An organization has multiple users that are using Azure resources and services via the Azure portal. A new user joined this organization. How can he use Azure resources and services?

Solution

Within an organization, a new user must first register into the default directory list using Azure Active Directory. Then the user will be able to use Azure resources and service via

the Azure portal. This lab is a step-by-step procedure to register a new user into the Azure Active Directory.

1. Log in to the Microsoft Azure portal and go to the portal menu.
2. Click on "Azure Active Directory" from the portal menu.

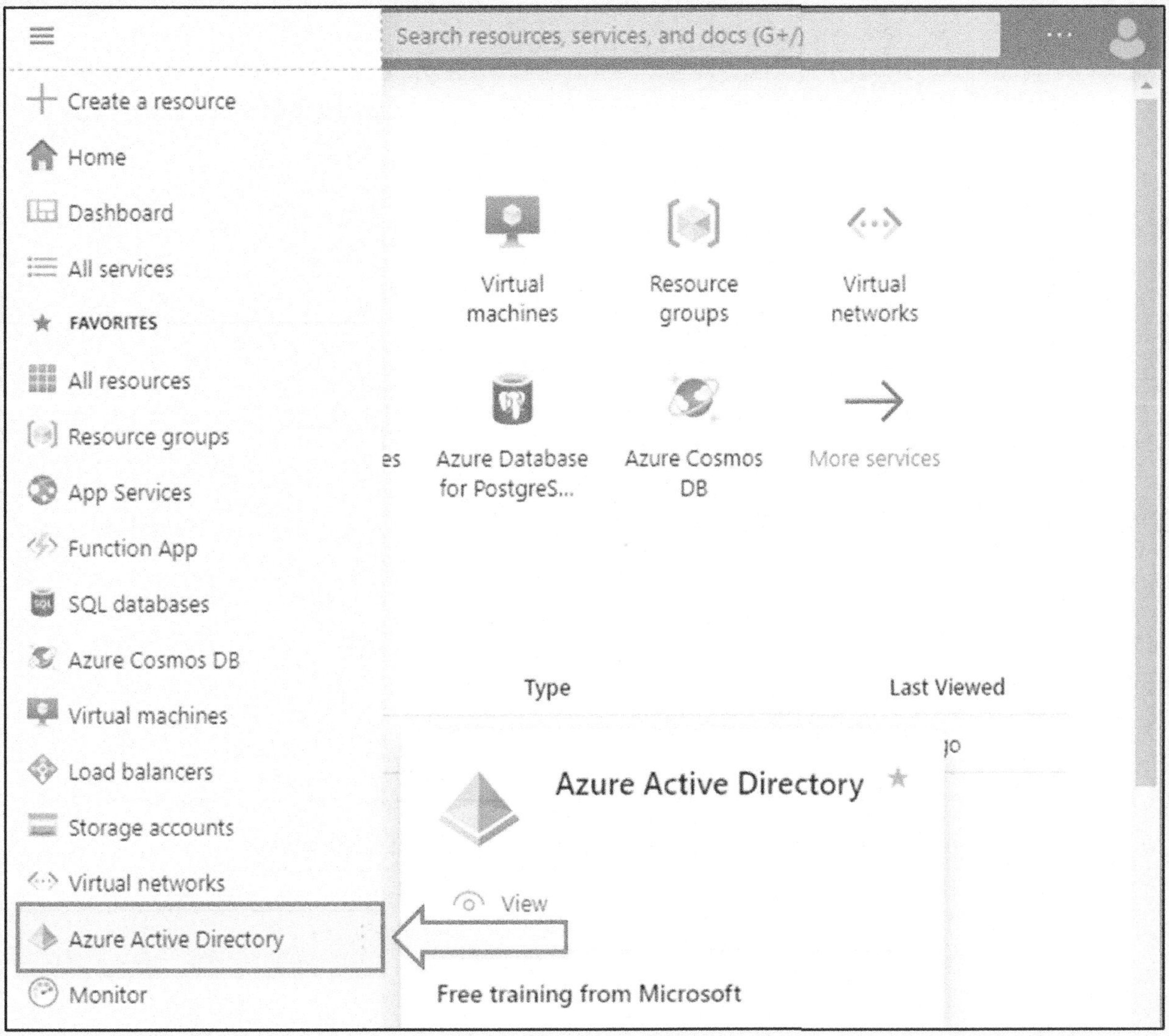

3. The current Active Directory is opened, AAD is the first resource that is created with a user's Azure account. The Default Directory shows an overview of the active directory.

Microsoft Azure
Search resources, services, and docs (G+/)
Home > nomykhannedianhotmail (Default Directory) - Overview
nomykhannedianhotmail (Default Directory) - Overview
Azure Active Directory
Documentation
Search (Ctrl+/)
Switch directory
Delete directory
Create a directory
Overview
Getting started
Diagnose and solve problems
Manage
Users
Groups
Organizational relationships
Roles and administrators
Enterprise applications
Devices
App registrations
Identity Governance
Application proxy
Licenses
Azure AD Connect
Custom domain names
Mobility (MDM and MAM)
Overview
nomykhannedianhotmail (Default Directory)
nomykhannedianhotmail.onmicrosoft.com
Tenant ID 71575372-8592-4097-b688-eb2a4e9abbac
Your role Global administrator More info
Azure AD for Office 365
Find
Users
Search
Azure AD Connect
Status Not enabled
Last sync Sync has never run

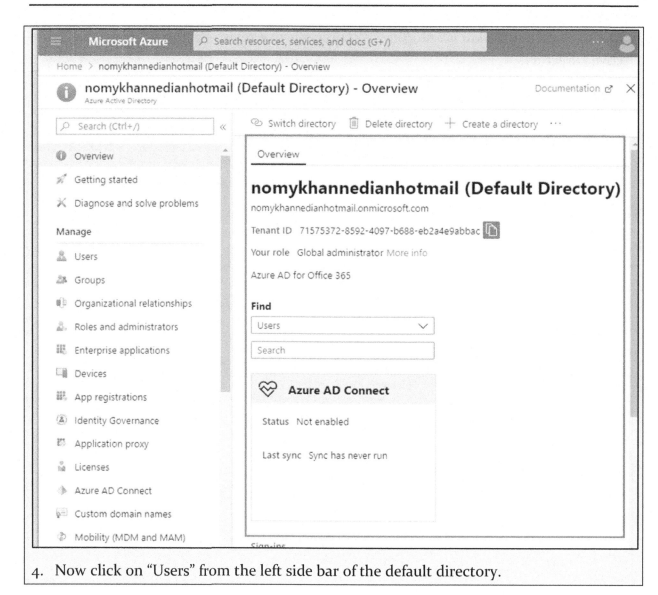

4. Now click on "Users" from the left side bar of the default directory.

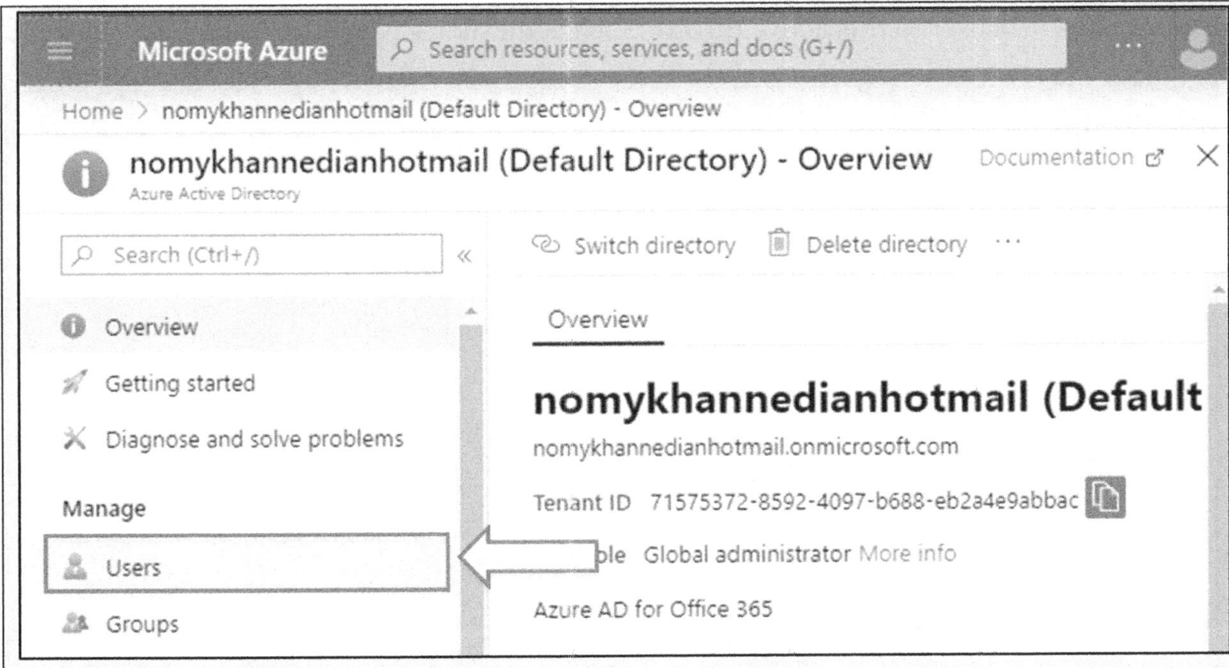

5. The “Users” tab shows the list of all users that are currently in the tenant. Tenant is the first Azure Active Directory.

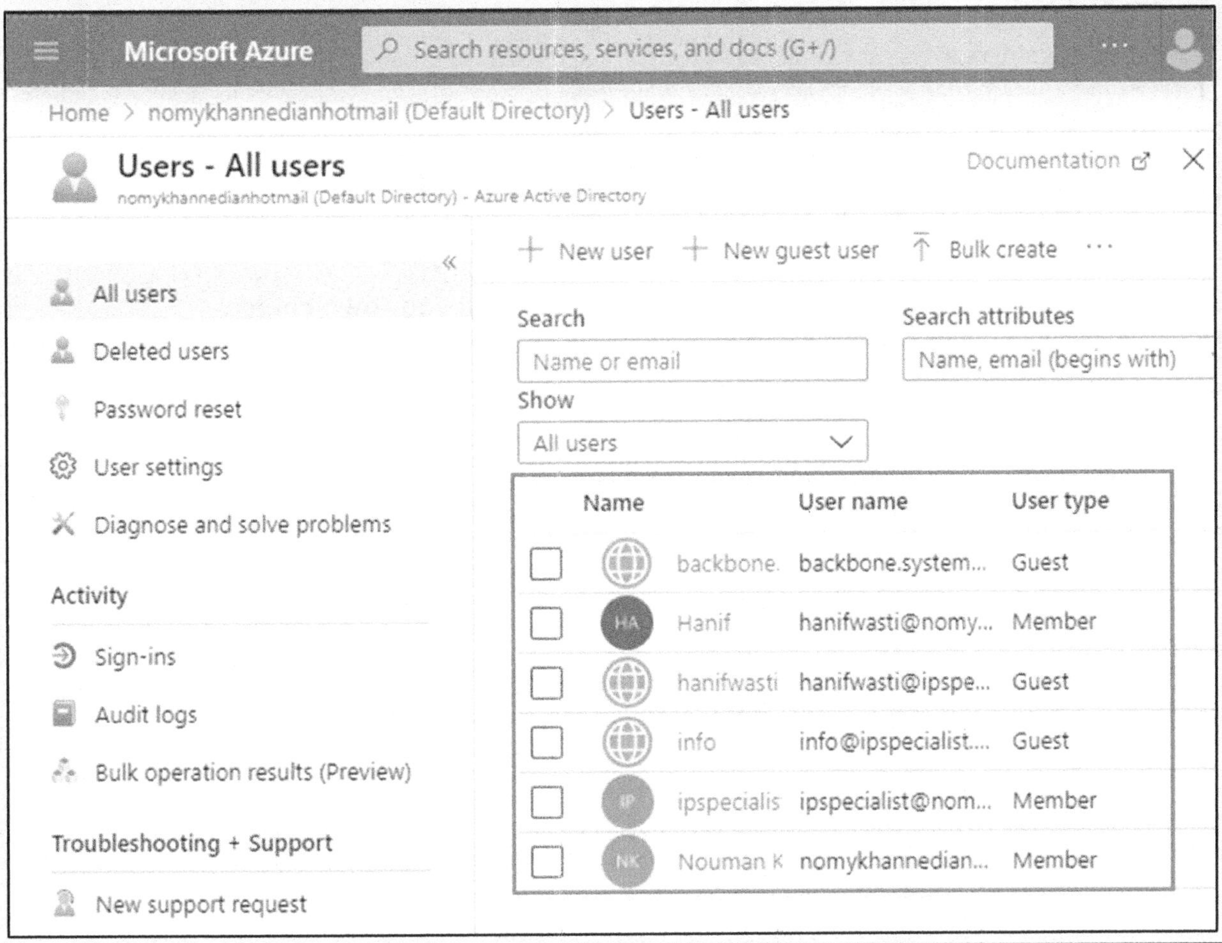

6. To add a new user to this active directory, click on the "+ New user" tab.

Microsoft Azure   Search resources, services, and docs (G+/)

Home > nomykhannedianhotmail (Default Directory) > Users - All users

Users - All users
nomykhannedianhotmail (Default Directory) - Azure Active Directory

Documentation

+ New user   er   Bulk create

All users
Deleted users
Password reset
User settings
Diagnose and solve problems

Activity
Sign-ins
Audit logs
Bulk operation results (Preview)

Troubleshooting + Support
New support request

Search: Name or email
Search attributes: Name, email (begins with)
Show: All users

Name	User name	User type
backbone.	backbone.system...	Guest
Hanif	hanifwasti@nomy...	Member
hanifwasti	hanifwasti@ipspe...	Guest
info	info@ipspecialist....	Guest
ipspecialis	ipspecialist@nom...	Member
Nouman K	nomykhannedian...	Member

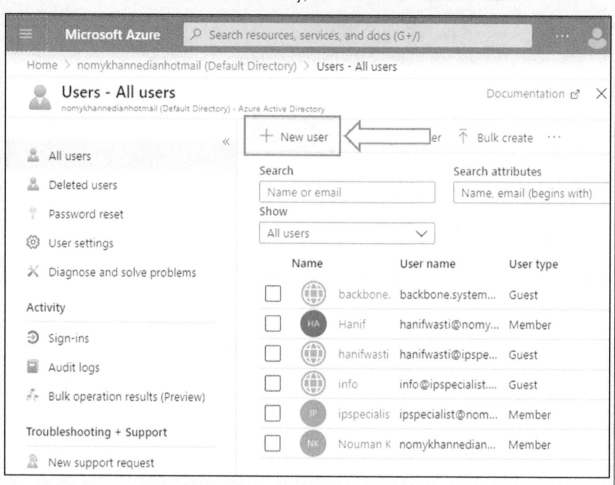

7. Write the names given in the "Identity" option.
8. Write user name, name, first name, and last name of your own choice.

Microsoft Azure
Search resources, services, and docs (G+/)
Home > nomykhannedianhotmail (Default Directory) > Users - All users > New user
New user
nomykhannedianhotmail (Default Directory)
Got a second? We would love your feedback on user creation →

Create user
Create a new user in your organization. This user will have a user name like alice@nomykhannedianhotmail.onmicrosoft.com.
I want to create users in bulk

Invite user
Invite a new guest user to collaborate with your organization. The user will be emailed an invitation they can accept in order to begin collaborating.
I want to invite guest users in bulk

Help me decide

Identity
User name * IPS_user @ nomykhannedianhotmail.o...
Name * New_user
First name IP
Last name Specialist

Password
Create

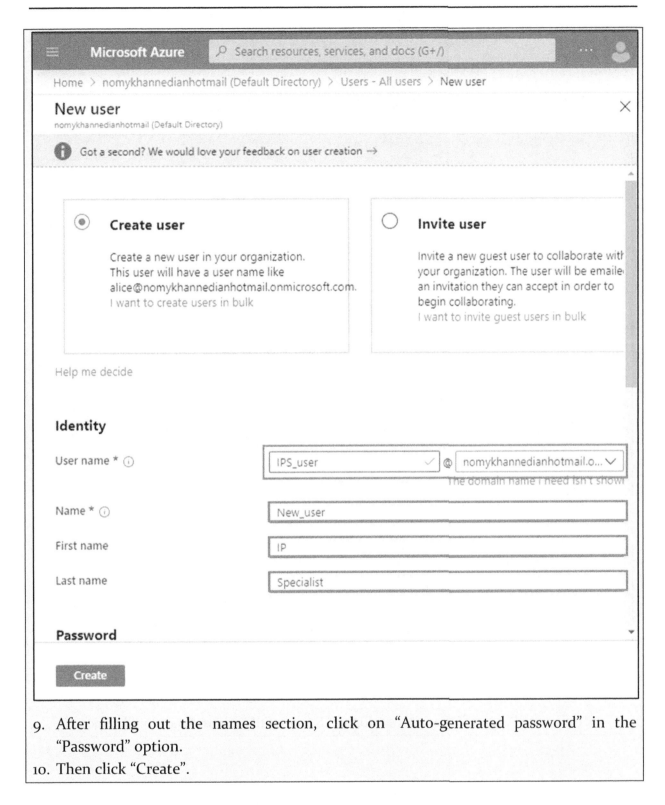

9. After filling out the names section, click on "Auto-generated password" in the "Password" option.
10. Then click "Create".

Microsoft Azure
Search resources, services, and docs (G+/)

Home > nomykhannedianhotmail (Default Directory) > Users - All users > New user

New user
nomykhannedianhotmail (Default Directory)

Got a second? We would love your feedback on user creation →

Password

Auto-generate password
Let me create the password

Initial password ••••••••

Show Password

Groups and roles

Groups 0 groups selected

Roles User

Settings

Block sign in Yes No

Usage location Filter usage locations

Job info

Create

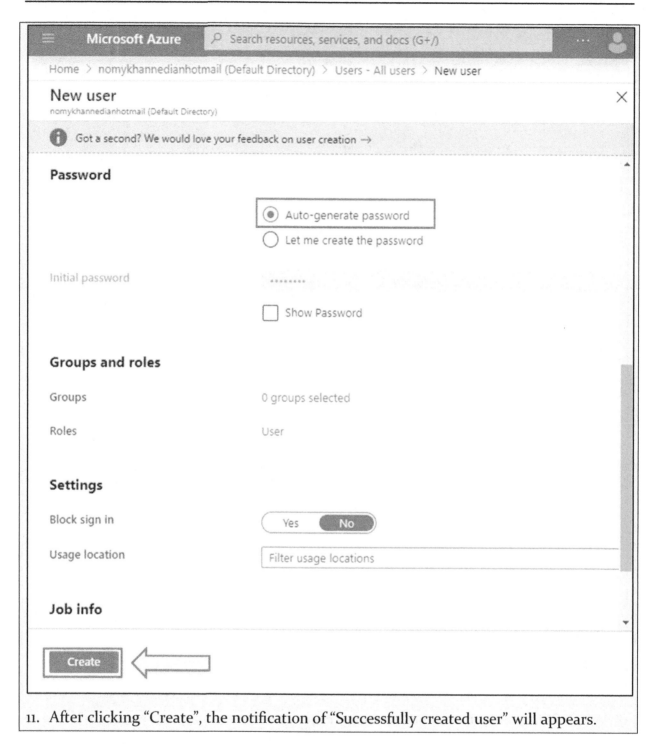

11. After clicking "Create", the notification of "Successfully created user" will appears.

Microsoft Azure
Search resources, services, and docs (G+/)

Home > nomykhannedia
Users - All use
nomykhannedianhotmail

All users
Deleted users
Password reset
User settings
Diagnose and solve p

Notifications

More events in the activity log → Dismiss all

Successfully created user
Successfully created user New_user.
a few seconds ago

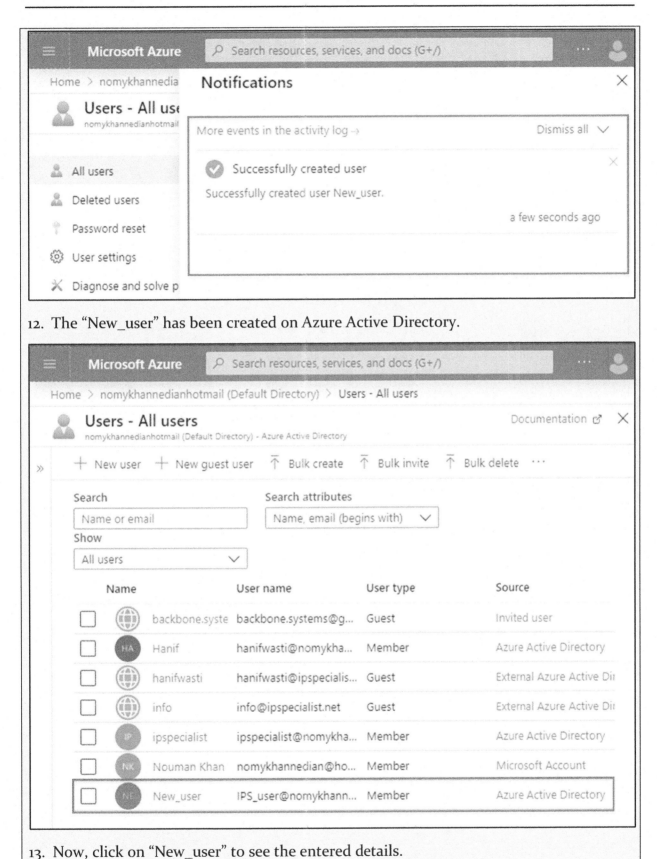

12. The "New_user" has been created on Azure Active Directory.

Microsoft Azure
Search resources, services, and docs (G+/)

Home > nomykhannedianhotmail (Default Directory) > Users - All users

Users - All users
nomykhannedianhotmail (Default Directory) - Azure Active Directory
Documentation

+ New user + New guest user Bulk create Bulk invite Bulk delete ...

Search
Name or email
Search attributes
Name, email (begins with)
Show
All users

Name	User name	User type	Source
backbone.syste	backbone.systems@g...	Guest	Invited user
Hanif	hanifwasti@nomykha...	Member	Azure Active Directory
hanifwasti	hanifwasti@ipspecialis...	Guest	External Azure Active Di
info	info@ipspecialist.net	Guest	External Azure Active Di
ipspecialist	ipspecialist@nomykha...	Member	Azure Active Directory
Nouman Khan	nomykhannedian@ho...	Member	Microsoft Account
New_user	IPS_user@nomykhann...	Member	Azure Active Directory

13. Now, click on "New_user" to see the entered details.

Microsoft Azure

Search resources, services, and docs (G+/)

Home > nomykhannedianhotmail (Default Directory) > Users - All users

Users - All users

nomykhannedianhotmail (Default Directory) - Azure Active Directory

Documentation

+ New user + New guest user Bulk create Bulk invite Bulk delete ...

Search

Name or email

Search attributes

Name, email (begins with)

Show

All users

Name	User name	User type	Source
backbone.syste	backbone.systems@g...	Guest	Invited user
Hanif	hanifwasti@nomykha...	Member	Azure Active Directory
hanifwasti	hanifwasti@ipspecialis...	Guest	External Azure Active Di
info	info@ipspecialist.net	Guest	External Azure Active Di
ipspecialist	ipspecialist@nomykha...	Member	Azure Active Directory
Nouman Khan	nomykhannedian@ho...	Member	Microsoft Account
New_user	@nomykhann...	Member	Azure Active Directory

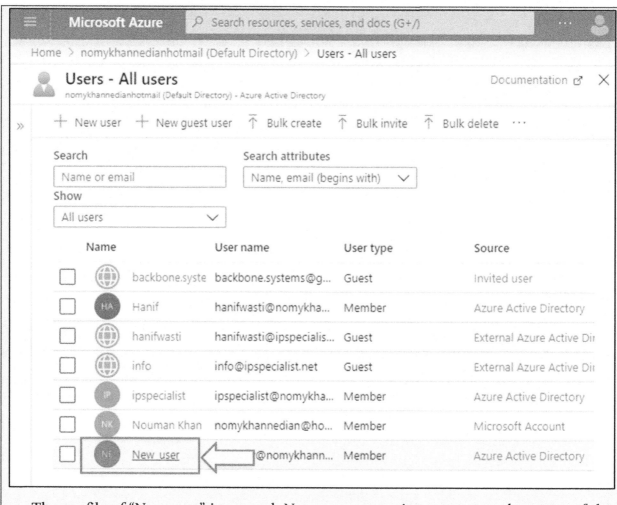

14. The profile of "New_user" is opened. Now, you can assign access to other parts of the Azure account.

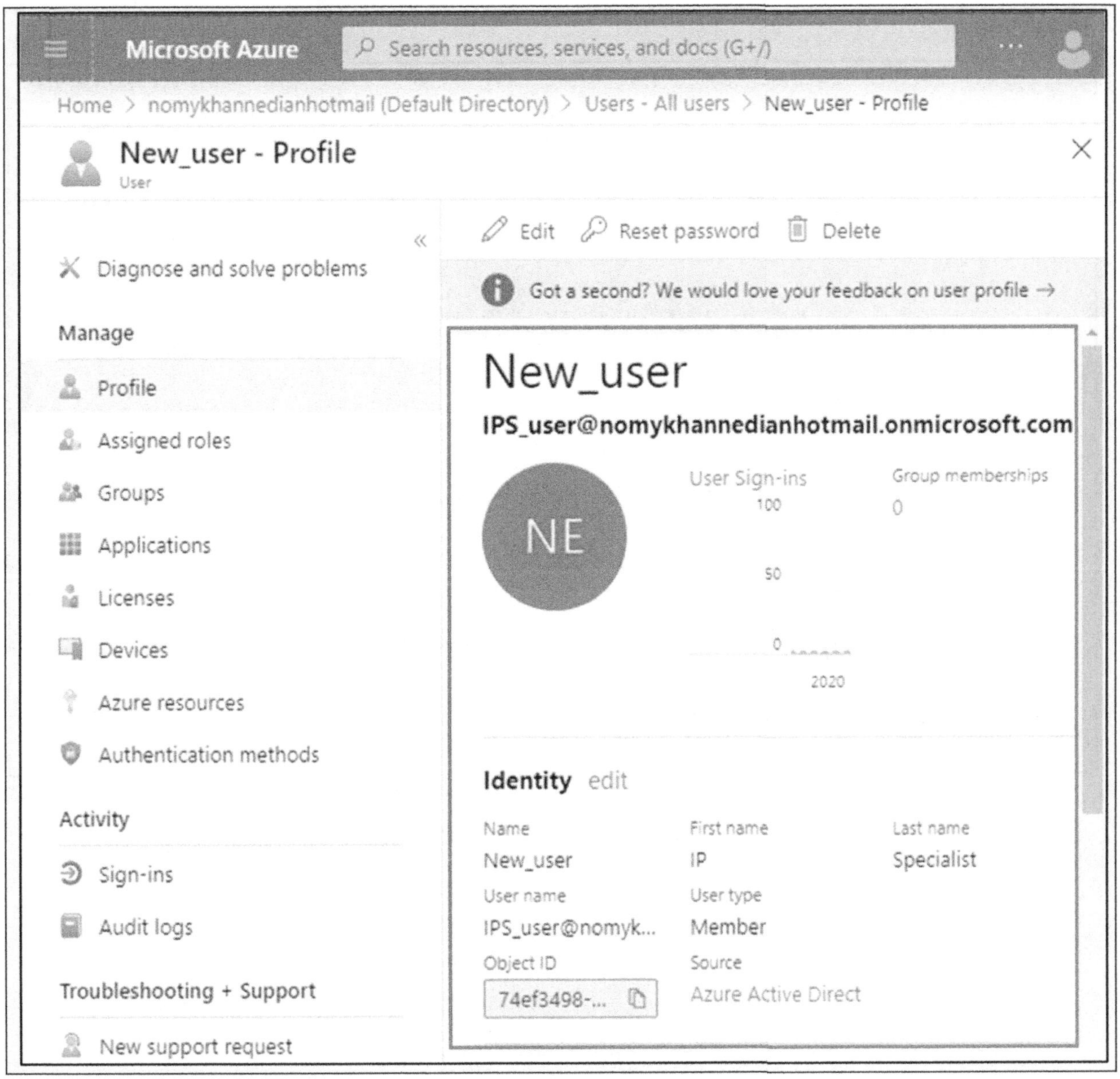

Microsoft Azure
Search resources, services, and docs (G+/)

Home > nomykhannedianhotmail (Default Directory) > Users - All users > New_user - Profile

New_user - Profile
User

Diagnose and solve problems

Manage

Profile
Assigned roles
Groups
Applications
Licenses
Devices
Azure resources
Authentication methods

Activity

Sign-ins
Audit logs

Troubleshooting + Support

New support request

Edit Reset password Delete

Got a second? We would love your feedback on user profile →

New_user

IPS_user@nomykhannedianhotmail.onmicrosoft.com

NE

User Sign-ins
100
50
0
2020

Group memberships
0

Identity edit

Name
New_user

First name
IP

Last name
Specialist

User name
IPS_user@nomyk...

User type
Member

Object ID
74ef3498-...

Source
Azure Active Direct

MindMap

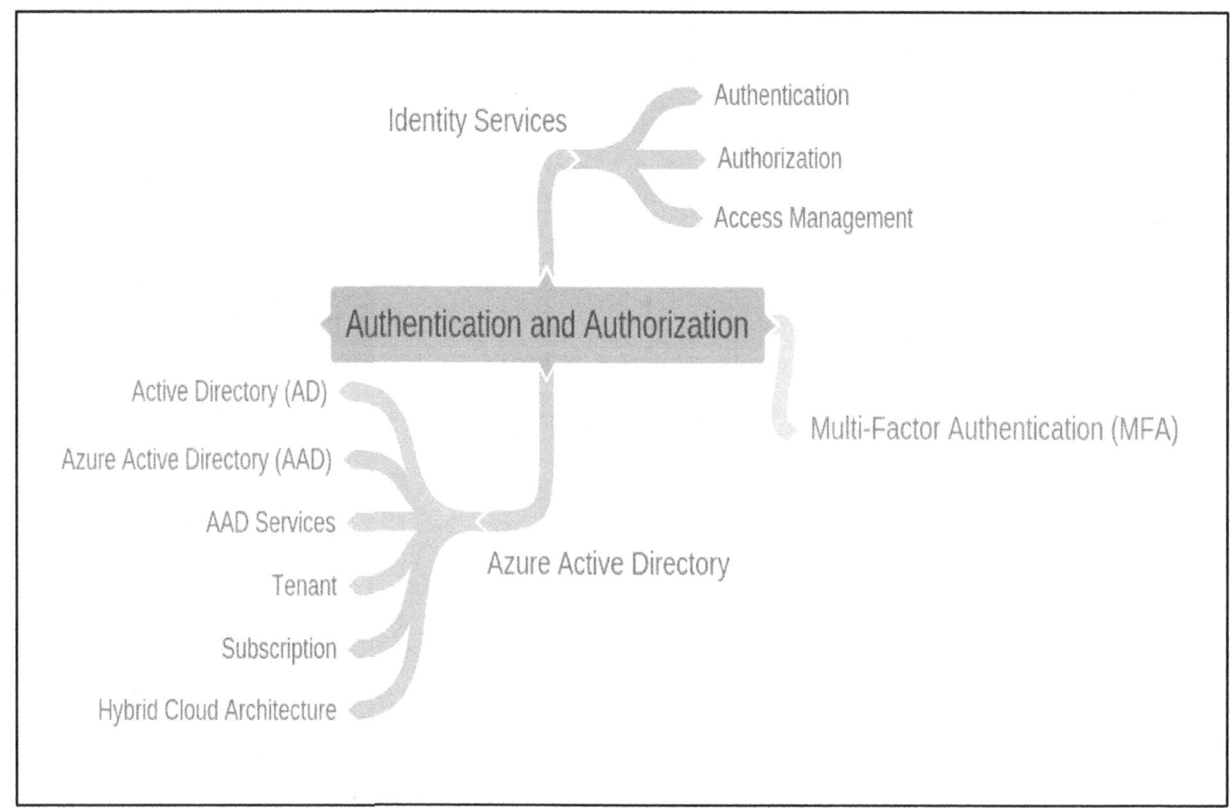

Figure 6-07: MindMap

Practice Questions

1. Which service is responsible for providing the platform to users for verification?
A. Identity Services
B. Authentication
C. Azure Active Directory (AAD)
D. Multi-Factor Authentication (MFA)

2. The two main steps toward a secure environment in Azure are ______________.
A. Encryption and Decryption
B. Authentication and Authorization
C. Authentication and Encryption
D. All of the above

3. Identity service is responsible for which one of the following?
A. Managing the traffic load
B. Routing Services
C. Subscription and Directory
D. Access Management

4. The identity of a user is called ______________.
A. Authorization
B. User profile
C. Authentication
D. None of the above

5. Which term allows an authenticated user to access data?
A. Authentication
B. Authorization
C. Security
D. Azure Active Directory

6. Which principle is followed by MFA for providing the advanced level of security?
A. Something you know, you have, you are
B. The code of 6 letters
C. Non-repudiation
D. Keystroke Monitoring

7. The user cannot be authorized until the user has gone through the process of ___________.
A. Modulation
B. Encryption
C. Authentication
D. Data Diddling

8. What is the first AAD instance after creating an account in Azure?
A. Tenant
B. Credential
C. Proxy Server
D. None of the above

9. Which directory service is commonly used in traditional offices?
A. AWS Directory Service
B. Google Directory Service
C. Microsoft Directory Service
D. Opera Directory Service

10. If a user has some data on Azure cloud and some present on the on-premises network, which service enables us to build a hybrid cloud architecture?
A. Content Delivery Network (CDN)
B. Multi-Factor Authentication (MFA)
C. Azure DNS
D. Azure Active Directory (AAD)

11. How many authentication ways are provided by MFA?
A. Only one
B. Two or more
C. At least four
D. Depends on the security requirement

12. Which of the following is a granular part of the identity service?
A. Active Directory (AD)
B. Tenant
C. Authorization
D. Cipher key

13. How is AAD different from AD?
A. AD is unable to provide service toward web apps
B. Both directory services are the same

C. AAD is easy to use
D. All of the above

14. If the subscription charges are not paid in time, the user will not able to use Azure resources. True or false?
A. True
B. False

15. Which of the following type of authentication processes are present in MFA?
A. Binary codes
B. Use of alphabets only
C. User must say "Security"
D. Biometric

16. Which of the following is responsible for providing the restriction of access to the data towards unauthorized users?
A. Authorization
B. Access Management
C. Traffic Manager
D. None of the above

17. Which of the following is considered as a compulsory service within Azure?
A. Multi-Factor Authentication
B. Azure DNS
C. Azure Active Directory
D. Account Creation

18. Which service is responsible for managing a user's information?
A. Traffic Manager
B. Azure Active Directory (AAD)
C. Express Route
D. Identity Service

19. Which of the following is the limitation of Microsoft Active Directory (AD)?
A. It is used for traditional offices only
B. It is unable to provide a secure environment
C. It supports administration and control
D. None of the above

20. A single user may belong to how many tenants at a time?

A. Two

B. More than five

C. Only one

D. At least three

Chapter 07: Azure Solutions

Introduction

Microsoft Azure is also known as Windows Azure and it is the public cloud computing platform used by Microsoft. It provides a variety of cloud services, including computing, analytics, storage, and networking services. Users can choose to build and scale new applications in the public cloud, or run existing applications, from these services. Microsoft Azure offers both a Platform as a Service (PaaS) and an Infrastructure as a Service (IaaS).

Azure has a lot of products, features, and services. In this lesson, we will focus on some of the core products of Azure. You will learn about some of the most cutting-edge technologies available today in Azure, which includes the Internet of Things (IoT), Big Data, Artificial Intelligence (AI), serverless computing in Azure and DevOps. These all are solutions built by Azure to solve their clients' problems.

Internet of Things

The Internet of Things (IoT) is a collection of interconnected computing devices, mechanical and digital machines, objects, or individuals. All of them are equipped with Unique Identifiers (UIDs) and the ability to transfer data over a network without requiring any human intervention.

Azure Internet of Things (IoT) is a collection of cloud services managed by Microsoft, which connects, monitors, and controls billions of IoT assets. Simply, an IoT solution is made up of one or more IoT devices and one or more back-end services running in the cloud that communicate with each other.

IoT Services

There are many IoT related services that the Azure offers to help you out. Two of the main IoT services are described here.

IoT Hub

IoT Hub is a cloud-hosted, managed service that serves as a central hub, which collects the data feeds from all devices. It is for bi-directional communication between your IoT application and the devices it manages. Using Azure IoT Hub, you can build IoT systems with efficient and secure communication between millions of IoT devices and a cloud-hosted backend solution. Virtually any computer can be connected to an IoT Hub.

As we know, it supports bi-directional communication, which means from cloud to device and device to cloud. IoT Hub monitoring helps you keep your solution healthy by tracking actions such as device creation, device failures, and device connections.

The capabilities of IoT Hub help you build scalable, full-featured IoT applications such as controlling industrial equipment used in manufacturing, tracking valuable healthcare assets and monitoring the use of office buildings.

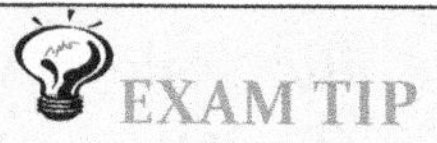

IoT Hub can receive and manage the data from million and even billions of devices.

IoT Hub Features

- **Scaling:** IoT Hub scales to millions of connected devices simultaneously and millions of events per second to support your IoT workloads
- **Securing**: IoT Hub gives you a secure communication channel for your devices to send data
- **PaaS**: It is a Platform as a Service in Azure
- **Integrating**: To build complete, end-to-end solutions, you can integrate the IoT Hub with other Azure services
- **Ease of Deployment:** With an array of built-in features, you can control your devices connected to an IoT Hub

IoT Central

Azure IoT Central is a fully managed, highly scalable IoT SaaS solution that reduces the complexity and costs of developing, managing and maintaining IoT solutions of an enterprise-grade nature. Build with Azure IoT Central gives you the opportunity to concentrate on your time, money and energy on transforming your company with IoT data, rather than simply maintaining and upgrading a complex and constantly evolving IoT infrastructure as it has no need of code to deploy your infrastructure. In this, you have pre-made connectors that you can use in IoT Central.

Its user-friendly interface allows easy monitoring of device requirements, developing guidelines, and managing millions of devices and their data over their life cycle. Additionally, it enables you to act on device insights by extending IoT intelligence into line-of-business applications.

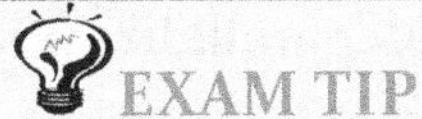

IoT central is a Software as a Service (SaaS) offering with templates and dashboards for a quick start.

So in short, we can say that to start an IoT project, there are two solutions: IoT Hub which is the solution where you need more control over the IoT process that means collecting and processing. While IoT Central is the solution that provides all the dashboard your infrastructure needs to create an IoT solution without any cloud nor IoT knowledge.

Big Data

Big Data is a term used to describe the collection of millions of data that is large in size and keeps growing exponentially over time. Although colleting a data from large number of sources is not such a difficult thing, but getting any value from any of these data is difficult. That is why Big data is ideal here. It is a combination of structured, semi-structured and unstructured data collected by companies that can be stored for information and used in predictive modeling, machine learning projects, and other advanced analytics applications. Systems that process and store big data have become a common component of data management architectures in organizations. Big data in terms of business value is used for better service, better products and more profits.

In Azure, there are many services and tools that deals with Big Data, some of them are defined below:

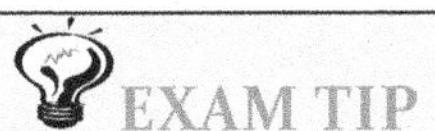

The value of big data keeps changing as the industry processes more and more data.

Azure Data Lake Analytics

Azure Data Lake Analytics is an on-demand job analytics service that simplifying big data. The data lake is a very large body of data on which you can perform analytical procedures. In Data Lake analytics there is parallel processing which means that same data is processed by two or more processors at the same time. Instead of hardware tuning, deploying, and configuring, you write queries to transform the data and abstract valuable insights.

Data Lake Analytics works for the highest performance, throughput and parallelization with Azure Data Lake Storage and works with Azure Storage blobs, Azure SQL Database, and Azure Warehouse.

HDInsight

Azure HDInsight is Microsoft's cloud-based big data analytics service, which helps organizations process large amounts of streaming or historical data. Azure HDInsight allows storing massive amounts of data easily, efficiently and cost-effectively. It is similar to Azure Data Lake Analytics but it uses most popular open-source frameworks such as Hadoop, Spark, Hive, LLAP, Kafka, Storm, R, and more. With these frameworks, a wide range of scenarios such as Extracting, Transforming, and Loading (ETL), data warehousing, machine learning, and IoT can be enabled.

Azure Databricks

Azure Databricks is an analytics platform based on Apache Spark, which is an open source cluster computing framework to enhance the Microsoft Azure platform. Databricks is integrated with Azure to provide one-click configuration, an open workspace, and streamlined workflows that enables data scientists, data engineers and business analysts to collaborate together. Databricks run and process a dataset on many computers simultaneously. When using Databricks, you do not need a lot of computers nor its maintenance. Azure provides all the computing powers and also the integration with other Azure Storage Services, such as Azure Data Lake Storage, Azure Blob Storage, Azure SQL Data Warehouse or Azure Cosmos DB. The data from all these storages are used to find insights and analyze the data in Apache Spark.

Big Data Outcomes

Collectively, the services of big data can bring the following outcomes for you.

Speed: Speed and efficiency for processing large amount of data, provided by the big data on Azure is the real value. You can find trends and insights to act accordingly.

Cost Reduction: Big data technology, such as cloud based analytics brings significant cost advantages when it comes to storing large amount of data.

Better Decision Making: Faster and better decision making with the speed of in-memory analytics combined with the ability to analyze new sources of data.

New Products and Services: Understand the customer demands and provide them with much better products and services.

Artificial Intelligence

Artificial Intelligence (AI) is the capability of a machine to imitate intelligent human behavior. With AI, machines can analyze images, comprehend speech, interact in natural ways and make predictions using data. In the Microsoft, AI is often called Machine Learning or AI is the sub-category of Machine learning, although AI and Machine learning are often placed in the same bucket.

Microsoft focuses on three main parts to how machine learning can be used on the cloud platform.

1. **Models**
   The definition of what your machine learning application is learning - A model is a set of rules that define how to use the data provided. The model finds patterns based on the rules.
2. **Knowledge Mining**
   Use Azure Search to finding existing insights in your data. File relationships, geography connections, and much more.
3. **Built-in Apps**
   Azure has a number of built-in apps that you can use for machine learning and AI straight away. These include cognitive services and bot services.

Azure AI use Rules and Models to train your AI implementation.

Azure Cognitive Services

Cognitive services bring AI within every developer's reach — without requiring expertise in machine-learning. All it takes is an API call to embed the feature to see, hear, speak, search, understand, and accelerate decision-making into your apps.

Vision

Identify and recognize the pictures, images, and digital ink automatically.

Decisions

The apps make content-based decisions by detecting the potential offensive languages, IoT anomalies and leverage data analytics.

Speech

Integrate speech processes into apps and services by converting speech into text as transcription. It also identifies unique voices and even verifies as speaker based on the speech.

Azure Machine Learning Studio

The Azure Machine Learning Studio is the top-level tool for the machine learning service. It is visual tool through which you can manage all of your needs for ML. It provides a centralized location for data scientists and developers to work with all the artifacts for developing, training, and deploying machine learning models.

In this, you have pre-made modules that you can use is as they are ready to be used immediately. Some use cases for Azure Machine Learning Studio are: Twitter Sentiment analysis, movie recommendation, and photo grouping.

Machine Learning Services

1. **End-to End Service:** The service to use AI and machine learning almost anywhere on Azure.
2. **Tooling:** The Machine Learning service is a collection of tools to help you build AI applications.
3. **Automation:** Azure automatically recognizes trends in your applications and creates models for you.

Serverless

Serverless is such an important part of modern cloud computing. Serverless model allows developers to build applications faster by eliminating the need for them to manage the infrastructure. It is an extreme PaaS. The cloud service provider automatically offers, scales, and manages the infrastructure required for running the code with serverless applications.

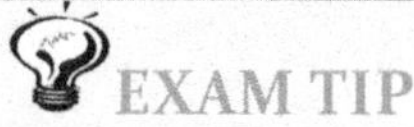

It is important to understand that "serverless" does not mean that no VMs are involved. It simply means that the VM running your code is not explicitly allocated to you, which means that you do not manage them. Your code is moved to the VM, it is executed, and then it is moved off.

Benefits of Serverless Model

No Infrastructure Management: Use fully managed infrastructure - developers are able to avoid administrative tasks and concentrate on the core business logic. You simply deploy the code with a serverless platform, and it runs with great availability.

Dynamic Scalability: For serverless computing, the infrastructure can automatically scale up and down within seconds to match any workload requirements.

Faster Time to Market: Serverless applications reduce the dependencies of operations on each development cycle, increasing the agility of development teams to produce more features in less time.

More Efficient Use of Resources: Shifting to serverless technology allows companies to reduce TCO and resource reallocation to speed up the pace of innovation.

Azure Functions

Azure Functions is the compute component of serverless services offered by Azure. It is called function as it has a single task to perform every time. Meaning that you can use Functions to write code without having to worry about deploying that code or creating VMs to run your code. The code runs only once for every invocation. Apps using Azure Functions are often referred to as Function Apps. It can be able to run millions of times per second if needed. Using an event-driven model, serverless functions accelerate development, with triggers that automatically execute code to react to events and bindings to seamlessly incorporate extra services.

Azure Logic Apps

Azure Logic Apps is a cloud service that connects the systems both inside and outside the Azure Platform; you can integrate apps, data, and services or even an entire system across organizations. With this you can automate, and orchestrate business processes, tasks, activities, and workflows. Unlike Function Apps, in order to create some efficient workflows with Logic Apps, you do not have to write the code. Everything is customizable in Azure Portal. Logic Apps simplifies how you design and build flexible applications for application integration, data integration, system integration, Enterprise Application Integration (EAI) and Business-to-Business (B2B) communication, whether in the cloud, at the premises, or both.

Use Case

Every time a new order is creating in your ordering system, you can create a logic app to create a record for how long it took. It inserts that into a database and sends an email to the requested person. You can also have a conditional path, like when an order is over 100$,

you can send a different email to customer service to ask them to thank the customer. You can connect a ton of applications either manually or using templates, there is no code need, no service to setup and you can get started very quickly.

Azure Event Grid

An event, in a computing concept, it is an action or occurrence that can be identified by a program and has significance for system application. Azure Event Grid lets you easily build applications with event-based architectures. First, pick the Azure resource you would like to subscribe to, and then send the event to the event handler or WebHook endpoint. Event Grid has built-in support for events such as storage blobs and resource groups, coming from Azure services. Event Grid also supports your own events, using custom-made themes. Event Grid is a serverless service so there is no need of management of infrastructure.

You can use filters to route specific events to different endpoints, multicast to multiple endpoints, and ensure your events are reliably delivered. Azure Event Grid is deployed to maximize availability by native distribution across multiple fault domains in every region, and across availability zones. Event Grid connects data sources and event handlers. You can use Event Grid to trigger a serverless function that analyzes images when added to a blob storage container.

DevOps

DevOps is a combination of the terms development and operations, meant to reflect a collective or cooperative approach to the activities performed by the application development departments of an organization and IT operations. The term DevOps is used in various ways, it is an organizational concept in its broadest sense that promotes better coordination and collaboration between these teams and others within an enterprise to generate a better and more reliable product.

DevOps is all about how Developers, Engineers, and System Administrators organize themselves and work as a team to deliver better products faster.

Azure DevOps

Azure DevOps offers developer tools to support teams in preparing projects, working on application creation, and designing and deploying new products.

Azure DevOps provides integrated features that can be accessed via your web browser or client IDE. Depending on your business needs, you may use one or more of the following services:

1. **Azure Boards:** Allows project manager to keep track of work task, timelines, planning and monitoring, code bugs, and issues.
2. **Azure Pipelines:** Provides services to develop and test, automatically and continuously.
3. **Azure Repos:** Provides the source control of your code to Git repositories or Team Foundation Version Control (TFVC). It is a store where your code is securely managed.
4. **Azure Test Plans:** Provides various tools for testing the software, including manual/exploratory testing and continuous testing automatically.
5. **Azure Artifacts:** Allows teams to share public and private Maven, Npm, and NuGet packages and incorporate package sharing into your CI/CD pipelines.

Azure DevTest Labs

Azure DevTest Labs helps team developers handle Virtual Machines (VMs) and PaaS tools effectively, without waiting for approvals. It focuses in the environment management. With this, developers and engineers are allowed to create an environment for test and development.

DevTest Labs creates labs that consist of pre-configured bases or templates for Azure Resource Manager. These have all the tools and applications you can use to create environments. You can create environments in a couple of minutes, instead of hours or days. It is also helpful for cost management as it minimizes the waste of resources in accounts. Creation of environment can also be automated.

Lab 7-01: Azure AI

Scenario

A company want to improve the attendance and surveillance system in its office by enabling face recognition service. How can this be done?

Solution

The company can use Azure Artificial Intelligence (AI) service of Face Recognition. This service will analyze the picture of a person by face expression, hairs, age, and accessories then declare the result based on the information collected.

Step-by-Step Guide

1. Open Microsoft AI.

Microsoft

Microsoft AI

Hands on with AI

Dive in to interactive demos that showcase a selection of the capabilities of the Microsoft AI platform.

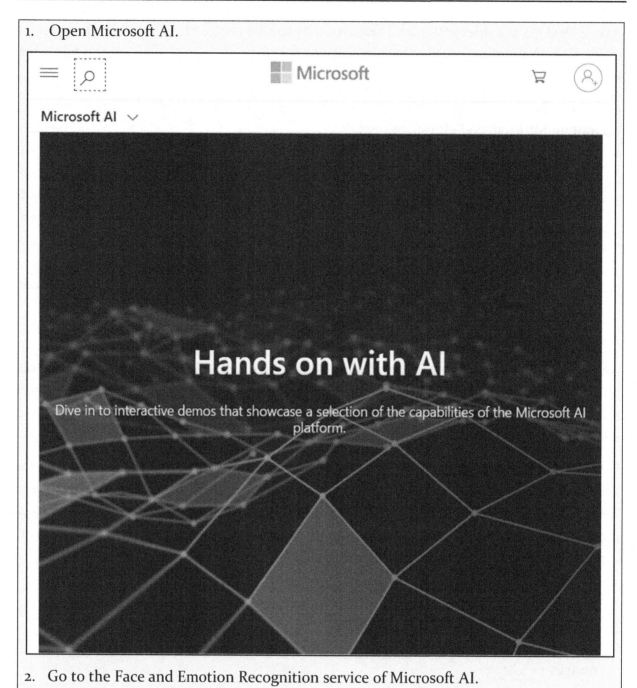

2. Go to the Face and Emotion Recognition service of Microsoft AI.
3. Click on the "Try it out" button.

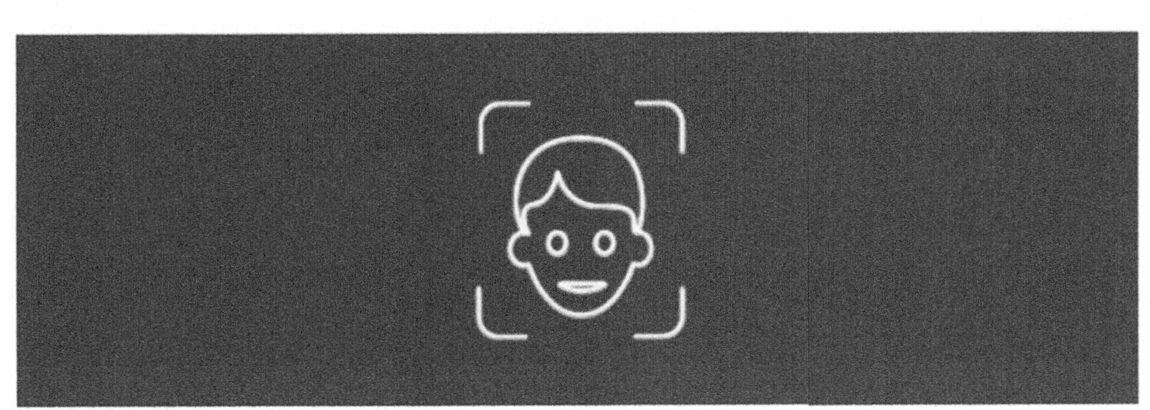

Face and Emotion Recognition
Microsoft Cognitive Services Face API can quickly analyze and compare to determine if two photos contain the same person or not. Test it out with your own photos or with a friend.

4. Face and Emotion Recognition service page will open and display as shown below.
5. Click on “Add Photo” in both PHOTO 1 and PHOTO 2.

Microsoft

Microsoft AI

Hands on with AI

Face and Emotion Recognition

Facial recognition can be a great security tool. See how Microsoft AI is able to quickly analyze and compare photos. Upload or take two photos and we will use our Face API to tell you if the photos are of the same person. We'll also provide the approximate age, gender, and emotion. Really test the system by making different faces or getting a friend involved to take one of the photos.

Add Photo

PHOTO 1

Add Photo

PHOTO 2

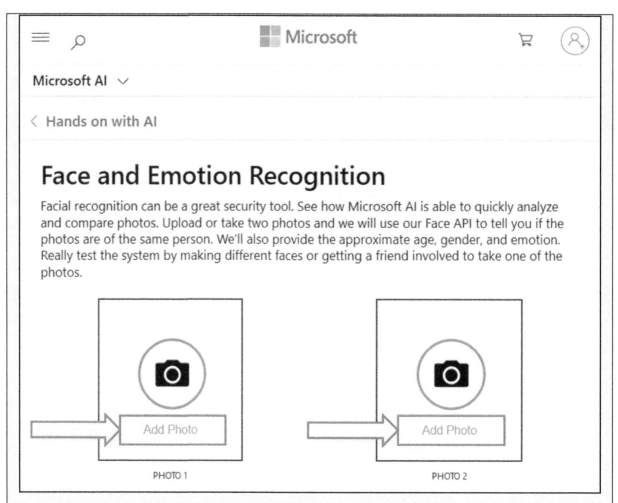

6. On PHOTO 1, upload the picture of company's employee from company's library.
7. On PHOTO 2, upload the picture of an unknown person.
8. The face recognition service will scan the photos and declare the result as shown below.

Microsoft AI

< Hands on with AI

Face and Emotion Recognition

PHOTO 1

GENDER:	Male
AGE:	46 years
EMOTION:	Happiness
ACCESSORIES:	None
FACIAL HAIR:	Yes

PHOTO 2

GENDER:	Male
AGE:	35 years
EMOTION:	Happiness
ACCESSORIES:	None
FACIAL HAIR:	Yes

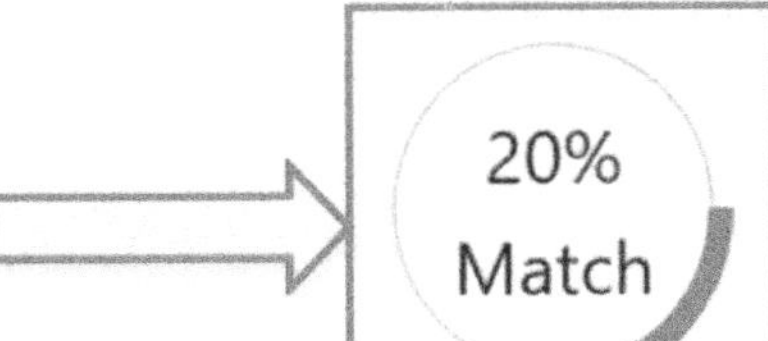

They're not the same person!

9. Now take the pictures of the same person for PHOTO 1 and PHOTO 2.
10. The result will show a 100% match, which means both persons are the same.

Microsoft AI

< Hands on with AI

Face and Emotion Recognition

PHOTO 1

PHOTO 2

	PHOTO 1		PHOTO 2
GENDER:	Male	GENDER:	Male
AGE:	46 years	AGE:	46 years
EMOTION:	Happiness	EMOTION:	Happiness
ACCESSORIES:	None	ACCESSORIES:	None
FACIAL HAIR:	Yes	FACIAL HAIR:	Yes

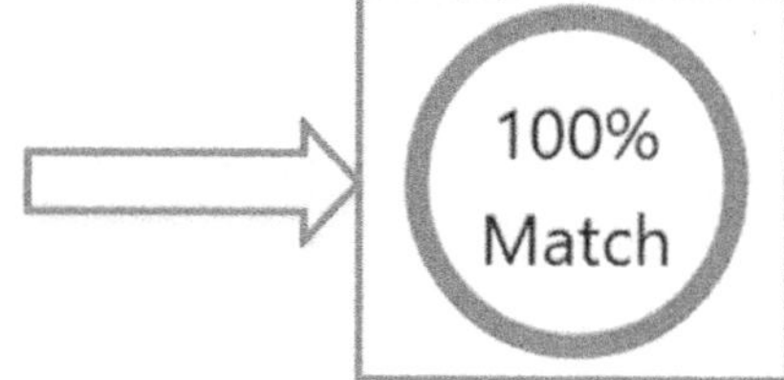

That's the same person!

Mind Map

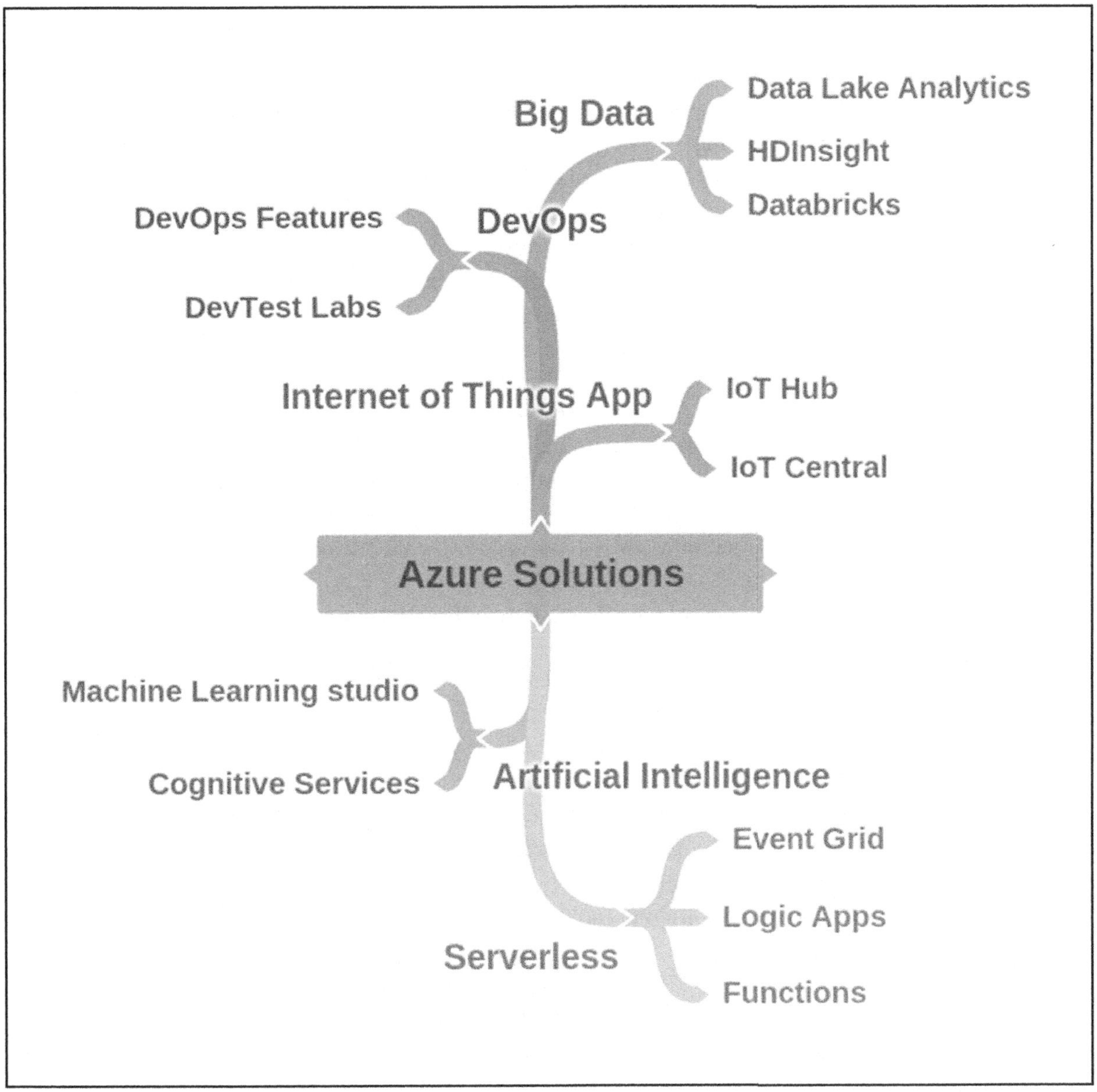

Big Data
Data Lake Analytics
HDInsight
Databricks
DevOps Features
DevOps
DevTest Labs
Internet of Things App
IoT Hub
IoT Central
Azure Solutions
Machine Learning studio
Cognitive Services
Artificial Intelligence
Event Grid
Logic Apps
Serverless
Functions

Figure 7-05: Mind Map of Azure Solutions

Practice Questions

1. What is the purpose of "models" in Machine Learning and Artificial Intelligence?
   A. The definition of what you want your Machine Learning implementation to learn
   B. The framework for integrating other Azure services with your particular Machine Learning instance

C. Defining the version of your Machine Learning application
D. The size and capacity of the Machine Learning service

2. What are some of the likely outcomes from using Big Data analytics? (Choose 3)
A. Cost reduction on data storage
B. Cheaper and more accessible cloud computing products
C. Products created better aligned to customer needs
D. Better decision making from immediate analysis
E. A decoupling of business decisions from the development of new products
F. More secure access to company infrastructure

3. When would you use Azure Logic Apps to solve a problem?
A. When a function is not able to solve a problem as a single task
B. When you have to send emails as part of your workflow while processing data from multiple data sources
C. When you have to integrate different systems inside and outside of Azure
D. When you have to use more than one Azure subscription
E. When there are too many integration points to handle with Azure Functions

4. What is the best definition of Azure DevOps?
A. It is a specific section of the Azure Portal where you can manage operational parts of your infrastructure
B. It is a way to write better code and find bugs faster
C. It is a platform to manage Azure resources meant for development, such as App Services, Azure Functions and Visual Studio Online
D. Azure DevOps is a suite of 5 different tools to create more robust software, faster

5. Which of the following are tools in Azure DevOps? (Choose 3)
A. Azure Automation
B. Azure Artifacts
C. Azure Deployment
D. Azure Operations
E. Azure Pipelines
F. Azure Boards

6. Which are Internet of Things services on Azure? (Choose 2)
A. IoT Services
B. IoT Management Studio
C. IoT Central
D. IoT App Services

E. IoT Hub
F. IoT Virtual Box

7. What is the purpose of "Knowledge Mining" in Machine Learning and Artificial Intelligence?
   A. The definition of what you want your Machine Learning implementation to learn
   B. The framework for integrating other Azure services with your particular Machine Learning instance
   C. Defining the version of your Machine Learning application
   D. Finding existing insights in your data. The size and capacity of the Machine Learning service

8. What are some of the likely outcomes from using HDInsight? (Choose 2)
   A. Cheaper and more accessible cloud computing products
   B. Allows storing massive amounts of data easily, efficiently and cost-effectively
   C. Wide range of scenarios such as Extracting, Transforming, and Loading (ETL), data warehousing, machine learning, and IoT can be enabled
   D. A decoupling of business decisions from the development of new products

9. Which Azure service is based on Events?
   A. HDInsight
   B. Databricks
   C. Logic Apps
   D. Event Grid

10. Which of the following two services are likely similar to each other?
    A. HDInsight
    B. Databricks
    C. Logic Apps
    D. Azure Functions

11. What are the three main features of Cognitive service?
    A. Vision
    B. Emotion
    C. Decisions
    D. Speech

12. What is the best definition of Azure Machine Learning studio?
    A. A specific section of the Azure Portal where you can manage operational parts of your infrastructure
    B. A way to write better code and find bugs faster
    C. It provides a centralized location for data scientists and developers to work with all the artifacts for developing, training, and deploying machine learning models

D. Azure Machine Learning studio is a suite of 5 different tools to create more robust software, faster

13. What are the three main services of Machine Learning?
    A. End-to End Service
    B. Tooling
    C. Automation
    D. Orchestration

14. What are the Benefits of Serverless Model?
    A. Dynamic scalability
    B. End-to End delivery
    C. Faster time to market
    D. More efficient use of resources

15. What is the purpose of Azure DevTest Labs?
    A. To offer developer the tools to support teams in preparing projects, working on application creation and designing and deploying software
    B. To create labs that consist of pre-configured bases or templates for Azure Resource Manager
    C. To provide customizable team dashboards with configurable widgets to share information, progress, and trends
    D. To test the latest versions of your software

16. Which Azure service provides serverless workflow orchestration to let you integrate apps, data, systems, and service across enterprises or organizations?
    A. Logic Apps
    B. Functions
    C. Apps Grid
    D. Bot Service

17. You need to use an Azure Big Data solutions that allow you to query and transform data to extract insights. What is the most appropriate solution for this?
    A. Azure SQL Database
    B. Data Lake Analytics
    C. Cosmos DB
    D. Blob Storage

18. In which situation should you use an Azure Function app?
    A. When you want to execute a visual studio graphical workflow that provisions an order when the order is received
    B. When you want to execute Java script code that sends a maintenance email every Sunday evening

C. When you want to execute a batch file that removes records from an Azure SQL Database on Demand
D. When you want to use Functions to write code without having to worry about deploying that code or creating VMs to run your code

19. Which Azure analytics service is based on Apache Spark?
A. HDInsight
B. Data Lake
C. Databricks
D. Event Grid

20. What are the outcomes from using Big Data to business value?
A. Better service
B. Better products
C. More profits
D. All of the above

Chapter 08: Security

Introduction

Microsoft is responsible for the security of the cloud. User as a cloud administrator is responsible for the security in the cloud. Azure security is the most important part of Azure. Azure security services provide protection of data, technologies, and infrastructure to work simultaneously. With Microsoft, security can successfully achieve the role of both Microsoft and cloud administrator. Microsoft administrator follows the principle of security, compliance, and integrity to ensure the protection of customer's data and their access. To get access to data, the administrator needs to follow the rules and regulations according to the Microsoft trusted cloud.

Why Security is Important

Security is a set of policies or rules, which allow the traffic to be directed to the network in the right way. Security of the network is very important, especially when there is a communication of infrastructure with the internet. On the internet, multiple access is possible at a time, so there a need to secure the cloud infrastructure with a set of security rules.

For example, there are multiple subnets present in VNet as shown in Figure 8-01. By default, all virtual machines within the subnet are communicated with each other. Within the same VNet, some Virtual Machines (VMs) store complex and sensitive data. For this, especially, security policies are required for the protection of data within the same network. For security purposes, the VM with sensitive data is separately available in a subnet with no connection with other subnets in VNet.

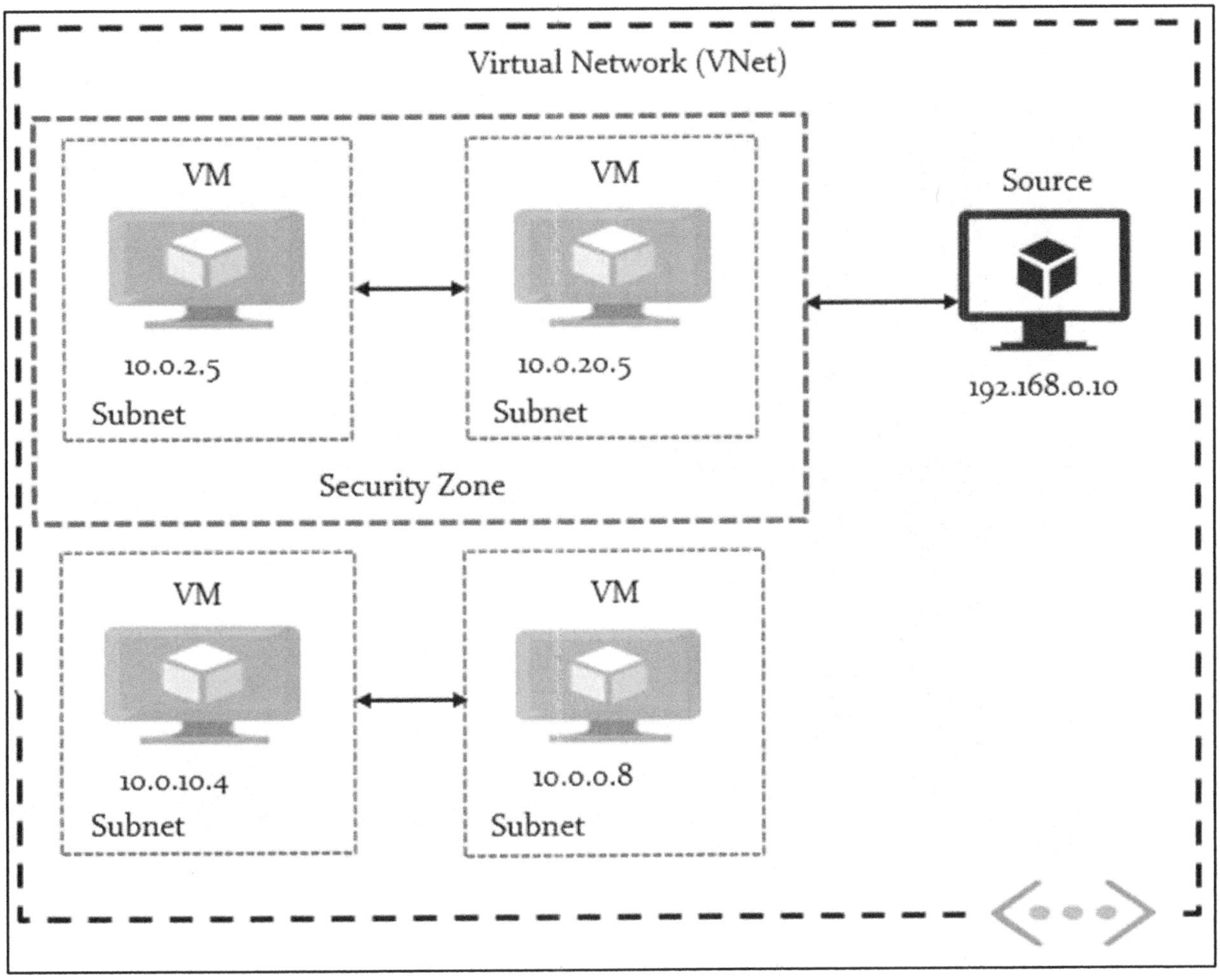

Virtual Network (VNet)
VM
10.0.2.5
Subnet
VM
10.0.20.5
Subnet
Security Zone
Source
192.168.0.10
VM
10.0.10.4
Subnet
VM
10.0.0.8
Subnet

Figure 8-01: VNet with Security feature

This chapter explains the Azure security aspects that make strong cybersecurity of the cloud.

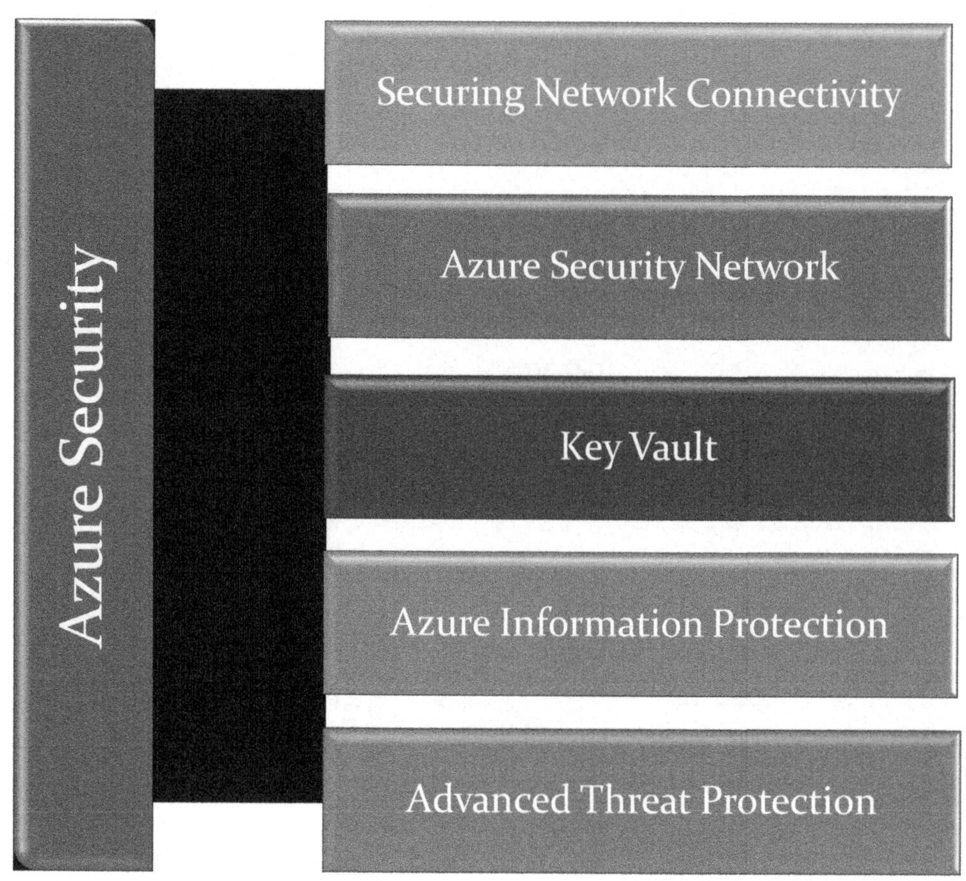

Figure 8-02: Azure Security Services

Azure security services include:

- **Securing Network Connectivity:** Network connectivity can be efficiently secured by Azure build-in resources and services. Azure user can make the entire network secure or just some small parts of the network depending on their cloud architecture needs
- **Azure Security Center:** Azure Security Center helps and guides Azure users to make Azure platform secure for the utilization of optimum services
- **Azure Key Vault:** Azure Key Vault is an amazing way to hide and save key passwords and uses key hardware for the provision of security when needed
- **Azure Information Protection:** Azure Information Protection (AIP) provides the protection of email, complex information, and sensitive data
- **Advanced Threat Protection (ATP):** Advanced Threat Protection (ATP) identifies special users and device activity. It enables the protection of sensitive data and applications against hacking approaches. It also provides a way of single-console management for protection

Securing Network Connectivity

The networks on Azure give access to everything for users. All the resources and services of Microsoft Azure are connected to a network to provide communication between users, processes and other services. To run this, smooth network behavior is required that efficiently provides all the network services within Azure. In order to achieve optimum network performance, secure network connectivity is very important. Figure 8-03 shows ways to ensure secure network connectivity.

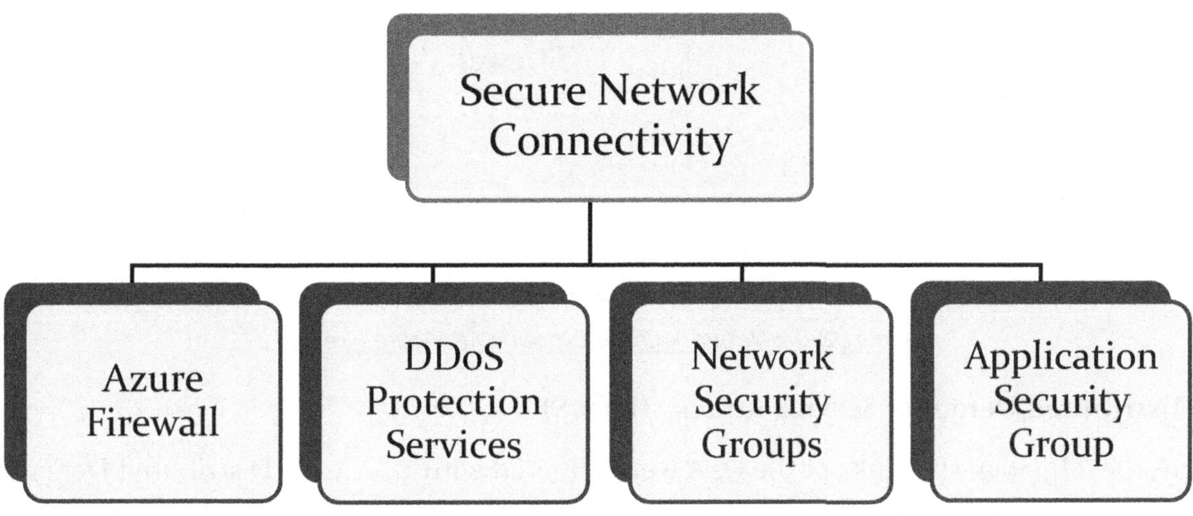

Figure 8-03: Ways of Secure Network Connectivity

Azure Firewall

An Azure firewall is a crucial service that protects and safes the network from unwanted traffic load.

- **Rules:** Azure firewall must have a certain set of rules that gives permission to allow and not allow the traffic according to the connected devices and services attached to the network
- **Variation:** The firewall may have certain hardware and software according to the size of the network
- **Compulsory Bit:** To ensure network security, a firewall is considered as a compulsory section in the network

Figure 8-04 shows the network performance that employes network security with the help of the Azure Firewall.

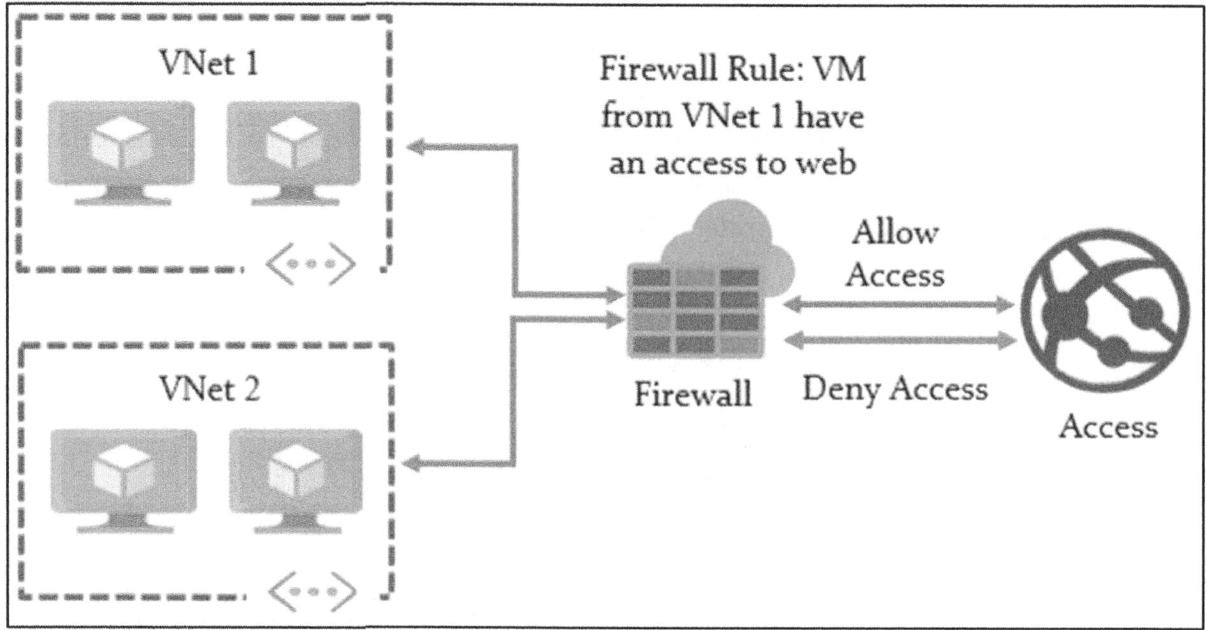

Figure 8-04: Network Configuration with Azure Firewall

Distributed Denial of Service Attacks (DDoS)

History: In 2012, six banks of the USA were targeted with a series of Distributed Denial of Service (DDoS) attacks. These banks were located in a small town and other areas as well. The attack was created from a large number of hackers' servers with each creating a 60 Gb traffic load per second. In 2014, the security provider and content delivery network "Cloud Flare" was targeted with DDoS attacks. The attack was created with a 400 Gb traffic load per second. In 2018, a famous development platform "GitHub" was targeted by DDoS attack with 1.35 Tb of traffic load per second. All these DDoS made the companies suffer a massive disaster. Companies lost business and users' trust due to this attack. In addition to that, the companies also needed to invest billions of dollar to remake the networks.

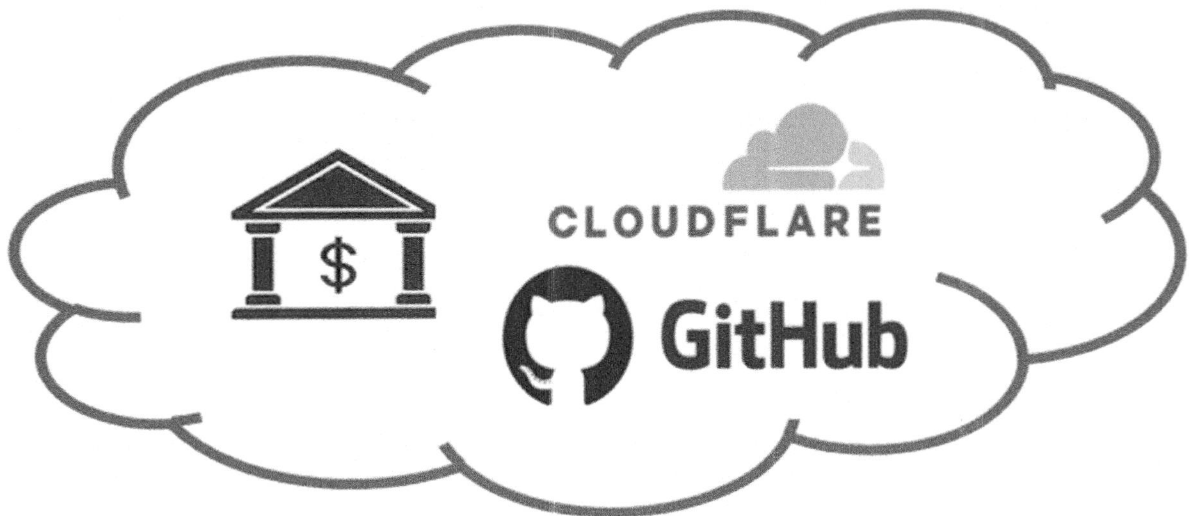

Figure 8-05: Companies Affected by DDoS Attack

DDoS Scenario

Distributed Denial of Service (DDoS) is the most common attack on services attached to the internet. Let's suppose, there is a website running on a server as shown in Figure 8-06. This server has the ability to serve a limited number of user requests. The number of users in the given network is 50,000 and the web server serves at most 5,000 requests every second. When all the users send the request at the same time, the webserver would not be able to serve the demands of the user request. In the end, the webserver will suddenly stop working due to the large number of user requests. This is because of the Denial-of-Service (DoS) attack. If the same number of requests was received by the webserver from many different sources and computers, the webservers would suddenly stop working due to the multiple simultaneous requests. This type of attack on the service is called a Distributed-Denial-of-Service (DDoS) attack.

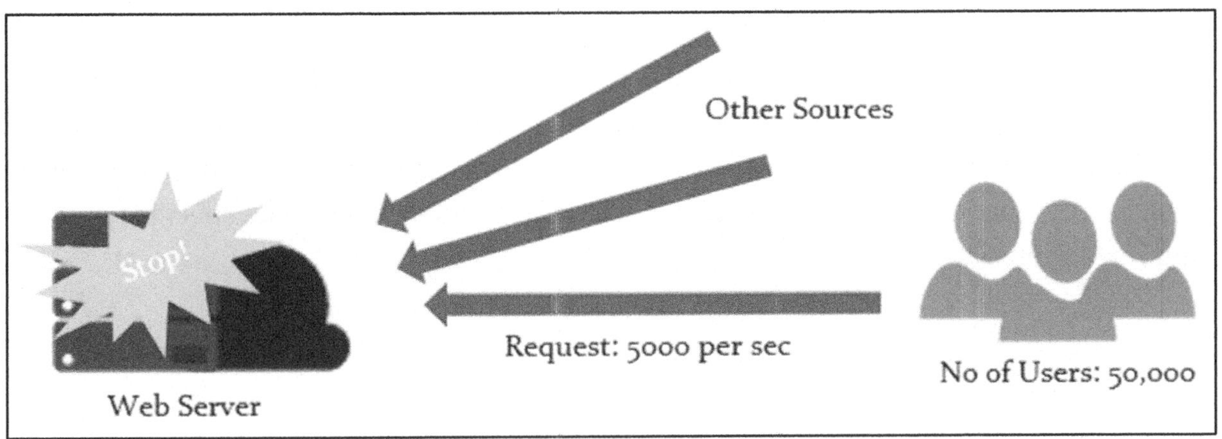

Figure 8-06: DDoS Attack

DDoS Protection Service

- **Target a Website:** A lot of servers target the same website or computer in order to stop its working. For example, GitHub was a target with 127 Mb requests every second
- **Azure Protection Service:** Microsoft Azure has protection service against DDoS attacks. This service has a different level of protection services depending upon the user needs of the application. Azure protection service detects DDoS attacks and work against it
- **No Halt:** Azure Protection service would not interrupt the routine process of other services on the website due to Azure global presents

Azure Firewall controls which traffic comes inside and goes outside the network based on a set of rules.

The DDoS attack is an attack of a huge amount of traffic from many different sources to a single website and server. Azure protection service protects from this type of attack globally with no downtime.

Network Security Groups

The security group provides a secure management environment for the network. Network Security Group (NSG) is required in the configuration of a Virtual Network (VNet) where different Virtual Machines (VMs) within the subnet are connected with each other.

- **Resource Firewall:** NSG has a private resource firewall that allows the connection of VNet, subnet or another network interface with VM
- **Rules:** NSG has a set of security rules that enable some special VMs to allow or not allow the inbound and outbound traffic load from other resources

Figure 8-07 illustrates the concept of the Network Security Group (NSG) in the network. There is a virtual machine present in the VNet. The network can be behind Azure firewalls for the protection of everything (i.e., complex information, sensitive data, resources or devices) present on the network. A virtual machine has its own NSG that specifies the rules and regulations for the machine.

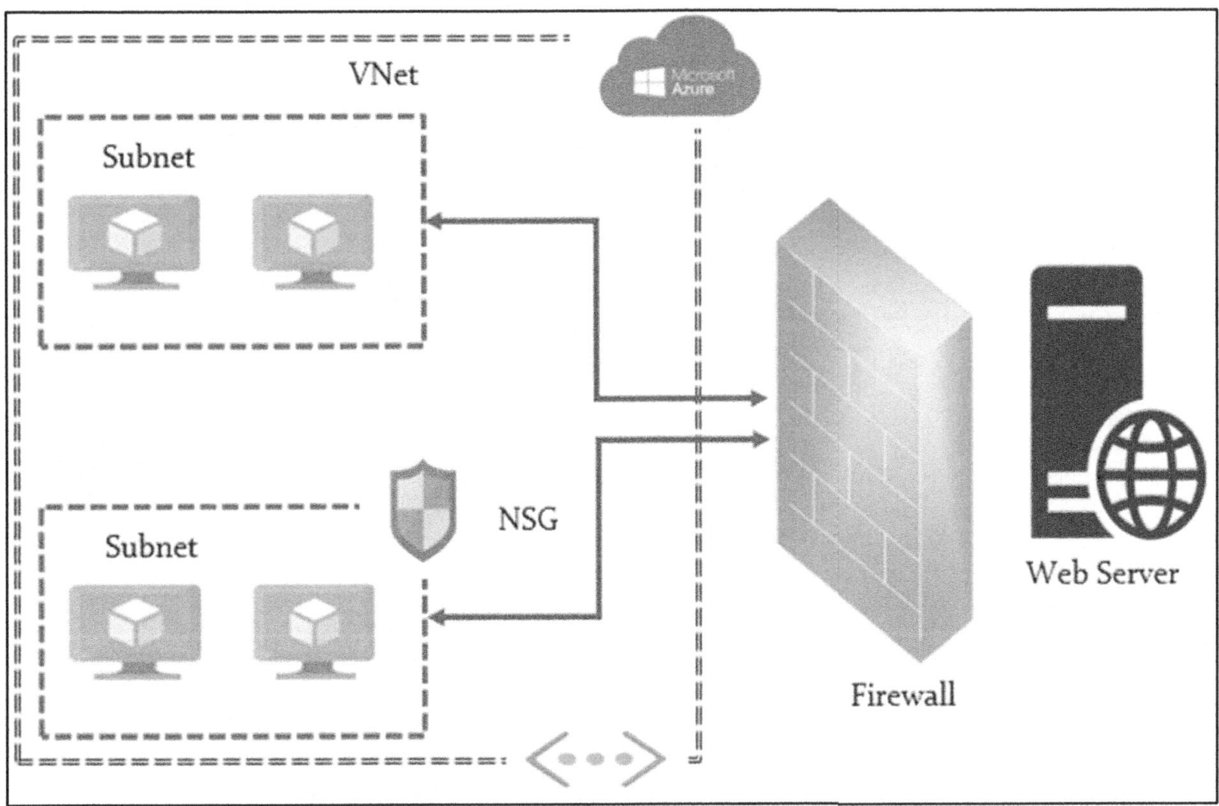

Figure 8-07: Network Configuration with NSG

Application Security Group

Network Security Group (NSG) protects the traffic flow from and to the specific virtual machine or subnet in the network. Application Security Group (ASG) protects the application running on that particular VM or subnet in the network. ASG provides the security of application and NSG provides the security of traffic flow.

- **Shielding Application Infrastructure**: ASG is responsible for providing security to the application (website or Azure resources) running on a particular VM in the network
- **Natural Integration:** With ASG, network performance is optimized with multiple levels of security rule for application and traffic flow. VMs from a different subnet combine into NSG based on the application running on those VMs.

Figure 8-08 shows a network configuration with both NSG and ASG.

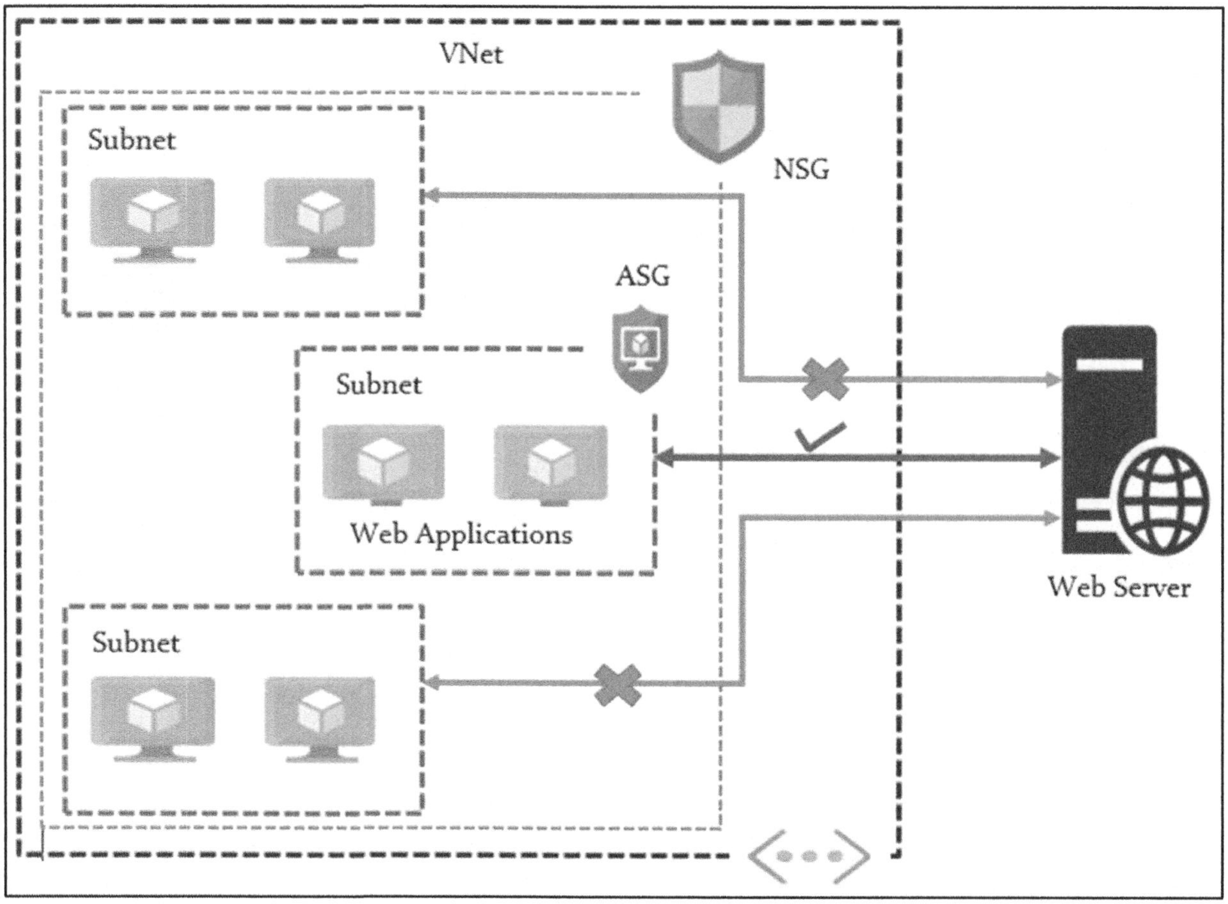

Figure 8-08: Network with ASG and NSG

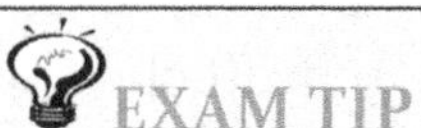

Network Security Group (NSG) is required in the configuration of a virtual network where different virtual machines within the subnet are connected with each other. NSG uses Access Control List (ACL) rules to allow or deny the access of network traffic to subnet or VM.

Application Security Group (ASG) protects the application running on that particular VM or subnet in the network.

Azure Security Center

Azure Security Center allows users to monitor the security features for Azure resources and on-premises as well. The security of each part of cloud infrastructure is a big challenge to handle. Azure Security has itself a portal within the Azure portal known as Azure Security Center. Azure Security Center indicates a threat alert that Azure detects and finds a way to protect its users from. Azure Security center works in a hybrid cloud infrastructure as well.

The security center can monitor all the security posture of on-premises data and Azure data. All VMs on a network has a special agent that sends the data towards a security center. Azure can analyze this data to make sure that data is free from all threats.

Azure Security Center portal contains a summarized view of policy, compliance and subscription coverage, networking, and resource integrity hygiene as shown in Figure 8-09.

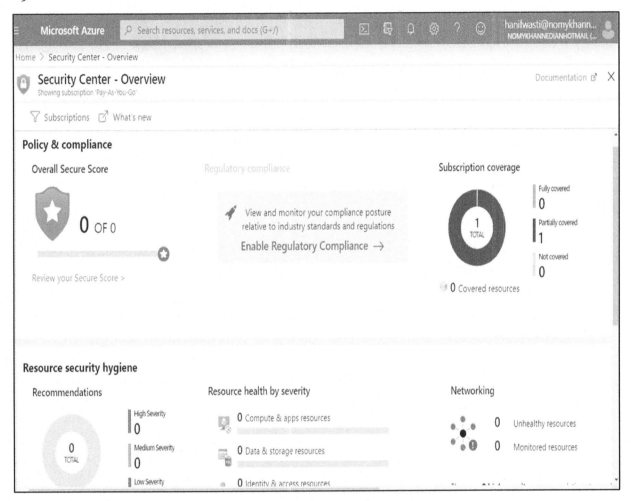

Figure 8-09: Security Center

Sections in Azure Security Center

Each section in the Azure Security Center portal shows an individual performance behavior of security features in graphical representation.

- **Policy, Compliance, and Subscription Coverage:** Policy, compliance, and subscription coverage are monitored by Azure. There is a secure score that represents the implementation of the Azure resource as securely as possible

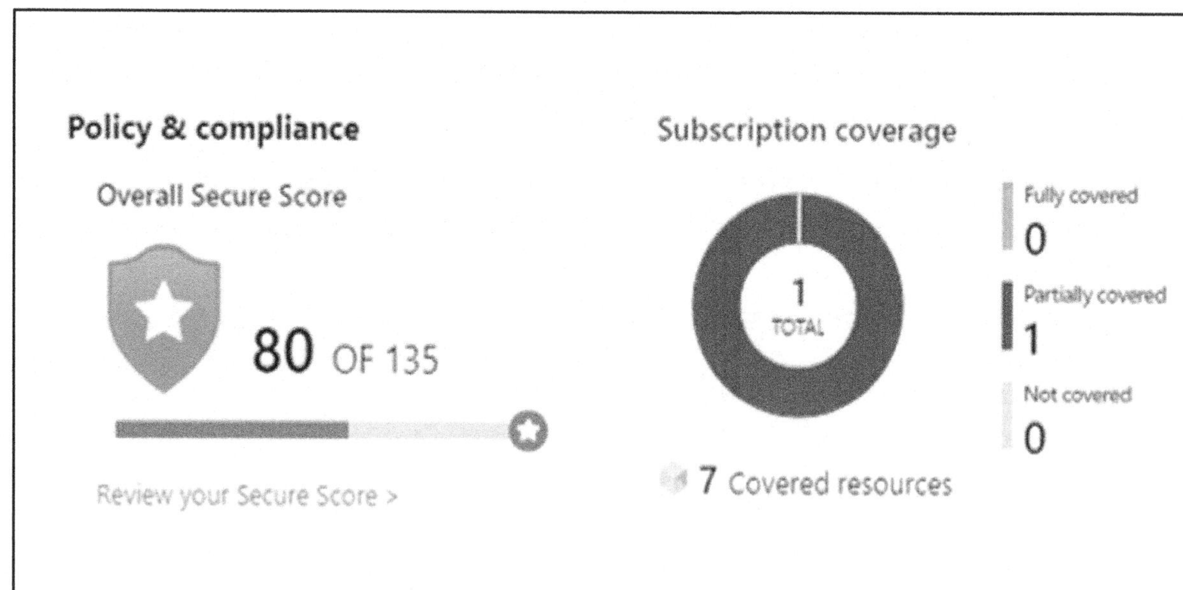

Figure 8-09(a)

- **Integrate with Other Cloud Providers:** With this, you can get security information from multiple cloud providers like AWS and GCP directly into Azure Security Center
- **Alerts for Resources Security:** If any of the VM is not updated, the security center quickly updates the VM, stores encrypted data that have an IP address, and traffic loads for processing

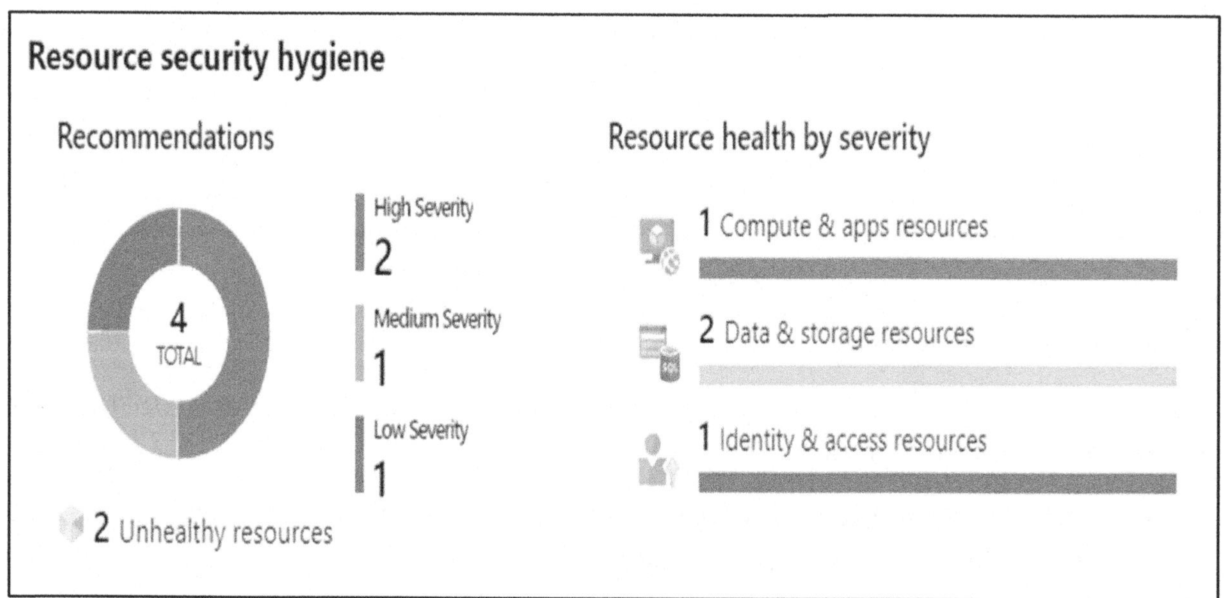

Figure 8-09(b)

- **Networking:** The configuration of secure resources in the network within Azure is successfully represented in the networking block of the security center

Networking

0 Unhealthy resources

3 Monitored resources

There are **0 high severity** recommendations to resolve.

Secure your network resources

Figure 8-09(c)

How to use the Security Center?

To take advantage of Azure Security Center for the security of cloud infrastructure, Azure users need to follow these three-step process.

- **Define Policies:** User needs to define the security policies that Azure can use to monitor cloud infrastructure. Security policies are a set of rules (such as Access Control List) that Azure uses to evaluate the valid configuration of service
- **Resource Protection:** Users need to protect resources and security centers that can help user protect the resources against a threat
- **Response:** In case of any security incident, the security center can raise the alerts. Users can investigate the traffic load within Azure implementation after the security alert

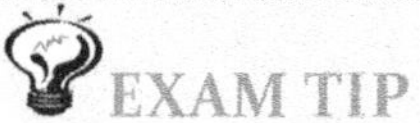

Azure Security Center is a portal within the Azure portal that monitors the resource security hygiene for Azure VMs resources. It contains a security alert timeline that defines the policy for efficient protection response in case of any incident.

Key Vault

As most of the cloud users need numbers of IDs and passwords as per their usage, it is very difficult to remember the entire list of passwords. One option is that users may share their password with different people for which users need to rely on them. However, with this, there is a problem that arises; how many people remember multiple passwords and secrets for different users? As the number of secret increases, this approach fails to protect the user's key from hackers.

To hide the key password and other information, Microsoft gives you a service known as Azure Key Vault. It is the best option for key storage. With Azure Key Vault, you can share your secrets with others without revealing the actual secrets. Azure Key Vault is present in the storage account of VMs. Storage account store keys in disk-encrypted form. Azure Key Vault allows users to store their key passwords in an encrypted form that nobody else can view. This key protection is defined by some set of rules and should follow the access policy criteria. On the application level, the app developer needs such type of protection based on their information that no one can expose.

Figure 8-10 shows the application of the Azure Key Vault. There is a database in a network. The data in the network is successfully used for internal services such as the application. For example, a user wants to share the access of the network to other trusted outsiders. However, outsiders need ID and password for accessing the application. In a way, password is a place in Azure Key Vault that efficiently allows an outsider to access individual applications easily. The application identifies itself using the Azure Key Vault to grant access to the database. This way, the password is never sent itself to others.

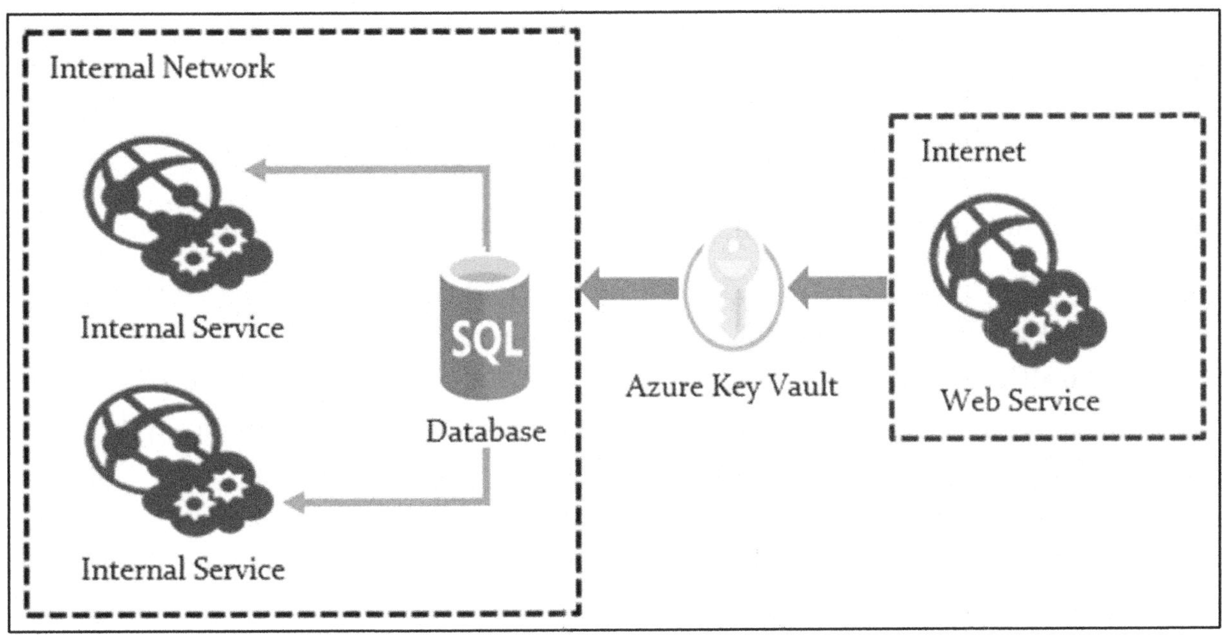

Figure 8-10: Azure Key Vault

Features of Key Vault

Azure Key Vault has a number of key features, some of which are:

- **Secure Hardware:** Azure Key Vault has hardware and software protection. Azure Key Vault uses Hardware Security Module (HSM) to store a password and a secret that no one else can see
- **Application Isolation:** Using Azure Key Vault, applications cannot pass on secrets. Access to the application can be removed easily without having to change the password
- **Global Scaling:** Azure Key Vault can be scaled globally as other managed Azure services result in cryptographic high performance

EXAM TIP

Azure Key Vault is a secure way to share secrets and passwords to applications and other resources outside the organization using a defined access policy. It can be scaled globally and not even Microsoft can reveal the actual secret.

Azure Information Protection

When you store your data on the company's server, how can you know who can access that data? Azure Information Protection (AIP) provides a way of protected sharing of resources. Azure Information Protection enables the sharing of files, documents and sensitive

information inside and outside Azure while maintaining full control over that data. Microsoft 365 takes full advantage of Azure Information Protection service. It makes a lot of new enhancement with AIP such as support PDF document protection, Outlook relicensing, and message protection for the shared mailbox.

With Azure Information Protection, the data can be secure in the following ways:

- **Data Configuration:** An organization can establish data and protection parameters according to AIP services for security purposes
- **Classification of Data**: Organization can make more secure data by classifying it according to sensitivity and priority. This can be done automatically by Azure Information Protection services or manually by users themselves
- **Track Activities:** With AIP, an organization has full control over data activities. If there is some irregular activity that occurs, an organization may cancel the access to that data
- **Share Data with others:** An organization has full control over data sharing. In addition, an organization can manage and carefully supervise who can edit, view, print and forward the data
- **Integration:** Control, protecting and classifying are integrated with applications like Microsoft Office and other applications that give the security of data and document with a click

An application of Azure Information Protection (AIP) is discussed in the scenario as shown in figure 8-11. There are two users, User 1 and User 2. User 1 wants to send an email with a sensitive document attachment to User 2 within Azure. The security of a document can be guaranteed by using Azure Information Protection services. User 1 uses a secure label that is defined in Azure to tag the document and create a link to information protection. The email will then be securely received by User 2. If User 2 is a valid user, then the document will open.

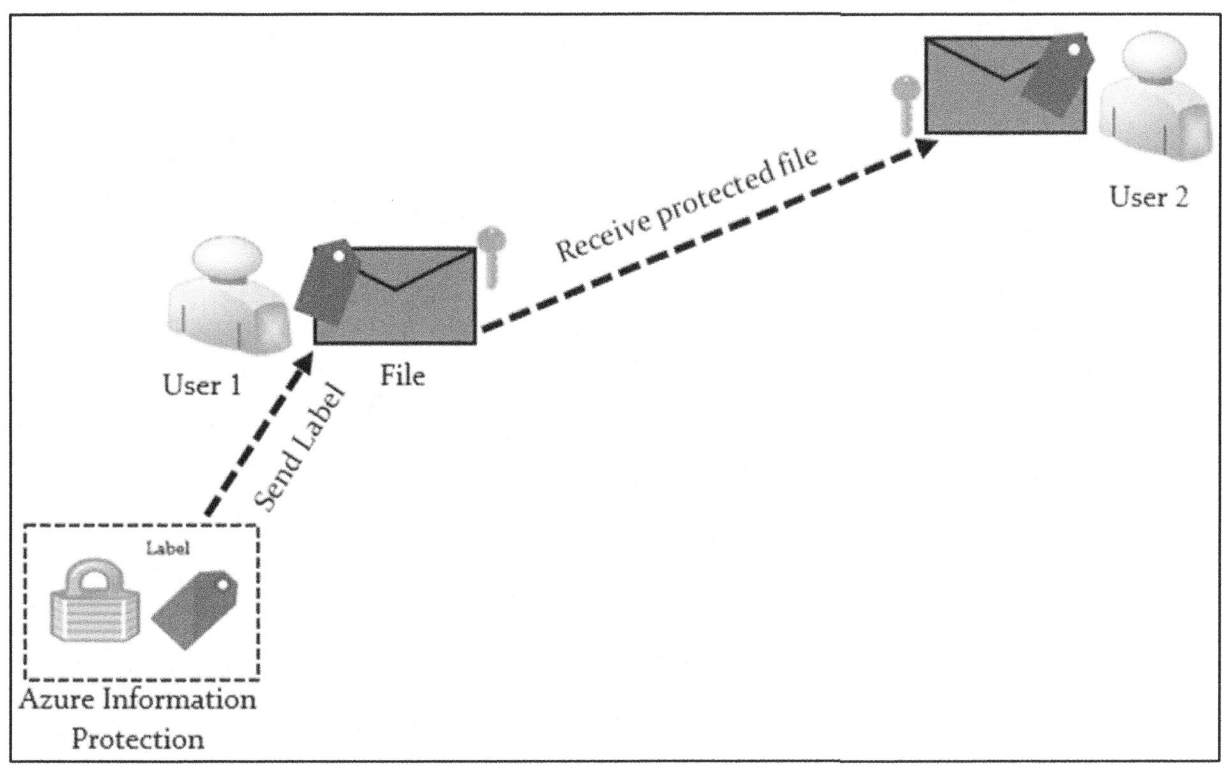

Figure 8-11: Azure Information Protection

Advanced Threat Protection (ATP)

Advanced Threat Protection (ATP) is the advanced and secure option for providing the security of the links as compared to the standard one. It gives an extra layer of security and management of the users in order to make a more secure and protected system.

Are Users Unreliable?

The need for Advanced Threat Protection is due to the users, whether they are customers or employees. If users have access to the organization's server, file or document, then they might be a weak link to attackers or hackers. For example, an organization has continuously received threats from the user side as shown in figure 8-12. The Business Corporation has some sensitive data that make the attackers target that corporation. One way to get sensitive data is through users. Users often have the weakest link within the organization and attackers usually take this as their target point. Attackers continuously pin one specific user to give them access to a corporation and hack the sensitive data.

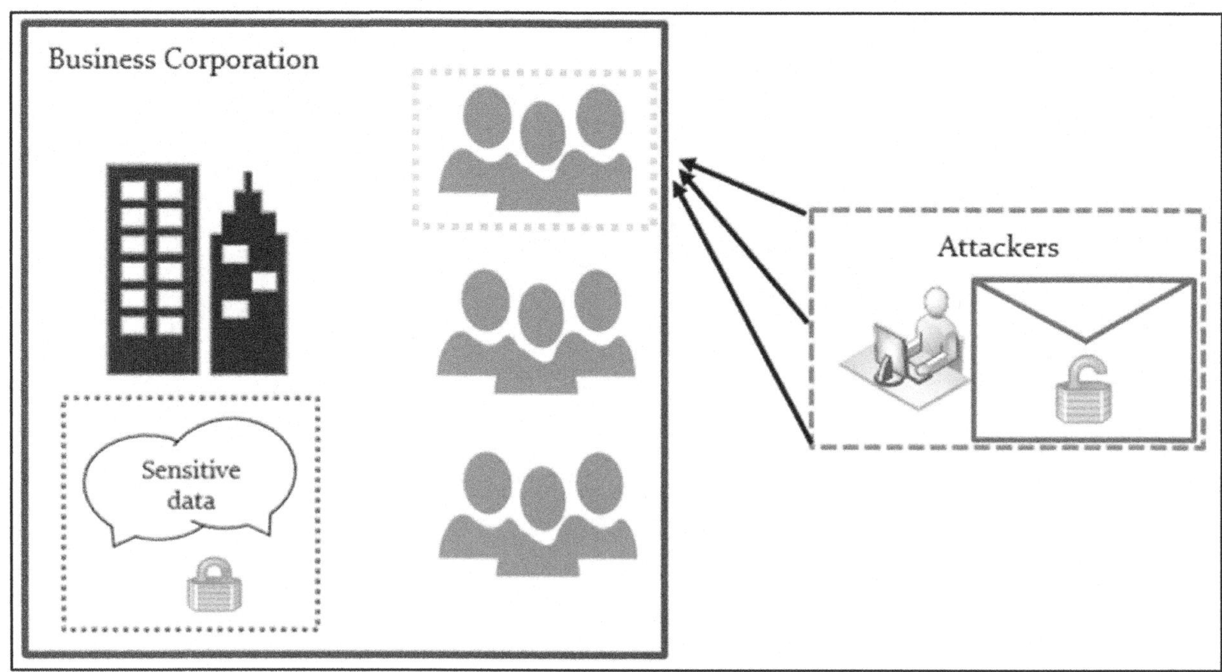

Figure 8-12: Attacker's target in the network

Features of Advanced Threat Protection (ATP)

Azure Advanced Threat Protection (ATP) has a number of features that provide the safety of links and analyze the security threats.

- **Monitor Users:** Azure ATP helps to monitors users in an on-premises environment and their behavior. Azure ATP analyzes user's activity and information across the network including permission and membership across each user
- **Supervised User's Behavior:** Azure ATP continuously focuses on user's activities. If some irregular activity occurs, ATP will be logged as a doubtful activity
- **Propose Changes:** ATP also offers some suggestions regarding security policy to provide the best security practices. Profiling and analyzing users will help to reduce the risk against threats both on-premises and in the cloud. ATP makes changes based on the required security policy

Cyber-Attack Kill-Chain

The cyber-attack kill-chain is a chain of phases that define how the attack is prepared and execute. This deployed model allows detecting and reacting upon the attack. The model reveals seven stages according to which reaction and detection on cyber-attack are available.

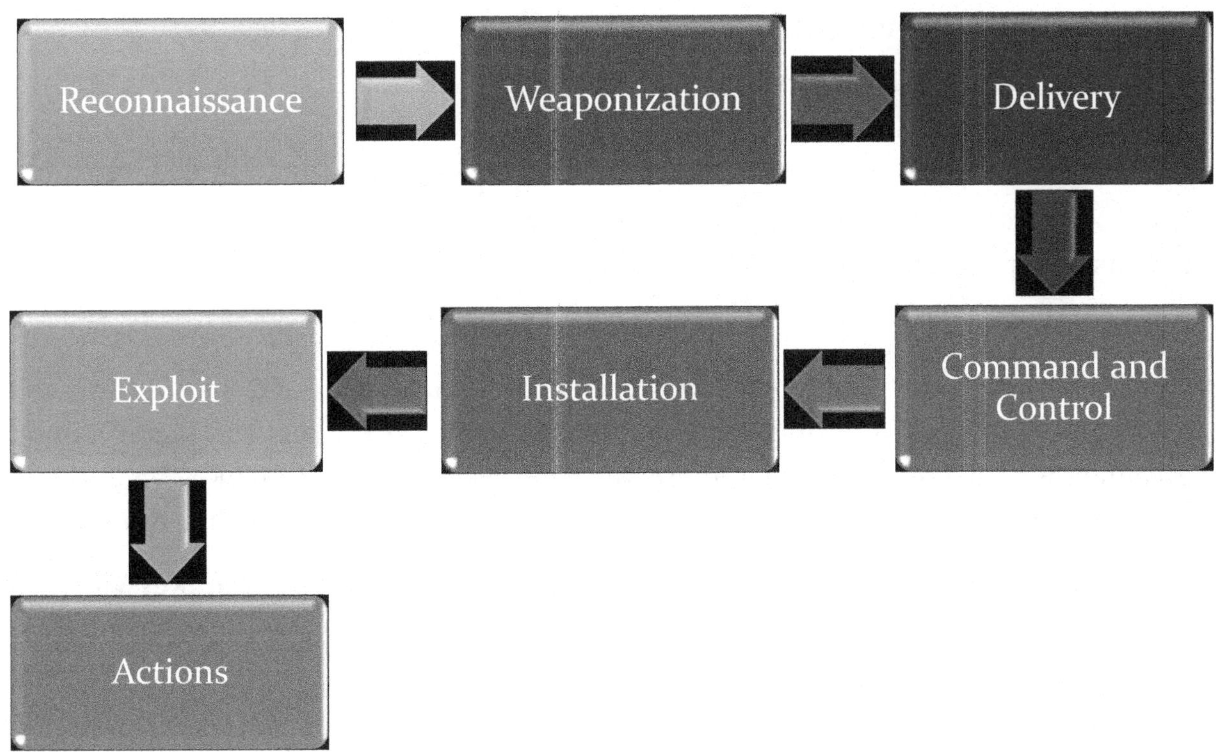

Figure 8-13: Cyber-Attack Kill-Chain

Azure Advanced Threat Protection is responsible for monitoring any aspect of cyber-attack kill-chain. Here, we will discuss the cyber-attack kill chain as per Azure.

- **Reconnaissance:** If the user is carrying out reconnaissance, it means that the user is searching the device IP address and finding the other's information to check out the system. ATP will raise the alert to protect the system from any inappropriate incident
- **Brute Force:** Identifying attempts to compromise user's credentials using brute force is the process of trying various combinations of user names and passwords
- **Increasing Privileges:** Any attempt to gain access to a user with access to more resources and areas within the network

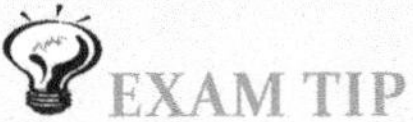
EXAM TIP

Azure Information Protection (AIP) enables the secure sharing of the file, document and sensitive data inside and outside an organization using protection labels and tags. Azure users have full control of who can edit, view, print the information.

Azure Advanced Threat Protection (ATP) provides advanced-level security to prevent the network from threats. It monitors user behavior, creates a baseline and immediately reports in case of any anomalies.

Lab 8-01: Azure Key Vault

Scenario

An organization needs to share a secret with a third party for business enhancement. To ensure secure internet traffic, how can the organization build an access policy for others to share its secret without revealing the encryption and security rules?

Solution

Azure Key Vault is considered to be a very useful tool for managing and sharing the secret. In the given situation, the organization can allow others to access the secret without revealing the actual secret by using Azure Key Vault. For this, first Azure Key Vault should be created, then a secret is built in the given Key Vault that can be accessible by others.

1. Log in to the Microsoft Azure portal and go to the search bar and type "Key Vaults" in the given space.

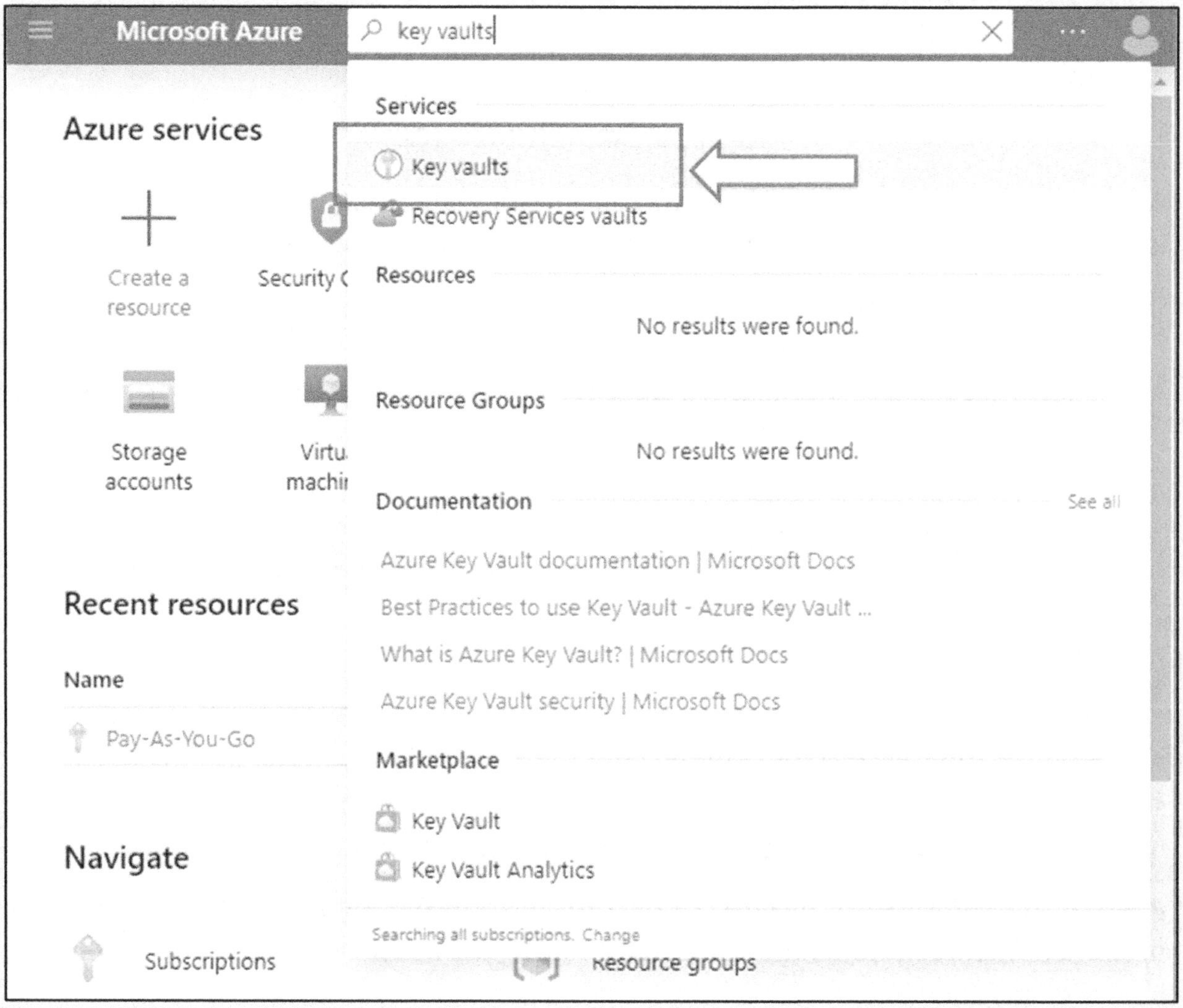

2. When the “Key Vaults” tab appears, click on “+ Add” to create a Key Vault.

Microsoft Azure
Search resources, services, and docs (G+/)
Home > Key vaults
Key vaults
nomykhannedianhotmail (Default Directory)
+ Add
Refresh
Assign tags
Subscriptions: Pay-As-You-Go
Filter by name...
All resource gr...
All locations
All tags
No grou...
0 items
Name ↑↓
Type ↑↓
Resource group ↑↓
Location ↑↓

3. Click on “Create new” to enter the resource group.

Microsoft Azure
Search resources, services, and docs (G+/)

Home > Key vaults > Create key vault

Create key vault

Basics Access policy Networking Tags Review + create

Azure Key Vault is a cloud service used to manage keys, secrets, and certificates. Key Vault eliminates the need for developers to store security information in their code. It allows you to centralize the storage of your application secrets which greatly reduces the chances that secrets may be leaked. Key Vault also allows you to securely store secrets and keys backed by Hardware Security Modules or HSMs. The HSMs used are Federal Information Processing Standards (FIPS) 140-2 Level 2 validated. In addition, key vault provides logs of all access and usage attempts of your secrets so you have a complete audit trail for compliance. Learn more

Project details

Select the subscription to manage deployed resources and costs. Use resource groups like folders to organize and manage all your resources.

Subscription * Pay-As-You-Go

Resource group * Select existing...

Create new

Instance details

Key vault name * Enter the name

Region * North Central US

Review + create < Previous Next : Access policy >

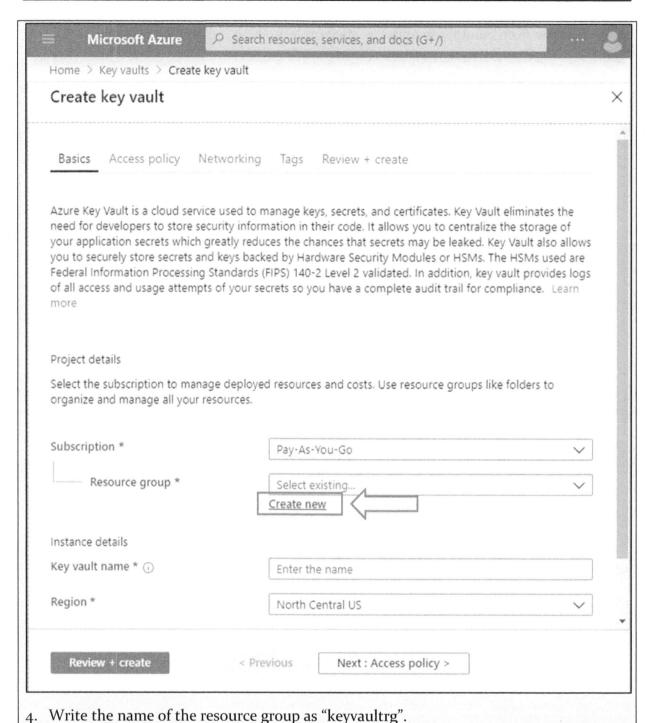

4. Write the name of the resource group as “keyvaultrg”.
5. Then click on “OK”.

Microsoft Azure
Search resources, services, and docs (G+/)
Home > Key vaults > Create key vault
Create key vault
Subscription *
Pay-As-You-Go
Resource group *
(New) keyvaultrg
Create new
A resource group is a container that holds related resources for an Azure solution.
Name *
keyvaultrg
OK
Review + create
< Previous
Next : Access policy >

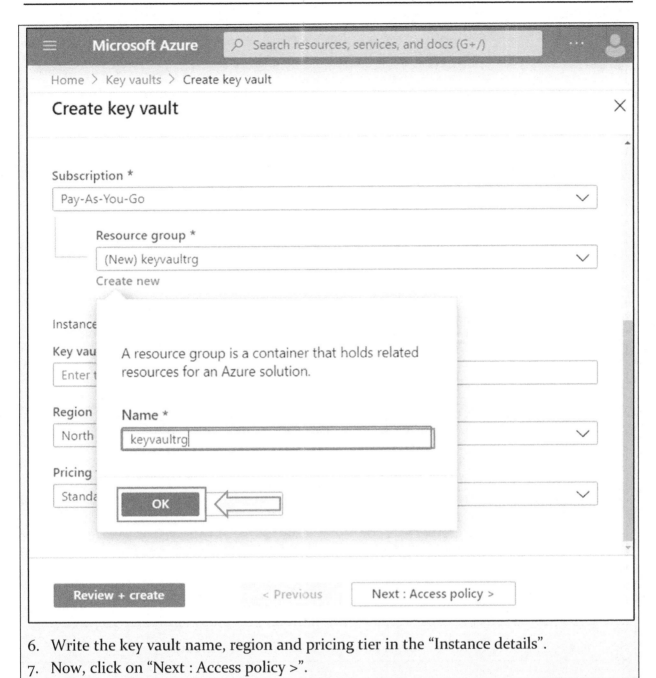

6. Write the key vault name, region and pricing tier in the "Instance details".
7. Now, click on "Next : Access policy >".

Microsoft Azure
Search resources, services, and docs (G+/)

Home > Key vaults > Create key vault

Create key vault

Subscription *
Pay-As-You-Go

Resource group *
(New) keyvaultrg
Create new

Instance details

Key vault name *
IPSkeyvault1

Region *
Australia Southeast

Pricing tier *
Standard

Review + create
< Previous
Next : Access policy >

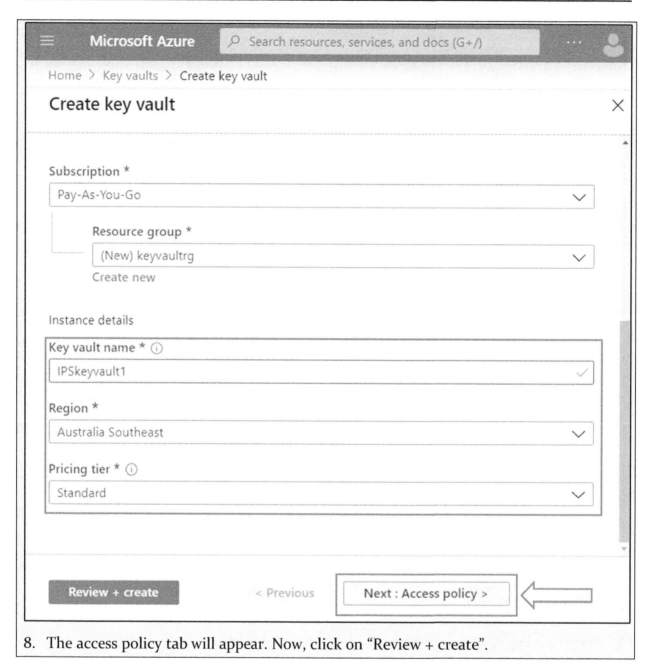

8. The access policy tab will appear. Now, click on "Review + create".

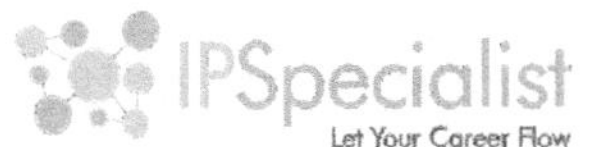

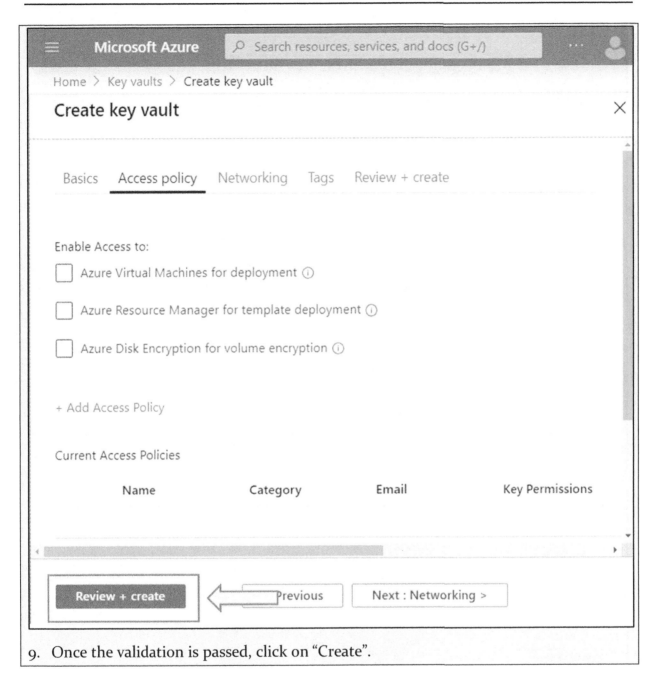

9. Once the validation is passed, click on "Create".

Microsoft Azure

Search resources, services, and docs (G+/)

Home > Key vaults > Create key vault

Create key vault

Validation passed

Basics Access policy Networking Tags Review + create

Basics

Subscription	Pay-As-You-Go
Resource group	keyvaultrg
Key vault name	IPSkeyvault1
Region	Australia Southeast
Pricing tier	Standard
Enable soft-delete	Disabled
Enable purge protection	Disabled

Access policy

Azure Virtual Machines for deployment	Disabled
Azure Resource Manager for template deployment	Disabled
Azure Disk Encryption for volume encryption	Disabled
Azure Disk Encryption for volume	Disabled

Create < Previous Next > Download a template for automation

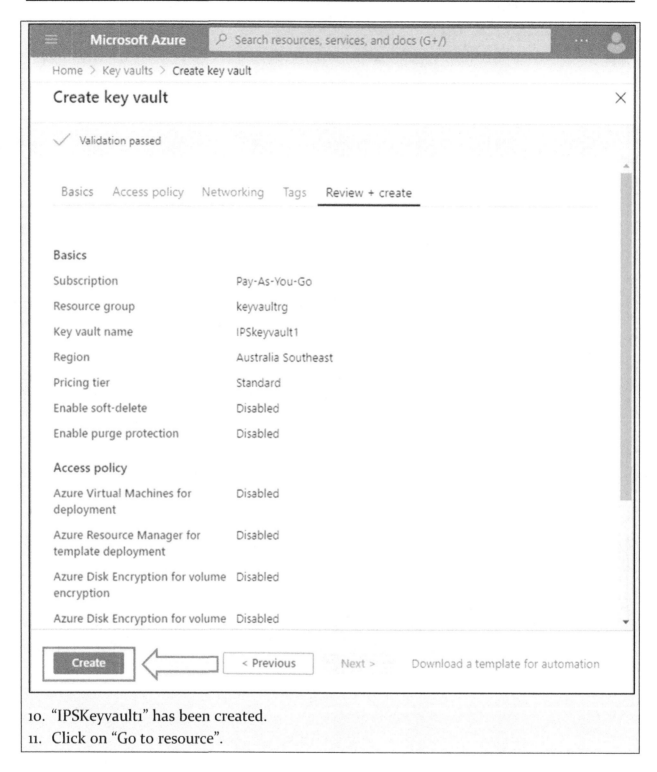

10. "IPSKeyvault1" has been created.
11. Click on "Go to resource".

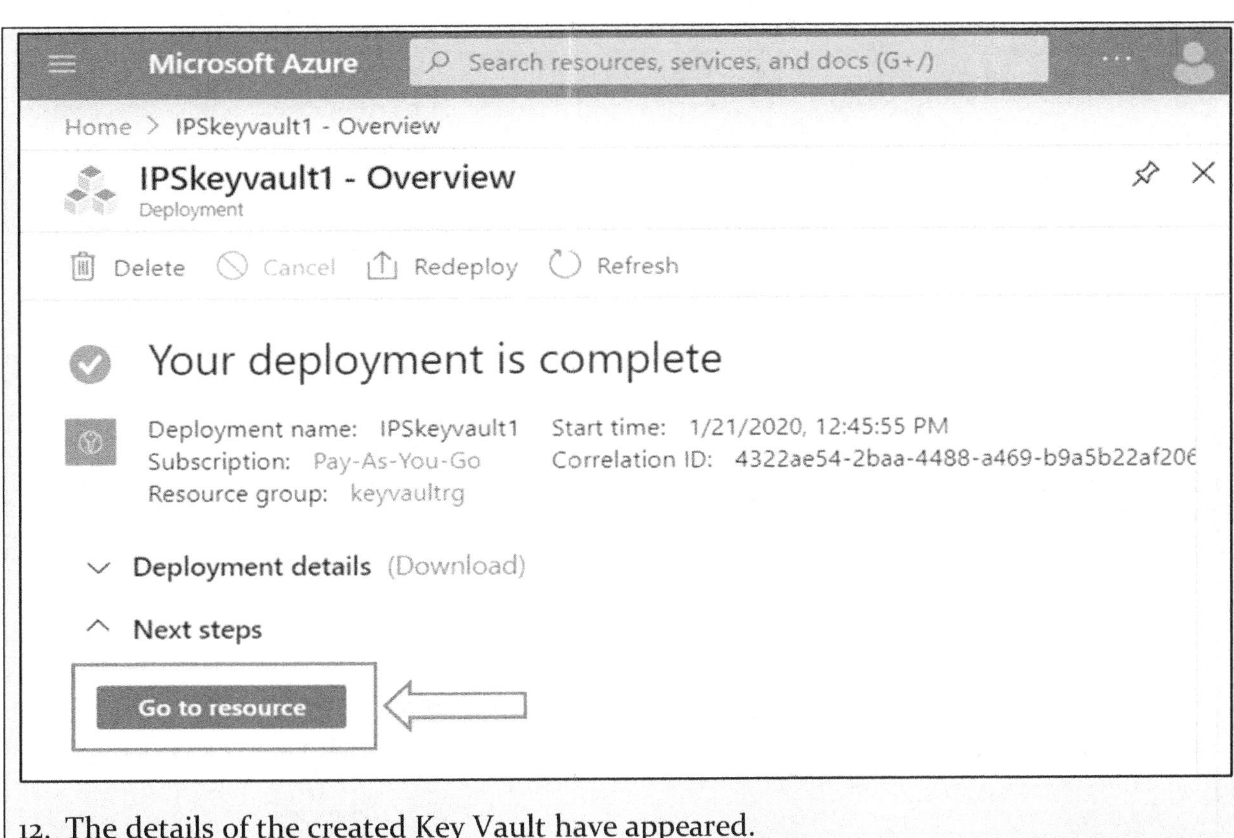

12. The details of the created Key Vault have appeared.

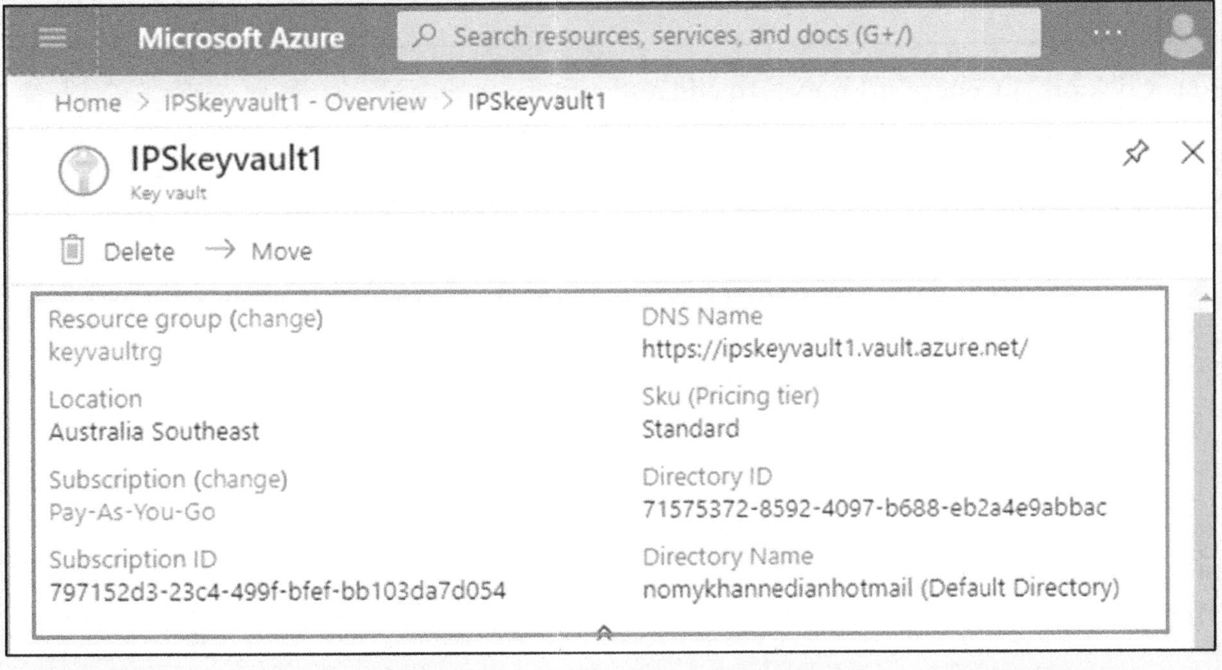

13. To add a secret, click on “Secret” from the left side of the IPSkeyvault1 tab.

Microsoft Azure
Search resources, services, and docs (G+/)
Home > IPSkeyvault1 - Overview > IPSkeyvault1
IPSkeyvault1
Key vault
Search (Ctrl+/)
Delete
Move
Overview
Activity log
Access control (IAM)
Tags
Diagnose and solve problems
Events (preview)
Settings
Keys
Secrets
Certificates
Resource group (change)
keyvaultrg
Location
Australia Southeast
Subscription (change)
Pay-As-You-Go
Subscription ID
797152d3-23c4-499f-bfef-bb103da7d054
DNS Name
https://ipskeyvault1
Sku (Pricing tier)
Standard
Directory ID
71575372-8592-40
Directory Name
nomykhannedianhc
Monitoring
Show data for last:
6 hours
12 hours
1 day
7 days
30 days
Click for additional metrics.

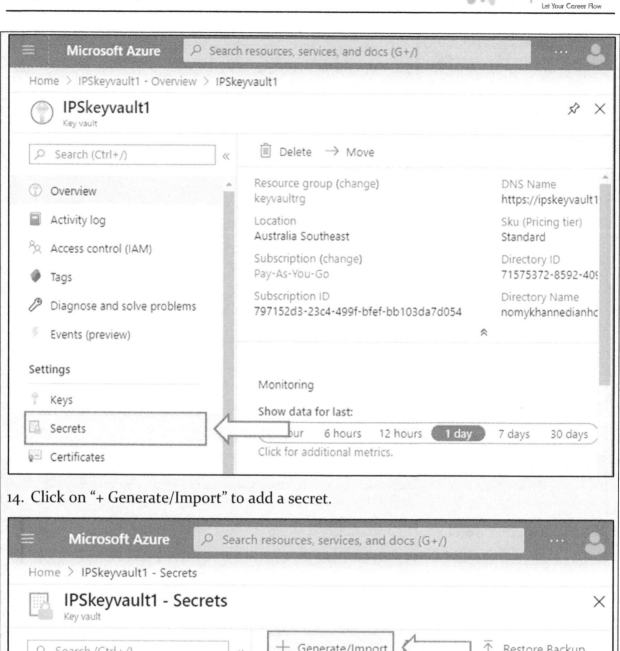

14. Click on "+ Generate/Import" to add a secret.

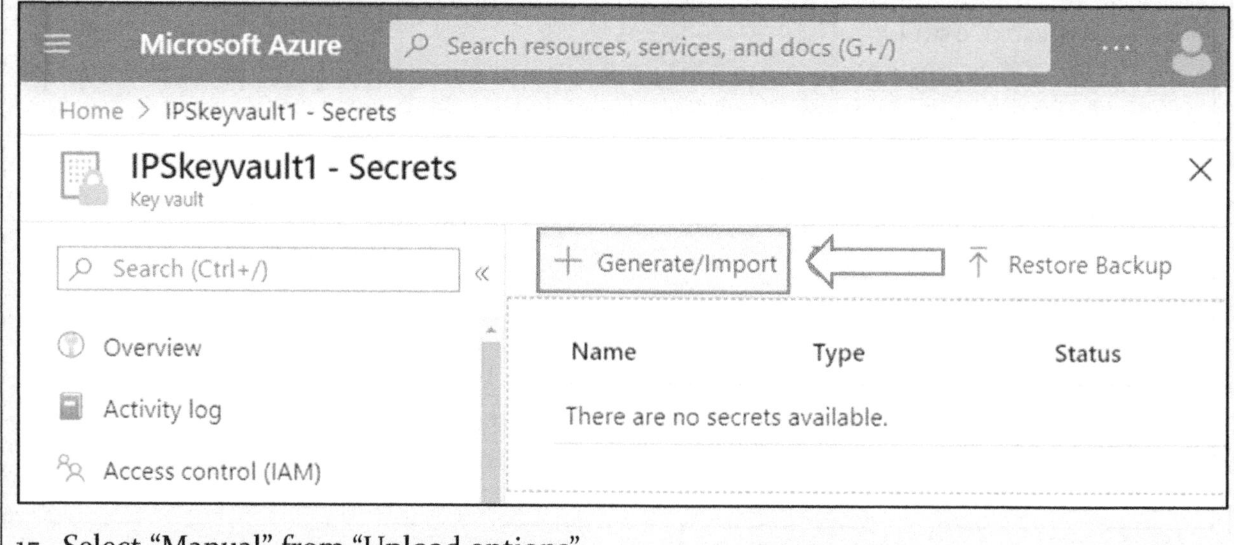

15. Select "Manual" from "Upload options".
16. Write the name and value of the secret.
17. Click on "Create".

Microsoft Azure

Home > IPSkeyvault1 - Secrets > Create a secret

Create a secret

Upload options

Manual

Name *

IPSsecret

Value *

••

Content type (optional)

Set activation date?

Create

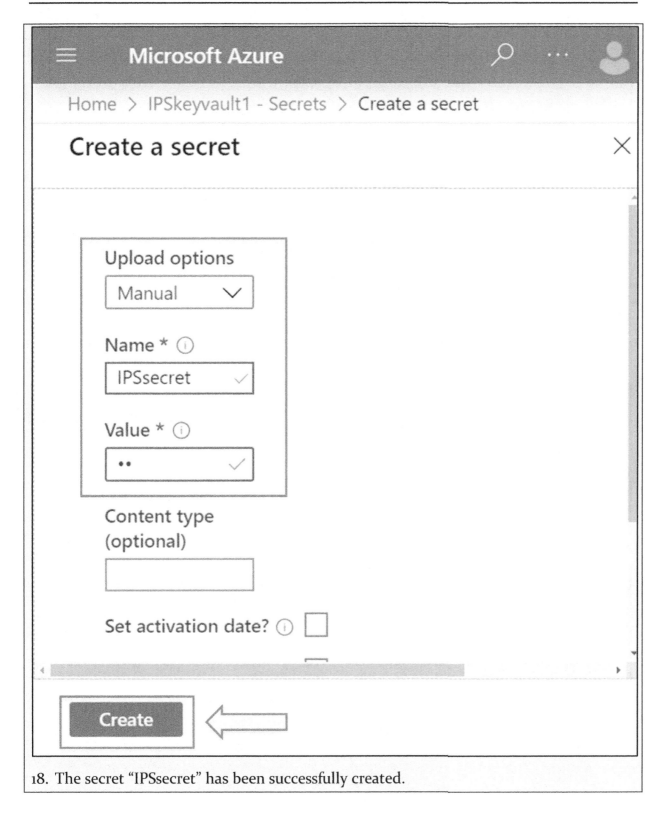

18. The secret "IPSsecret" has been successfully created.

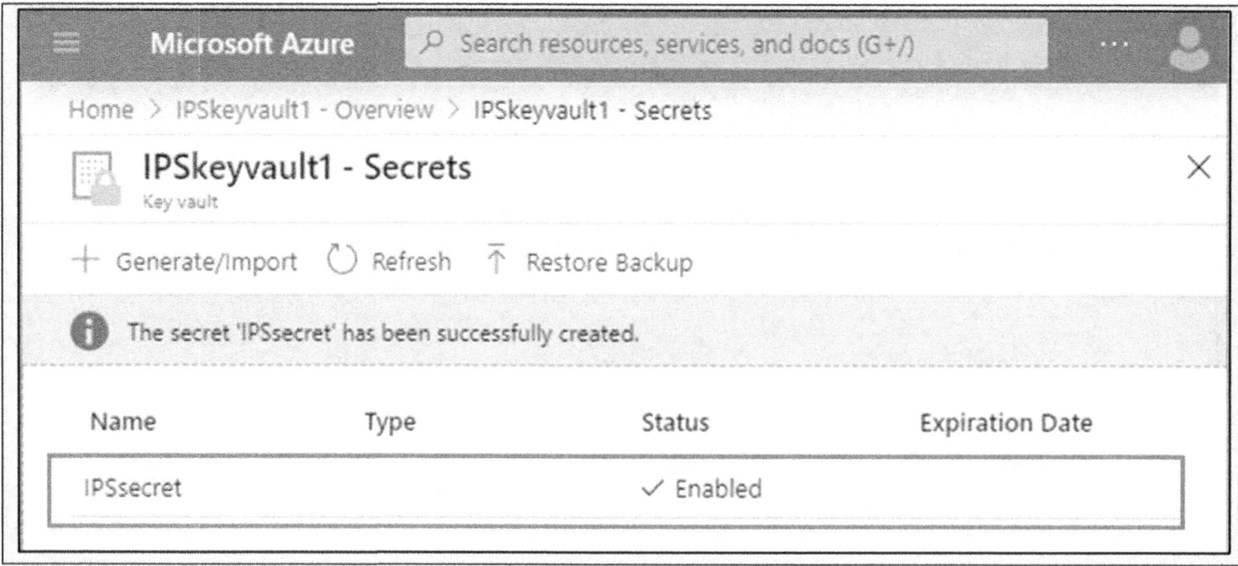

MindMap

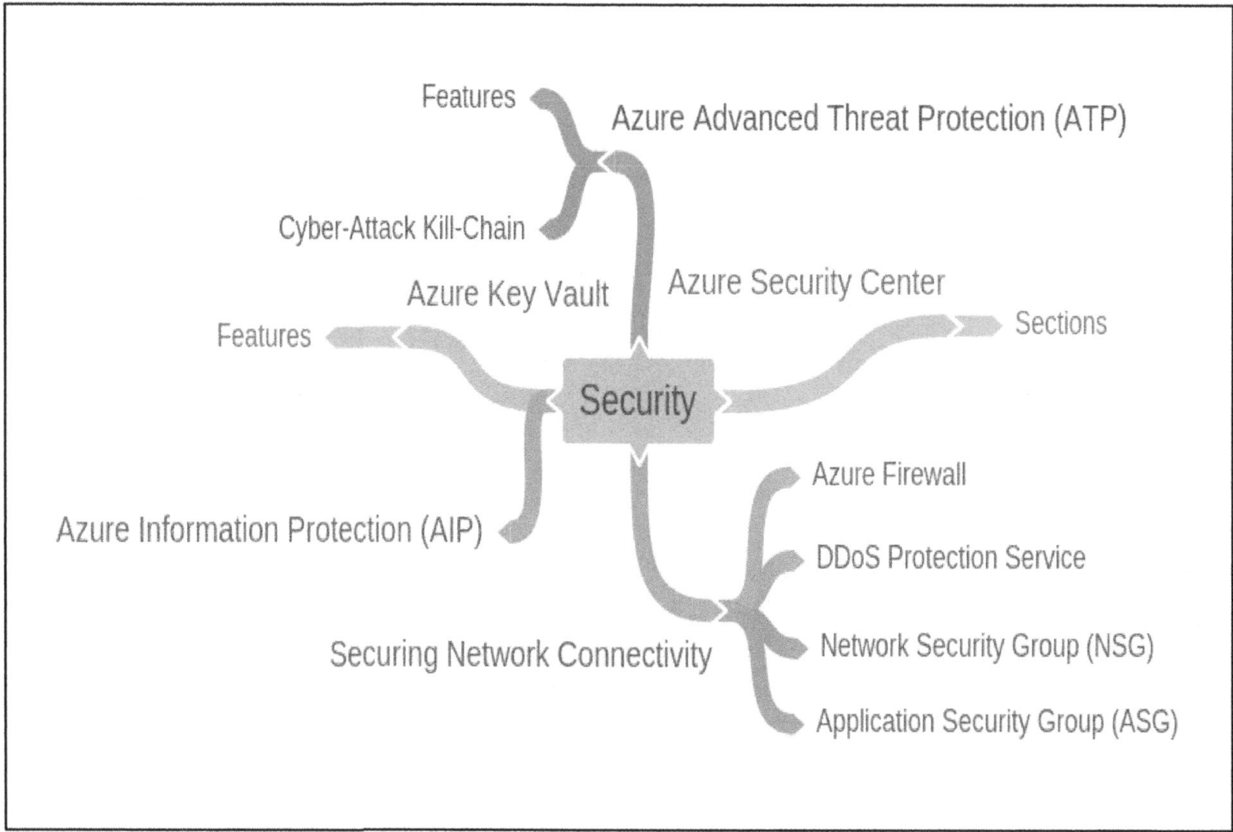

Figure 8-14: MindMap

Practice Questions

1. What is the most crucial part of Microsoft Azure in the configuration of a network?

A. Security

B. Networking

C. Authentication and Authorization

D. Computation

2. How many ways of securing network connectivity can be possible in Microsoft Azure?

A. Only one

B. Four

C. One hundred

D. Infinite

3. What is the purpose of the Azure Firewall?

A. Protect sensitive information

B. Help monitor user's behavior in on-premises and cloud environment

C. Set of rules to provide the security of network resources

D. All of the above

4. Which of the following Azure service may use secure hardware to make the password and secret secure?

A. Azure Information Protection

B. Network Security Group

C. Advanced Threat Protection

D. Azure Key Vault

5. There is a web server that receives a consecutive number of requests from different sources at the same time and these continuous requests make the server stop working abruptly. What is this type of attack called?

A. Cross-site Scripting (XSS) Attack

B. Password Attack

C. Distributed Denial-of-Service (DDoS) Attack

D. Malware Attack

6. How is Network Security Group different from the Application Security Group?

A. NSG defines traffic policies and ASG defines network security based on application policies

B. NSG is responsible for tracking the attacks whereas ASG configures attacks

C. ASG is limited to two VMs whereas NSG has unlimited resources

D. None of the above

7. Which of the following service uses the Access Control List (ACL) to allow or deny the access of network traffic to subnet or VM?

A. Azure Key Vault

B. Azure Firewall

C. Network Security Group

D. Azure Information Protection

8. Which of the following is responsible for the protection of subnets and VMs?

A. Azure Privacy Services

B. Secure Network Connections

C. Azure Key Vault

D. Azure Active Directory

9. What is the function of the Azure Key Vault?

A. Provide secure access to secrets

B. Ensure the network connectivity

C. Allow sharing of user's credential

D. Prevent the use of resources

10. Which of the following service is helpful for sharing files and sensitive information inside or outside Azure?

A. Advanced Threat Protection

B. Azure Key Vault

C. Application Security Group

D. Azure Information Protection

11. Which Azure service can monitor user behavior?

A. Azure Firewall

B. Azure Security Center

C. Advanced Threat Protection

D. Azure Networking services

12. Which Azure Service can you use to share the secret with the third party without revealing the actual secret?

A. Azure DNS

B. Azure Key Vault

C. Azure Monitor

D. Azure ATP

13. Which of the following service has its own portal within the Azure portal?

A. Azure Security Center

B. Azure Key Vaults

C. Azure Active Directory

D. Azure SQL

14. In 2018, a popular developer platform "GitHub" was targeted by DDoS attack with ________________.

A. 60 Gb traffic per second

B. 400 Gb traffic per second

C. 1.23 Gb traffic per second

D. 1.35 Tb traffic per second

15. Which Azure service acts as a resource firewall?

A. Azure Monitor

B. Azure DNS

C. Network Security Group

D. Content Delivery Network

16. Which Azure service configures network security as a network extension of an application structure?

A. Network Security Group

B. Application Security Group

C. Azure Firewall

D. Advanced Threat Protection

17. Which of the following service gives the single unified view of security in hybrid cloud architecture?

A. Azure Active Directory

B. Storage Account

C. Azure Security Center

D. SQL Database

18. When data is stored in company servers and resources, both customers and employees are eligible to get that data and share it inside and outside the company. Which Service can you use to provide the protected sharing of data?

A. Azure Information Protection

B. Advanced Threat Protection

C. Azure App Services

D. None of the above

19. Why does Azure ATP need a security alert timeline?

A. It protects resources from threats

B. It enables attackers to get access to resources through users

C. It monitors the protection of sensitive data

D. All of the above

20. Which of the following allows us to limit the access of Key Vault to the users?

A. Networking Policy

B.	Access Policy
C.	Tags
D.	All of the above

Chapter 09: Privacy, Compliance, and Trust

Introduction

Every company has a need for privacy of its data. They want to trust that their data is stored quickly and privacy is looked after. In Azure, you have a service that performs the privacy, trust and compliance factor for your company. In this chapter, we will discuss Governance in Azure; what is its context, why it needs to be done with perfection, and which tools Azure provides you for governance. Azure Monitor has a collection of tools to detect, diagnose, visualize and analysis the response and integrate the data from Azure services' logs and metrics.

As we all know that down time is a serious problem in the world, with Azure Service Health, you can ensure the maximum uptime of your business. We will also discuss the compliance and privacy of your applications. In Azure, Microsoft has its own Trust Center, which they want you to read in order to get more trust.

Governance

We all know that most of the companies use the Azure platform for its agility to make it easier for the developers to create, manage, update and delete the resources as per requirement. However, sometimes unwanted access to the resource may cause unintended cost consequences. In order to overcome this, Azure provides a solution of resource access governance, which is the process of managing, monitoring and auditing the resource usage in order to meet the goals and requirements.

Consider you have developers and a system administrator who both have their own thoughts of upgrading the resource at its best. This may cause a mess and there is a lot of resources that maybe wrongly created. So by using Governance, you can overcome this, as it has a set of rules, policies and roles that define acceptable use of Azure resources. In order to implement good governance, Azure provides you multiple tools.

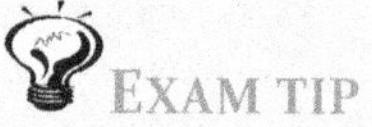

Governance keeps you compliant and out of trouble.

Azure Policy

Azure Policy is used to create policies in Azure. With Azure Policy, you can manage and assign policies to the resources with multiple rules, so that specific resources are complaint

with your business standard and SLAs. You can use Azure Policy to make sure that the use of resources does not become a mess. Azure Policy is a default allow and explicit deny system.

If you have a group of resources with the policies for each of the resource, then Azure Policy is a service, which ensures that these resources are compliant with the policies. Azure enforces that.

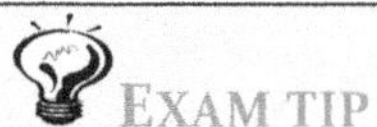

EXAM TIP

Azure Policy ensures that policies applied to the resources are compliant. A policy is set of rules to ensure compliant resources.

Role-Based Access Control (RBAC)

Role-based Access Control is one of the critical components in the governance of uses and access to Azure resources. With RBAC, you can outline fine grained access management to the resources. You can also define specific user access to an individual resource like what they can do with that specific resource and in what specific area of resource they have access. In any infrastructure, best practice is to give minimum access to the necessary resource to each user. With this, you can target specific use cases for assigning access for example, you can allow an application to access certain resources while allowing the user to access all resources in a specific resource group.

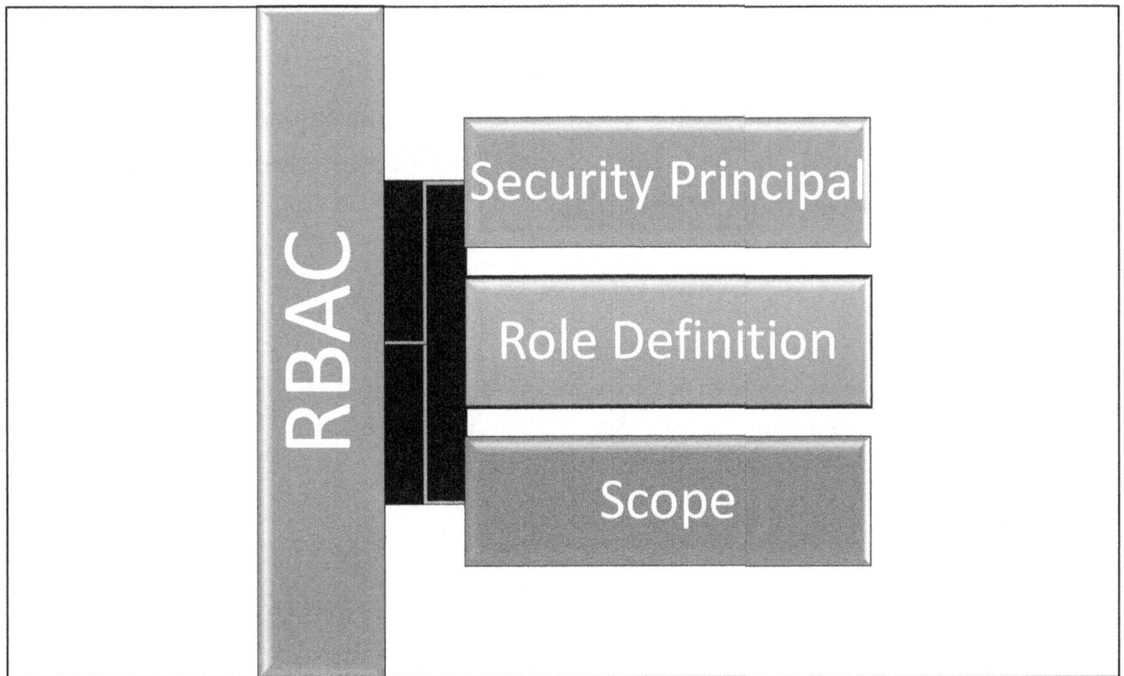

Figure 9-01: RBAC Elements

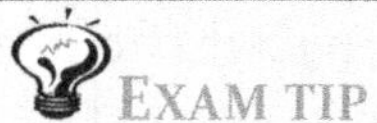

EXAM TIP

RBAC ensures your compliance by assigning roles to a user which is a combination of security principal, scope and role definition.

RBAC works by assigning roles to users and this role assignment is based on three elements, which are:

Security Principal

It is an object representing an entity that can get access to Azure resources like the user, group, etc.

- The user is an individual profile with in Microsoft AD
- The group is the set of users inside the Azure AD
- The service principal is a user identity used to access different Azure resources through applications or services
- Managed Identity is the identity that is managed by Azure in AD

Role Definition

It is a collection of permissions like read, write, or delete. With this, you can define a list of permissions to the resources. In Azure, there are some built-in roles that you can use to grant permissions.

Scope

It is a resource to which you grant access by specifying which role can access a resource or resource group. By defining scope, you can further limit the actions. The scope is in the parent-child structure. It can be applied at different levels: management group, subscription, resource group, or resource.

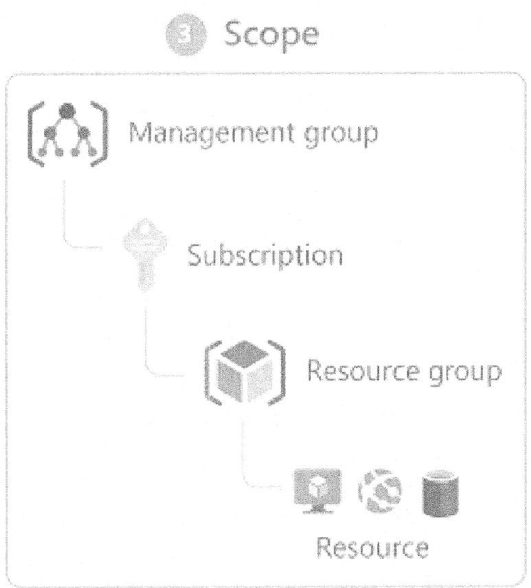

Figure 9-02: Scope Architecture

Role Assignment

Role Assignment is the process of combining all these together to grant proper action to Azure resources. Access is granted by the creation of a role assignment and deleted by the deletion of that role assignment.

Consider an example, your enterprise has three virtual machines; one for admin, one for billing, and one for general use. If you want to create a role based access for these resources, then you can assign it in the following ways:

- The admin role has access to all three VMs with all permissions
- The accountant role has access to general and billing VMs. It has read/write access to the billing VM and only read access to the general VM
- The standard user role has only read access to the general VM

With RBAC, you have the advantage of assigning any role to any number of users. If you want to make any change in the role, then perform changing only on the role rather than on individual users. In this way, all users that are assigned to this role will automatically be updated.

Locks

It is a simple tool to manage the changes and remove resources. It is used for the resource which you do not want to change or delete. It can be assigned to subscription, resource group, or resources. It is of two types: delete or read only. In delete lock type, you cannot delete the resource while in read only lock type, you cannot make any changes to the

resource. Once "locked" is defined to any of the resources, it needs to be deleted to perform any action.

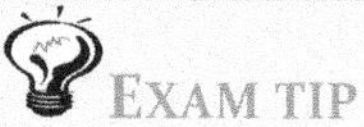
EXAM TIP

Locks ensure that the resources can neither be deleted nor changed.

Azure Blueprint

It is a template for creating Azure resources. Everything you need to deploy in the standard cloud environment of Azure is defined in the blueprint. Consider an example where you have to create a new Azure environment and you have to meet specific governance rules and regulations. Now, doing this manually can be quite difficult. With Azure Blueprint, you get a package of everything including templates for which resources to create user permissions using RBAC and any necessary policies. For some common scenarios, they have built-in samples like situations with specific governance, regulations and guidelines.

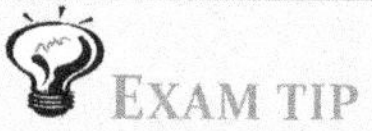
EXAM TIP

To create a standard Azure Environment, Azure Blueprint is used.

Azure Advisor for Security Assistance

Azure Advisor is a separate portal within Azure that has Security Assistance as a part of the Azure Security Center. You already know about the Azure Security Center, as we discuss it in chapter 8.

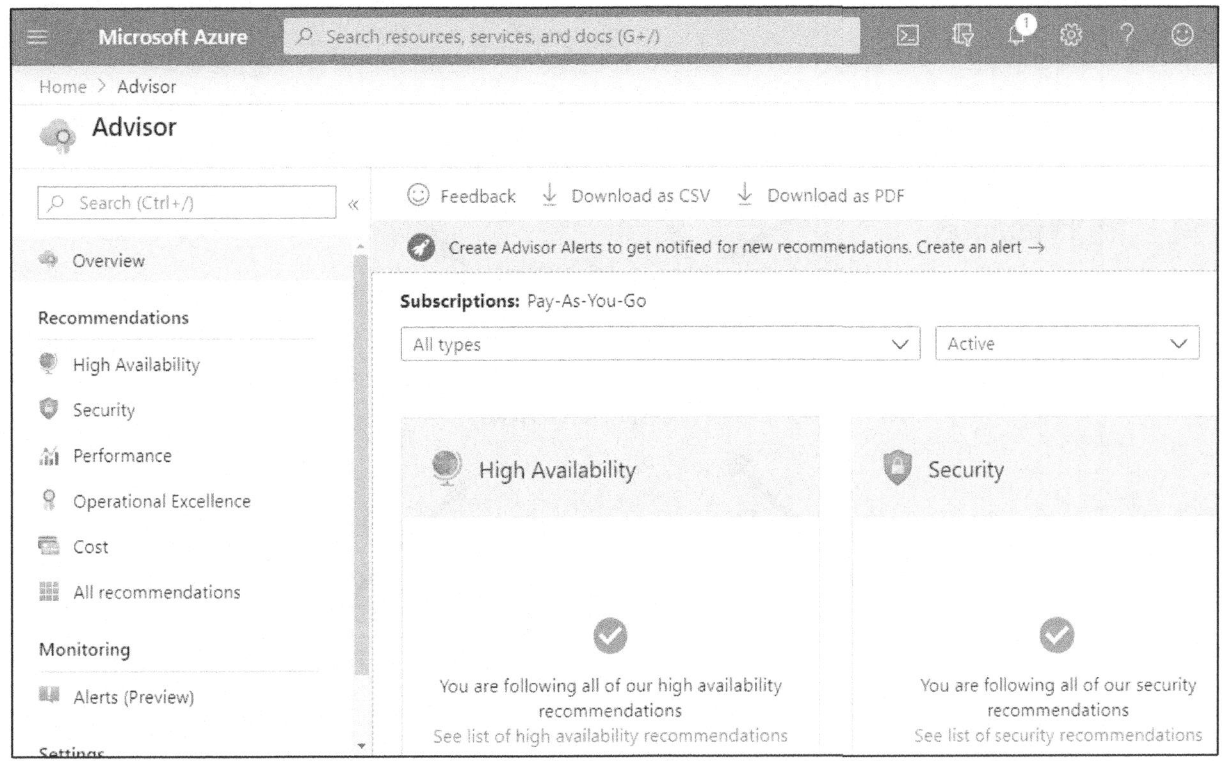

Figure 9-03: Azure Advisor

Azure Monitor

In order to improve your Azure experience, Azure Monitor uses the telemetry data. Azure Monitor maximizes flexibility and application efficiency by offering a comprehensive solution to capture, monitor, and use the cloud and on-site telemetry. It helps you understand how your applications operate and detect problems and the resources on which they depend proactively.

We know that managing cloud services means lots of resources and a lot of individual processes. And on top of that, you need to monitor the health of system in order to check whether things are running smoothly or not. In a scenario where one of the services is not performing well or it fails, then identifying it becomes the aim of the Azure Monitor.

Telemetry is the collection of measurements or other data that are at remote or inaccessible points and their automatic transmission to the receiving equipment for monitoring and analyzing. It is the information about how services or devices are performing. This information is then passed to the central server in order to perform analysis.

The data collected in Azure of two types: logs and metrics. Metrics are in the form of numerical value while logs are different kinds of data like events or traces.

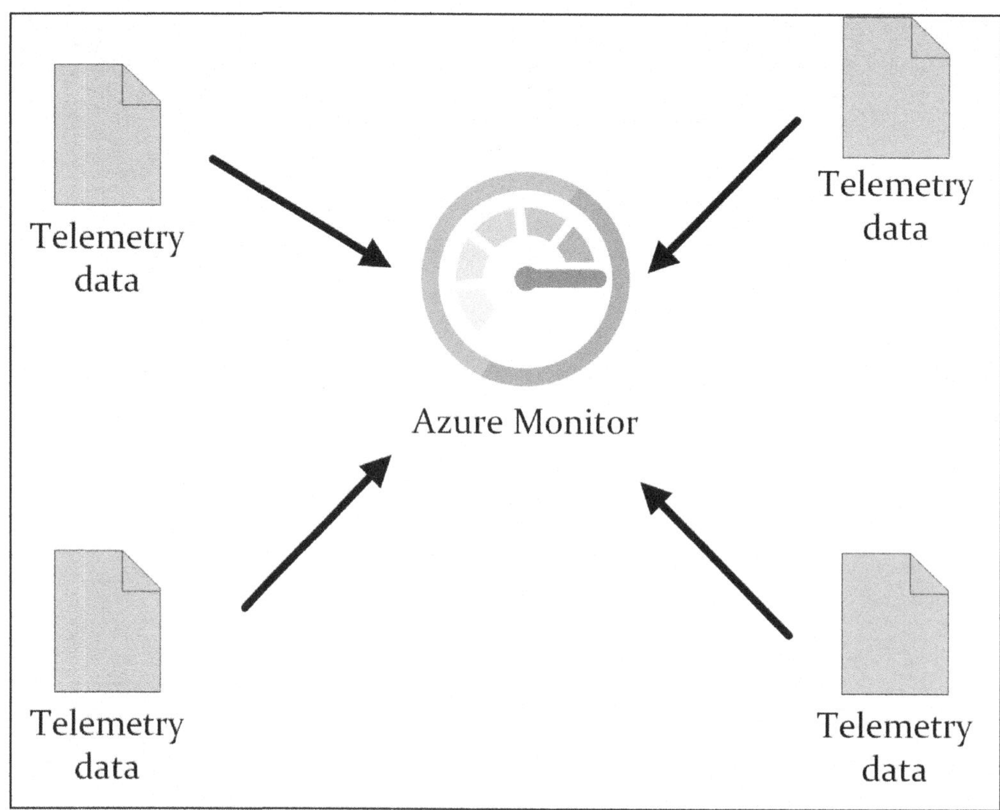

Figure 9-04: Pushing Telemetry Data to Azure Monitor

In Azure, all the telemetry data goes into Azure Monitor. Consider an example in which multiple VMs are running, Azure Monitor verifies that all of them are running smoothly. If any one VM is not performing, then you need to know which one and for that, you need telemetry data about the machine. This telemetry data constantly feeds into the Azure Monitor. Through Azure Monitor, you can analyze all of your data in one place. It is a fully managed centralized service. You can also use interactive query language in order to query the telemetry data. For detecting problem faster, you can use Machine Learning with your resources.

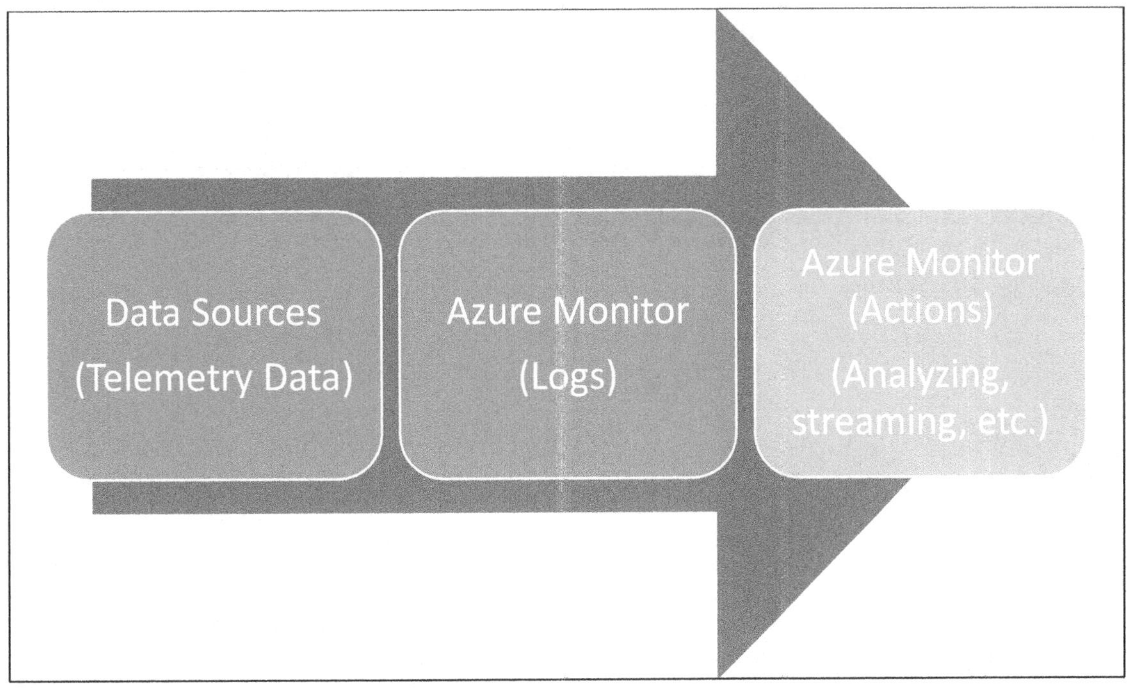

Figure 9-05: Azure Monitor Working

Outcomes

The outcome of using Azure Monitor:

- Maximize performance
- Maximize availability
- Identify issue

Azure Service Health

Whenever there is a plan of maintenance or service incident, you get notified about it with the use of Azure Service Health. The Azure platform needs to be updated and maintained like any infrastructure by mitigating the risk and taking necessary steps to protect your infrastructure and applications. Downtime is one of the enemies of your application or service. To help with this, there is a Service Health Dashboard in Azure.

With Azure Service Health, you get notified about the planned or unplanned maintenance of the platform. It has the following features:

- **Dashboard** – There is a personalized dashboard to highlight the service issues which effects your resources
- **Custom Alerts** – There are custom alerts to notify about any outages. These are simple to setup and customize

- **Real-time Tracking** - In case any issue occurs, it finds the root cause of the issue in real-time and after resolving the issue, it downloads the official report
- **Free Service** - It's a free service

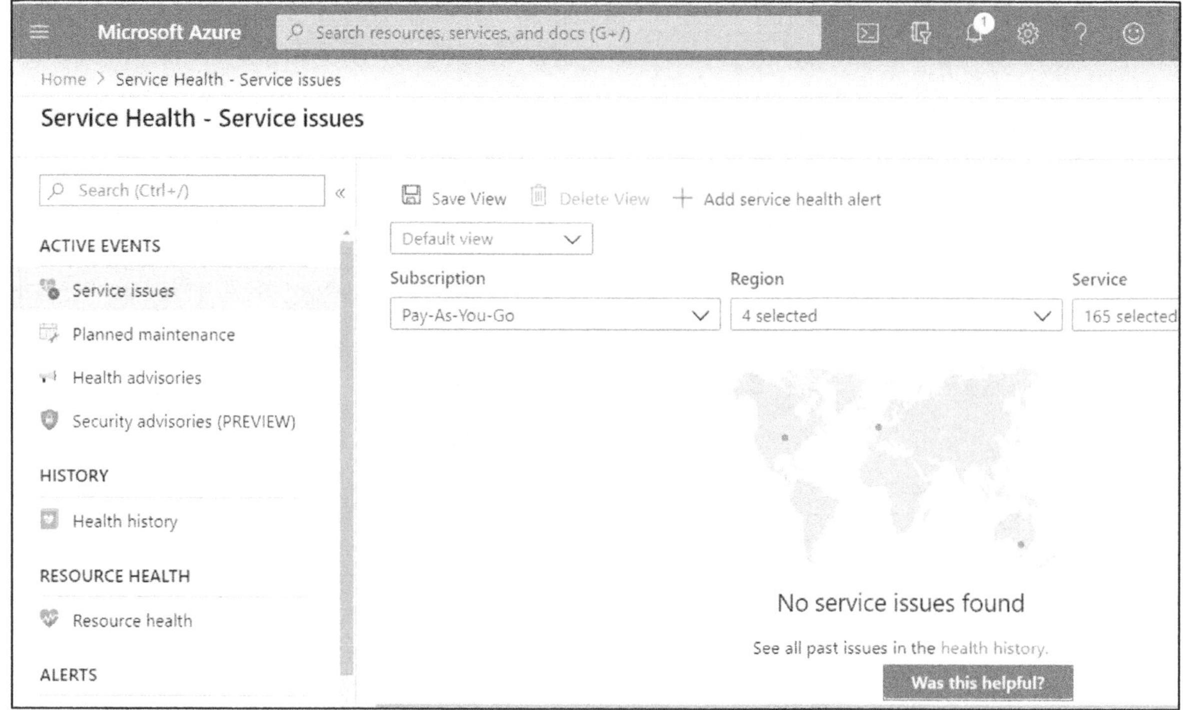

Figure 9-06: Service Health Dashboard

Demo of using Azure Monitor

1. Login to Azure Portal and go to "Monitor".

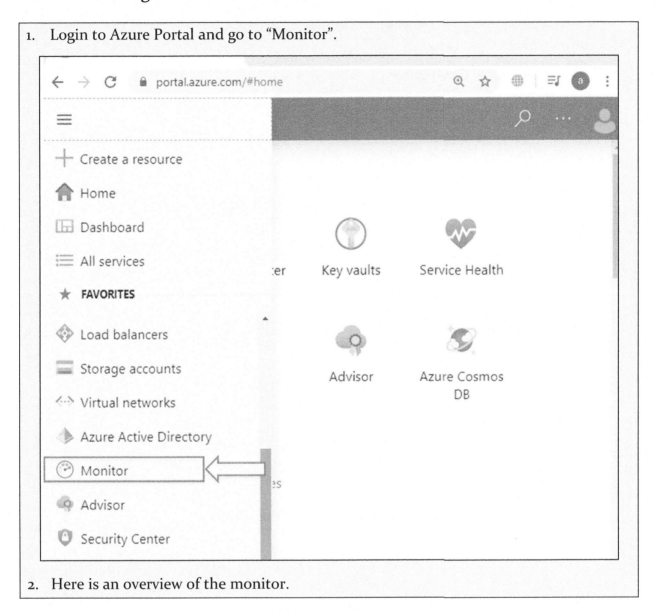

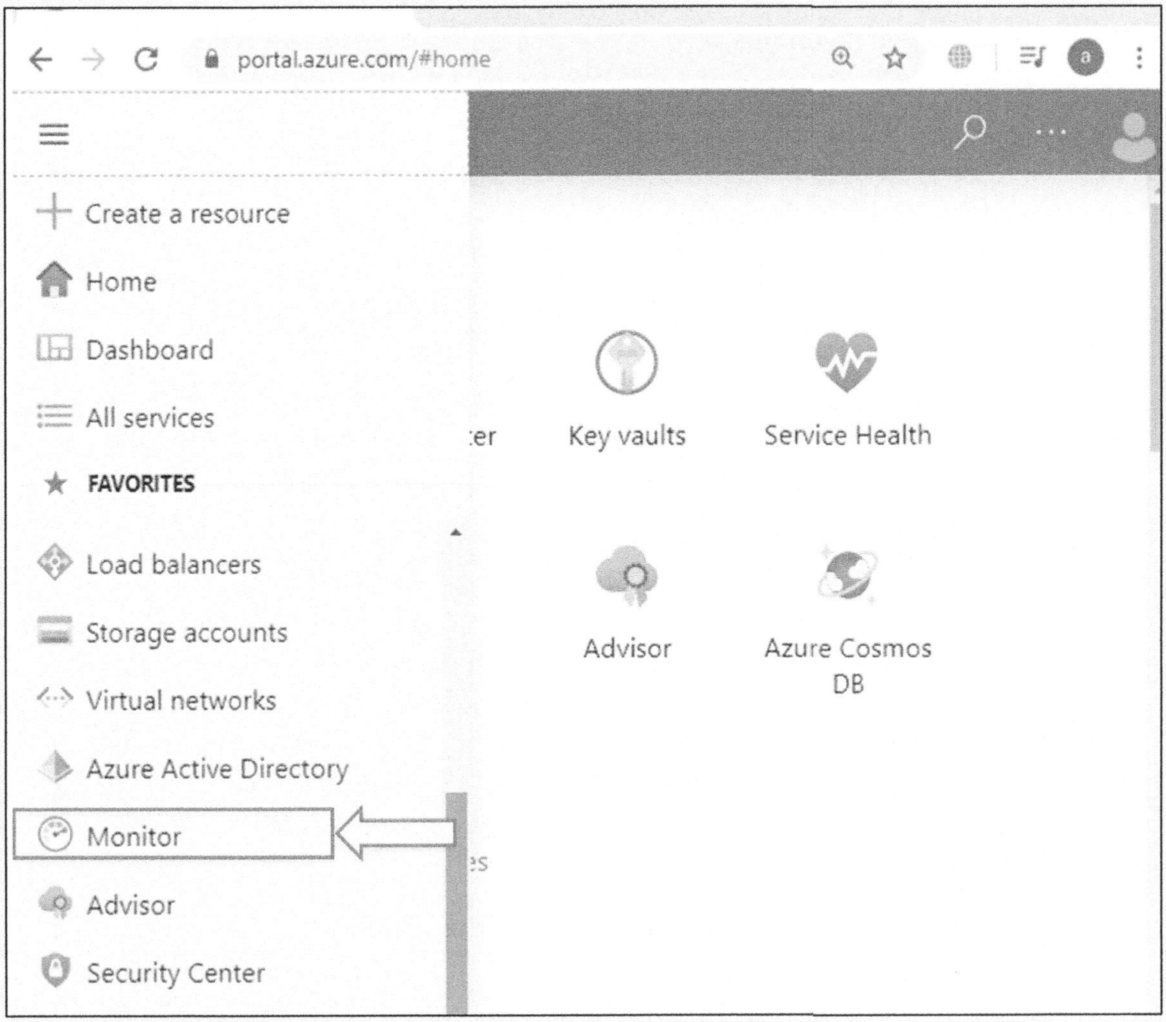

2. Here is an overview of the monitor.

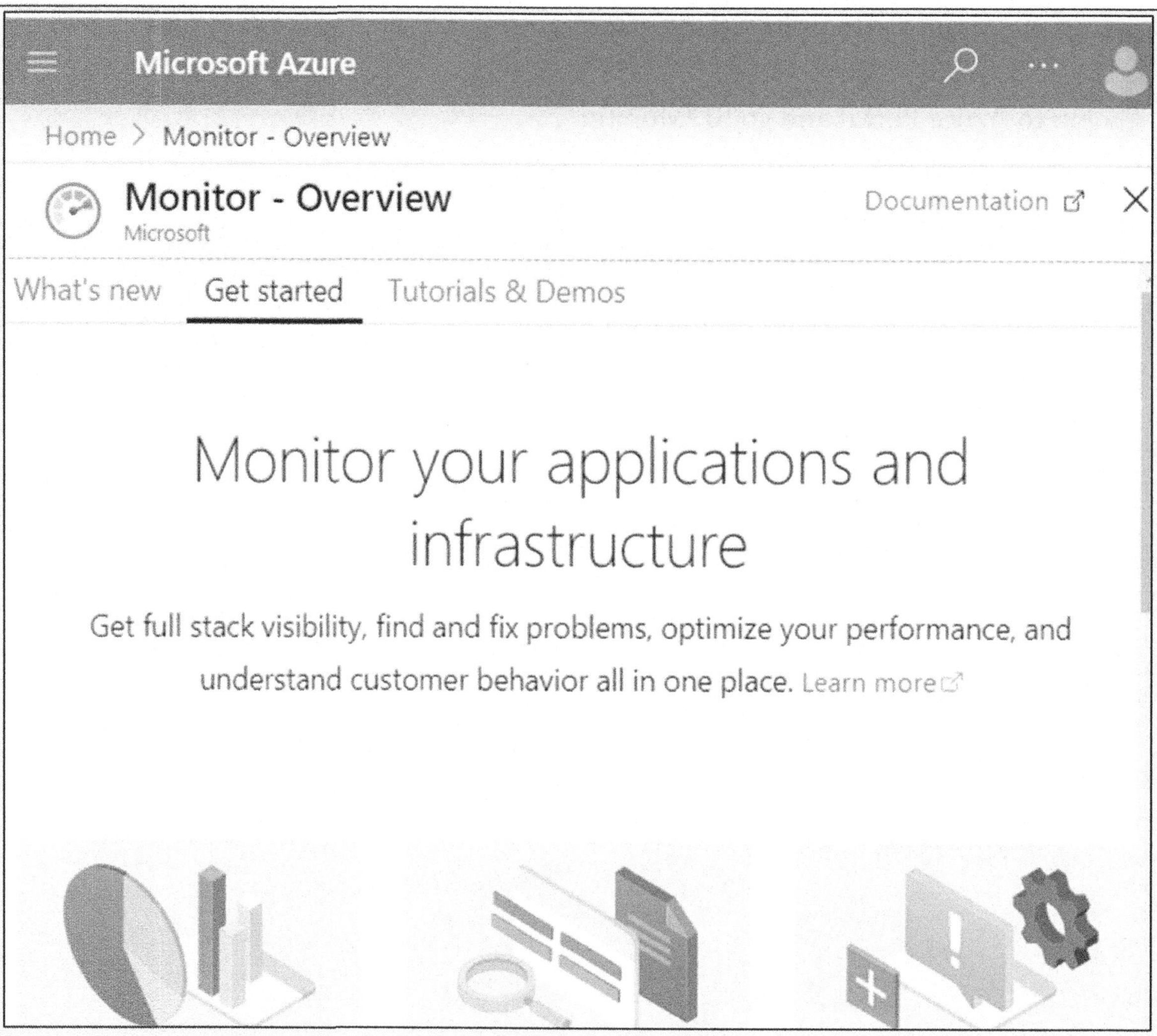

3. Now, go to “Service Health” from the left side of the window.

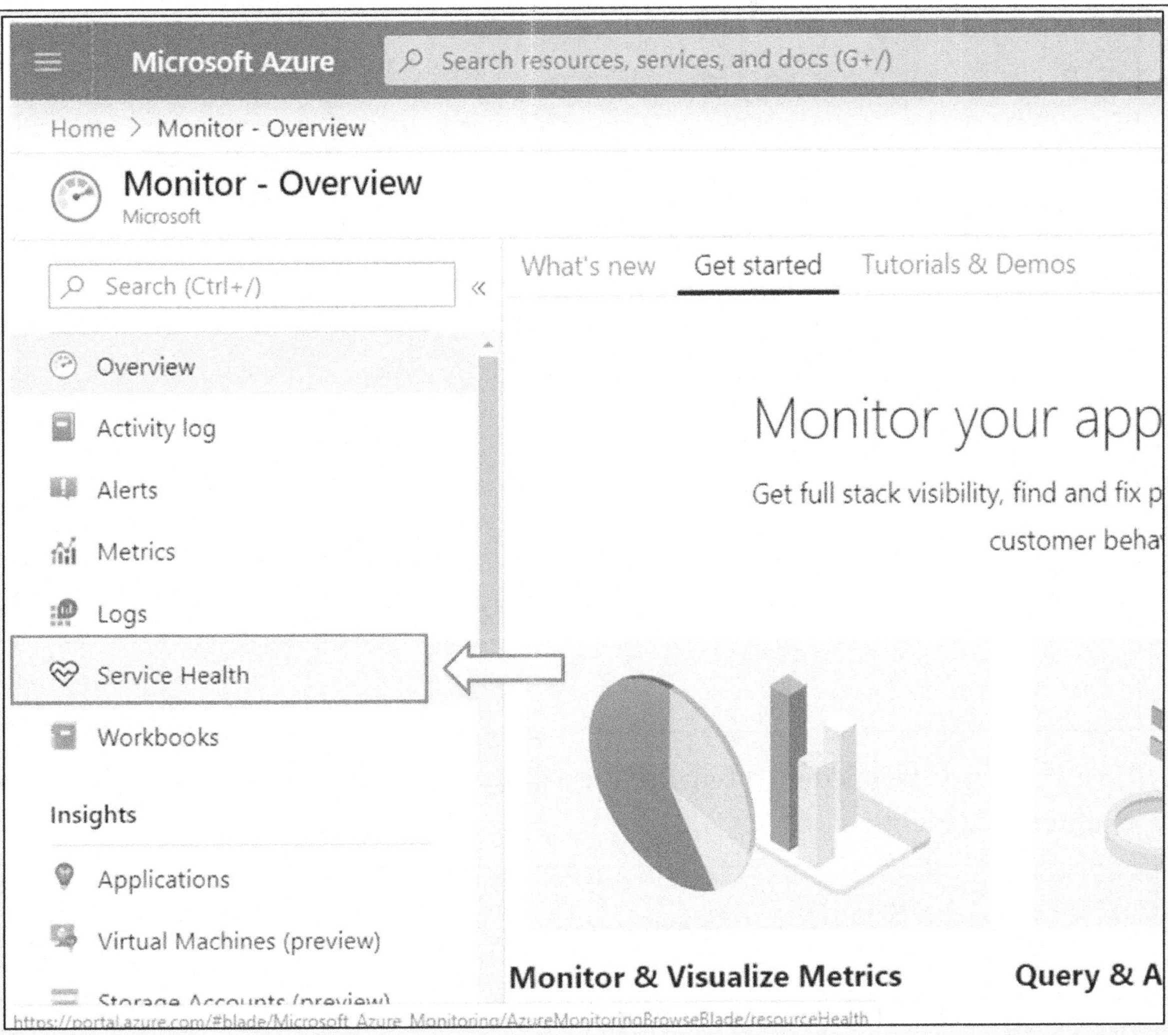

4. Currently, it shows that no issue is found. It will alert you of any issue in the services if found.

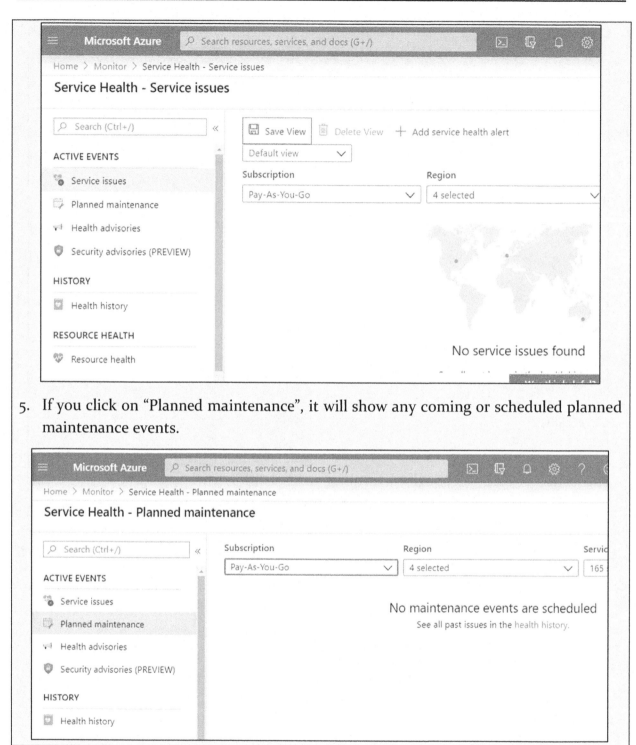

5. If you click on “Planned maintenance”, it will show any coming or scheduled planned maintenance events.

Compliance

The general principle that cloud services deliver must adhere to the requirements faced by cloud customers is strongly compliant. This is a very important issue with new cloud

computing services, and many IT professionals are looking at it very thoroughly. If any company in the EU does not take compliance seriously, they then have to pay a massive fine. For example, if any company is dealing with paying customers and does not comply with privacy and regulations about personal data, the company could be fined 4% of the annual global turnover. There are different standards and regulations that cloud customers need to comply.

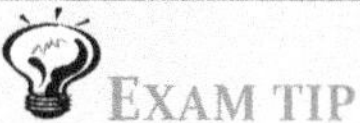

Compliance is not negotiable.

Industry Compliance

This refers to the legislation and rules the industry, in general, has to comply with. The most common three legislations and rules are:

- **General Data Protection Regulation (GDPR)** - Its main objective is to protect individuals and the processing of their data. With this, you get personal data to get back to an individual rather than company ownership In order to control consumer's data, it forces companies to implement a lot of tools to protect data.

GDPR compliance is needed to interact with EU-based customers.

- **ISO Standards** - ISO is the International Standardization Organization and they have a huge number of compliance categories. Generally, it is compliant with quality and customer satisfaction, which is ISO 9001:2008
- **NIST** – NIST it is the National Institute of Standards and Technology and it focuses purely on the technical industry. NIST guidelines are designed in such a way that compliance with NIST also means compliance with multiple Federal US regulations. CyberSecurity Framework is one of the most famous frameworks there is.

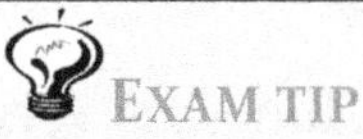

GDPR, NIST, and ISO are the regulations and standards that ensure your application legislation.

Azure Compliance Manager

For compliance in Azure, Azure Compliance Manager is available, because Azure knows about compliance and about your resources, so it combines the tools and gives you a

recommendation as per that. There are many benefits of using Compliance Manager, some of which are:

- It gives you a recommendation on ensuring compliance with GDPR, NIST, ISO, or others
- It also assigns tasks to your team and tracks the progress of the task; each member is responsible for a certain compliance area
- With that, you have a compliance score to chase perfect compliance
- It gives you secure storage for uploading the compliance documents to prove compliance
- It also gives you a report on compliance of data so that you can give that report to your managers and auditors

Azure Government Cloud

In order to know what is compliance, who make guidelines bodies and framework, and how Azure manages it all, you have two regions and offerings that are unique when there is compliance.

First is Azure Government Cloud, if you are US government body or are contracted for one, then you can get access to Azure resources in Azure Government Cloud regions. They are separate dedicated datacenters. With these dedicated datacenters, you get exclusivity which means that it is guaranteed that only US federal, state and local government have access to this dedicated instance with operations control by Screened US citizens.

It ensures compliance with required US government agencies and level 5 Department of Defense approval. With this, you can get all the benefits of Azure like HA, scalability, and managed resources.

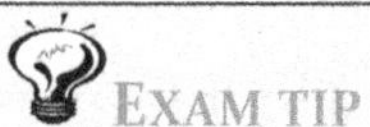

EXAM TIP

Azure Government Cloud provides dedicated datacenters purely for US government bodies.

China Region

It is the second specific region when it comes to compliance. As a country, China has very specific and strict requirements when there is data, internet, or online entities, so when you need to provide cloud services here, you have to use the China region in Azure. This means that Azure has physically separated datacenters located in China without any connection to the other regions of Azure. All data is stored in China at all times, for example if China is included in the region for DynamoDB then it will not work on a global scale.

Within that, you are completely compliant with all Chinese regulations. All of these physically separated locations are managed by Chinese companies.

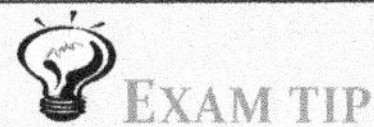

EXAM TIP

Azure China region is fully compliant with Chinese regulation; both datacenters, and data.

Privacy

Privacy is an extension of compliances. In Azure, privacy is the core power of the platform so there is no single service or place for it. Microsoft also has its own privacy statement which you can see from the following link: https://privacy.microsoft.com/en-gb/privacystatement.

- **Azure Information Protection** - it is used for classifying, labelling and helping protect data based on its sensitivity
- **Azure Policy** – as discussed earlier, it is used to define and enforce the rules to ensure regulations and privacy
- **Guides** - when dealing with GDPR privacy request from European user data, then Guides are used on Azure to comply with these
- Use Compliance Manager in order to follow the privacy guidelines

Trust

In Azure, there are two services in terms of Trust. One is Trust Center and the other is Service Trust Portal. Trust Center is a shortcut of knowing all the things that Microsoft does to make sure that you do not lose trust in Azure and other services. With this, you have a link to learn about security, privacy, GDPR, location of your data, compliance and more. With this link, you get know more about security implementations, privacy implementations and so on.

Service Trust Portal is a location to review all the independent reports about Azure. It is a portal of proof that they are compliant with many millions of different standards and certifications. It is crucial to know that Azure is compliant with all of the various quality and security standards, in fact, more than any other cloud provider. In short, we can say that it is a one-stop shop for security, regulatory and compliance, and privacy information related to Azure Cloud.

MindMap

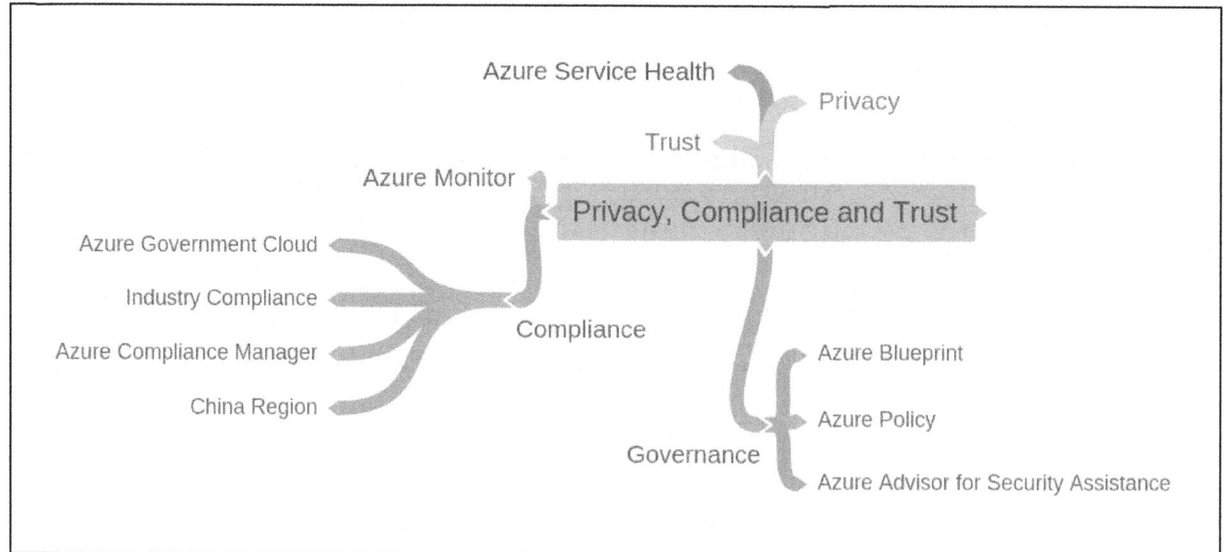

Figure 9-07: Mindmap

Practice Questions

1. Which two customers can develop a cloud solution using Azure Government?

A. A European government entity
B. A Canadian government contractor
C. A European government contractor
D. A United States government entity

2. From the following options, which one provides organizations the ability to manage compliance of Azure resources across multiple subscriptions?

A. Azure App Service Plans
B. Azure Policy
C. Azure Resource Group
D. Management Group

3. If you want to restrict access to Azure resources as per the policy of company so that only the admin is allowed to create a resource in the region where their office is located, then which Azure resource will you use to define this policy?

A. A Reservation
B. A Management Group
C. An Azure Policy
D. Read the only lock

4. For migrating the services from on-premises to Azure cloud, you need to identify the compliance of Azure with your organization's regional requirement. From the following which one is helpful?

A. Azure Trust Center
B. Azure Portal
C. Azure Market Place
D. None of the above

5. For what region the GDRP compliance is needed?

A. US Region
B. EU Region
C. Asia Region
D. All of the above

6. From the following, which one is used for tracking an incident in real time and then getting its report.
A. Azure Network Watcher
B. Azure Policy
C. Azure Service Health
D. Azure Blueprint

7. RBAC has a feature to define which action is allowed to be performed by which user on specific resources. True or false?
A. True
B. False

8. In Azure Monitor, which services can feed data?
A. On-premises
B. Azure Services
C. Both On-premises and Azure Services
D. Only Premium Services

9. In Azure, what types of locks can you apply? (Choose 2)
A. Closed
B. Read-only
C. Update
D. Create only
E. Delete

10. In order to trust more on Azure Portal, you can view the Service Trust Portal and Azure Privacy Portal in Azure. True or false?
A. True
B. False

11. In the China region, all Azure Services are globally located. True or false?
A. True
B. False

12. In RBAC, how many elements are present?
A. 2
B. 3
C. 4

D. 5

13. In order to create a standard Azure Environment, you can take help from _______.
A. Azure Advisor
B. Azure Policy
C. Trust Center
D. Azure Blueprint

14. For compliance in Azure, which service can be used?
A. Azure Trust Center
B. Azure Privacy Portal
C. Azure Compliance Manager
D. Azure Monitor

15. In order to classify, label, and help protect data based on its sensitivity, which Azure Service can you use?
A. Key Vault
B. Security Center
C. Azure Dedicated HSM
D. Azure Information Protection

Chapter 10: Pricing

Introduction

For migration to the cloud; we have discussed a lot of topics but we did not examine the primary concern, which is pricing. It is one of the most important part of any Cloud computing. Pricing does not only mean understanding the price of Azure services. Organizations often want to know about the cost of computing services before applications are deployed to the cloud. After the application is deployed, they want to reduce costs as much as possible and have insights in Azure's resource costs.

There are some areas in pricing that you need to be familiar with, i.e., Subscriptions, Cost Management, Pricing Factors, and Best Practices in Azure for managing costs.

Azure Pricing Structure

Azure pricing structure depends upon the following criteria:

- Pay for the resources you access
- Pay for the number of hours you use
- Pay depending upon the size of the resource
- Service payment is tiered
- Pricing as per the location of service

Subscriptions

The pricing structure of Microsoft Azure works on a subscription price that is tied to what you are using within the Azure infrastructure. All resources in Azure resides within the subscription, you cannot access any resources until you are subscribed.

Once you sign up for Azure, you immediately get an Azure subscription, and all the services you create are created within that subscription. Additional subscriptions are useful in cases where you want to have some logical groupings for Azure resources, or if you want to be able to report on resources used by specific groups of people.

You can manage your subscription in the Azure portal like any other Azure resources. You can monitor and manage costs, you can give access to it through RBAC to other users, you can add locks to it, and much more.

Subscription in Azure can be defined as:

Multiple Subscriptions: Any Azure account can have multiple subscriptions. It is very useful for organizing like who pays for what.

Billing Admin: One or more users can be a 'billing admin', which manages anything and everything that has to do with billing and invoicing on Azure. It ensures invoice separation of responsibility.

Billing Cycle: A billing cycle on Azure is either 30 or 60 days.

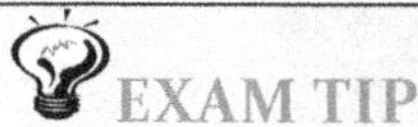

Each subscription is associated with a unique identifier called a subscription ID. To help you identify it, you may assign your subscription a descriptive name, but Azure will always use the ID to identify your subscription. If you inquire about your Azure account with Microsoft, you will often be asked for your subscription ID too.

Offer Types

At any given time, Azure has a lot of active offer types. You can get the offer depending upon your subscription type. Popular subscription type such as pay-as-you-go and enterprise level agreement, you can get many more offers as well. You can check the offer types when you are signing up for Azure.

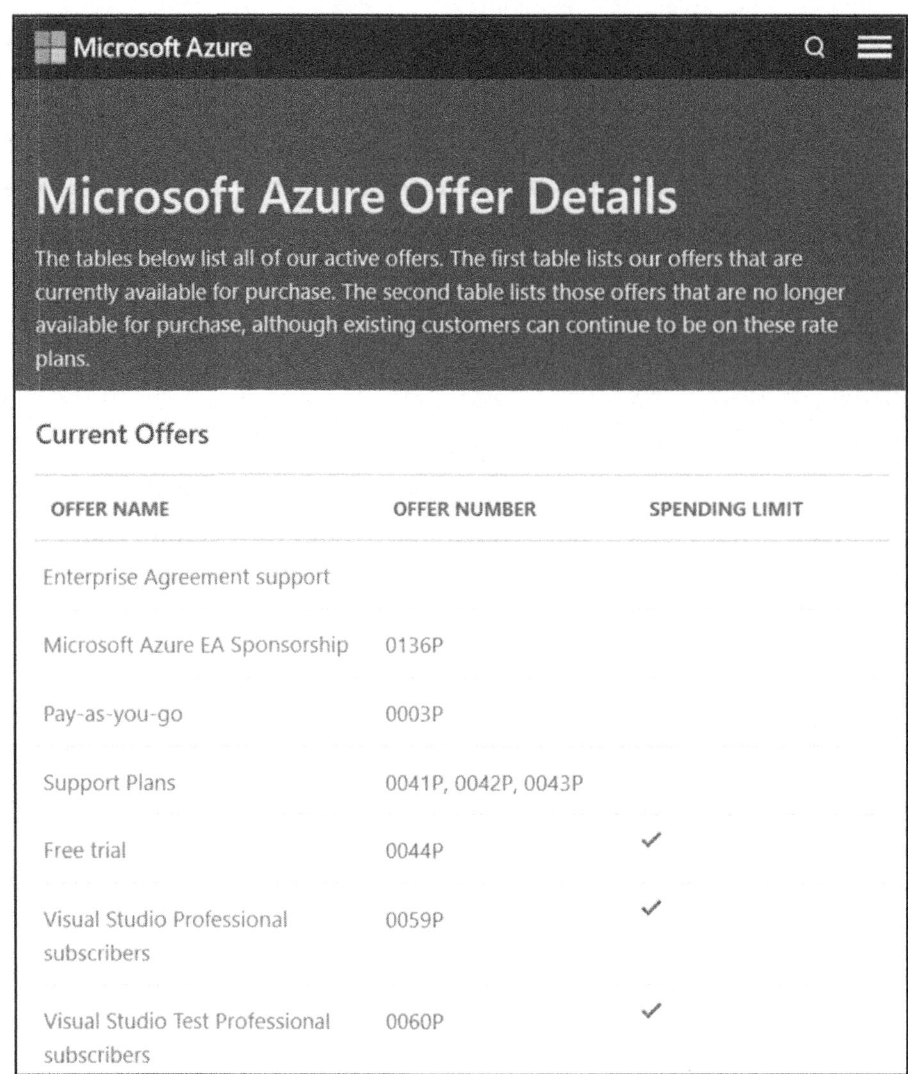

Microsoft Azure

Microsoft Azure Offer Details

The tables below list all of our active offers. The first table lists our offers that are currently available for purchase. The second table lists those offers that are no longer available for purchase, although existing customers can continue to be on these rate plans.

Current Offers

OFFER NAME	OFFER NUMBER	SPENDING LIMIT
Enterprise Agreement support		
Microsoft Azure EA Sponsorship	0136P	
Pay-as-you-go	0003P	
Support Plans	0041P, 0042P, 0043P	
Free trial	0044P	✓
Visual Studio Professional subscribers	0059P	✓
Visual Studio Test Professional subscribers	0060P	✓

Figure 60-01: Azure Offer Types

Management Groups

Management Groups is a very useful feature on Azure when it comes to subscription. Management groups may indicate the following:

Group Subscriptions: You can group your subscriptions to allow taking actions in bulk across subscriptions. This is very useful in organizations that deal with many subscriptions.

Organize: You can manage access, policies, and compliance in multiple subscriptions at the same time.

Billing Logic: You maintain the billing associated with the right budgets. You have the Nest management groups to indicate the hierarchy, which means each management group has a single parent group but many child groups and their relationship.

Cost Management

We know that when resources and services are running, its cost management can be quite an expensive task. In order to manage all of these costs, you have cost management. When you use resources or services in Azure you need to buy them as without that you cannot use it. You need a service that automates the cost management because tracking of every single cost is such a difficult thing to do. When you start thinking about moving to the cloud, the first thing you will probably want to do is decide about the cost of the resource as per resource needs. Once you have started deploying and using Azure services, it becomes important to manage your costs to remain within your budget. Azure has tools to help you schedule and manage your Azure costs. The management of cost in Azure can be done in many different ways; some of these are given below:

Azure Free Account

If you have never had a free Azure trial and have never been a paying Azure user, then you are eligible for a free Azure account. A free account gives you free access to the most popular Azure services for 12 months, and many other Azure services offer free usage even after the 12 months have passed. You also get a $200 credit, which you can use for a 30-day span of Azure services after you sign up for a free account.

Free accounts provide a range of benefits such as 12 months' free access which includes 750 hours of computing on virtual machines, 5 GB of storage, 250 GB of SQL database, 5 GB storage on Cosmos DB and a bundle of Artificial Intelligence services.

Microsoft places a $200 free-account spending limit. If you reach the spending limit, you are allowed to upgrade your subscription to a Pay-As-You-Go subscription with which you can create additional resources.

At the end of the 30-day span, any resources that are not free for 12 months or more are automatically deleted. So if you want to continue using your resources, you must make sure you upgrade your Azure subscription before the 30 days expire.

EXAM TIP

The $200 credit cannot be used to pay for Azure Marketplace offerings. Many Azure Marketplace offerings, however, provide their own free trials.

You can have only one free account per Microsoft Account.

Azure Cost Management

Azure Cost Management is a handy tool in Azure that allows the study of your costs on a granular level. Cost management allows you to create a budget for your Azure expenses, set up configurable notifications as so you will know if you are hitting a budgeted limit and evaluate your costs in detail.

Azure Cost Management is accessible from the Azure portal. You can get a detail view of the current and future projected costs of all the resources that are within your area of accountability. Azure Cost Management is free of cost and included with all Azure subscriptions.

You can download reports on spending and get recommendations on how to save on costs and analyze them. You can optimize your current resources to save money and also monitor the charges of other cloud service providers such as Amazon Web Services.

To get started with Cost Management, open the Azure portal and search for Cost Management, and click on Cost Management + Billing.

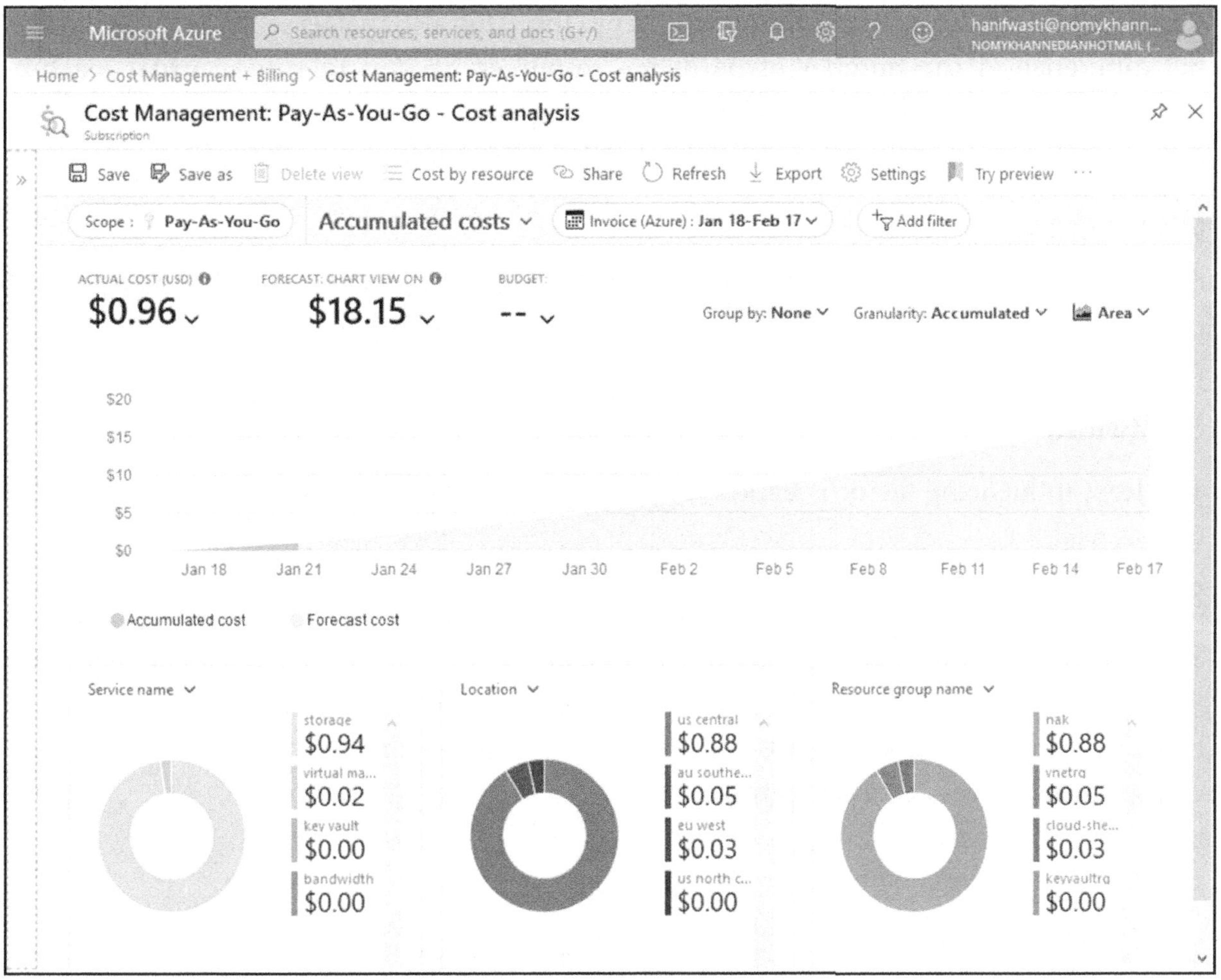

Figure 10-07: Azure Cost Management

Pricing Factors

Pricing in cloud computing is very tricky to predict and calculate. Any Azure account has a lot of resources such as networks, connections, virtual machines, firewalls, storage accounts, functions, etc.

When you plan your Azure deployments; you should keep in mind the factors that can influence your costs. The primary factors influencing costs are the size of resources, type of resource, the Azure regions you are using, and the bandwidth.

Resource Size

The pricing depends upon the size of the resource. A more powerful virtual machine will cost more than the less powerful one.

Resource Type

Resource type is also an important factor in pricing. This also makes sense as there is a very big difference in the number of hardware resources needed to run a virtual machine compared to a machine learning service or big data analytics, and there is also big difference in the complexity of maintaining and running various Azure services.

Location

Azure has a global network of datacenters from US to Australia and from Norway to South Africa, they are all treated equally with slightly different pricing. Exchange rates, labor costs, etc. have an influence on the prices.

Bandwidth

The least influencing factor is bandwidth. The bandwidth your services are using incurs a cost as well.

Zones & Bandwidth

To make things clear, Azure has designed three billing zones, each of these zones has many Azure regions. Any data transfer between the regions located in the same billing zone is free, this process is called Ingress. Any data transfer between two different billing zone is charged, this process is called Egress.

Billing Zone 1

Region Region

Free Free

Region Region

Ingress (data in) = free
Egress (data out) = not free

Ingress (data in) = free
Egress (data out) = not free

Billing Zone 2

Region Region

Free Free

Region Region

Ingress (data in) = free
Egress (data out) = not free

Billing Zone 3

Region Region

Free Free

Region Region

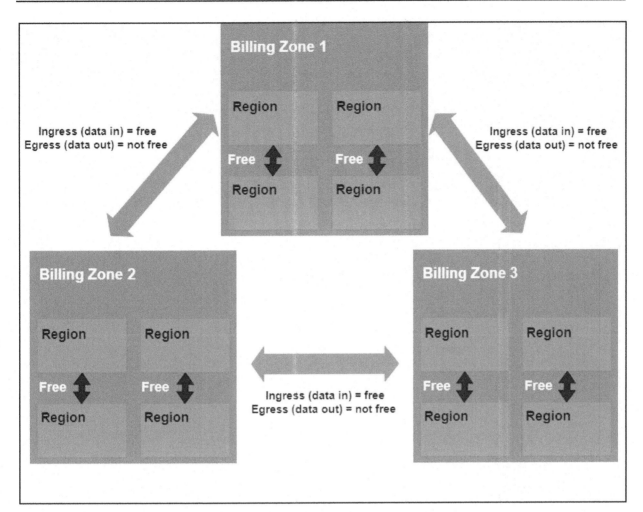

Figure 10-08: Data Transfer in Billing Zones

Each Azure service has a pricing page that outlines the estimated pricing for that resource based on typical usage.

Pricing Calculator

The Azure pricing calculator helps you get an estimate of costs depending on the products that you plan to use, as well as where those products will be deployed, and so on. You can access the pricing calculator by going to https://azure.microsoft.com/en-us/pricing/calculator.

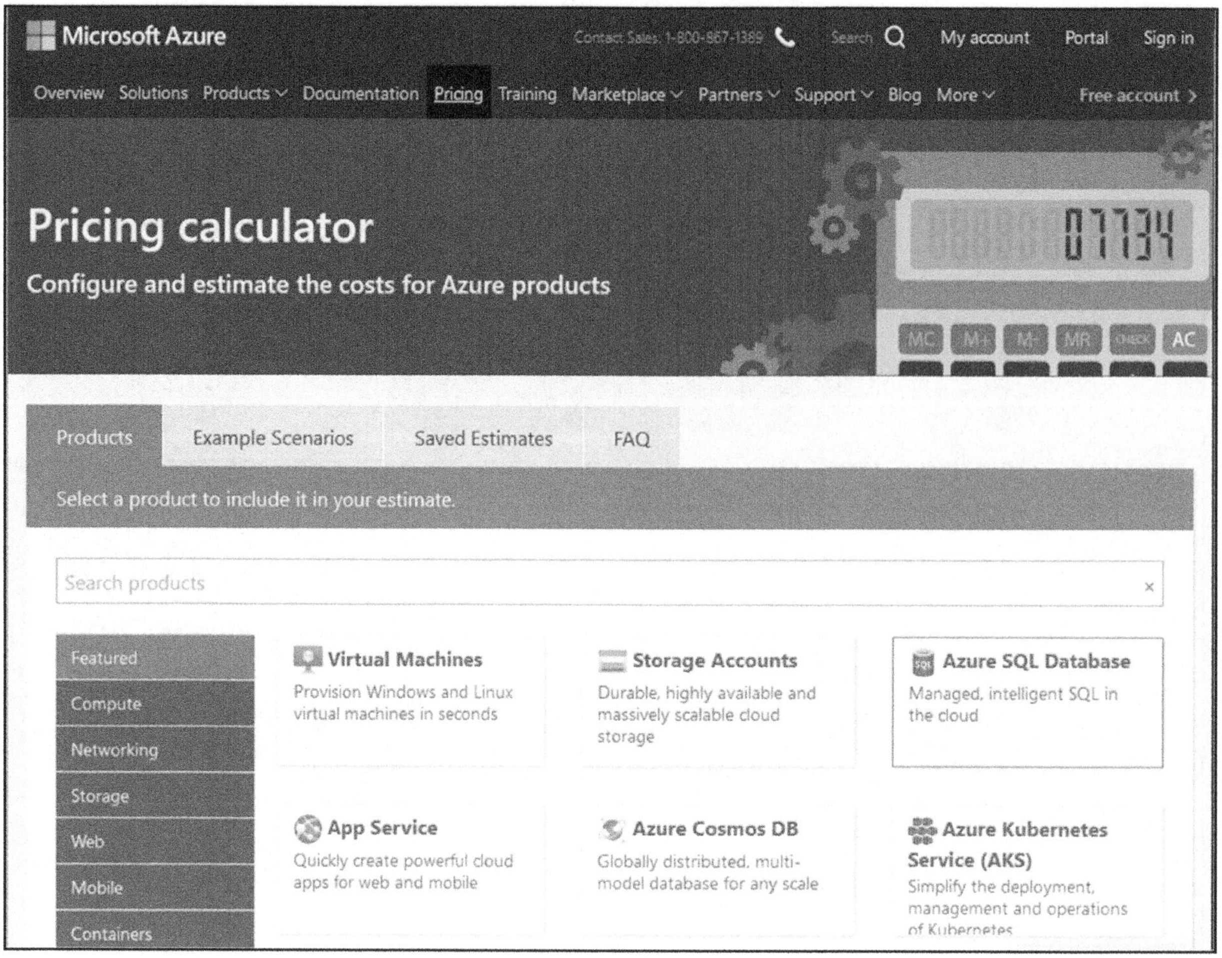

Figure 10-09: Pricing Calculator

Steps for Using Pricing Calculator

1. The first step in calculating your Azure expense estimate is to select which products you wish to use. Some of the more popular Azure products are shown by default, and by clicking on its tile, you can select any of those products.
2. Then scroll down to customize the specifics of each service after you select the products you want to use. These specifics vary according to how Microsoft pays for the product.
3. Clicking on "Pricing Details" will open the product pricing page in a new tab.
4. You can also click on "Product Details" or "Documentation" to read more about the service to help you make better decisions about the options you select.
5. Once you have configured the product according to your needs, you can click the "Clone" button to add another instance of the product to your estimate.
6. To check your estimate of prices, scroll down to the bottom of the page.
7. You can pick a support plan to add to your estimate.

8. You can click "Export" to save your estimate as an Excel file, then select "Save" to save your estimate in the price calculator to make changes later, or select "Share" to build a sharable link to your estimate so that others can view it too.

Total Cost of Ownership (TCO) Calculator

The pricing calculator is helpful for estimating your expenses for new applications in Azure, but if you have on-premises applications that you want to migrate to Azure and you want an estimate of how much you can save, the TCO calculator is a better choice. You can access the TCO calculator by browsing to:

https://azure.microsoft.com/en-us/pricing/tco/calculator.

Information about your on-premises servers, databases, storage and network usage should be included when using the TCO calculator. Figure 10-05 configures an on-premises server for a Web App.

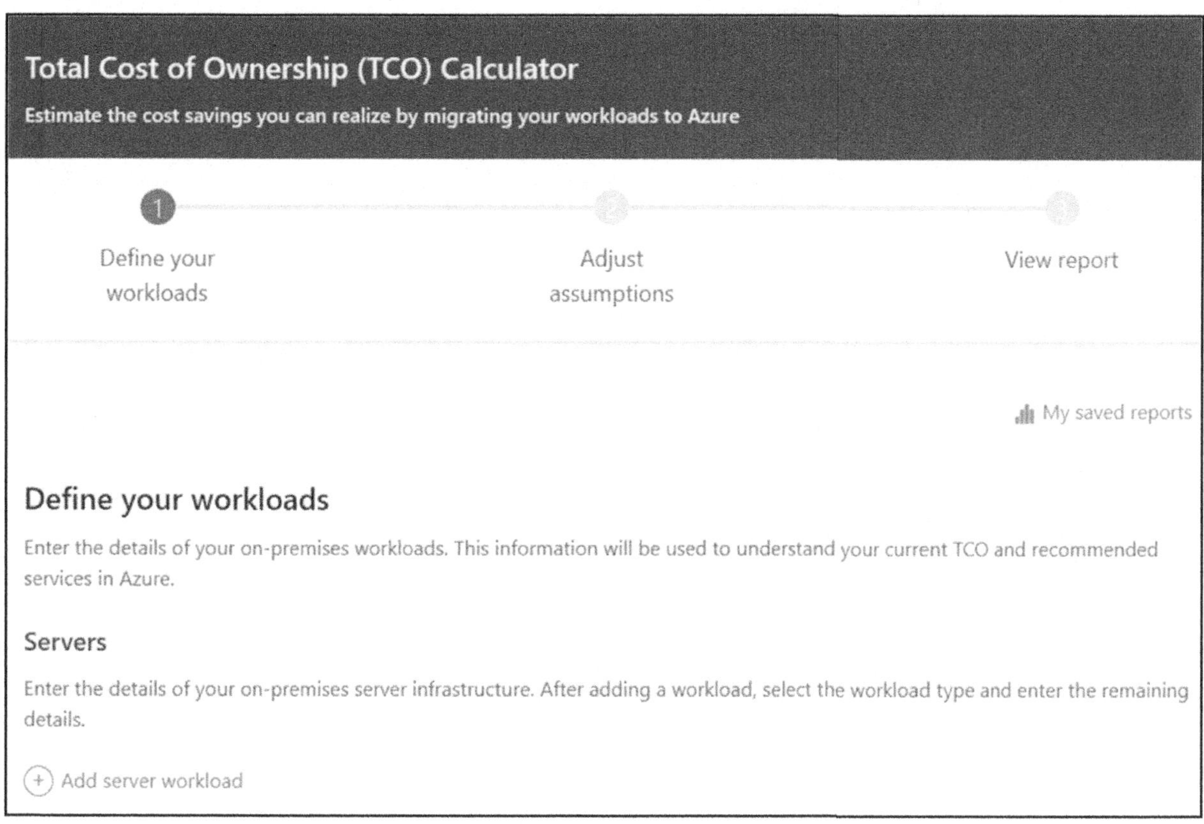

Figure 10-010: TCO Calculator

Your TCO report shows you how much you can save by moving your app to Azure over the next 5 years, as shown in Figure 10-06.

Over 5 year(s) with Microsoft Azure, your estimated cost savings could be as much as $14,349

Total on-premises vs. Azure cost over time

Savings from running workloads in Azure accrue over time. The following shows how those savings add up over years.

On-premises cost
Microsoft Azure cost
20K
15K
10K
5K
0
1 Year
2 Years
3 Years
4 Years
5 Years

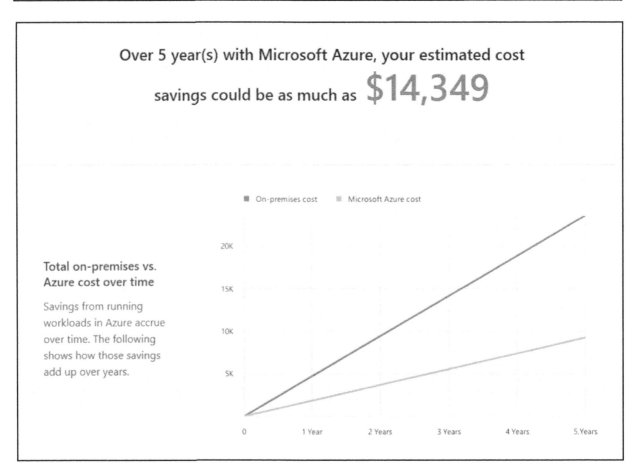

Figure 10-011: TCO Report

A TCO report includes detailed charts of expenses. You will also find a breakdown of on-premises costs and Azure costs at the bottom of the report so that you can easily determine where you will be saving money.

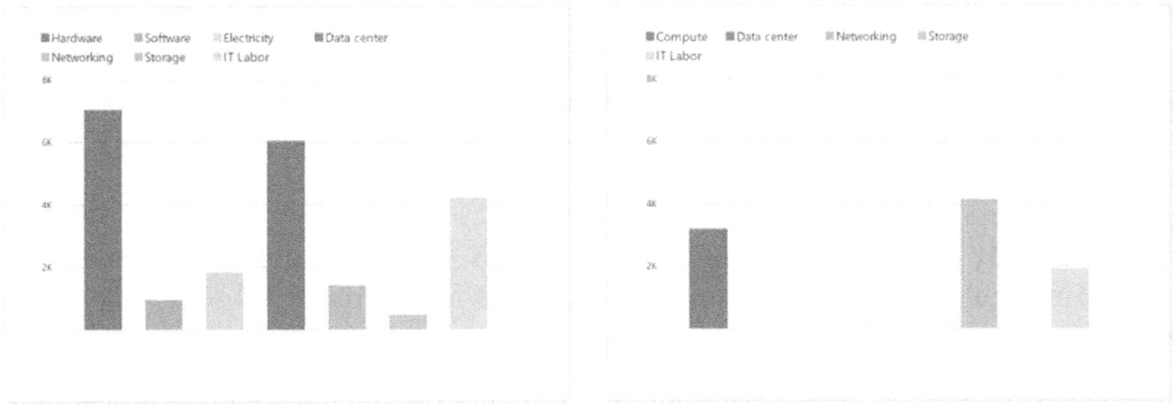

Hardware Software Electricity Data center
Networking Storage IT Labor

Compute Data center Networking Storage
IT Labor

$23,588

Cost over 5 year(s)

On-premises cost breakdown summary

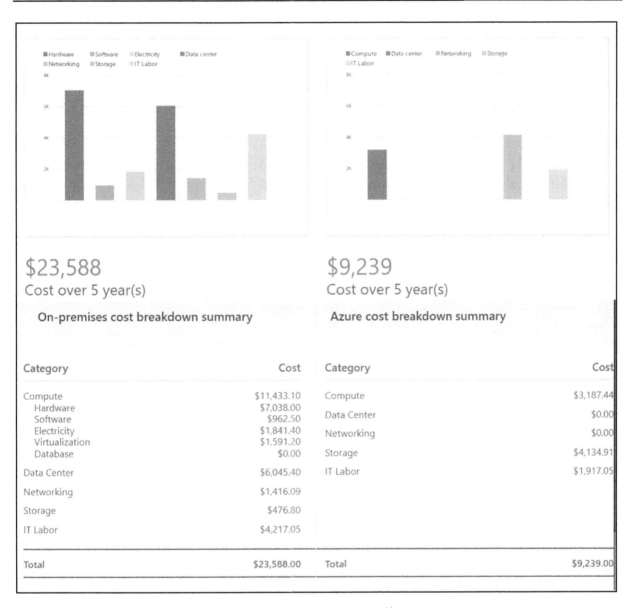

Category	Cost
Compute	$11,433.10
Hardware	$7,038.00
Software	$962.50
Electricity	$1,841.40
Virtualization	$1,591.20
Database	$0.00
Data Center	$6,045.40
Networking	$1,416.09
Storage	$476.80
IT Labor	$4,217.05
Total	$23,588.00

$9,239

Cost over 5 year(s)

Azure cost breakdown summary

Category	Cost
Compute	$3,187.44
Data Center	$0.00
Networking	$0.00
Storage	$4,134.91
IT Labor	$1,917.05
Total	$9,239.00

Figure 10-012: TCO Report Chart

Best Practices for Minimizing Azure Costs

Cost management is an operational challenge and should be an ongoing practice that begins before spending money on cloud services. In order to implement cost control effectively and reduce costs, you need to:

- Be equipped with the right tools for performance
- Be responsible for costs
- Take appropriate action to reduce expenses

Spending Limits

Azure spending limits are the recommended in order to prevent you from spending over your credit and manage your Azure subscription's total spending. When your usage leads to charges that exhaust your spending limit, the services you deployed will be disabled for the rest of that billing period.

Default Limit: Some Azure accounts with monthly credits, will have default spending limits. This could be 0$ for a free account and 150$ for Microsoft subscription account. When the credits are used, the limit kicks in.

No Increase: When the credits are gone, either remove the spending limit entirely or leave it in effect.

No Spending Limit: Pay-as-you-go subscription has no spending limit functionality.

An important part of cutting off Azure costs is to ensure that all the cloud services are fully utilized. Since most cloud use is based on resource consumption, not using parts of a network reflects unnecessary expenses. Proper planning can help avoid unused resources in the cloud.

Quotas

A quota is the limit on certain properties of an Azure service. For example, a maximum of 100 namespaces per subscription is allowed for Event Hub. The quotas are necessary to ensure Azure can maintain its high service level. If you need to increase the quota for a particular service, you can ask Microsoft to increase them.

Tags

Tags are non-functional labels attached to resources or resource groups in order to manage the cost of resources. You can attach as many to each resource as you want. Tags provide an excellent way of attributing costs. The tags can be used as a filter and as well as when you analyze data to evaluate costs, you can use them to group the resources together that have same tags. They are non-functional attributes.

Some common best practices for using tags are:

Identify Roles: Protect sensitive data by defining which roles can access a resource.

Related Resources: To make bulk processing and updating easier, define which resources are related.

Filter: Filter resources per project, customer, or for reporting purposes.

Unambiguous: Create a list for tags used that includes: description, tag name, and potential values.

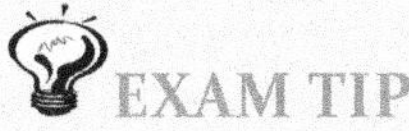

EXAM TIP

Pay-as-you-go is a very common pricing model in which you pay only for what you use on per month basis. It is one of the most expensive model for Azure usage.

Reserved Instances

With Reserved Instance, you are allowed to prepay for the virtual machine or SQL Database computing capacity for one or three years. Pre-paid allows you to get a discount on the resources you are using. You cannot reserve all the services. It will dramatically reduce the cost of computing up to 72 percent on pay-as-you-go pricing with an upfront commitment of one year or three years. Reservations offer a discount on billing does not affect the runtime status of your instance.

Azure Advisor

Azure Advisor is a tool that detects the low-usage virtual machines from a CPU or network cost standpoint. From there, you can choose to either shut down or resize the system to continue running the machines, based on estimated costs. Advisor also makes recommendations for purchases in reserved instances. The recommendations are based on your virtual machine usage for the last 30 days. With the help of this recommendation, you can reduce your expenditure when you act upon them.

Microsoft Azure

Search resources, services, and docs (G+/)

All services > Advisor - All recommendations

Advisor - All recommendations

Documentation

Feedback | Download as CSV | Download as PDF | Create alert | Manage alert rules

Create Advisor Alerts to get notified for new recommendations. Create an alert →

Subscriptions: Pay-As-You-Go

All types | Active | No grouping

Total recommendations 3

Recommendations by impact: 0 High impact, 1 Medium impact, 2 Low impact

Impacted resources 3

IMPACT	DESCRIPTION	POTENTIAL BENEFITS	IMPACTED RESOURC...	UPDATE...
Medi	Enable Soft Delete to protect your blob data	Save and recover your data when blobs or blob snapshots are accidentally overwritten or deleted	1 Storage Account	1/23/2020 2:12:53 PM
Low	Diagnostic logs in Key Vault should be enabled		1 Key vault	1/23/2020 3:24:46 PM
Low	Create an Azure service health alert	Get notified when Azure service issues affect you	1 Subscription	1/23/2020 1:56:51 PM

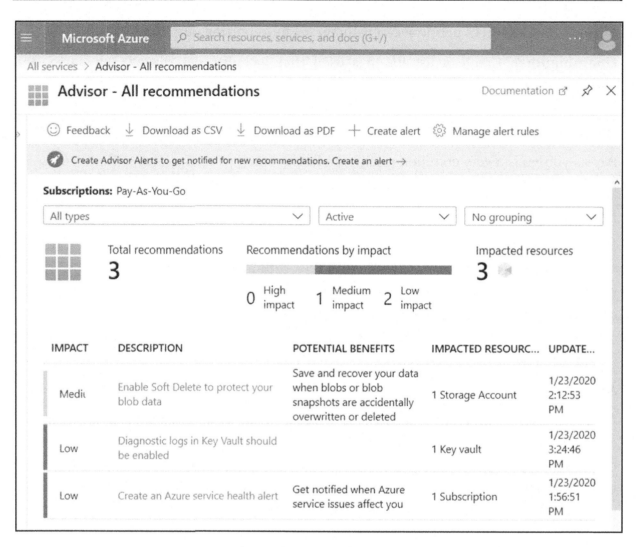

Figure 10-013: Azure Advisor

Lab 10-01: Using the Pricing Calculator

Scenario

An organization is planning to upgrade its infrastructure with Azure services, but wants to know the estimated cost for requesting the service of Virtual Machine and Azure Function.

Solution

Microsoft Azure provides a free pricing calculator to estimate the cost of any services. You just select the service and add the features you want to find the estimated result of the cost that you can download in the form of Excel Sheet, which can be useful for decision making.

1. Open a browser and go to the Azure pricing calculator https://azure.microsoft.com/en-au/pricing/calculator/ as shown below.

Microsoft Azure

Pricing calculator

Configure and estimate the costs for Azure products

Products | Example Scenarios | Saved Estimates | FAQ

Select a product to include it in your estimate.

Search products

Featured

Virtual Machines
Provision Windows and Linux virtual machines in seconds

Storage Accounts
Durable, highly available and massively scalable cloud storage

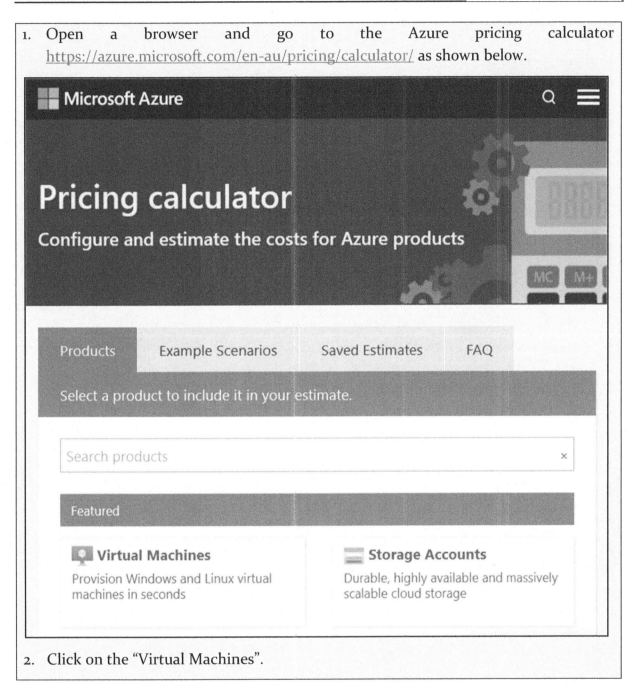

2. Click on the "Virtual Machines".

azure.microsoft.com/en-au/pricing/calculator/

Products | Example Scenarios | Saved Estimates | FAQ

Select a product to include it in your estimate.

Search products

Featured

Virtual Machines

Provision Windows and Linux virtual machines in seconds

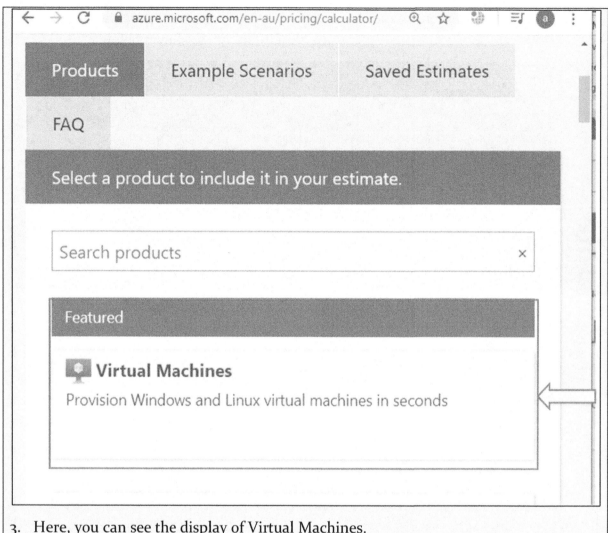

3. Here, you can see the display of Virtual Machines.
4. Configure Virtual Machines as needed.
5. Select the Region, OS, Tier, and Instance.

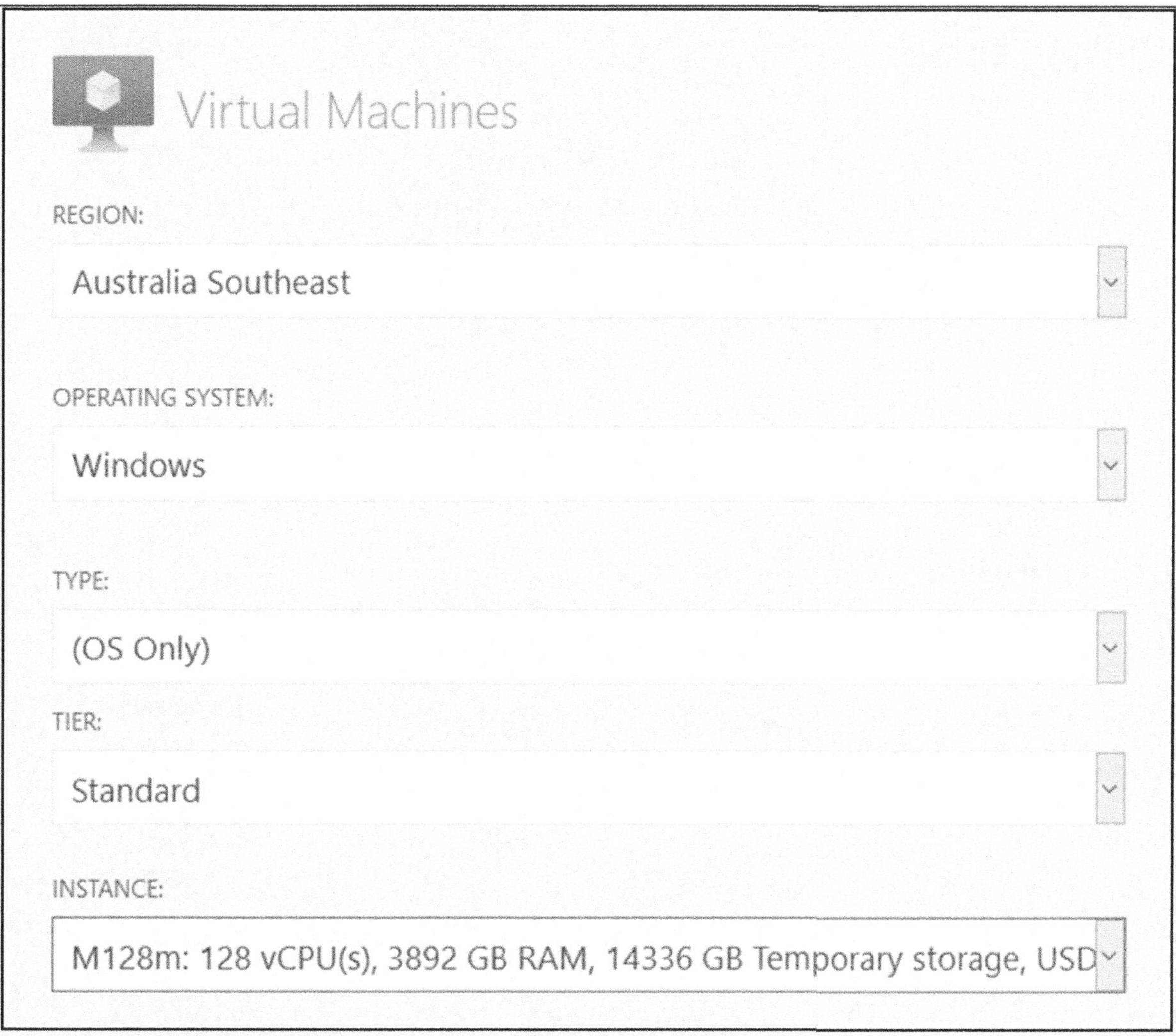

Virtual Machines

REGION:

Australia Southeast

OPERATING SYSTEM:

Windows

TYPE:

(OS Only)

TIER:

Standard

INSTANCE:

M128m: 128 vCPU(s), 3892 GB RAM, 14336 GB Temporary storage, USD

6. On the billing options, select the number of Virtual Machines and the number of hours for utilizing this VM.
7. You can see the estimated cost of 1 VM with 1 hour of utilization.

Billing Option

Save up to 72% on pay-as-you-go prices with 1-year or 3-year Reserved Virtual Machine Instances. Reserved Instances are great for applications with steady-state usage and applications that require reserved capacity. Learn more about Reserved VM Instances pricing.

- ◉ Pay as you go
- ○ 1 year reserved (~41% savings)
- ○ 3 year reserved (~65% savings)

Save up to 40% with Windows Server Licenses you already own. Learn more about Azure Hybrid Benefit to save compute costs.

8. Now, click on "Azure Functions" to add functions.

Featured

Virtual Machines

Provision Windows and Linux virtual machines in seconds

Storage Accounts

Durable, highly available and massively scalable cloud storage

Azure SQL Database

Managed, intelligent SQL in the cloud

App Service

Quickly create powerful cloud apps for web and mobile

Azure Cosmos DB

Globally distributed, multi-model database for any scale

Azure Kubernetes Service (AKS)

Simplify the deployment, management and operations of Kubernetes

Azure functions

Process events with serverless code

Cognitive Services

t API capabilities to enable contextual interactions

9. Configure Azure functions by selecting regions, memory size, execution time, and number of executions.
10. You can see the estimated cost for 4 million requests in 100 seconds as shown below.

Azure functions

REGION:

Australia Southeast

The first 400,000 GB/s of execution and 1,000,000 executions are free.

Executions

Memory size: 128 × 100000 Execution time (in milliseconds) × 4000000 Executions per month = USD 793.60

Requests

4,000,000 Execution count = USD 0.60

Sub-total USD 794.20

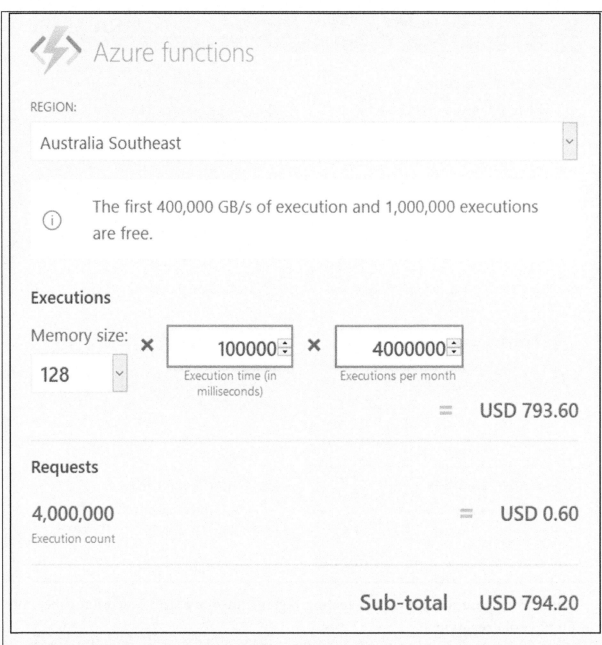

11. Select the support level that charges 100 USD.
12. See the total estimated cost of all the added services.
13. Save and export the result.

Support

SUPPORT:

Standard

USD 100.00

Estimated monthly cost

Export

Save

Share

USD 942.08

US Dollar ($)

Mind Map

Pricing

Pricing Factors
Resource Size
Resource Type
Location
Bandwidth
Pricing Calculator
TCO Calculator

Subscriptions
Management Groups
Offer Types

Cost Management
Azure Free Account
Azure Cost Management

Best Practices
Azure Advisor
Tags
Spending Limits
Quotas
Azure Reservations

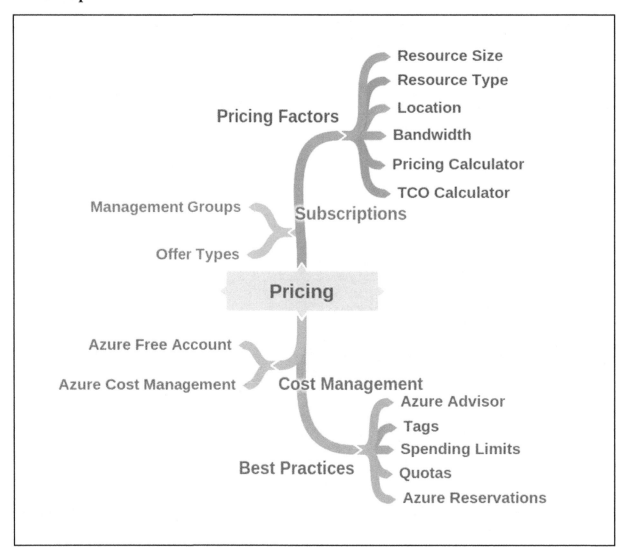

Figure 10-014: Mind Map of Azure Pricing

Practice Questions

1. A billing cycle on Azure is ________.
   A. Bi-monthly
   B. Yearly
   C. Monthly
   D. Hourly

2. Which of the following terms is not indicated by the Management Group?
   A. Group Subscriptions
   B. Organize
   C. Billing Admin
   D. Billing Logic

3. A free account gives you free access to the most popular Azure services for ______.
   A. 30 days
   B. 60 days
   C. 6 months
   D. 12 months

4. Which of the following allows you to create a budget for your Azure expenses, set up configurable notifications so you will know if you are hitting a budgeted limit, and evaluate your costs?
   A. Management Groups
   B. Cost Management
   C. Pricing Calculator
   D. TCO Calculator

5. With which of the following can you download reports on spending and get recommendations on how to save on costs and analyze them?
   A. Cost Management
   B. Management Groups
   C. Pricing Calculator
   D. TCO Calculator

6. Which of the following is the least influencing factor of pricing?
   A. Resources Size
   B. Resources Type
   C. Bandwidth
   D. Location

7. Any data transfer between the regions located in the same billing zone is free, this process is called Egress. True or false?
   A. True
   B. False

8. Any data transfer between two different billing zone is charged, this process is called Egress. True or false?
   A. True
   B. False

9. From the following, which one will help you get an estimate of costs depending on the products that you plan to use, and also get to know where those products will be deployed?
   A. Cost Management
   B. Azure Advisor
   C. Pricing Calculator
   D. TCO Calculator

10. You have on-premises applications that you want to migrate to Azure. Now, if you want to estimate of how much you can save in Azure, which of the following should be the best choice?
    A. Cost Management
    B. Azure Advisor
    C. Pricing Calculator
    D. TCO Calculator

11. TCO report shows the estimated result of how much money you can save by moving your app to Azure over the next _____________.
    A. 3 years
    B. 4 years

C. 5 years
D. 1 year

12. Select the three primary groups that need to be coordinated within the company to ensure you handle the costs effectively.
    A. Finance
    B. Managers
    C. App teams
    D. Billing Admin

13. Which cost analyzing tool can monitor the charges of other cloud service providers such as Amazon Web Services?
    A. Cost Management
    B. Azure Advisor
    C. Pricing Calculator
    D. TCO Calculator

14. What are the best practices to implement cost control effectively and reduce costs?
    A. Be equipped with the right tools for performance
    B. Be responsible for costs
    C. Take appropriate action to reduce expenses
    D. Resize your resources

15. Which tool can make recommendations for purchases in reserved instances?
    A. Azure Reservations
    B. Azure Advisor
    C. Pricing Calculator
    D. TCO Calculator

16. How are Azure subscriptions related to pricing?
    A. If you lock subscriptions in for 1 or 3 years, the services within it go down in price
    B. The more subscriptions you have, the cheaper each service will get
    C. The billing of each service in your account is within a single subscription
    D. The price of a subscription depends on the location of your company or personal address

17. To manage expenses on Azure, what is a recommended best practice?
    A. Monitor frequently used services and keep track of any excess usage using the Azure Spending Manager
    B. Use Azure Alerts to get notified of when spending exceeds the subscription limits
    C. Use the subscription credit limits, which are built into all Azure subscriptions
    D. Use Azure spending limits on resources and services

18. Which Azure calculator would you use to figure out monthly costs for Azure services?
    A. Azure Service Calculator
    B. Azure Portal Service Estimation
    C. Total Cost of Ownership Calculator
    D. Azure Pricing Calculator

19. From the following, which features are in Azure Cost Management? (Choose 2)
    A. Recommendations to move services between Azure regions to save on cost
    B. Visualize future costs for your Azure account
    C. Visualize current costs for your Azure account
    D. Automatic shutdown of services that have not been used for a set period of time

20. Which factors have an influence on the cost of using products and services on Azure? (Choose 3)
    A. The location of the service or resource
    B. Resource usage. The more you use it, the cheaper it gets
    C. The age of the resource
    D. Resource size
    E. How much bandwidth you will use

Chapter 11: Support

Introduction

Support plays an important role in the cloud environment. As we have learned, when we move to the cloud, at least some portion of infrastructure management moves to the cloud provider. When something goes wrong, it is important you get the help you need to keep your applications available. It is also important to understand what level of support is being provided for specific services, in particular services that may be in previewing and not published officially. We also know that there are always some changes that have been performed to upgrade features or new products coming for which you need an extensive support infrastructure for Azure and its users.

In this lesson, we will look at all the aspects related to Azure. We will cover some various support plans that you can purchase and benefit from, tickets to generate query, available support channels, knowledge center, Service Level Agreements and the release cycle for Azure services.

Plans

Microsoft offers numerous support plans for Azure customers in order to find right level of support for your organization. There are five different support plans available in Azure; Basic, Developer, Standard, Professional Direct, and Premier. Choosing the right plan is a balance between how much access you need for help and support and how much you are willing to spend.

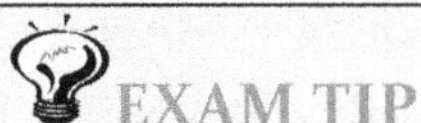

The higher the support plans, the higher the amount you need to pay.

The things which are included in all support plans are:

- ***24/7 Access:*** Around the clock access to billing and subscription support as Microsoft wants to make sure you can pay them
- ***Online Self-Help:*** Includes Azure documentation and white papers that guides you about complex issues or scenarios
- ***Forums:*** Support forums that offer a great way to ask questions to other Azure users about what they use and how they use it
- ***Azure Advisor:*** Best practice recommendations for multiple Azure services from Azure Advisor

- ***Service Health:*** Access to service health status of current issues and future planned maintenance on the Azure platform

These are included in all the support plans free of charge and coincidentally, these all are a part of Basic Support Plan, which is free as well.

Plans Inclusions- Paid Plans

The following table is shows features of various Azure paid plans.

	Developer	Standard	Professional Direct	Premier
Price	$	$$	$$$	$$$$
Technical Support	Access to support engineers via email only during business hours	Access to support engineers 24x7 via email or phone	Access to support engineers 24x7 via email or phone	Access to support engineers 24x7 via email or phone
Support Cases	Unlimited	Unlimited	Unlimited	Unlimited
Azure Configuration	Guidance Troubleshooting	Guidance Troubleshooting	Guidance Troubleshooting	Guidance Troubleshooting
Response Time	Sev. C: < 8 hours	Sev. C: < 8 hours Sev. B: < 4 hours Sev. A: < 1 hour	Sev. C: < 4 hours Sev. B: < 2 hours Sev. A: < 1 hour	Sev. C: < 4 hours Sev. B: < 2 hours Sev. A: < 1 hour <15 minutes (with Azure Rapid Response or Azure Event Management)
Architecture Support	General Guidance	General Guidance	Architecture Guidance	Customer Specific
Operations Support			Onboarding Reviews	Tech Reviews Reporting Tech Account Manager
Training			Webinars	On-demand

Table 11-01: Azure Paid Plans

Apart from premier, these all support services can be used by signing up online. Your support service will start immediately.

Tickets

To contact a support there is medium called "Tickets". Tickets are what the enquiry issue makes support A ticket is usually a number that uniquely identify your enquiry. All communication and details of your support request are recorded with a ticket number attached to them. So, a ticket is a single reference to the whole support request.

Submitting a Ticket

There are number of steps to submit a ticket.

1. You submit a ticket through the Azure portal after logging in.

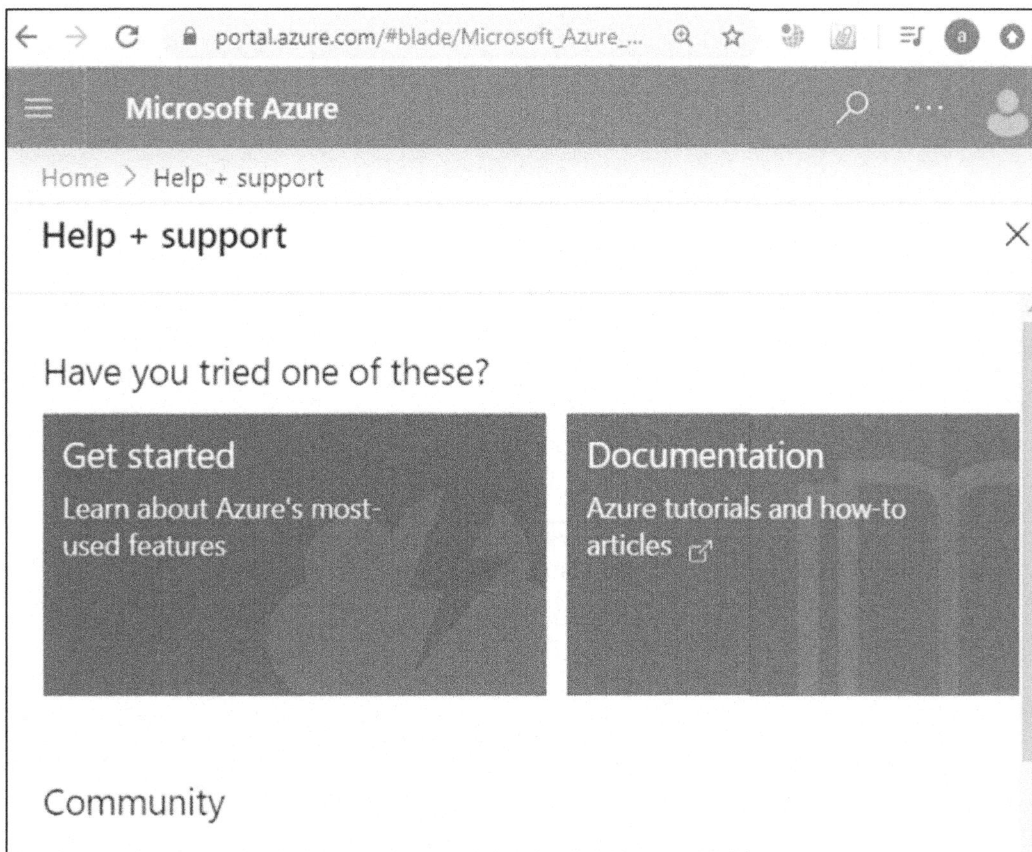

2. Choose the support ticket type from the four support ticket types as shown in the figure below.

Microsoft Azure

Home > Help + support - New support request

Help + support - New support request

Basics | Solutions | Details | Review + create

Create a new support request to get assistance with billing, subscription, technical (including advisory) or quota management issues.
Complete the Basics tab by selecting the options that best describe your problem.
Providing detailed, accurate information can help to solve your issues faster.

* Issue type

Select an issue type

Billing

Service and subscription limits (quotas)

Subscription management

Technical

Next: Solutions >>

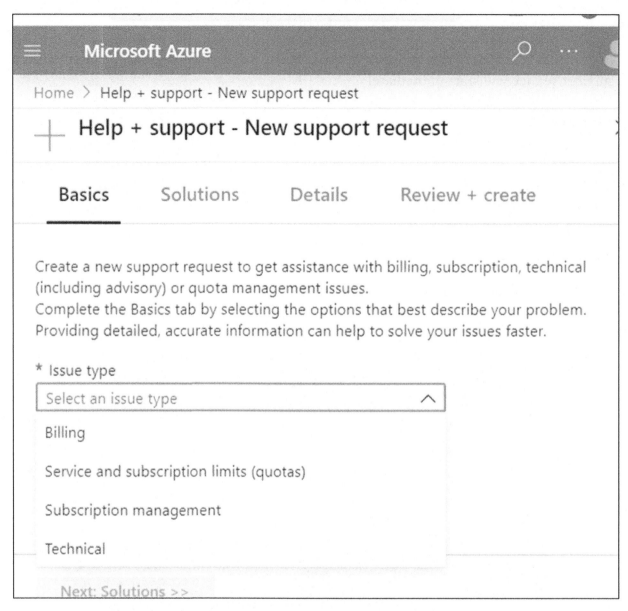

3. Fill in the details regarding the issue you are creating a ticket for.

Microsoft Azure

Search resources, services, and docs (G+/)

Home > Help + support - New support request

Help + support - New support request

Basics | Solutions | Details | Review + create

Create a new support request to get assistance with billing, subscription, technical (including advisory) or quota management issues.
Complete the Basics tab by selecting the options that best describe your problem. Providing detailed, accurate information can help to solve your issues faster.

* Issue type

Billing

* Subscription

Pay-As-You-Go (797152d3-23c4-499f-bfef-bb103da...

Can't find your subscription? Show more

* Summary

In a few words, describe your issue

* Problem type

Let's begin by understanding more about your issue

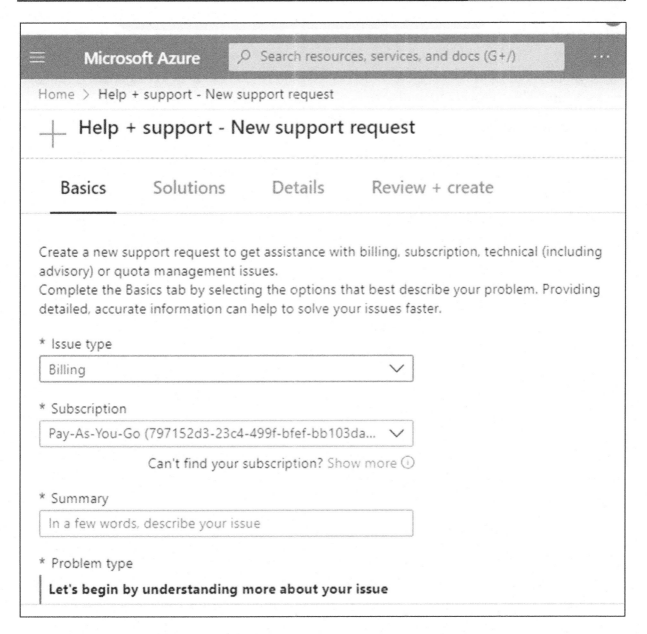

4. Microsoft's support person will attend to your request within the specific time and according to your support plan.

EXAM TIP

Azure basic support plan allows to create a ticket for billing and subscription only, nothing technical.

Channels

Azure supports various channels that are free to everyone through which you get more help from Azure. The support channels are:

1. **Azure Documentation:** Azure documentation is a collection of thousands of articles written on Azure products and services. They are written by the Azure product managers, technical experts and the community contributes. These are constantly updated and they provide in-depth knowledge of products and services.
2. **Forums:** Forums attracts everyone from beginners to experts. On forums, people ask questions, some give answers, and some search for past knowledge.
   https://azure.microsoft.com/en-au/support/community/
3. **Social Media:** Social media is an effective way to get direct support from Azure and the team behind every service. You can ask questions by searching experts on various social media platforms.

Knowledge Center

Knowledge center is the place of a common Azure knowledge. In knowledge center, you can find basic questions that are common for all those who are new to Azure, these questions are called Common questions. Azure knowledge center aims to answer those common questions.

In knowledge center, you are provided with the following guidelines:

1. **No New Question:** You cannot add a new question or add to an existing one.
2. **Search:** Search the knowledge center by category, product and free text. Azure knowledge center also give links to Azure documentation and more.
3. **Complements to other Channel:** You cannot find all the answers in knowledge center, so you can use the other support channels as well.
   https://azure.microsoft.com/en-au/resources/knowledge-center/

Service Level Agreement

When you are using Azure Services, you need some form of guarantee that the service will be running stably. This is called Service Level Agreement, which helps to ensure the services you are subscribed for is available to you as mentioned in the agreement. It describes the Microsoft's commitment for uptime and connectivity.

It is like a contract between the service provide and client. It is an agreement on certain levels of service like how long the service will be available in case of any unavailability. If your service does not go up for the given time defined in the agreement, then you will be compensated by claiming it from the Microsoft.

Properties

Some properties of SLAs are:

1. **Confidence:** SLAs give confidence to customers by ensuring uptime and reliability of services.
2. **Contract:** SLAs ensure a contract between Microsoft and customers that states a commitment for uptime and connectivity.
3. **Multiple SLAs:** There are a lot of SLAs in Azure, generally one for each product. It automatically comes when you subscribe for the service.
4. **Complex:** Some SLAs are very complex as they have various levels depending on the number and variety of services, which region you use, and much more.
5. **Mandatory:** SLAs are given from Microsoft; if you have an Azure account, various service levels apply. No SLAs are associated with free products and services.

Service Life Cycle

Every product and the service in Azure has its lifecycle known as Service Lifecycle. Azure is an always-changing environment, and new services are always being introduced. Existing services also evolve over time and introduce new features. It is important to understand the service lifecycle in Azure, how you can keep up with changes, and how a service's lifecycle might impact your support and your SLA.

Gathering Customers Data

When the services are developed by the Microsoft for the Azure platform, it is necessary to ask questions to customers regarding the new features before adding. This act can save large investments if the services fail.

Stages

There are two main stages in Service Life Cycle:

1) **Preview:** Most of the Azure product will go through the preview phase before becoming fully available at the Azure platform. It is categorized into two forms: private preview and public preview.

   a) *Private Preview:* It ensures that *specific* Azure customers have an Azure feature available for assessment. This is typically by invite only and issued directly by the product team responsible for the feature or service.
   b) *Public Preview:* This ensures that all Azure customers have an Azure feature available for evaluation.
2) **General Availability:** In this, all the services are generally available to all the customers as normal service. These services have an SLA, support team and all other support that the services need. Azure technologies, which are reviewed and tested successfully will typically be made available as part of the generally available Azure-based product to customers. Before going fully global, generally, services are rolled out in few regions. https://azure.microsoft.com/en-au/updates/

Demo on Using Preview Services

1. Go to the following preview portal link: https://preview.portal.azure.com/#home. Now here, you see a preview option is showing on top of the portal. It is different from the Azure portal, as it contains all the services and products that are in preview state.

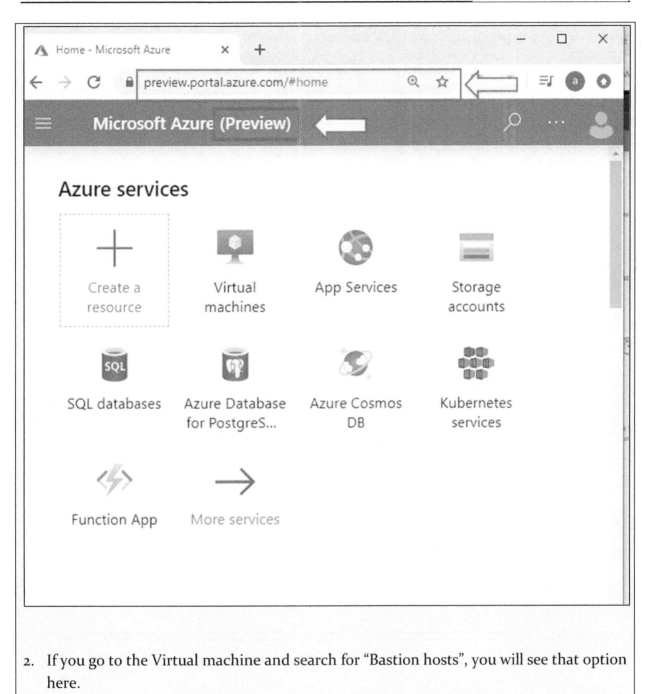

2. If you go to the Virtual machine and search for “Bastion hosts”, you will see that option here.

IPSpecialist
Let Your Career Flow

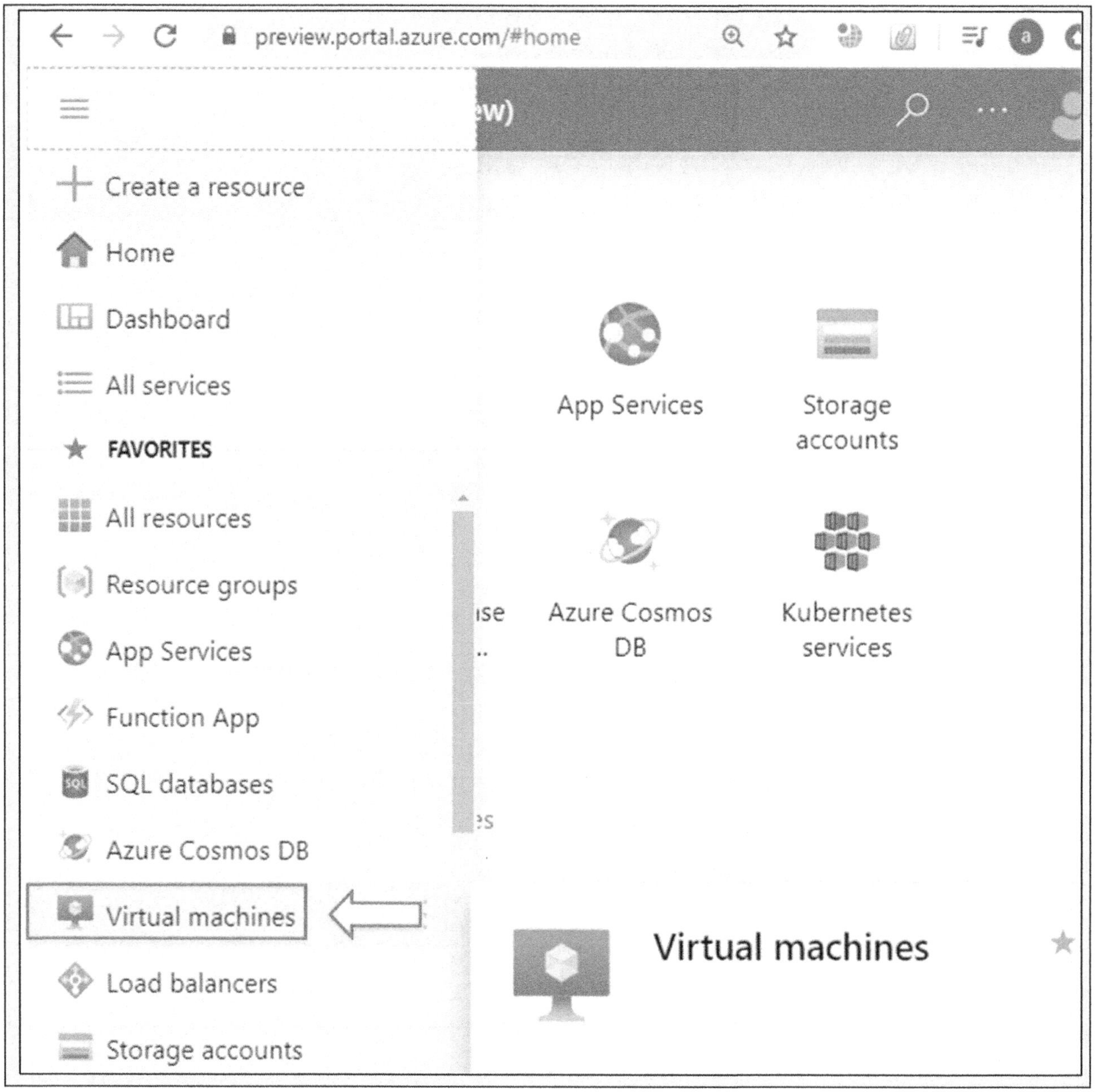

preview.portal.azure.com/#home
Create a resource
Home
Dashboard
All services
FAVORITES
All resources
Resource groups
App Services
Function App
SQL databases
Azure Cosmos DB
Virtual machines
Load balancers
Storage accounts
App Services
Storage accounts
Azure Cosmos DB
Kubernetes services
Virtual machines

preview.portal.azure.com/#blade/HubsExte...

bastion

Services

Bastions

Azure Maps Accounts

Resources

Marketplace

Documentation

Resource Groups

Searching all subscriptions. Change

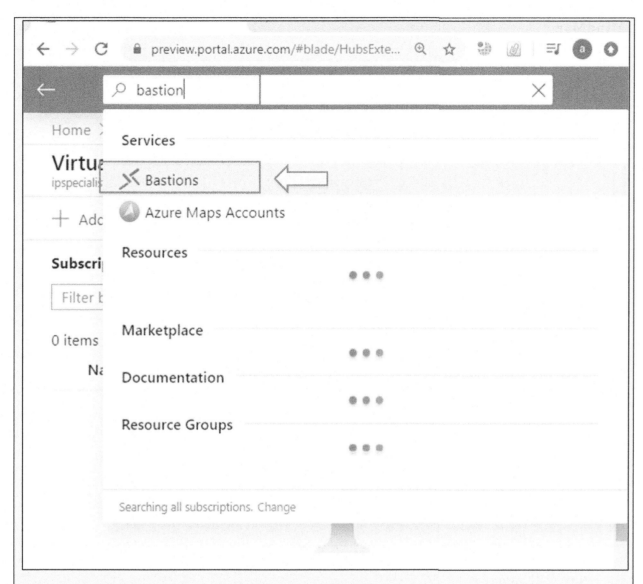

Note: Go into that service and create it if you want. From this preview portal, you can view of all the products that are currently not available on Azure portal.

MindMap

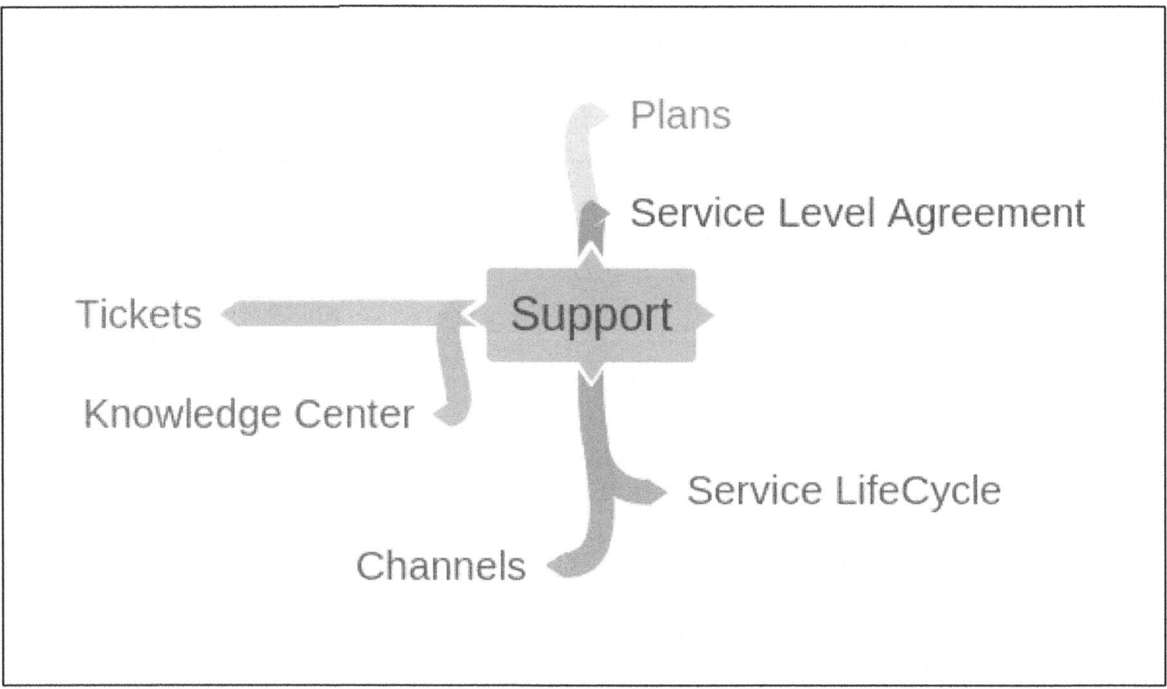

Figure 11-01: Mindmap

Practice Questions

1. From the following options, which are the valid support channels in Azure?
A. Azure Call Support
B. Phone a Friend
C. Azure Documentation
D. Social Media

2. How will you submit a ticket in Azure?
A. Through the Azure Support Portal, which comes with any paid support plan.
B. Through the Azure Portal
C. Using the email address support@azure.com
D. Use the phone number for your region and support level

3. What is the response time for Severity B on the Professional Direct Support Plan?

A. 1 hour
B. 3 hour
C. 2 hour
D. 5 hour

4. What is the response time of Severity C cases in Standard Support Plan?
A. 8 hour
B. 3 hour
C. 2 hour
D. 5 hour

5. How many support plans are available in Azure?
A. 2
B. 3
C. 4
D. 5

6. From the following support plans, which one is free of costs and available with free account?
A. Standard
B. Basic
C. Developer
D. Premier

7. What questions and answers can the Azure Knowledge Center give you?
A. Architectural diagrams
B. A selection of the Azure documentation and articles found on TechNet
C. Common questions asked when first starting to use Azure
D. Over 100,000 user submitted questions and answers

8. In Azure Knowledge Center, users are able to submit new questions as well. True or false?
A. True
B. False

9. How do you sign up for a service level agreement with Azure?
A. Call the regional support number as provided in the Azure Portal to discuss the desired level of the agreement
B. In the Azure Portal, go to the service in question and click on the "Service Level Agreement" section
C. Fill out the form on the Microsoft Azure main support page
D. Service level agreements are included with every Azure service automatically

10. In private preview, the services will be available for evaluation to all customers. True or false?
A. True
B. False

11. There is no SLAs with the free products. True or false?
A. True
B. False

12. What is SLA?
A. A contract between user and Azure
B. A contract between user and free services
C. A contract between user and preview services
D. None of the above

13. From the following support plans, which support give < 15 minutes response time for critical business impact cases?
A. Standard
B. Basic
C. Developer
D. Premier

14. Which support plan has only technical support via email?
A. Standard
B. Professional Direct
C. Developer

D. Premier

15. Which support channel is a collection of thousands of articles written on Azure products and services?

A. Azure Documentation

B. Azure Call Support

C. Phone a Friend

D. Social Media

Answers:

Chapter 01: Introduction to Azure

1. 1. **Answer:** B

Explanation:

Consumption-based pricing is pricing based on usage of resource and it is not time based. It is not limited to free accounts and the services are not necessarily consumed all the time.

2. **Answer:** C

Explanation:

IaaS is the backbone of cloud computing, and in some way, all Azure services depend on IaaS. IaaS Azure services must never be purchased in advance, but may be used as required.

3. **Answer:** A

Explanation:

It collects data from various sources and visualizes the data from sources like on premise and cloud.

4. **Answer:** C

Explanation:

Instead of providing and managing services, Cloud Agility lets them concentrate on other issues such as security, monitoring, and analysis.

5. **Answer:** A

Explanation:

In Azure, this is called Scalability, which means adding or removing the resources in an easy and quick way as per demand. It is important in such situations where you do not know the actual amount of the resource that is needed.

6. **Answer:** D

Explanation:

In this way, you get high availability for your servers by replacing the failed server instantly with the new one. HA depends on the number of VM that you setup to eventually cover in case one goes down.

7. **Answer:** C

Explanation:

Capital Expenditure (CapEx) is the expenditure to maintain or acquiring fixed assets by spending money. This includes land, equipment, etc.

Operational Expenditure (OpEx) is the cost of a product or a system that is running on a day to day basis like electricity, printer papers, etc.

8. **Answer:** A

Explanation:

Availability Zones are locations within an Azure region that are physically separate. It is composed of one or more independently operating power, and network datacenters.

9. **Answer:** B

Explanation:

Each region has a minimum of three zones.

10. **Answer:** C

Explanation:

Regions are geographical areas where Azure is present to deploy the Azure resources. It is a set of data centers with latency-defined perimeter connected via a dedicated regional low-latency network.

11. **Answer:** D

Explanation:

PaaS is designed to facilitate the fast development of web or mobile apps for developers without the need to take concern over the setting or maintaining the underlying server, storage, network, and database infrastructure needed for development.

12. **Answer:** B

Explanation:

VMs are Linux and Windows VM on demand with your desired configuration hosted in Azure. It is an IaaS resource.

13. **Answer:** B

Explanation:

Resource Manager Template is a JavaScript Object Notation (JSON) file that defines the resources deployed in the resource group. It also defines the dependencies between the deployed resources. With this template, resources can be deployed in a consistent and repeatable way.

14. **Answer:** B

Explanation:

In Azure Storage, you can build a storage account for up to 500 TB of cloud data because it has a limit of 500TB per storage account.

15. **Answer:** D

Explanation:

It is a cloud based identity and access management service in Azure. It is one of the core services of Azure. With this service, the user can sign in and access the internal or external resources.

16. **Answer:** C

Explanation:

In CLI, command changes rarely, so you can automate the commands for future purposes.

17. **Answer:** A

Explanation:

An interactive browser, accessible shell for managing Azure resources. The shell experience is the best option, whether you work with Bash or PowerShell as it offers flexibility.

18. **Answer:** B

Explanation:

The limitation of free Azure Account is that you get free services for 12 months with credit expiration after 30 days.

19. **Answer:** D

Explanation:

Most Azure features for PowerShell are made up of cmdlets. This simplifies the interaction with Azure resources to be consistent and efficient. It is a small lightweight group of commands to perform actions.

20. **Answer:** B

Explanation:

You can use the Azure portal with any form of subscription to access all generally available Azure products and services.

Chapter 02: Compute

1. **Answer: C**

Explanation:

Virtual machines are an IaaS offering, where you can manage the entire machine.

2. **Answer: B & C**

Explanation:

Azure charges for Virtual Machines on hourly basis and the resources you used. In another way; if you use more CPUs and RAMs on your VMs, the more you pay per hour.

3. **Answer: D**

Explanation:

Azure Container Instances is the simplest and fastest way to run an Azure container without having to manage any virtual machines and without having to follow a higher-level service.

4. **Answer: C**

Explanation:

With respect to Azure, compute is a term that covers any services in Azure enabling computation in the cloud.

5. **Answer: A**

Explanation:

Azure App Service is a fully managed Platform as a Service (PaaS), meaning servers, networks, storage and other fundamental infrastructures are all managed and controlled by Azure.

6. **Answer: D**

Explanation:

Scale sets support up to 1,000 VM instances. If your own custom VM images are created and uploaded, the limit is 600 VM instances.

7. **Answer: A**

Explanation:

API is an Application Programming Interface that host your data backend services and does not have graphical user interface, i.e., no user interface, no front end.

8. **Answer: C**

Explanation:

Containers are the preferred way for cloud applications to be packaged, deployed and managed.

9. **Answer: B**

Explanation:

Kubernetes is an open-source container orchestration system for automating application deployment, management, and scaling.

10. **Answer: A, C, & D**

Explanation:

Azure Kubernetes Service cluster architecture is based on Node, Node pools, Node selector, Pods.

11. **Answer: A**

Explanation:

Azure Functions is the serverless computing service that is hosted on the public cloud of Microsoft Azure.

12. **Answer: C**

Explanation:

Easy to create and manage multiple VMs

- It is important to maintain a consistent configuration across your environment when you have multiple VMs that operate your application. The VM size, disk configuration, and device configurations should be the same across all VMs for reliable performance of your application
- All VM instances are created from the same base OS image and configuration in the scale set. This approach allows you to easily control hundreds of VMs without additional network management or configuration tasks
- Scale sets allow the use of the Azure load balancer for basic layer-4 traffic distribution, and Azure Application Gateway for further advanced layer-7 traffic distribution and SSL termination.

13. **Answer: C**

Explanation:

Azure Functions is a great solution for data processing, systems integration, internet-of-things (IoT) work, and simple APIs and microservices development.

14. **Answer: C**

Explanation:

With respect to Azure, compute is a term that covers any services, enablinf computation in the cloud.

15. **Answer: B**

Explanation:

Function Service belong to Serverless cloud service model.

16. **Answer: C**

Explanation:

Azure virtual machine scale sets allow you to create and manage a pool of load balanced VMs that are identical. In response to a demand or a given schedule, the number of VM instances will automatically increase or decrease. Scale sets make your applications highly accessible and allow you to centrally manage, configure and upgrade a large number of VMs.

17. **Answer: C**

Explanation:

Azure Functions is an easy way to run small pieces of code or "functions" in the cloud. A user can create and upload code with serverless, and then define the triggers or events to execute the code. Triggers may come from a wide variety of sources, including the application of another user or other cloud services, such as databases and events and hubs for notification.

18. **Answer: B**

Explanation:

Azure App Service is a fully managed Platform as a Service (PaaS). This means servers, networks, storage and other fundamental infrastructures are all managed and controlled by Azure; you just have to focus on business values and logics.

19. **Answer: A, D, E**

Explanation:

Azure provides three types of app services. Web Apps, Web Apps for Containers and API Apps all cover a specific use case. App Services can all run on Linux, but it is not a particular type of service. Event Grid is a separate service on Azure.

20. **Answer: C**

Explanation:

Each virtual machine has its own virtual hardware, including CPUs, memory, hard drives, network interfaces, and other devices. On the physical computer, the virtual hardware is then mapped to the actual hardware, which saves costs by reducing the need for physical hardware systems along with the related maintenance costs, also the power and cooling demand.

Chapter 03: Networking

1. **Answer: A**

Explanation:

Azure networking provides the connectivity between Azure resources and the on-premises network.

2. **Answer: C**

Explanation:

Azure load balancer and application gateway are both able to distribute the traffic load among the service.

3. **Answer: A**

Explanation:

CDN with Dynamic Site Acceleration (DSA) provides the web application update features to the customers. It enables the user to route the dynamic request through CDN without cache.

4. **Answer: D**

Explanation:

Azure CDN places the replicas of data at the datacenter present closest to the user side. The datacenter present closest to the users is called edge nodes, which contain a cache of files that provides the edge of the internet to users.

5. **Answer: A**

Explanation:

VPN gateway provides secure connectivity between Azure and on-premises network. A VPN gateway is made up of VNet gateway and virtual private network.

6. **Answer: A**

Explanation:

It is considered as the most advanced load balancer that enables the balancing of web traffic to manage the web applications using an HTTP request. Because of its services, the gateway is called layer 7 load balancer within Microsoft Azure.

7. **Answer: B**

Explanation:

CDN is able to provide information like image, dynamic changes of video or website content that is regularly changing. Users can experience good performance and access the resources more quickly.

8. **Answer: C**

Explanation:

VPN gateway is useful for establishing the private connection between Azure resource and an on-premises environment, office, the cloud or other premises within the cloud in order to establish a private secure connection.

9. **Answer: A**

Explanation:

The main purpose of creating a subnet is to make multiple networks within the same VNet. With multiple subnets, two or more VM is developed within the subnet. Such subnet is called gateway subnet and a virtual network gateway is used to connect these gateway subnets.

10. **Answer: C**

Explanation:

Azure load balancer provides the load-balancing feature to the connected virtual machines within Microsoft Azure. It is responsible for managing the network traffic load and also enables the use of all VMs for processing.

11. **Answer: D**

Explanation:

Azure portal is the console of Microsoft Azure, providing numerous features, services, and a way to create networks with multiple Azure resources and services. It gives GUI representation for the customer to use Azure services. It provides constant availability for using these services.

12. **Answer: A**

Explanation:

Cloud networking enables cloud computing in order to develop network with low latency, better security and optimized performance of devices.

13. **Answer: B**

Explanation:

There are 3 possible connections for connecting the hybrid networks. These are:

1. Site-to-Site Connection
2. Point-to-Site Connection
3. Multi-Site Connection

14. **Answer: D**

Explanation:

The data of a company is distributed in Azure and on-premises infrastructure for making it a hybrid solution. A specific type of VNet gateway called VPN gateway is used for providing the connection between the two. VPN gateway is responsible for creating encrypted communication within the hybrid cloud architecture.

15. **Answer: A**

Explanation:

A simple VNet must consist of virtual machine (one or more than one), the internet resource and an on-premises network. VNet is able to provide secure connections using gateways.

16. **Answer: A**

Explanation:

Content Delivery Network (CDN) provides networking services but it can lead toward the chance of network failure. CDN proves reliability to its end-users, but when it stops working due to some technical issues, the end-users are unable to get any information from the server-side.

17. **Answer: C**

Explanation:

Azure load balancer delivers high availability and network performance to online applications. It distributes the traffic load to the virtual machine present in the network.

18. **Answer: B**

Explanation:

The attributes of VNet while being created in the Azure portal, define a way to improve network performance and provide scalable service from the designed network. These attributes include address space, public IP address, location, and subnet.

19. **Answer: B**

Explanation:

Using the Azure portal, a VNet should first be create, once the VNet has been deployed, the next step is to add a number of resources from the resource group to VNet present in Azure portal. The resources can be added as long as there is space available in address space and each resource should have a unique IP address.

20. **Answer: C**

Explanation:

The load balancer belongs to layer 4. It has multiple virtual IP addresses to route TCP/UDP traffic. It is also responsible for providing the connection between the virtual network and on-premises. Whereas, application gateway is an advanced load balancer that provides gateway services to the application layer. It is responsible for routing traffic to specific applications like web apps. Application gateway secures application services using firewalls.

Chapter 04: Storage

1. **Answer: D**

Explanation:

Disk storage is a complete virtual hard drive to be accessed. It is ideal as a disk for a virtual machine. Basically, disk storage is created when you create a virtual machine.

2. **Answer: C**

Explanation:

In file types and sizes, Azure blob containers are the most flexible. Any type of file sizing up to 2GB can be stored in an Azure blob container.

3. **Answer: B**

Explanation:

Drive mapping is how operating systems, like Microsoft Windows, link a local drive to another device (such as File Server), via a network using a shared storage area. So the shared storage solution is File storage.

4. **Answer: B**

Explanation:

Archive storage is the cheapest form of blob storage to store data, which is very rarely used, like, device backups.

5. **Answer: B**

Explanation:

When creating a Storage Account, the name must be in between 3 to 24 characters in length and may only contain numbers and lowercase letters.

6. **Answer: A**

Explanation:

Every storage account on Azure must have a unique name, which is used by giving it a web address to identify it on the Internet. Access management of storage account is done via Azure Active Directory

7. **Answer: C**

Explanation:

You can use the file storage as an extension to your on-premises file system so that it never runs out of space and also prioritizes which data you keep on-site.

8. **Answer: B and D**

Explanation:

Azure offers four types of manage disk storage: Standard HDD, Standard SSD, Premium SSD, and Ultra Disk.

9. **Answer: B**

Explanation:

All storage accounts are encrypted for data at rest using SSE (Storage Service Encryption).

10. **Answer: D**

Explanation:

Append blobs are used for log data and can be up to 195GB in size. It is usually used for optimizing the append operation.

11. **Answer: B**

Explanation:

Hot tier - it is for frequently accessed data and is the most optimized. Access costs are lower (read-write) but storage costs are the highest.

12. **Answer: C**

Explanation:

Premium SSD- it is a super-fast and high performance storage for critical workloads. It is recommended for database installation in particular with low latency.

13. **Answer: C**

Explanation:

Data on your Azure Storage Account are durable, highly accessible, safe and scalable. The unique namespace means that every storage data has its webpage with its unique name. It is written in the format: "https://<Storage-Account-Name>.<Storage-type>.core.windows.net.

14. **Answer: A**

Explanation:

A Storage Account is like an access point for Azure Storage. All of your Azure Storage Data Objects like blobs, files, queues, tables, and disks are on an Azure storage account. So first, you need to create a storage account then use any storage option.

15. **Answer: D**

Explanation:

Block blobs store text and binary data up to 4.7 TB. It is made up of blocks of data that can be managed individually. In one block blob, you can have 50,000 blocks.

Chapter 5: Databases

1. **Answer: B**

Explanation:

Cosmos DB is a NoSQL, globally distributed DB.

2. **Answer: B**

Explanation:

Latency is the time taken by the data to travel. The higher the latency, the longer the data takes time to reach the user.

3. **Answer: A**

Explanation:

With Cosmos DB, latency is limited to single digit millisecond (0-9) to anywhere in the world.

4. **Answer: D**

Explanation:

With Azure SQL, you can easily migrate your on-premises SQL database to Azure SQL and get all its benefits, this is done without any change in code and with a frictionless process.

5. **Answer: C**

Explanation:

With Azure SQL, you can store 100TB of data within a minute.

6. **Answer: A**

Explanation:

With Azure SQL, you can also take advantage of integrated Machine learning tools. Depending on the usage pattern, database optimization and performance improvement suggestions are given. With ML, you get the benefit of getting notified about any degradation or anything bad happening in your database.

7. **Answer: D**

Explanation:

Azure Server for MySQL was designed to provide high availability with 99.99% SLA and does not require additional setup, replica features, or costs to guarantee that your apps run as necessary.

8. **Answer: C**

Explanation:

Azure Database for MySQL is the database built-in by the community while Azure SQL is Microsoft's product. MySQL is an open source project where anyone can contribute to the community.

9. **Answer: C**

Explanation:

Azure database for MySQL is PaaS, which is managed by Microsoft.

10. **Answer: B**

Explanation:

PostgreSQL is the default database for MacOS.

11. **Answer: D**

Explanation:

It is the ability of a database to sort and index the data as well as the flexibility to get the data out again and to be able to retrieve them in an exact format. Databases are not cheaper, but more safer and have more efficient space than other data storage options.

12. **Answer: A**

Explanation:

Cosmos DB has a distributed database that is globally distributed and includes an extremely low latency, a number of collaborative software and unlimited scaling in order to meet demand. Cosmos DB is not meant for cheap storage or data backup.

13. **Answer: C**

Explanation:

Database Migration Service on Azure has a range of destinations to which the data can be migrated. These include Azure SQL, Azure SQL Server, and Cosmos DB. Big data tools like Azure Data Lake or HDInsight are not currently supported.

14. **Answer: A**

Explanation:

It is deployed as a single server and as a Citus cluster. The Hyperscale (Citus) choice scale queries in a horizontal manner through multiple sharding tools and offers more scaled and productive applications.

15. **Answer: C**

Explanation:

For geometric data (GIS) the government mostly uses Postgres. PostGIS is the GIS extension that gives hundreds of functions to process geometric data in multiple formats.

16. **Answer: C**

Explanation:

When large volumes of data that are not frequently used are needed to be stored, then search for a data warehouse or data lake. Transactional applications such as SQL, PostgreSQL, and CosmosDB are useful for data that are frequently accessed.

Chapter 6: Authentication & Authorization

1. **Answer: A**

Explanation:

Identity services of Microsoft Azure are responsible for providing the platform to the users and ensure the validity of users for the application through the process of authentication, authorization and access management tool.

2. **Answer: B**

Explanation:

Authentication is a way to verify the customer's or user's identity. Once authenticated, the user is allowed to access files, databases, emails, etc. This is called authorization.

3. **Answer: D**

Explanation:

Identity service is responsible for access management, ensuring the restriction of access to service towards other or unauthorized users. It provides confidentiality, integrity, and availability.

4. **Answer: C**

Explanation:

Authentication is the identification of the user through user ID and password. Other verification approaches are also used to authenticate Azure users.

5. **Answer: B**

Explanation:

Identity service is the management tool that secures the identity of the user by first authenticating it. After authentication, authorization will be done to give the access right to Azure users.

6. **Answer: A**

Explanation:

Multi-Factor Authentication provides the most advanced level of security and protection features to Azure users. MFA has the most efficient throughput protection using multiple authentication processes. MFA uses the principle of "something you know (user ID and password), something you have (app on mobile to receive the confirmation code) and something you are (biometric)".

7. **Answer: C**

Explanation:

Authorization is a part of identity management that provides access rights to Azure users after the authentication process.

8. **Answer: A**

Explanation:

Tenant is the first AAD instance after creating an Azure account. One user belongs to a single tenant only.

9. **Answer: C**

Explanation:

Microsoft Active Directory (AD) provides directory services for physical access only. It is most commonly used in on-premises networks like offices, educational institutes, etc.

10. **Answer: D**

Explanation:

Hybrid cloud architecture is the requirement for many organizations. Azure Active Directory (AAD) can help the user manage resources and services on both on-premises and Azure clouds.

11. **Answer: B**

Explanation:

Multi-Factor Authentication (MFA) performs authentication of the user in multiple steps. The first step is to verify the user with a user ID and password. The second step is to send a code on the user phone for further verification. The third step is the biometric verification. This step is optional.

12. **Answer: C**

Explanation:

Authorization is considered as a granular part of identity service that provides the rights to authenticated users to access particular data.

13. **Answer: A**

Explanation:

Both Azure Active Directory (AAD) and Active Directory (AD) are directory services. Directory services are databases, which store information distributed across different locations. AAD is the main tool to manage services on Azure. Whereas, AD is the management tool for the on-premises network.

14. **Answer: A**

Explanation:

Azure subscription is very important for both the end-user and Microsoft. Azure subscription allows the user to use Azure resources for cloud computing.

15. **Answer: D**

Explanation:

Multi-Factor Authentication combines multiple authentication processes for the provision of an advanced level of secure environment for accessing the data. Sometimes, biometric is taken to be the only authentication way to provide security.

16. **Answer: B**

Explanation:

Access management provides user access to IT resources. Access management only allows a correct user (i.e., authorized user) to access the system applications for the sake of security.

17. **Answer: C**

Explanation:

Azure Active Directory is the first service when a user creates an Azure account. Without AAD, Azure users are able to use Azure resources and services.

18. **Answer: B**

Explanation:

Azure Active Directory is a very important tool in the Azure portal because it is also responsible for handling user's information and assigning access to other resources such as Cosmos DB, Virtual Machine, etc.

19. **Answer: A**

Explanation:

Active Directory is designed for access to on-premises network resources and users. AD does not support the management of web-based services.

20. **Answer: C**

Explanation:

Tenant is the first directory service when a new user creates an account in Azure. A user belongs to single-tenant and tenants may have multiple users. Sometimes, the user can be guests of other tenants.

Chapter 7: Azure Solutions

1. **Answer: A**

Explanation:

A model is a set of rules of how to use the data provided. The model finds patterns based on the rules.

2. **Answer: A, C, & D**

Explanation:

Azure Data Lake Analytics is an on-demand job analytics service that simplifies big data. Instead of hardware tuning, deploying, and configuring, you write queries to transform the data and abstract valuable insights. The analytics service can promptly handle jobs of any size by changing the dial to how much power you need. You pay for your job only when it is working, making it cost-effective.

3. **Answer: C**

Explanation:

Logic Apps simplifies how you design and build flexible applications for application integration, data integration, system integration, Enterprise Application Integration (EAI) and Business-to-Business (B2B) communication, whether in the cloud, at the premises, or both.

4. **Answer: D**

Explanation:

Azure DevOps offers developer tools to support teams in preparing projects, working on application creation, and designing and deploying software. Developers can use Azure DevOps Services or on-premises with Azure DevOps Server to operate in the cloud. Azure DevOps provides integrated features that can be accessed via your web browser or client IDE.

5. **Answer: B, E, & F**

Explanation:

There are currently 5 services in Azure DevOps:

Azure Boards- Provides a suite of Agile tools to help with planning and monitoring, code bugs, and issues using Kanban and Scrum process.

Azure Pipelines- Provides services to develop and release continuous integration and distribution of your apps.

Azure Repos- Provides the source control of your code to Git repositories or Team Foundation Version Control (TFVC).

Azure Test Plans- Provides various tools for testing the software, including manual/exploratory testing and continuous testing.

Azure Artifacts: Allows teams to share public and private Maven, Npm, and NuGet packages and incorporate package sharing into your CI/CD pipelines.

6. **Answer: C & E**

Explanation:

There are many Azure services for Internet of Things. Two of them are IoT Hub and IoT Central. The others listed are not valid Azure services.

7. **Answer: D**

Explanation:

Use Azure Search to find existing insights in your data. File relationships, geography connections and much more.

8. **Answer: B & C**

Explanation:

Azure HDInsight allows storing massive amounts of data easily, efficiently and cost-effectively. The most popular open-source frameworks such as Hadoop, Spark, Hive, LLAP, Kafka, Storm, R, and more are available. With these frameworks, a wide range of scenarios such as Extracting, Transforming, and Loading (ETL), data warehousing, machine learning, and IoT can be enabled.

9. **Answer: D**

Explanation:

Azure Event Grid lets you easily build applications with event-based architectures.

10. **Answer: C & D**

Explanation:

Logic Apps are similar to Function Apps because they are kicked off by a trigger, but what happens after that is completely different. Unlike Function Apps, in order to create some efficient workflows with Logic Apps, you do not have to write code.

11. **Answer: A, C & D**

Explanation:

Cognitive services bring AI within every developer's reach — without requiring expertise in machine-learning. All it takes is an API call to embed the feature to see, hear, speak, search, understand, and accelerate decision-making into your apps.

12. **Answer: C**

Explanation:

The Azure Machine Learning studio is the top-level tool for the machine learning service. It provides a centralized location for data scientists and developers to work with all the artifacts for developing, training, and deploying machine learning models.

13. **Answer: C**

Explanation:

Machine Learning Services are:

End-to-End Service: The service to use AI and machine learning almost anywhere on Azure.

Tooling: The Machine Learning service is a collection of tools to help you build AI applications.

Automation: Azure automatically recognizes trends in your applications and creates models for you.

14. **Answer: A, C & D**

Explanation:

Benefits of Serverless Model are:

No Infrastructure Management: Use fully managed infrastructure. Developers are able to avoid administrative tasks and concentrate on the core business logic. You simply deploy the code with a serverless platform, and it runs with great availability.

Dynamic Scalability: For serverless computing, the infrastructure can automatically scale up and down within seconds to match any workload requirements.

Faster Time to Market: Serverless applications reduce the dependencies of operations on each development cycle, increasing the agility of development teams to produce more features in less time.

More Efficient Use of Resources: Shifting to serverless technology allows companies to reduce TCO and resource reallocation in order to speed up the pace of innovation.

15. **Answer: B & D**

Explanation:

DevTest Labs creates labs which consist of pre-configured bases or templates for Azure Resource Manager. These have all the tools and applications you can use to create environments. With this, you can create environments in a couple of minutes instead of taking hours or days.

By using DevTest Labs, you can test the latest versions of your software when performing the following tasks:

- Using interchangeable templates and artifacts to quickly provision Windows and Linux environments
- Easily integrating the DevTest Labs delivery system for the provision of on-demand environments
- Scaling up the load testing by providing multiple testing agents and building pre- provisioned training and demo environments

16. **Answer: A**

Explanation:

Azure Logic Apps is a cloud service that helps you plan, automate, and orchestrate business processes, activities, and workflows when businesses or organizations need to integrate apps, data, and services.

17. **Answer: B**

Explanation:

Azure Data Lake Analytics is an on-demand job analytics service that simplifying big data. Instead of hardware tuning, deploying, and configuring, you write queries to transform the data and abstract valuable insights.

18. **Answer: D**

Explanation:

Azure Functions is the compute component of serverless services offered by Azure. This means that you can use Functions to write code without having to worry about deploying that code or creating VMs to run your code.

19. **Answer: C**

Explanation:

Azure Databricks is an analytics platform based on Apache Spark, enhanced for the Microsoft Azure cloud services platform.

20. **Answer: D**

Explanation:

Businesses use the big data accumulated in their systems to improve operations, provide better customer service, create customized marketing campaigns based on specific customer preferences and, ultimately, increase profitability.

Chapter 8: Security

1. **Answer: A**

Explanation:

In the configuration of networks, network security is a very important part that protects access to files, directory, and information in a computer network against hacking and unauthorized changes in the network.

2. **Answer: B**

Explanation:

There are four possible ways that are defined to make secure network connections. The Azure firewall defines a set of rule for the protection of resources. Distributed Denial of Service (DDoS) protection services prevent the system from an excessive number of requests. Network Security Group (NSG) makes the security of network resources and Application Security Group (ASG) is used for the provision of application-level security.

3. **Answer: C**

Explanation:

Azure firewall is a layer 7 protocol introduced by Microsoft. It defines the set of rules for the incoming and outgoing traffic in the network to make sure of the security of resources in the network.

4. **Answer: D**

Explanation:

To hide the key password, secrets and other information from a third party, Azure Key Vault is the best option for key storage. It allows the sharing of a secret with others without revealing the actual credential for security reasons. Azure Key Vault has hardware and software protection. Azure Key Vault uses Hardware Security Module (HSM) to store passwords and secrets that no one can view.

5. **Answer: C**

Explanation:

When the same number of requests is received by the webserver from many different sources and computers at a time, the webserver would then suddenly stop working due to the multiple simultaneous requests. This type of attack on the service is called a Distributed Denial of Service (DDoS) attack.

6. **Answer: A**

Explanation:

Network Security Group (NSG) is required in the configuration of a virtual Network (VNet) where different Virtual Machines (VMs) within the subnet are connected with each other. Network Security Group is capable of securing the traffic load across the network whereas Application Security Group (ASG) protects the application running on that particular VM or subnet in the network.

7. **Answer: C**

Explanation:

Network Security Group (NSG) is required in the configuration of a virtual Network (VNet) where different Virtual Machines (VMs) within the subnet are connected with each other. NSG uses Access Control List (ACL) rules to allow or deny the access of network traffic to subnets or VMs.

8. **Answer: B**

Explanation:

To provide secure and protected communication between the resources, services, and processes, a secure network connection should be required in the configuration of a network.

9. **Answer: A**

Explanation:

Azure Key Vault is a useful service that hides the actual passwords and keys from other parties. It secures the network by defining the access policy that allows a secure access to secrets and passwords.

10. **Answer: D**

Explanation:

Azure Information Protection provides a way of protecting the sharing of resources. Azure Information Protection (AIP) enables the sharing of files, documents, and sensitive information more securely outside the organization.

11. **Answer: C**

Explanation:

Advanced Threat Protection (ATP) is an advanced and secure option for providing the security of the links as compared to the standard one. It gives an extra layer of security and management of the users in order to make a more secure and protected system.

12. **Answer: B**

Explanation:

Azure Key Vault stores the secret and password. It allows the sharing of passwords and secrets with others in a hidden form so that nobody can view the actual secret.

13. **Answer: A**

Explanation:

Azure Security Center is itself a portal that monitors the various security features of Azure. Security features include policy, compliance, networking, and subscription coverage and resource security hygiene. Security Center enables threat alerts as well.

14. **Answer: D**

Explanation:

DDoS attack is the attack of excessive number requests at a time from different sources resulting in server failure or website failure. GitHub experienced a recent record break DDoS attack with 1.35 Tb traffic per second.

15. **Answer: C**

Explanation:

Network Security Group (NSG) acts as a resource firewall to prevent network resources from unwanted traffic loads. It defines rules called the Access Control List (ACL) to make the security of network resources as secure as possible.

16. **Answer: B**

Explanation:

Application Security Group (ASG) is responsible for providing protection to an application that is running on a particular VM or subnet.

17. **Answer: C**

Explanation:

Azure Security Center provides an overview of security features in Azure. It also provides its advantage towards a hybrid cloud infrastructure where data is present on both on-premises and cloud.

18. **Answer: A**

Explanation:

Azure Information Protection (AIP) provides the protected sharing of email, file or sensitive data inside and outside an organization. It uses a label for sensitive information that protects the information from threats and other activities throughout the process.

19. **Answer: A**

Explanation:

Azure Advanced Threat Protection service has a security alert timeline that contains a timeframe for the activities in the network. It also highlights and detects the issues in the network.

20. **Answer: B**

Explanation:

Azure Key Vault is the limit access to secret and password. It defines access policy to make decide who can access the secret.

Chapter 09: Privacy, Compliance, and Trust
1. **Answer: D** **Explanation:** First is Azure Government Cloud, if you are US government body or are contracted for one, then you can get access to Azure resources in Azure Government Cloud regions. It is a physically separated instance of Azure, dedicated to U.S. government workloads only. 2. **Answer: B** **Explanation:** Azure Policy is used to create policies in Azure. With Azure policy, you can manage and assign policies to the resources with multiple rules so that specific resource is complaint with your business standard and SLAs. 3. **Answer: C** **Explanation:** With the use of Azure Policy, you can define the company policy so it will enforce the resource to comply with this policy. 4. **Answer: A** **Explanation:** Trust Center is a shortcut of knowing all the things that Microsoft does to make sure that you do not loss trust in Azure and other services. With this, you have a link to learn about security, privacy, GDPR, location of your data, compliance and more. 5. **Answer: B** **Explanation:** Any company that wishes to interact with users located in the European Union must adhere to the many GDPR rules around privacy. 6. **Answer: C** **Explanation:** Azure Service Health informs you of incidents and planned maintenance related to Azure Service. This information can be used to take adequate measures to limit downtime. Data from any of your applications or third-party services cannot be received from Azure Service Health. It is Azure only. 7. **Answer: A** **Explanation:** With RBAC you can outline fine grained access management to the resources. You can define specific user access to an individual resource for example, what they can do with that specific resource and in which specific area of resource they have access to.

8. **Answer: C**

Explanation:

In order to monitor their activities and health, Azure Monitor can accept data from almost any application. You have a single dashboard for all the current measurements, or you can use the collaborative query language to dive into the archived data.

9. **Answer: B and E**

Explanation:

Locks are of two types: delete or read only. In delete lock type, you cannot delete the resource while in read only lock type, you cannot make any changes to the resource.

10. **Answer: B**

Explanation:

The Trust Center can be used to find evidence of all the various compliance specifications Azure complies with. You can read audit reports on any part of Microsoft products, like Azure, through the Service Trust Portal.

11. **Answer: B**

Explanation:

Azure has physically separated datacenters located in China without any connection to the other regions of Azure. All data is stored in China at all times with Chinese regulations.

12. **Answer: B**

Explanation:

In RBAC, there are three main elements present: Security Principal, Scope and Role Definition.

13. **Answer: D**

Explanation:

Azure Blueprint is a template for creating Azure resources. Everything you need to deploy in the standard cloud environment of Azure is mentioned in the blueprint.

14. **Answer: C**

Explanation: For compliance in Azure, there is Azure Compliance Manager, because Azure knows about compliance and about your resources, so it combines the tools and gives you a recommendation as per that.

15. **Answer: D**

Explanation:

Azure Information Protection is used for classifying, labelling and helping protect data based on its sensitivity.

Chapter 10: Pricing

1. **Answer: C**

Explanation:

A billing cycle on Azure is either 30 or 60 days.

2. **Answer: C**

Explanation:

Management groups may indicate the following:

Group Subscriptions: You can group your subscriptions to allow taking actions in bulk across subscriptions. This is very useful in organizations that deal with many subscriptions.

Organize: You can manage policies and compliance in multiple subscriptions at the same time.

Billing Logic: You maintain the billing associated with the right budgets. You have the Nest management groups to indicate the hierarchy and their relationship.

3. **Answer: D**

Explanation:

A free account gives you free access to the most popular Azure services for 12 months.

4. **Answer: B**

Explanation:

Cost management allows you to create a budget for your Azure expenses, set up configurable notifications so you will know if you are hitting a budgeted limit, and evaluate your costs in detail.

5. **Answer: A**

Explanation:

By Azure Cost Management, you can download reports on spending and get recommendations on how to save on costs and analyze them.

6. **Answer: C**

Explanation:

The bandwidth slightly influences the pricing factor; the bandwidth your services are using incurs a cost as well.

7. **Answer: B**

Explanation:

Any data transfer between the regions located in the same billing zone is free, this process is called Ingress.

8. **Answer: A**

Explanation:

Any data transfer between two different billing zone is charged, this process is called Egress.

9. **Answer: C**

Explanation:

The Azure price calculator will help you get an estimate of costs depending on the products that you plan to use, and also where those products will be deployed, and so on.

10. **Answer: D**

Explanation:

When you have applications on site that you want to migrate to Azure, and you want an estimate of how much you can save in Azure, the TCO calculator is the best choice.

11. **Answer: C**

Explanation:

TCO report shows you how much you can save by moving your app to Azure over the next 5 years.

12. **Answer: A, B, & C**

Explanation:

Three primary groups that are listed below, need to be coordinated within the company to ensure you handle the costs effectively.

1) **Finance:** Person responsible for authorizing budget requests across the enterprise based on projections of cloud spending. To drive accountability, they pay the corresponding bill and assign the costs to different teams.
2) **Managers:** Business decision-makers in an organization needs to understand cloud spending to find the best outcomes for spending.
3) **App Teams:** Engineers manage cloud infrastructure on a daily basis, and create applications that meet the needs of the enterprise. These teams need flexibility in their defined budgets to deliver the most value.

13. **Answer: A**

Explanation:

By Azure Cost Management, you can optimize your current resources to save money and also monitor the charges of other cloud service providers such as Amazon Web Services.

14. **Answer: A, B, & C**

Explanation:

In order to implement cost control effectively and reduce costs, you need to:

- Be equipped with the right tools for performance
- Be responsible for costs
- Take appropriate action to reduce expenses

15. **Answer: B**

Explanation:

Advisor makes recommendations for purchases in reserved instances. The recommendations are based on your virtual machine usage for the last 30 days. The recommendations can help you reduce your expenditure when you act upon them.

16. **Answer: C**

Explanation:

The pricing structure of Microsoft Azure works on a subscription price that is tied to what you are using within the Azure infrastructure. All resources in Azure requires a subscription; you cannot access any resources until you subscribed.

17. **Answer: D**

Explanation:

Azure spending limits are the recommended means to manage your Azure subscription's total spending. When your usage leads to charges that exhaust your spending limit, the services you deployed will be disabled for the rest of that billing period. Manual monitoring of the spending of Azure services is ineffective.

18. **Answer: D**

Explanation:

The Azure price calculator will help you get an estimate of costs depending on the products that you plan to use, as well as where those products will be deployed.

19. **Answer: B & C**

Explanation:

Azure Cost Management is accessible from the Azure portal. You can get a detailed view of the current and future projected costs of all the resources that are within your area of accountability. Azure Cost Management is free of cost and is included with all Azure subscriptions.

20. **Answer: A, D, & E**

Explanation:

The primary factors influencing costs are;

Resource Size

Different sizes of resources will have different pricing. A more powerful virtual machine will cost more than the less powerful one.

Resource Type

The choice of resource type has a big influence on price. This also makes sense as there is a very big difference in the number of hardware resources needed to run a virtual machine as compared to a machine learning service or big data analytics. There is also a big difference in the complexity of maintaining and running various Azure services.

Location

Azure has a global network of datacenters from US to Australia and from Norway to South Africa, they are all treated equally with slightly different pricing. Exchange rates, labor costs, etc. have an influence on the price.

Bandwidth

The bandwidth your services are using incurs a cost as well.

Chapter 11: Support

1. **Answer: C and D**

Explanation:

The supported channels required in order to interact with experts and professionals of Azure are: The Azure documentation, technical forums and official Azure social media accounts.

2. **Answer: B**

Explanation:

For support tickets, you can go through the "Support" section of the Azure Portal. There, you will have a choice of various tickets and you can choose the kind of support level you want.

3. **Answer: C**

Explanation:

The response time for Severity B cases in Professional Direct Support plan is <2 hours.

4. **Answer: A**

Explanation:

The response time of the severity C cases in Standard Support plan is <8 hours and it is also the same in Developer support plan.

5. **Answer: D**

Explanation:

There are five different support plans available in Azure; Basic, Developer, Standard, Professional Direct, and Premier.

6. **Answer: B**

Explanation:

Basic support plan is free of costs and given along with the Azure Free account.

7. **Answer: C**

Explanation:

Knowledge center is the place of a common Azure knowledge. In knowledge center, you can find basic questions that are common for all those who are new to Azure, these questions are called Common questions. Azure knowledge center aims to answer those common questions.

8. **Answer: B**

Explanation:

No New Question: You cannot add a new question or add to an existing one.

9. **Answer: D**

Explanation:

All Azure services are subject to Service Level Agreements. Each SLA includes subscription and support level.

10. **Answer: B**

Explanation:

Public preview: This ensures that all Azure customers have an Azure feature available for evaluation.

11. **Answer: A**

Explanation:

SLAs are given from Microsoft; if you have an Azure account, various service levels apply. No SLAs are associated with free products and services.

12. **Answer: A**

Explanation:

SLA describes the Microsoft's commitment for uptime and connectivity. It is like a contract between the service provider and client. It is an agreement on certain levels of service like how long the service will be available in case of any unavailability.

13. **Answer: D**

Explanation:

For high severity business impact cases, the response time is <15 minutes (with Azure Rapid Response or Azure Event Management).

14. **Answer: C**

Explanation:

Access to support engineers via email only during business hours is given in the developer support plan.

15. **Answer: A**

Explanation:

Azure documentation is a collection of thousands of articles written on Azure products and services. They are written by the Azure product manager, technical experts and the community contributes.

Acronyms:

AAD	Azure Active Directory
ACI	Azure Container Instances
ACL	Access Control List
AD	Active Directory
ADC	Application Delivery Controller
AES	Advanced Encryption Standard
AI	Artificial Intelligence
AIP	Azure Information Protection
AKS	Azure Kubernetes Service
API	Application Program Interface
APU	Accelerated Processing Unit
ARM	Azure Resource Manger
ASG	Application Security Group
AWS	Amazon Web Service
AZ	Availability Zone
Azure ATP	Azure Advanced Threat Protection
B2B	Business-to-Business
CapEx	Capital Expenditure
CDN	Content Delivery Network
CLI	Command Line Interface
CPU	Central Processing Unit
DB	Database
DC/OS	Distributed Cloud Operating System
DDoS	Distributed Denial of Service
DevOps	Development and Operations
DMS	Database Migration Services
DNS	Domain Name System
DoS	Denial of Service
DR	Disaster Recovery
DSA	Dynamic Site Acceleration

EAI	Enterprise Application Integration
ETL	Extracting, Transforming, and Loading
EU	European Union
FaaS	Function as a Service
FIPS	Federal Information Processing Standards
GCP	Google Cloud Platform
GDPR	General Data Protection Regulation
GPU	Graphics Processing Unit
HA	High Availability
HDD	Hard Disk Drive
HDFS	Hadoop Distributed File System
HSM	Hardware Security Model
HTTP	Hyper Text Transfer Protocol
HTTPS	HyperText Transfer Protocol Secure
IOPS	Input/Output Operations Per Second
IoT	Internet-of-Things
IP	Internet Protocol
ISO	International Standardization Organization
IT	Information Technology
JSON	JavaScript Object Notation
KEDA	Kubernetes-based Event Driven Autoscaling
MFA	Multi-Factor Authentication
ML	Machine Learning
MPLS	Multiprotocol Label Switching
NIST	National Institute of Standards and Technology
NSG	Network Security Group
OpEx	Operational Expenditure
OS	Operating System
PaaS	Platform as a Service
PCI	Payment Card Industry
POP	Point of Presence
RBAC	Role Based Access Control

SLA	Service Level Agreement
SOC	Standard Occupational Classification
SQL	Structured Query Language
SSD	Solid State Drive
SSE	Storage Service Encryption
SSL	Secure Sockets Layer
SSO	Single Sign On
TCO	Total Cost of Ownership
TCP	Transmission Control Protocol
TFS	Team Foundation Server
TFVC	Team Foundation Version Control
UIDs	Unique Identifiers
URL	Uniform Resource Locator
US	United State
VM	Virtual Machine
VMs	Virtual Machines
VNet	Virtual Network
VPN	Virtual Private Network

References:

Chapter 1:

https://azure.microsoft.com/en-gb/global-infrastructure/regions/

https://docs.microsoft.com/en-us/learn/paths/azure-fundamentals/

https://searchcloudcomputing.techtarget.com/definition/Windows-Azure

https://searchcloudcomputing.techtarget.com/definition/cloud-computing

https://azure.microsoft.com/en-us/global-infrastructure/locations/

http://www.azurespeed.com/Information/AzureRegions

https://docs.microsoft.com/en-us/azure/azure-resource-manager/management/overview

https://docs.microsoft.com/en-us/azure/azure-resource-manager/management/resource-providers-and-types

https://azure.microsoft.com/en-us/product-categories/compute/

https://docs.microsoft.com/en-us/learn/modules/welcome-to-azure/3-tour-of-azure-services

https://azure.microsoft.com/en-us/product-categories/networking/

https://www.dataversity.net/key-cloud-agility/

https://docs.microsoft.com/en-us/azure/storage/common/storage-introduction#types-of-storage-accounts

https://docs.microsoft.com/en-us/cli/azure/get-started-with-azure-cli?view=azure-cli-latest

https://docs.microsoft.com/en-us/cli/azure/install-azure-cli?view=azure-cli-latest

Chapter 2:

https://docs.microsoft.com/en-us/azure/app-service/

https://docs.microsoft.com/en-us/azure/app-service/overview

http://www.informit.com/articles/article.aspx?p=2423911

https://www.techopedia.com/definition/6580/compute

https://azure.microsoft.com/en-us/overview/what-is-a-virtual-machine/

https://www.techopedia.com/definition/4805/virtual-machine-vm

https://docs.microsoft.com/en-us/azure/aks/intro-kubernetes

https://docs.microsoft.com/en-us/azure/aks/concepts-clusters-workloads#kubernetes-cluster-architecture

https://azure.microsoft.com/en-in/services/kubernetes-service/

https://azure.microsoft.com/en-us/services/container-instances/

https://searchcloudcomputing.techtarget.com/definition/Microsoft-Azure-Functions

https://docs.microsoft.com/en-us/azure/azure-functions/functions-overview

https://docs.microsoft.com/en-us/azure/virtual-machine-scale-sets/overview?toc=%2Fazure%2Fvirtual-machines%2Flinux%2Ftoc.json

Chapter 3:

https://www.pluralsight.com/paths/managing-microsoft-azure-networking

https://www.microsoftpressstore.com/store/microsoft-azure-essentials-fundamentals-of-azure-9781509302963

https://www.youtube.com/watch?v=kgwqrqKrox8

https://www.vmware.com/topics/glossary/content/cloud-networking

https://en.wikipedia.org/wiki/IP_address

https://www.techopedia.com/definition/4763/address-space

https://www.accessagility.com/blog/benefits-of-subnetting

https://www.c-sharpcorner.com/article/azure-virtual-networks/

https://docs.microsoft.com/en-us/azure/load-balancer/load-balancer-overview

https://kemptechnologies.com/glossary/source-ip-hash-load-balancing/

https://docs.microsoft.com/en-us/azure/vpn-gateway/vpn-gateway-about-vpngateways

https://docs.microsoft.com/en-us/azure/vpn-gateway/vpn-gateway-howto-site-to-site-resource-manager-portal

https://docs.microsoft.com/en-us/azure/vpn-gateway/vpn-gateway-vpn-faq

https://mindmajix.com/microsoft-azure-application-gateway

https://acloud.guru/course/az-900-microsoft-azure-fundamentals/learn/networking/a5b8496d-4af7-8ad6-eef8-9ec04f34103c/watch

https://www.f5.com/services/resources/glossary/ssl-offloading

https://docs.microsoft.com/en-us/azure/application-gateway/overview

https://docs.microsoft.com/en-us/azure/dns/dns-overview

https://practical365.com/blog/how-to-use-azure-cdn-content-delivery-network/

https://docs.microsoft.com/en-us/azure/architecture/best-practices/cdn

https://docs.microsoft.com/en-us/azure/cdn/cdn-dynamic-site-acceleration

Chapter 4:

https://cloud.netapp.com/blog/storage-tiers-in-azure-blob-storage-find-the-best-for-your-data

https://docs.microsoft.com/en-us/azure/storage/blobs/storage-blob-storage-tiers?tabs=azure-portal

https://docs.microsoft.com/en-us/azure/storage/blobs/storage-blobs-overview

https://aidanfinn.com/?p=18415

http://techgenix.com/azure-storage-accounts/

https://docs.microsoft.com/en-us/azure/storage/common/storage-account-overview

https://intellipaat.com/blog/tutorial/microsoft-azure-tutorial/azure-storage/#Azure_Disk_Storage

https://www.dremio.com/azure-storage-explained/

https://docs.microsoft.com/en-us/azure/virtual-machines/windows/disks-types#disk-comparison

https://azure.microsoft.com/en-us/services/storage/archive/

Chapter 5:

https://docs.microsoft.com/en-us/azure/cosmos-db/introduction

https://stackify.com/what-is-azure-cosmos-db/

https://azure.microsoft.com/en-us/services/cosmos-db/

https://docs.microsoft.com/en-us/azure/sql-database/sql-database-technical-overview

http://www.davidchappell.com/writing/white_papers/Introducing_the_Windows_Azure_Platform,_v1.4--Chappell.pdf

https://azure.microsoft.com/en-us/services/sql-database/

https://docs.microsoft.com/en-us/azure/mysql/overview

https://docs.microsoft.com/en-us/azure/postgresql/overview

https://azure.microsoft.com/en-au/resources/videos/azure-database-services-mysql-postgresql-mariadb/

https://azure.microsoft.com/en-us/services/database-migration/

https://docs.microsoft.com/en-us/azure/dms/faq

Chapter 6:

http://www.differencebetween.net/technology/difference-between-authentication-and-authorization/

https://docs.microsoft.com/en-us/azure/app-service/overview-authentication-authorization

https://www.youtube.com/watch?v=NRRK3DYeqXU

https://www.youtube.com/watch?v=IopoT4UxFxE

https://www.youtube.com/watch?v=oxmg-6zUVwc

https://www.slideshare.net/IdentityDays/gouvernance-multitenant-didentits-et-ressources-azure-avec-azure-active-directory-par-marius-zaharia

https://en.wikipedia.org/wiki/Active_Directory

https://searchwindowsserver.techtarget.com/definition/Active-Directory

https://docs.microsoft.com/en-us/azure/active-directory/authentication/concept-mfa-howitworks

https://acloud.guru/course/az-900-microsoft-azure-fundamentals/learn/authentication-and-authorization/quiz/watch?backUrl=~2Fcourses

https://docs.microsoft.com/en-us/power-bi/developer/create-an-azure-active-directory-tenant

Chapter 7:

https://acloud.guru/course/az-900-microsoft-azure-fundamentals/learn/azure-solutions/

https://searchitoperations.techtarget.com/definition/DevOps

https://whatis.techtarget.com/definition/HDInsight

https://docs.microsoft.com/en-us/azure/lab-services/devtest-lab-overview

https://azure.microsoft.com/en-us/overview/ai-platform/

https://azure.microsoft.com/en-us/services/cognitive-services/

https://docs.microsoft.com/en-us/azure/devops/user-guide/what-is-azure-devops?view=azure-devops

https://docs.microsoft.com/en-us/azure/event-grid/overview

https://docs.microsoft.com/en-us/azure/logic-apps/logic-apps-overview

https://docs.microsoft.com/en-us/azure/azure-databricks/what-is-azure-databricks

https://azure.microsoft.com/en-us/overview/serverless-computing/

https://docs.microsoft.com/en-us/azure/data-lake-analytics/

Chapter 8:

https://en.wikipedia.org/wiki/Cloud_computing_security

https://www.forcepoint.com/cyber-edu/cloud-security

https://acloud.guru/course/az-900-microsoft-azure-fundamentals/learn/security-/introduction/watch?backUrl=~2Fcourses

https://digitalguardian.com/blog/what-advanced-threat-protection-atp

https://docs.microsoft.com/en-us/azure/security/fundamentals/network-overview

https://azure.microsoft.com/en-us/services/azure-firewall/

http://techgenix.com/network-security-groups/

https://docs.microsoft.com/en-us/azure/virtual-network/security-overview

https://www.petri.com/understanding-application-security-groups-in-the-azure-portal

https://medium.com/awesome-azure/azure-application-security-group-asg-1e5e2e5321c3

https://azure.microsoft.com/en-us/blog/applicationsecuritygroups/

https://docs.microsoft.com/en-us/azure/security-center/security-center-intro

https://azure.microsoft.com/en-us/services/security-center/

https://azure.microsoft.com/en-us/services/key-vault/

https://www.winwire.com/azure-key-vault/

https://azure.microsoft.com/en-us/services/information-protection/

https://www.microsoft.com/en-us/itshowcase/protecting-files-in-the-cloud-with-azure-information-protection

https://docs.microsoft.com/en-us/azure/information-protection/reports-aip

https://techcommunity.microsoft.com/t5/azure-information-protection/new-enhancements-to-office-365-message-encryption-with-azure/ba-p/1042617

http://download.microsoft.com/download/B/2/7/B2763D5D-E72A-45CA-AA3A-AD13519886B2/Data_in_Motion_Infographic_EN_US.pdf

https://azure.microsoft.com/en-us/features/azure-advanced-threat-protection/

https://docs.microsoft.com/en-us/azure-advanced-threat-protection/what-is-atp

https://docs.microsoft.com/en-us/azure-advanced-threat-protection/working-with-suspicious-activities

https://en.wikipedia.org/wiki/Kill_chain

Chapter 9:

https://docs.microsoft.com/en-us/azure/role-based-access-control/overview

https://docs.microsoft.com/en-us/azure/role-based-access-control/overview

https://www.petri.com/getting-started-with-role-based-access-control-in-azure

https://docs.microsoft.com/en-us/azure/governance/policy/overview

https://azure.microsoft.com/en-us/solutions/governance/

https://docs.microsoft.com/en-us/azure/governance/blueprints/overview

https://docs.microsoft.com/en-us/azure/azure-monitor/overview

https://www.techopedia.com/definition/30551/cloud-compliance

https://docs.microsoft.com/en-us/azure/azure-government/

https://docs.microsoft.com/en-us/azure/azure-government/documentation-government-welcome

https://docs.microsoft.com/en-us/azure/china/overview-operations

https://azure.microsoft.com/en-us/overview/trusted-cloud/privacy/

https://servicetrust.microsoft.com/

https://docs.microsoft.com/en-us/microsoft-365/compliance/get-started-with-service-trust-portal

Chapter 10:

https://learning.oreilly.com/library/view/exam-ref-az-900/9780135732199/ch04.xhtml#ch04

https://docs.microsoft.com/en-us/azure/cost-management-billing/costs/cost-mgt-best-practices

Chapter 11:

https://daryusman.wordpress.com/2019/01/24/access-public-and-private-preview-features/

https://azure.microsoft.com/en-us/support/legal/preview-supplemental-terms/

https://www.lynda.com/Azure-tutorials/Understand-service-lifecycle-Azure/2815127/2246786-4.html

About Our Products

Other products from IPSpecialist LTD regarding AWS technology are:

AWS Certified Cloud Practitioner Technology Workbook

AWS Certified SysOps Admin - Associate Workbook

AWS Certified Solution Architect - Associate Technology Workbook

AWS Certified Developer Associate Technology Workbook

AWS Certified Advance Networking – Specialty Technology Workbook

AWS Certified Security – Specialty Technology Workbook

AWS Certified Big Data – Specialty Technology Workbook

Microsoft Certified: Azure Fundamentals

Note from the Author:

Reviews are gold to authors! If you have enjoyed this book and it has helped you along your certification, would you consider rating and reviewing it?

Link to Product Page: